The IMF and the Politics of Austerity in the Wake of the Global Financial Crisis

The IMF and the Politics of Austerity in the Wake of the Global Financial Crisis

Ben Clift

OXFORD
UNIVERSITY PRESS

OXFORD
UNIVERSITY PRESS
Great Clarendon Street, Oxford, OX2 6DP,
United Kingdom

Oxford University Press is a department of the University of Oxford.
It furthers the University's objective of excellence in research, scholarship,
and education by publishing worldwide. Oxford is a registered trade mark of
Oxford University Press in the UK and in certain other countries

First Edition published in 2018
Impression: 1

Published in the United States of America by Oxford University Press
198 Madison Avenue, New York, NY 10016, United States of America

British Library Cataloguing in Publication Data
Data available

Library of Congress Control Number: 2017950106

ISBN 978–0–19–881308–8

Printed and bound by
CPI Group (UK) Ltd, Croydon, CR0 4YY

For my wonderful wife Rachel and our two amazing boys,
Charlie & Sam—thanks so much for all your love and support.

Acknowledgements

The research underpinning this book was conducting in the context of a Research Fellowship funded by the Leverhulme Trust. I am very grateful for the support of the Leverhulme Trust for the research fellowship funding (RF-2012-340) entitled 'It's Mostly Fiscal—the IMF, Evolving Fiscal Policy Doctrine and the Crisis' which enabled the research for this book to be undertaken. Anna Grundy at Leverhulme was especially helpful and patient in answering all my queries. The final phases of completing the manuscript were made possible by a period of study leave awarded by the University of Warwick, and I am most grateful to the Department of Politics and International Studies for granting me the time and head space needed to finish this book. Jill Pavey, the Research Grant administrator in the PAIS Research office, provided first-rate logistical support throughout the duration of the project. Naomi Falkenburg provided assistance by transcribing a series of my interviews.

An especially warm thank you is extended to Marjorie Henriquez, Public Affairs Communications Officer at the IMF for her tremendous support in facilitating the setting up of interviews, providing security passes, and general logistical know-how. Her unstinting efforts made my series of research trips to the IMF pass off so smoothly. Christoph Rosenberg, Assistant Director of the Communications Department at the International Monetary Fund, was also helpful in securing permissions and access to Fund staff. Premela Isaacs was, as ever, supremely helpful in helping locate archival material and navigate the IMF's electronic and paper archives. I am especially indebted to all my interviewees at the IMF for giving up their valuable time and engaging in open, reflective dialogue with me: Vivek Arora, Larry Ball, Craig Beaumont, Andrew Berg, Olivier Blanchard, James Boughton, Ajai Chopra, Carlo Cottarelli, Jorg Decressin, Hervé De Villeroche, Giovani Del Arrichia, Nicolas End, Luc Eyraud, Steve Field, Kevin Fletcher, Edouard Gardner, Martine Guerguil, Sanjeev Gupta, Jean-Jacques Hallaert, Laura Jaramillo, Tom Josephs, Doug Laxton, Daniel Leigh, Alessandro Leipold, Prakash Loungani, David Lipton, Paolo Mauro, André Meier, Jonathan Ostry, Antonio Spilimbergo, Krishnan Srinivasan, Hajime Takizawa, Teresa Ter-Minassian, José Viñals, and Irina Yakadina. Whilst in DC, I also benefited from fruitful conversations about economic and fiscal policy with a number of researchers at the Brookings Institution—notably Alice Rivlin, Bill Gale, and Doug Elliott. Thanks go to Martin Bailly for facilitating this, and for his kind hospitality. I am also grateful to Sargon Nissan of the Bretton Woods Project and to members of the IMF's Independent Evaluation Office, notably Charles Collyns, Ruben Lamdany, and Louellen Stedman, for inviting me to an event to discuss Fund issues in London in March 2017.

Thanks go to Cornelia Woll, both for long-standing research collaboration and friendship, but also for facilitating two visiting research fellowships at Sciences Po's Maxpo research centre in Paris. This was the perfect launch pad for fieldwork interviews with French policy elites and officials. Whilst at Sciences Po, I benefited from fruitful research conversations with, amongst others, Marion Fourcade, Colin Hay, Emiliano Grossman, Patrick le Lidec, and Miguel Otero-Iglesias. It also gave me the opportunity to present research findings on the French case to the Sciences Po 'Conversations on Ökonomie, Politics and Society (COOPS)' seminar in November 2013. A number of friends and colleagues helped put me in touch with interviewees and other research contacts, notably Nicolas Veron, Cornelia Woll, Miguel Oero-Iglesias, and Nicolas Jabko. I am grateful to all those French policymakers, advisors, and officials who were kind enough to take time out of their busy schedules to accord me an interview: Marie-Anne Barbat-Layani, Gérard Bélét, Antoine Deruennes, Christian Durand, Anne Epaulard, Ambroise Fayolle, Jean Pisani-Ferry, Philippe Gudin, Thibault Guyon, Michel Houdebine, Alexis Kohler, Philip Martin, Emmanuel Moulin, Emmanuel Jessua, William Roos, Etienne Wasmer, and Eric Woerth. At the UK Treasury, I am very grateful to Dave Ramsden for granting me an interview. The project also benefited from a series of conversations with Treasury economists during a lecture on the IMF and the Treasury, organized by Duncan Needham, which Jim Tomlinson and I gave in May 2015.

A number of friends and colleagues were kind enough to read parts of the book and provide invaluable comments on draft chapters at various stages of development. They were Cornel Ban, Benjamin Braun, Liam Clegg, Andrew Gamble, Alex Kentikelenis, Manuela Moschella, Jonathan Perraton, Ben Richardson, Chris Rogers, Gabriel Siles-Brugge, Tim Sinclair, Ben Thirkell-White, Jim Tomlinson, Kate Weaver, and Wes Widmaier. I hope I have been able to do justice to their first-rate suggestions in my revisions.

I have presented the ideas for chapters of this book in numerous academic fora, and I am grateful to the organizers of those events for giving me the opportunity to receive feedback on earlier drafts of my work. At an Agora Workshop, convened by Len Seabrooke in the Centre for the Study of Globalisation and Regionalisation at the University of Warwick in September 2014, I was able to use the collected brains trust to try out some of the central arguments of the book. Parts of the book's research and arguments were also presented at: the International Studies Association conferences in Toronto (March 2014), New Orleans (Feburary 2015), and Baltimore (2017); the American Political Science Association conference in Washington DC, (August–September, 2014); the British International Studies Association conference, Dublin (June 2014) and Brighton (June 2017); the Politics Studies Association Conference Cardiff (March 2013) and Manchester (April 2014); and the Council of European Studies, Paris (July 2015). It was also presented at seminars at the University of Reading, University of Sheffield, the University of Oxford, and the University of Warwick.

My thanks go to fellow panellists, discussants, and audience members for their comments and criticisms—responding to which has made the book's arguments stronger and richer. Those who provided insightful comments on my work in seminars, workshops, and so on include Andrew Baker, Cornel Ban, James Brassett, André Broome, Chris Clarke, Aitor Erce, Daniela Gabor, Dermot Hodson, Chris Holmes, Wade Jacoby, Matthias Matthijs, Manuella Moschella, Stephen Nelson, Abe Newman, Lena Rethel, Len Seabrooke, Gabriel Siles-Brugge, Wes Widmaier, Mat Watson, and Kate Weaver.

A number of my PhD students are working on topics related to the focus of this book, and I am grateful to them for many fruitful discussions, notably Matthias Kranke, Te-Anne Robles, Sean McDaniel, David Yarrow, Lorenzo Genito, Jack Copley, Iacopo Mugnai, and Nick Taylor. I also presented portions of the book at the Politics and International Studies Department Annual Research Conference, Warwick (June 2016 and June 2017). I am, as ever, grateful to my colleagues in the department for their positive and friendly engagement with my ideas, my research, and my arguments. In my department I am especially grateful for the general intellectual support from Mat Watson, Nick Vaughan-Williams, Shirin Rai, Mike Saward, Matthew Clayton, Richard Aldrich, and Shaun Breslin, to name but a few.

A number of research collaborations have been particularly important in shaping some of the ideas and arguments underpinning this book. In particular, working with Jim Tomlinson over more than a decade on the politics of economic ideas, the IMF, and UK economic policy was crucial groundwork for this book. Secondly, work with Magnus Ryner on the political economy of French and German approaches to EU integration and Eurozone governance—which began fifteen years ago—continues to bear fruit. I sincerely hope we carve out time to warm up our slow-burning research collaboration now this book is complete. Thirdly, my current collaboration with Wes Widmaier on the politics of economic ideas focusing on monetary policy has been a rich source of new insights which have fed into the thinking about fiscal policy detailed in this book. His suggestions about structuring my theoretical contribution were especially instructive. Fourthly, working with Ben Rosamond on the lineages of British international political economy has been important in shaping my thinking about the field, and what it is to be a political economist. All of this underpins the approach taken in this book and indeed all my work. I look forward to more research discussions and wonderful hospitality in Copenhagen and Lund.

At Oxford University Press I am very thankful for the enthusiastic support of Dominic Byatt, who helped shepherd the project through the various stages before publication. Sarah Parker's and Olivia Wells' conscientious efforts have also made the publication process a smooth one. I am grateful to Andrew Hawkey for his assiduous proofreading. Two reviewers selected by OUP read a number of draft chapters and provided useful and helpful suggestions for minor amendments and additions.

My wife Rachel was kind enough to proofread the final manuscript and iron out many glitches. Finally, and most importantly, I am hugely grateful to all my family, and especially to Rachel, and my sons Charlie and Sam, for all their love, encouragement, and support.

Ben Clift

Garsington, Oxfordshire
July 2017

Contents

List of Abbreviations xv

1. The IMF and the Politics of Austerity in the Wake of the Global Financial Crisis 1
   Introduction 1
   Constructing Economic Orthodoxy 4
   Economics, Ideology, and Fiscal Policy 9
   The Social Construction of Crisis, and of Economic Policy Orthodoxy 15
   Shared Understandings within the Fund of the Economy and Policy 18
   Outline of the Book 23

2. Ideational Change at the IMF after the Crash 27
   Introduction 27
   Ideational Change but *not* Paradigm Change 29
   Constructivist Institutionalism and Ideational Change at the IMF 31
   Putting the CI Approach into Practice: Mechanisms of Ideational Change in the Fund 35
   Power Relations and Practices of IMF Economic Policy Knowledge Production 41
   Hierarchy and Path-Contingent Change in IMF Economic Ideas after the Crash 48
   IMF Bricolage and the 'New Normal' 50
   Conclusion 54

3. The IMF, Economic Schools of Thought, and Their Normative Underpinnings 56
   Introduction 56
   The Fund's Repertoire of Economic Ideas and Academic Economics 59
   Schools of Thought in Economics and Their Normative Underpinnings 63
   Keynesianism 65
   The Neo-Classical Synthesis 66
   New Classical Macroeconomics 68
   New Keynesian Macroeconomics 70
   New Consensus Macroeconomics 72

The IMF's Repertoire of Fiscal Policy Thinking before the Crash 74
The Fund and its Post-Crisis Fiscal Policy Rethink 80
The Scope for Keynesian Thinking *within* the New Consensus 85
Conclusion 86

4. Analysing the IMF Surveillance of Advanced Economies: The Social Construction of Fiscal Space 88
Introduction 88
The IMF as an Actor in World Politics: Conceptions of Fund Autonomy and Agency 91
Fund Authority, its Surveillance Mandate, and Advanced Economies 93
Powerful Members, Fund Autonomy, and the Moveable Limits of 'Thinkable' Policy 98
Fund Influence over Advanced Economy Policies and Its Limits 100
Maximizing Traction? IMF Bricolage and Framing Policy Advice 103
The Politics of Austerity and the Social Construction of Fiscal Space 106
The Wax and Wane of Fund Influence over Advanced Economy Fiscal Policy Debates 110
Conclusion 111

5. The Fund's Fiscal Policy Views and the Politics of Austerity 113
Introduction 113
The Fund's Re-Evaluation of Fiscal Policy Potency and Efficacy for Advanced Economies 115
Fiscal Policy for the Crisis 117
The Evolving Crisis Narrative: From Macroeconomic Stimulus to Exit Strategies 123
The Troika and the Politics of Austerity 126
Growth Friendly Fiscal Consolidation? 128
Fiscal Policy Efficacy and Consolidation in Recessionary Conditions 132
The Eurozone Crisis and the Politics of Fiscal Rectitude 135
Both Too Much *and* Too Little Fiscal Consolidation Can Be Dangerous 142
The Second Revival of Counter-Cyclical Policy 144
Conclusion 147

6. The IMF, the UK Policy Debate, and Debt and Deficit Discourse 150
Introduction 150
UK/IMF Relations: IMF Intellectual Authority and the Limits of 'Traction' 151
UK/IMF Relations, Fiscal Policy, and the 2008 Crash 154
2012: Stagnation . . . and Hysteresis? 160
There Is No Alternative . . . or Osborne's Switch to 'Plan B'? 163
How Big Is the Output Gap? Supply Optimism/Pessimism and Its Policy Ramifications 166

Playing with Fire 168
The Politics of the UK Austerity Debate 170
Conclusion 175

7. The IMF and French Fiscal Rectitude amidst the Eurozone Crisis 178
Introduction 178
French Officials/Fund Relations and Article IV Consultations 180
French Fiscal Policy and the Crisis 181
Turning Off the Taps 185
Weak Growth and Fiscal Consolidation 191
The Fund's Shaping of the European Fiscal Policy Debate 2012–13 194
Franco-German Relations, the IMF, and Eurozone Crisis Narratives 199
The IMF, Breaking the 'Doom Loop', and the Politics of European Banking Union 202
Conclusion 205

8. Conclusion—IMF Intellectual Authority and the Politics of Economic Ideas after the Crash 208
Introduction 208
The Construction of Economic Rectitude 211
The Internal Politics of Economic Ideas within the IMF 213
The IMF and Its Quest for Traction 218
IMF Autonomy and Intellectual Authority—and Their Limits 223
Lasting Change? 225
Coda 230

Bibliography 233
Index 269

List of Abbreviations

CDU	Christian Democratic Union (Germany)
CI	Constructivist Institutionalism
CPE	Comparative Political Economy
DG	Ecfin Directorate General for Economic and Financial Affairs (of the European Commission)
DI	Discursive Institutionalism
DSGE	Dynamic Stochastic General Equilibrium
DSK	Dominique Strauss-Kahn
EA	Expansionary Austerity
EC	European Commission
ECB	European Central Bank
Ecofin	Economic and Financial Affairs Council (of the European Council)
EDP	Excessive Deficit Procedure
EFSF	European Financial Stability Facility
ESM	European Stability Mechanism
EU	European Union
FAD	Fiscal Affairs Department
FDP	Free Democratic Party (Germany)
G20	Group of Twenty
GDP	Gross Domestic Product
GEM	Global Economy Model
GFC	Global Financial Crisis
HI	Historical Institutionalism
IEO	Independent Evaluation Office
IMF	International Monetary Fund
IMFC	International Monetary and Financial Committee
IOs	International Organizations
IPE	International Political Economy
MAP	Mutual Assessment Process

MCM	Monetary and Capital Markets
MIP	Macroeconomic Imbalances Procedure
MIT	Massachusetts Institute of Technology
NIESR	National Institute of Social and Economic Research
NCS	Neo-Classical Synthesis
NCM	New Consensus Macroeconomics
NICE	Non-Inflationary Continuous Expansion
NKM	New Keynesian Macroeconomics
OBR	Office for Budget Responsibility
OECD	Organization for Economic Cooperation and Development
ONS	Office for National Statistics
PA	Principal/Agent
QE	Quantitative Easing
RBC	Real Business Cycle
SGP	Stability and Growth Pact
SI	Sociological Institutionalism
SPR	Strategy Policy and Review Department
UK	United Kingdom
US	United States
VAR	Vector Autoregression
WEO	*World Economic Outlook*
ZLB	Zero Lower Bound

1

The IMF and the Politics of Austerity in the Wake of the Global Financial Crisis

Introduction

A staff member once noted that the International Monetary Fund (IMF) really means it's mostly fiscal', an allusion to the Fund's reputation for harsh loan conditionality involving spending cuts, fiscal retrenchment, and budget deficit reductions as standard responses to economic difficulties and financial crises. As this book demonstrates, the Fund's reputation for conformity with 'Washington Consensus'-style fiscal and intellectual conservatism belies its ideational innovation and more differentiated prescriptive policy discourse since the global financial crisis (GFC). This study is interested in the politics of economic ideas in the wake of the crash and the Eurozone crisis. It explores this by analysing how the Fund's approach to fiscal policy evolved after 2008, and the IMF's role as an authoritative voice in shaping advanced economy policy responses during the Great Recession through its oversight, surveillance, and commentary.

The Fund's unique mandate and knowledge bank afford it influence in shaping how economic policy gets understood. Through its research, its flagship publications, and its surveillance interactions with member governments, the Fund works to impress its interpretation of sound policy upon others, and instil its thinking into international economic policy debates. In doing so, the IMF can shape the policy possibilities and the range of policy tools available to governments in pursuit of growth and economic stability. The IMF's intellectual authority means that its seal of approval plays a key role for countries seeking market access to fund their borrowing. For other countries, the Fund is an important source of credibility for their economic policies. As such, the interpretive framework through which the IMF assesses and evaluates policy is an important site of power in world politics.

Whilst many have focused on IMF conditionality as a means to influence member government economic policy, the relation between the Fund and advanced economies *not* borrowing from the Fund has gone underexplored. This book focuses on those neglected interactions and relations. As well as seeking to change behaviour through loan conditionality, the Fund also pursues strategies to shape and influence conventional wisdoms about appropriate economic policy through surveillance and commentary. The IMF dedicates vast resources to surveillance, which is what the organization spends most of its time doing. This is testament to the enormous importance the Fund attaches to shaping how economic policies get understood, even if it does not always succeed in its efforts. It has long been in the business of developing and corroborating a prescriptive discourse regarding appropriate (and, more importantly, inappropriate) economic policy.

The context of this exploration is the politics of austerity. From the 1980s to the 2000s, a consensus had built up around macroeconomic policy conduct in advanced economies that prioritizes low inflation and fiscal conservatism in the form of balanced budgets and low deficits (Alesina & Perotti 2000; Blyth 2002a; Eatwell 1995; Fischer 2001a & b; Hay 2001; Williamson 1990, 2002). With the onset of the GFC and the Great Recession in 2008, counter-cyclical fiscal stimulus was advocated on a vast scale to stave off another Great Depression *even though* deficit and debt levels were rising precipitously. Central banks began to pump billions into broken advanced economy financial systems through unconventional monetary policy, partly to restore bank balance sheets, but also to boost aggregate demand, compensate for broken credit channels, and counter deflationary threats. The full array of macroeconomic policy levers, both fiscal and monetary, were being actively deployed to boost demand and confidence, counter instabilities wrought by financial crisis, and ward off threats of depression, stagnation, and a prolonged downturn. The principles of sound economic management for advanced economies were thrown into flux. This book's central goal is to chart how the IMF sought to intervene in the ensuing economic policy debate, and how it worked to shape understandings of 'sound' fiscal policy in the wake of the GFC and Eurozone crises. In doing so, it unearths an important but underexplored link between the Fund's ideas, its ideational influence, and the economic policy 'room to manoeuvre' available to some national governments.

Another aim of the 'politics of economic ideas' approach taken in the book is to explore how economic ideas, even when espoused by technocratic and self-avowedly 'scientific' institutions like the IMF, are always rooted in understandings of the principles of political economy—normatively informed views of how the economy and policy work. Some interpretations argue that the Fund, after a brief flirtation with Keynesianism in 2008, reverted to pre-crisis fiscally conservative orthodoxy, embracing the 2010 Toronto G20 mantra of 'growth-friendly fiscal consolidation' and the efficient market hypothesis (Blyth 2013b: 206; Baker 2010; Radice 2011; Gamble 2014: 64). However, whilst that captures the approach to austerity policies taken in London, Berlin, and at the European Central Bank (ECB) to name but a few, the IMF followed a different path. As detailed in this book, the Fund's role within the politics of austerity has been more critical and unconventional, using its intellectual authority strategically to challenge important elements of both the pre-crisis economic orthodoxy, and the single-minded pursuit of austerity since 2010. As one former IMF Mission chief put it, 'the IMF stands in contrast or in juxtaposition to the more hawkish official positions within Europe.'[1] Deputy director of the Research Department Jonathan Ostry characterized the Fund's evolution since 2008 thus: 'I think there has been a fundamental rethinking on fiscal policy, on monetary policy, on managing capital flows, and on inequality.'[2] This matters because which economic ideas are drawn on, and how, to inform and underpin economic policy conduct and commentary can have important implications for macroeconomic policy space.

The Fund has promoted diagnostic economic ideas about the crisis which have led to a re-evaluation of financial markets and their relationship to economic stability. Fund thinking and practice has thoroughly rehabilitated fiscal policy as an active tool for economic stabilization, and its commentary has consistently emphasized the need to boost weak demand and strengthen anaemic growth. It has countered the single-minded focus on cutting public expenditure to bring debt and deficits down, using its commitment to credible medium-term frameworks to underpin a 'not too far, not too fast' approach to fiscal consolidation. Leveraging its mandated role as a guarantor of international coordination, the IMF consistently decried the damaging folly of all countries consolidating at once, encouraging more expansionary policies from surplus countries to boost global demand. For those advanced economies enjoying 'fiscal space' (not under threat of losing the confidence of financial markets), the Fund advised 'less now, more later', postponing fiscal adjustment until the post-crash downturn was over. This book explores the dynamics and the successes and failures of Fund attempts to gain wider acceptance for these ideas amongst advanced economy policymakers. It finds that the crisis presented relatively conducive conditions for the IMF to shape the climate of opinion, yet even with these comparatively favourable conditions, its ability to shape economic policy thinking in advanced economies had its limits.

1 Interview with Alessandro Leipold, September 2013.
2 Interview with Jonathan Ostry, Deputy Director of the IMF Research Department, June 2013.

Constructing Economic Orthodoxy

The prevailing economic policy wisdom at any time is rooted in contingent social constructions of economic assumptions. Which economic ideas are drawn on, and how, to inform and underpin economic policy orthodoxies changes over time. Within the intersubjective process of constructing economic policy rectitude, those who can make authoritative knowledge claims, such as prominent economists and institutions like the Fund, enjoy a privileged position. In analysing the IMF's role within international economic policy debates since the 2008 crash, another of the book's main goals is to analyse and reveal the malleability of economic orthodoxy. The Fund's track record and institutional memory of performing its surveillance and oversight roles for many decades make it an ideal focal point to unearth to what extent the combination of economic ideas invoked to assess economic policy have evolved. How this nexus of economic ideas and economic orthodoxy changes is a deeply political process in which the Fund, for all the emphasis the institution places on the technocratic, scientific nature of its work, is intimately involved.

The book's main contributions are to two bodies of literature, firstly, international political economy (IPE) explorations of international organizations (IOs) in general and the IMF in particular, analysing their internal workings, their sources of authority, and their influence in and impact on world politics. Secondly, constructivist IPE and comparative political economy (CPE) studies analysing the importance of ideational factors, especially economic ideas, in explaining change in contemporary world politics, in particular those analysing the construction and narration of the global financial and Eurozone crises, as well as their political economic implications.

This book substantially revises our understanding of the IMF's economic policy thinking and its effects on the room to manoeuvre enjoyed by governments. The Fund's reputation for conformity with fiscally conservative one-size-fits-all neo-liberalism is at odds with its significant shift since 2008 towards more growth-oriented, varied, and contingent prescriptive policy discourse that emphasizes, amongst other things, tackling inequality. Building on earlier analyses of the internal structures, politics, and culture of the Fund (Momani 2005a & b; Park & Vetterlein 2010), the research analyses how persuasive struggles play out amongst competing 'subcultures' of economic thinking within the Fund, shaped by internal power relations (Chwieroth 2010; Ban 2015a & b). It finds Fund thinking to be less homogenous than some earlier studies have implied (Blyth 2003b; Grabel 2003), and provides novel insights into internal processes of ideational interaction and their contemporary evolutions. It reveals the development of Fund thinking to be more iterative, contingent, and pragmatic than often appreciated

(Wade 2003a; Peet 2009). Feedback loops are identified within Fund practices which act as transmission mechanisms through which reflexive actors appreciate the limits of socially acceptable change, and reshape their institutional context.

The findings presented here challenge, advance, and update extant understandings of IMF economists' shared beliefs, charting a revival of more Keynesian and market-sceptical 'subcultures' in the Fund, and their increased influence since 2008. It reveals the wide range of economic insights—including unconventional elements—reconcilable to mainstream economic thought, and how this affords key IMF actors hitherto neglected scope to select and prioritize within this menu of respectable economic thinking. The Fund's leading lights thought their Keynesian interpretation of the crisis and appropriate responses was right, and the more orthodox approaches of, e.g. Germany and the ECB were misguided. Thus, part of the motivation was for the Fund to play its self-allocated role as a font of economic policy knowledge—and for the Fund to be 'on the right side of history' in the international economic policy debate.[3] This dimension of Fund policy commentary has gone under-reported and under-appreciated by scholars keen to critique the austerity-centric approach of the IMF (see e.g. Stiglitz 2002; Webb 2000; Wade 2001). The Fund of the New Classical 'silent revolution' during the 1980s prioritized low inflation and austerity as necessary preconditions for growth (Boughton 2001: 25–8; Babb & Buira 2005). By contrast, the post-crash IMF took a more activist approach which identified supporting aggregate demand through counter-cyclical policy, infrastructure investment, and tackling inequality as key macroeconomic components of securing growth in advanced economies.

The chapters which follow pull back the veil on the politics of economic ideas both within the IMF and in its interactions with major advanced economy governments. Combining close textual analysis with extensive, searching interviews with numerous Fund economists, this work comes close to inhabiting the 'lived in' space of IMF debates and practices. As senior IMF figure Paolo Mauro put it, 'this is a very intellectually live place, actually. We have big battles all the time. Those battles are usually fought between departments—one department being the advocate of one policy, another pushing back. So there's a lot of back and forth.'[4] The analysis opens the 'black box', situating internal Fund debates within hierarchical power relations to develop a novel theory of ideational change in IOs. This explains how prevailing economic ideas within the IMF can and do change.

[3] Interview with Research Department economist Daniel Leigh, September 2013. Similar sentiments were expressed by many IMF interviewees.

[4] Interview with senior IMF economist Paolo Mauro, a senior fellow at the Peterson Institute for International Economics at the time of the interview in 2014.

In situating IMF internal evolution in the wider context of world politics, this book addresses two blind spots in the IMF literature by focusing on relations with *advanced* countries *not* borrowing from the Fund. Surveillance, rather than loan programmes, is what the Fund spends most of its time doing, hence the focus on IMF views of advanced economies and their conduct of macroeconomic policy. This book updates and refines our understanding of how IOs seek to wield ideational power by analysing the Fund's post-crash ability to fix meanings attached to economic policies. Taking account of the role of powerful states within IOs, this monograph analyses the enduring scope for IMF autonomous action (Barnett & Finnemore 2004), and more specifically the ability of IMF innovators in influential positions to select and prioritize within the parameters of what Seabrooke terms 'thinkable' policy (2010: 141).

Fund surveillance and commentary confidently advances its assessment of 'what's going on', defining the nature of economic threats, risks, and downside possibilities and probabilities. Yet the IMF is often more circumspect in spelling out 'what was to be done', what constitutes appropriate economic policy settings and practices in the wake of the crash. As this book illustrates, this is because Fund leverage and 'traction' on non-borrowing advanced economy policymakers is limited. By developing a framework for understanding under what conditions Fund influence is more likely to prevail, it provides fresh insights into the sources, scope, and limits of IMF intellectual authority vis-à-vis advanced economies in the Great Recession.

The conditions of possibility for the IMF to convince advanced economy policymakers to adjust policy settings are context-dependent. As Blanchard noted of the Fund's fiscal multipliers research which gained sway within the economic policy agenda in 2012, it's a combination of message and opportunity...I have a sense that the papers made a difference. If you have a clear message then you have some effect, and you clearly have more effect if it fits the agenda.' 'I think you can move the compass a little bit.'[5] The Fund has to have a clear line, backed up by its evidence base, which aligns sufficiently with national authorities' policy agenda, and it needs the opportunity to press its case, such as an economic crisis and G20 or other meetings to discuss policy responses. The post-crash Fund has, on a contingent basis, worked to expand the economic policy possibilities for certain advanced economies, not all of whom have chosen to heed the Fund's counsel. This wider array of fiscal policy options were, however, not available to all—and crucially not to crisis-hit programme countries like Greece that arguably needed them most, a theme developed in Chapters 5 and 7.

[5] Interview with IMF Chief Economist Olivier Blanchard, June 2013.

In terms of constructivist IPE and CPE literatures, this book builds on debates about mechanisms of incremental change (Carstensen 2011a & b; Mahoney & Thelen 2010a & b; Campbell 2004; Streeck & Thelen 2005a & b). Its Constructivist Institutionalist (CI) approach (Hay 2008, 2015; Schmidt 2008, 2010; Clift 2012, 2014a) foregrounds the institutionally constituted cognitive filters, such as operating within the Fund's scientific and technocratic culture and its existing body of economic policy knowledge, through which actors make sense of their environment and their role as pragmatic policy economists. This research specifies four mechanisms of internal ideational change at the Fund—reconciliation, operationalization, corroboration, and authoritative recognition—developed at length in Chapter 2, which shape the politics of economic ideas within the Fund. These help explain which economic ideas prevail and why.

The post-crash Fund is engaged in reconstructing its prescriptive policy thinking. In this case, perhaps contrary to expectations, crises provide opportunities not for 'great transformations' (Blyth 2002a) or paradigm shifts (Hall 1993) but for ongoing struggles over the periodic, pragmatic readjustment of the Fund's repertoire of economic ideas. The self-understanding of IMF staff as non-doctrinaire, and their view of the institution as increasingly open-minded and willing to learn from past crises, are an important part of the way Fund actors make sense of their institutional environment and their role as policy economists. They use the building blocks of a range of economic perspectives, sustained by different Fund subcultures, to maintain a pragmatic relevance to ongoing policy debates. We find that the IMF is neither beholden to an outmoded ideology in the Washington Consensus, nor simply applying a one-size-fits-all neo-Classical model to macroeconomic policy debate. Rather, it is engaged in reflexive and pragmatic processes of 'bricolage', defined by Campbell as when actors 'craft new institutional solutions by recombining elements in their repertoire through an innovative process' (Campbell 2004: 69), and 'layering' new ideas over old (Mahoney & Thelen 2010b; Streeck & Thelen 2005b). The Fund's rethinking of the premises of its policy thinking proceeds iteratively, the composite added to as ideas get taken up by IMF 'bricoleurs' in powerful positions within the Fund hierarchy, such as Dominique Strauss-Kahn, Olivier Blanchard, and Christine Lagarde.

The book contributes to CPE and IPE literature on the politics and political economy of austerity, and the economic policy possibilities and dilemmas presented by the GFC and Eurozone crises and their narration. The construction of economic crises, like the construction and maintenance of economic policy orthodoxies, is a social phenomenon. It is a contingent, and an often open-ended, inter-subjective process (Kirshner 2003b: 265; Keynes 1937: 114–18; Blyth 2003b, 2007, 2013b; Widmaier 2003a; Widmaier et al. 2007). Economic crises provide more conducive conditions for Fund bricoleurs to reshape understandings of 'appropriate' policy. As political economists interested in ideas have highlighted, what matters is not just the material manifestations of any crisis, but also the construction and narration of crises, for these shape economic policy implications (see e.g. Baker 2015: 345; Ban 2016; Blyth 2007, 2013b; Hay 1996; Gamble 2014: 7; Widmaier 2004: 437–8, 2016). Crucially important for shaping economic policy thinking is how the crisis comes to be understood—and what kinds of economic policy responses that understanding supports. In addition to those insights, this account underscores the importance of the Fund's crisis-defining economic ideas, and crisis *legacy*-defining ideas, which construct interpretations of economic crises in ways which prioritize particular policies, mechanisms, and institutions, and rule out or marginalize others. It spells out how the IMF's construction of the crisis and crisis legacy inform a Keynesian (see Chapter 3) recalibration of prescriptive policy discourse for advanced economies enjoying fiscal space which stands apart from the austerity and crisis of debt narratives.

The Fund enjoys a degree of doctrinal flexibility, although this should not be overstated. There are limits imposed, both by powerful members of its Board and by the need for consistency and continuity linked to maintaining its reputation as an intellectual authority on economic policy (Broome 2008). Numerous interviewees reflected upon how the Fund cannot be seen to be changing position or admitting it was wrong often without seriously damaging its standing as an authoritative source of economic policy knowledge and expertise. That reputation is crucial to securing the 'traction' the IMF seeks in dealings with and advice to member governments of all kinds. At the same time, there is a keenness amongst staffers to show sufficient flexibility. As Lagarde noted in a speech in early 2013, the IMF does not operate under principles that are set in stone: 'the pride of this institution is to constantly question, challenge, revisit, reexamine, and test its findings and assumptions, in order to be as up to date as possible' (2013). The Fund's Independent Evaluation Office is something of an institutional manifestation of that ethos (see e.g. Schwartz & Rist 2016). It is a delicate balancing act. As Blanchard points out, 'it is dangerous for an institution like this to admit mistakes' but there is a 'trade-off between admitting mistakes and keeping credibility'. Nevertheless, 'if you think the way you are going to behave in the future is different from how you behaved in the past—you have to own up to it.'[6] The slight element of cognitive dissonance amongst staff when invited to reflect on the degree and nature of change on fiscal policy since 2008 is interesting. The normal pattern was for staff to insist that the Fund has not really changed its mind, and then, over the course of lengthy interviews, to outline a series of significant evolutions since 2008.

[6] Interview with IMF Chief Economist Olivier Blanchard, June 2013.

Economics, Ideology, and Fiscal Policy

In exploring the Fund's role within the social construction of economic policy orthodoxy, one of the book's contributions is to locate this often technocratic discussion within the politics of economic ideas, both within the Fund and outside it. Internally, the politics of economic ideas requires the production of knowledge to be presented in socially acceptable form. Most immediately, new thinking must be reconcilable to internal Fund scientific culture and norms, which includes integration with mainstream academic economic thinking. Earlier research has identified 'subcultures' within the Fund which develop 'different interpretations and applications' of policy thinking, drawing on 'ongoing debates within the economics profession' (Chwieroth 2010: 23–4; Ban 2015a & b; Boughton 2004). After 2008, these debates amongst economists involved considerable soul-searching. The self-congratulatory view that 'New Consensus Macroeconomics' (NCM, see Chapter 3), which emerged in the 1990s, had resolved economic growth and stability problems (Lucas 2003; cf. Mankiw 2006) was demolished by the GFC and the deep recession that followed. Whilst diehards like Lucas kept the faith in their versions of rational expectations and NCM, others felt fresh thinking was warranted. Conventional monetary policy, hitherto deemed the only stabilization tool policymakers required, offered no answers in a world where stagnating advanced economies faced deficient demand and interest rates were constrained by the Zero Lower Bound. As the recession deepened, and more financial fragilities and systemic risk emerged, faith in the assumed efficiency of financial markets and their tending towards socially optimal outcomes was also profoundly shaken (see e.g. Auerbach and Gorodnichenko 2012, 2013a & b; Delong & Summers 2012). Influential economists like Larry Summers and Brad Delong shifted their thinking in light of the evidence in ways which did not simply reaffirm their prior assumptions or what they had argued previously. Eminent academic economists such as these, in revisiting their economic policy thinking, generated openings for the questioning of conventional wisdoms. These parallel re-evaluations, much cited in post-crash Fund flagships, were helpful to Fund economists seeking to alter thinking.

The analysis highlights the role of key senior figures, notably IMF Managing Director Dominique Strauss-Kahn (referred to internally as DSK), who served from 2008 to 2011, in changing the Fund's prevailing fiscal policy ideas. His recruitment of the very highly regarded, open-minded, and Keynesian-sympathetic Olivier Blanchard as chief economist was also key. Strauss-Kahn's explicit call for all Fund staff to 'think outside the box' in approaching economic policy and economic stabilization in the context of the crisis was crucial. As then Director of the Fiscal Affairs Department (FAD), Carlo Cottarelli, put it in 2013, 'this change of position of the Fund regarding fiscal activism under [Strauss-Kahn] came from the top. And then, you know, the way the Fund works, the mentality; everybody aligns.'[7] In a deeply hierarchical organization, this steer from on high, allied with Fund staff's self-understanding as non-doctrinaire and pragmatic, guided by the facts and evidence, expanded the space for policy rethinking. For First Deputy Managing Director David Lipton, 'I think the Fund's thinking has been appropriately to have an open mind, to try and understand the different channels through which policies have an effect and then to calibrate advice to countries based on what each individual country needs.'[8] Strauss-Kahn and Blanchard, along with other like-minded individuals recruited or promoted to senior positions, strengthened the market-sceptical, Keynesian 'subculture' within the Fund. This bolstered an interpretive framework focused on post-crash deficiencies of aggregate demand and crises of confidence, and more positively disposed under certain conditions to using fiscal policy proactively. Fund 'flagships' like *World Economic Outlook* (*WEO*) and the newly introduced *Fiscal Monitor* were used to reflect and showcase the rehabilitation of fiscal policy as an economic stabilization and crisis management tool. This was timely given the post-crunch context where what 'sound' economic management entailed was up for redefinition. Blanchard and others sought to effect this redefinition in repeated interactions with national economic policymakers through surveillance, IMF autumn and spring meetings, the G20, European meetings, and other fora. They also hosted a string of conferences inviting leading economists to advance the post-crash rethink of economic policy.

One thing revealed by this revisiting of the premises of economic policy thinking was the breadth, along a wide continuum, of the policy approaches reconcilable to mainstream economic thinking (Blanchard, Romer et al. 2012; Akerlof, Blanchard et al. 2014). This was particularly true in the realms of fiscal policy—extending from the conviction that fiscal policy could have no beneficial effect to thoroughgoing revival of counter-cyclical Keynesianism (see e.g. Alesina & Giavazzi 2013b). Those seeking to adopt positions anywhere along this variegated spectrum could find corroboration from holders of Nobel prizes—from Lucas, Sargent, and Fama at one end to Krugman, Stiglitz, and Shiller at the other. This forms the backdrop to the contemporary politics of austerity debates about fiscal consolidation, debts, and deficits (Blyth 2013a; Quiggin 2012). These competing and divergent authoritative knowledge claims reveal what Kirshner calls the 'indeterminacy of economic theory as a guide to policy' (Kirshner 2003a: 7). This is a crucially important insight for analysing the politics of economic ideas. There are, in short, multiple different constructions of the economically 'sound'. This gives sources of authoritative

[7] Interview with Carlo Cottarelli, June 2013.

[8] Interview with David Lipton, September 2013.

economic policy recommendation such as the IMF scope to select and prioritize within this menu of respectable economic thinking.

How economic theory is invoked by the Fund in economic policy recommendation is a recurrent theme in this book. To unearth what is at stake in the selection of one set of economic concepts over another, it is necessary to delve into the intellectual building blocks and assumptive foundations of the economic theorizing that is presented as common sense or orthodoxy. The economic policy debate is conducted partly within the norms of academic economics discourse. It takes on a technocratic tone, and often dwells upon methodological justifications for techniques used to corroborate one set of claims or another. However, underlying this 'scientific' debate, deep down there are roots in debates over the principles of political economy; positions on what economic policy can and should do, about the nature, propensities, and appropriate roles of state and markets. This underlines the *political* role played by IMF bricoleurs seeking to shape economic policy conduct by foregrounding particular rationales, insights, and prioritizations. Whilst Fund surveillance and commentary is cloaked in scientific and technocratic parlance, the *selection* of *which* economic ideas and concepts are afforded primacy is a highly significant and a deeply political process.

Economic ideas are always rooted in underlying ideological assumptions about how the economy and policy work. Within the politics of austerity and post-crisis economic policy debates in advanced economies, this is sometimes all too apparent. Discussions of 'moral hazard' issues raised by sovereign bail-outs and then debt restructuring were conducted as morality plays, rather than technical economic debates (Fourcade et al. 2013; Matthijs & McNamara 2015). As Blyth underscores, the ideology of austerity foregrounds the failings of states and public powers, whilst sweeping private sector moral hazard issues raised by socialization of massive financial sector liabilities under the carpet (Blyth 2013a). Yet this ideological dimension of economic ideas is equally present even when it is less self-evident (Dow 2015).

As Best and Widmaier put it, economists deal in 'analytically prior ontological assumptions' about 'economic policy possibilities' (Best & Widmaier 2006: 626). These ideological assumptions about the nature of state/market relations hark back to and evoke the classical political economy debates of Smith, Ricardo, Say, Keynes, and many others (Watson 2005; Clift 2014a; Heilbroner 1992, 1996). They all posed the perennial questions about the principles of political economy: How effective is state intervention in the economy? To what extent will the market, left to its own devices, tend towards full employment and socially optimal outcomes? Under what conditions might this be more or less likely to occur? Different schools of economic theory encapsulate different worldviews on these questions, and essentially assert them a priori, rather than subjecting them to sustained interrogation (see Klamer & Colander 1990; Colander 2005: 177; Fourcade 2009; Fuchs et al. 1997, 1998; Chwieroth 2010: 11, 12). As Schumpeter put it, 'analytic work begins with material provided by our vision of things and that vision is ideological almost by definition' (1949: 359).

It is forbiddingly difficult to gauge empirically the precise impact of fiscal policy. This is partly because growth has effects on fiscal imbalances as well as vice versa, but also because one cannot isolate fiscal policy effects from other policy effects, nor from the range of complex causal factors affecting economic activity (IMF 2010g; Ball et al. 2011). Various techniques have been developed in economics to attempt to assess fiscal policy effects, but none is perfect. None escapes these 'endogeneity' problems to make wholly convincing causal claims. The fiscal policy debate, like others in economics, is impossible to resolve conclusively at the empirical level. No ultimate 'scientific' judgement is possible. Whilst some contend that almost all economists agree about how fiscal and monetary policies work (see e.g. Wren-Lewis 2016b), it is fair to say that the economics profession is and always will be divided on these issues to some degree. At some level, those making claims and policy recommendations are reliant upon underlying normatively driven prior assumptions on the efficacy and desirability of public spending, state intervention, and public power playing a major role in the market economy. It comes down to assumptive foundations about how the economy and policy works (Dow 2015; Fuchs et al. 1997, 1998; Jelveh et al. 2014; Rivlin 1987). Tracing the evolution of fiscal policy thinking over the decades prior to the crisis, and since the crisis, reveals how prevailing views on such assumptive foundations can and do shift—sometimes markedly and quickly.

The Keynesianism of the neo-classical synthesis (Samuelson & Solow 1960; see Chapter 3), which came to dominate economic policymaking from the 1940s through to the 1970s, and had a much longer shelf life within the IMF, assumed that fiscal and monetary policy could affect overall economic activity by managing levels of aggregate demand in the economy. One of Keynes' core contributions to economic theorizing was to point how postulates such as Say's law assuming the efficient operation of markets, 'happen not to be those of the economic society in which we actually live' (Keynes 1964 [1936]: 3). Say's law was a mainstay of the neo-classical economic orthodoxy Keynes was railing against. Markets under certain conditions could not be relied upon to tend to full employment, or deliver socially optimal outcomes. In particular, Keynes highlighted how sufficient aggregate demand, and indeed confidence, may be lacking. An economy could get 'stuck' below full employment for protracted periods, and free markets contained no inherent propensity to return to a full employment equilibrium. This insight into and assumption of potential market failure carved out a role for macroeconomic policy and governmental economic management. This was the essence of the post-war case for counter-cyclical macroeconomic policy and 'demand management'. Sometimes called 'Keynesian fine-tuning', or more compellingly 'hydraulic' Keynesianism, with government's economic management role involving pulling policy levers conceived as the sluice gates manipulating levels of demand (Coddington 1976: 1263–7).

After the 1970s, a 'conventional wisdom' grew up in academic economic circles, accepted yet under-reflected upon, taken-as-read but built on shaky foundations (see Galbraith 1958: 16–17), that fiscal policy was unreliable as an economic stabilization tool. This had its adherents within the Fund (see Chapter 3), but was more stridently embraced in academia. At the extremes of what is always a somewhat ideological debate about fiscal policy, even if it is carefully couched in the 'scientific' norms of economics, there is a meta-critique of fiscal policy suggesting that governments should not even attempt economic stabilization through macroeconomic policy. The 'New Classical' economics of Lucas, Sargent, and others used particular kinds of 'rational expectations' assumptions to build a radically anti-Keynesian reinvigoration of the neo-classical tradition. At the centre of this view is the notion of 'Ricardian equivalence' which has played a prominent role within the post-crash politics of austerity. The core assumption here is that forward-looking agents will anticipate fully future tax rises (to pay for higher debts), adjusting their behaviour to consume less. This will nullify any boost to economic activity or demand that a fiscal stimulus was designed to initiate (see e.g. Barro 1974, 1989). This rather unrealistic and decidedly anti-Keynesian view of economic actors holds that fiscal policy simply *cannot* be an effective tool for economic management. It is one manifestation of a broader concept which arises from the extreme rational expectations assumptions underpinning the New Classical school (see Chapter 3), termed the 'policy irrelevance' or 'policy ineffectiveness' proposition (Blyth 2013b; Blaug 1996: 686). The post-crash Fund set itself decidedly against these views. As Cottarelli put it in 2013, 'I think nobody is a Ricardian in the Fund any more'.[9]

Illustrating the intertwining of ideological and technocratic elements in economic policy conduct, monetary policy was deemed more effective because central banks would offset the fiscal expansionary impulse by raising interest rates. Central bankers' ideological opposition to big government and higher public spending, their 'deficit bias' concerns that governments are always prone to spend more money than they raise, would undermine the potency of the fiscal policy tool (Hilbers 2004). Thus, for many Fund economists, not only was monetary policy seen as a preferable economic stabilization tool, but also given the politics of fiscal policy and the ideological predispositions of central

[9] Interview with Carlo Cottarelli, June 2013; interview with Doug Laxton, Division Chief of the Economic Modelling Division, IMF Research Department, September 2013.

bankers, the interaction of fiscal and monetary policy under normal conditions rendered fiscal expansion considerably less effective.

A more pragmatic set of views continued to see economic stabilization as a necessary and good thing, but identified practical impediments to doing it through fiscal policy. These were part and parcel of 'New Consensus' Macroeconomics which sought to reconcile New Keynesian and New Classical approaches from the 1990s onwards (see Chapter 3). One concern was fiscal policy's implementation lags, reducing confidence that fiscal policy interventions could be relied upon to be sufficiently timely. By the time the demand impetus 'kicked in' the downturn could well be over. Secondly, in open economies there is a risk that, unless international coordination could be achieved, fiscal stimulus could simply 'leak out' and adversely affect the trade balance. These reservations were often harnessed to a more general anxiety amongst economists about 'deficit bias' of governments not able to finance their new spending commitments. One long-serving senior Fund economist noted 'an innate resistance to advocate fiscal expansion' at the Fund, especially for countries without a reputation for being spendthrift.[10] Fiscal policy struggled to be 'credibly temporary', since new spending, once introduced, would be very difficult to take away. The fourth major concern, again linked to a broader anxiety about government expenditure, was that spending might be captured by powerful vested interests as demonized by public choice theory (Niskanen 1971; Buchanan 1975; Tullock 1965, 1989). This Virginia School of political economy asserted the irresponsibility of politicians' behaviour if granted licence to use fiscal policy. Their rent-seeking behaviour would mean that new spending would not be directed towards efficient ends. These are dubbed 'political economy' considerations within Fund parlance.

What differentiates this array of positions on fiscal policy are varied responses to the perennial political economy questions discussed above. Similarly, different understandings of the principles of political economy underpin the diverse positions on the politics of austerity which have dominated national economic policy debates in many advanced economies since the GFC. What separates these viewpoints, at root, are normative predispositions towards fiscal policy. Reputable arguments, backed by robust methodological techniques, can be mounted on both sides. It comes down to taking a position on a spectrum of views about how far the market, left to its own devices, will likely deliver the most efficient outcomes, and to what extent (and under what conditions) public power can and should intervene in the economy using public investment and expenditure to improve the growth prospects and stability of the economy. It is, broadly speaking, the same ideological debate

[10] Interview with former Deputy Director of the IMF European Department Alessandro Leipold, September 2013.

which pitched Keynes against neo-classical orthodoxy in the 1930s. All of which is uncomfortable territory for a Fund deeply engaged in the debate, yet keen to retain a non-political character removed from such ideological considerations, and to assert its intellectual authority as a source of scientific, technocratic wisdom on economic policy.

The Social Construction of Crisis, and of Economic Policy Orthodoxy

The construction of economic policy knowledge is a social process, wherein authoritative voices can shape others' perceptions of what sensible economic policy conduct looks like. The IMF's quest for 'traction' for its economic analysis and policy recommendations is understood here as the Fund seeking to exercise ideational power through the shaping of meanings attached to 'sound' economic policy. The IMF, like other IOs, exercises authority by developing and spreading norms (Barnett & Finnemore 1999, 2004; Clegg 2013; Park & Vetterlein 2010), and shaping intersubjective understandings of appropriate economic policy conduct. A crucial aspect of what IO scholars term the Fund's 'productive power' is its ability to influence or determine 'what counts as legitimate knowledge', and to 'set and fix meanings' attached to economic policies (Barnett & Duvall 2005: 21–2; Chwieroth 2010; Broome & Seabrooke 2012; Best 2010). The analysis identifies mechanisms of incremental ideational change within the institution through which Fund thinking on this evolves. The IMF is able to mobilize its research resources, flagship publications, and its seat at the table of international summits such as the G20 to provide evidence and corroboration in support of its favoured economic policy approaches.

In executing its legal mandate for surveillance in pursuit of economic stability, whereby all members are accountable for the external effects of their domestic policies, the Fund works to build a consensus about appropriate macroeconomic policy (Pauly 1997). The Fund's intellectual framework for understanding economic policy is central to the process of attempting to fix meanings attached to economic policy (Clift & Tomlinson 2012; Ban 2015a; James 1996). The Fund works to promote its interpretive framework, and along with a small number of other authoritative bodies, shapes the limits of the credible in economic policy. Even though Fund advice is not always heeded, and policy recommendations arising out of IMF surveillance can be ignored, the Fund's assessment of the credibility of policies still matters (Stone 2002).

The Fund's success within what Baker terms 'the process of political and intellectual construction of crisis' which 'proceeds through persuasive struggles' (2015: 345) was greatest in the initial phase, when the threat of another Great

Depression loomed. With the global economic system on brink of collapse, in the autumn of 2008 Strauss-Kahn and Blanchard worked to construct what Widmaier calls a 'Keynesian understanding' or 'market failure construction of crisis' (see Widmaier 2004: 437–8), harnessed to corralling of advanced economy leaders to commit to coordinated fiscal stimulus to avert another Great Depression (Strauss-Kahn 2008a & b; Blanchard 2008b; Blanchard & Cottarelli 2008; Spilimbergo et al. 2008). The Fund's countercyclical fiscal stimulus recommendations sat outside the normal policy ideas of most advanced economy governments, and were not the lessons policymakers had drawn from academic economics up until the crisis. This Keynesian praxis involved Fund leadership seeking to stabilize expectations to tackle short-term market failure, working to orchestrate coordinated policy responses, and guiding the world's major economies away from the abyss. Amidst the global financial maelstrom, when the Fund had scope to be most influential, the conjuncture was most opportune to mobilize salient *short-run* Keynesian insights into liquidity traps,[11] demand deficiency, and higher fiscal multipliers (reflecting heightened potency of fiscal policy).

With the shift from the fiscal stimulus phase to the prioritization of fiscal consolidation *circa* 2010, the construction and framing of the economic crisis evolved. The revival of Keynesian insights was somewhat superseded. As Gamble notes of the post-2010 period, 'orthodox narratives around debt, retrenchment and austerity have for the most part defined the crisis and determined how it has been perceived' (Gamble 2014: 7). Debt and deficit discourse foregrounded the importance of 'living within our means', paying down the deficit and the debt, and 'paying our way in the world'. Economists have long pointed out the irrelevance of the household analogy for understanding the public finances (see e.g. Wren-Lewis 2016a: 5–6). The IMF's careful differentiation between medium-term goals of fiscal sustainability and the short-term goal of supporting growth and recovery enabled it to advance an alternative interpretation of the crisis, and the legacy of the crisis. The Fund's consistent highlighting of the ongoing need to boost weak demand and nurture economic growth offered a counterpoint, advocating a role for fiscal policy and unconventional monetary policy within economic stabilization. In reasserting the need for international coordination, the IMF worked to shift the prioritization of economic policy. As this book demonstrates, the Fund has sought—with at best limited success—to challenge the austerity-oriented definition of the crisis.

The post-crash strategic doctrinal flexibility of IMF bricoleurs has been enacted and operationalized through the concept of fiscal space. As we explore

[11] When central bank efforts to lower the long-term interest rates fail, and monetary policy becomes ineffective at stimulating the economy.

in Chapter 4, fiscal space is a social construction central to the more differentiated approach to economic policy advice which is a notable feature of the post-crash IMF. It is also crucial to Fund efforts to attenuate and challenge the single-minded myopic prioritization of austerity measures and debt and deficit reduction by governments in London, Berlin, and elsewhere. It explains how the Fund has seemingly changed its tune, apparently abandoning its reputation for harsh austerity, spending cuts, and restrictive macroeconomic policies (Meltzer 2010). The IMF worked to broaden the range of policy tools and appropriate policy responses to the crisis and the ensuing recession. As IMF Research Department Deputy Director Jonathan Ostry described the post-crash rethink of Fund policy advice, 'More policy activism across the board is a lesson. We now know we have a much richer toolkit with which to combat the kinds of crises that countries can experience: fiscal crises, growth crises, financial crises, and external crises.'[12] Ironically, though, the Fund did not deem some of these policy options open to those countries most in need of them. Programme countries in the Eurozone periphery such as Greece and Portugal, facing high unemployment and very low growth, did not, in the IMF's estimation, enjoy the fiscal space to delay fiscal consolidation. Nor could they pursue counter-cyclical policies injecting more demand into the economy to try and get the recovery off the ground (IEO 2016; see Chapters 5 and 7).

Fiscal space underlines the contingent differentiated nature of the Fund's economic policy message, mindful of national conditions and dependent upon shared understandings of a country's fiscal sustainability. Countries facing high borrowing costs and struggling for creditworthiness for reasons of track record, reputation, revenue-raising capacity or the scale and structure of their debts enjoy many fewer policy options and much reduced policy space. With the exception of the November 2008 blanket call for a 2 per cent coordinated global fiscal stimulus, most post-GFC Fund entreaties to boost aggregate demand using fiscal policy applied only to those countries *not facing financing constraints*. Fiscal space is not a scientific concept, but is drawn on widely within the Fund in a 'rule of thumb' manner to justify policy recommendations and advice, an example of how important subjective judgements are within Fund decision-making (Nelson 2017). As Fund economist Vivek Arora notes of Fund surveillance in general, 'at the end of the day a lot of it is based on the judgement of the review officer and the mission chief . . . there's a lot of judgement involved, but it is informed by the expertise, ongoing experience, and by the multilateral work'.[13] The non-quantifiable, intuitive, and not directly measurable quality of fiscal space provides latitude for Fund actors to

[12] Interview with IMF Research Department Deputy Director Jonathan Ostry, June 2013.

[13] Interview with then Assistant Director in the IMF Strategy, Policy and Review Department Vivek Arora, September 2013.

define what constitutes economic policy virtue in the contemporary economic conjuncture for advanced economies. Fiscal space also crucially insulates the case for more use of fiscal policy levers from the debt sustainability and 'deficit bias' concerns often voiced by those less convinced of fiscal policy's merits.

The IMF was designed as part of the Bretton Woods plan to create domestic policy space to pursue objectives, even if at odds with international financial market integration (Ruggie 1982, 1983). The initial Bretton Woods settlement curtailed short-term capital flows to enhance policy autonomy; as Keynes put it, 'the whole management of the domestic economy depends on being free to have the appropriate rate of interest without reference to the rate prevailing elsewhere in the world. Capital control is a corollary to this' (1980: 148–9). Scholarship on the IMF of the Washington Consensus era critiqued the Fund for betraying these principles, curtailing policy autonomy and inducing countries to adjust to international economic conditions in ways which harmed the domestic economy (Davidson 2007: 93–103). As Thirkell White summarized this view in the early 2000s, 'many currently feel the IMF has reversed these priorities... attempts to push countries to adapt their social and political environments to suit market imperatives' (2005: 7; Best 2003; Soederberg 2004). Unlike the confining and restricting of policy space which Robert Wade and others associate with an earlier phase of the Bretton Woods institutions' interactions with developing economies (Wade 2003a & b), the post-crash construction and deployment of fiscal space involves the IMF seeking to *expand* the policy space for a select group of advanced economies. It may also expand policy space for some developing economies, although that is beyond the scope of this study.

Shared Understandings within the Fund of the Economy and Policy

The focus of this book, then, is on how the IMF seeks to shape understandings of 'sound' economic policy in advanced economies not borrowing from the Fund. In this section we map the broad contours of the Fund's recalibration of its economic policy thinking since 2008. This provides the context for drilling down into the fiscal policy discussion in the remainder of the book. One conspicuous facet of Fund commentary and intellectual production after 2008 was a greater degree of scepticism towards the properties and propensities of markets, in particular financial markets. Market economies are understood to be more prone to instability than appreciated prior to 2008. It is striking how expansive the scepticism towards market pathologies became, and the extent and range of shortcomings of markets recognized and emphasized (Cottarelli & Jaramillo 2012; IMF 2014d; IMF 2015b) by senior Fund figures.[14] 'Efficient' market assumptions about inherent tendencies towards optimal outcomes, what economists call a 'Walrasian' view of market propensities (after the Swiss Economist Leon Walras), held much less sway in the post-crash IMF. Blanchard in September 2014 noted how the view that 'economic fluctuations' were 'regular, and essentially self-correcting' had gained ground in pre-crisis macroeconomics. Hence its linear assumptions about natural return to steady state over time and its particular variant of rational expectations. 'The problem', Blanchard notes, 'is that we came to believe that this was indeed the way the world worked', neglecting how 'small shocks could have large adverse effects, or could result in long and persistent slumps' (2014a: 28).

Fund assessments of the relationship between financial markets and stability changed markedly after 2008. Economic stability had to be actively pursued through a wide range of policy and regulatory measures by governments, central banks, the IMF and others, since it was not safe to assume an inherent tendency on the part of financial markets to deliver stability, full employment, and growth (Vinals 2010, 2011, 2016). This non-Walrasian, market-sceptical worldview opens space for a critique of market outcomes. Markets can exacerbate instabilities, and can exhibit herd behaviour and irrational exuberance, leading to bank runs and 'sudden stops' (Blanchard 2014a: 28–31), which can trigger broader crises through contagion effects. Further financial crises are considered more likely, and should be anticipated as the norm, not the exception. What is more, future crises will be hard to predict. A corollary of this broad recognition is thinking not just in terms of clearly calculable, linear, and predictable financial market 'risks' but appreciating pervasive 'uncertainty' as Knight or Keynes understood it (Blanchard 2009, 2012c; Keynes 1937; Knight 1921).

One of the most direct implications of this appreciation for the conduct of economic policy was in rethinking the nature of 'fiscal risks' facing states and their public finances, especially contingent liabilities arising in countries with large financial sectors (IMF 2011k). The revised, more sceptical assessment of financial markets led to new appreciation of potential vulnerabilities and instabilities inherent in market economies (IMF 2013j: 15). Financial markets are also now recognized to perform poorly in assessing risks and uncertainties, such that the price mechanism is unlikely to deal effectively with contingent liabilities. Given these sizeable likely impacts of an unpredictable financial crisis, and since hidden liabilities would probably end up on the public debt book, assessments of 'prudent' levels of public debt might need to be revised

[14] This was a view expressed by numerous Fund economists in interview.

downwards (IMF 2011c: 20–9). Advanced economy governments, after all, cannot afford another bail-out like 2008–9. In this context, it is all the more remarkable that the Fund in its dealings with many advanced economies enjoying fiscal space, has shifted away from a single-minded focus on reducing debt and deficits (IMF 2014d: 75–114; IMF 2015b: xvi, 1, 19–25).

The Fund's heightened post-GFC appreciation of the pervasive uncertainty in the global economy foregrounds the need for 'stabilising norms' (Best 2010: 203; see also Widmaier 2003a, 2004). This harks back to Keynes' account of the economy, wherein—amidst pervasive uncertainty—economic actors operating on incomplete information were guided by intersubjectively constituted 'conventions' (Keynes 1936, 1937; Blyth 2002a; Nelson & Katzenstein 2014; Baker & Widmaier 2014). Shaping these conventional understandings is something its surveillance and policy commentary work, as well as new fiscal risk assessment techniques, can contribute to. The understanding of economic actors, and their rationality, which underpins post-crash economic policy thinking in the Fund operates in terms of multiple possible equilibria. This is another departure from the linear world of markets tending towards efficient outcomes. Ideas about 'multiple equilibria' and 'belief-driven equilibria' bedevilling sovereign debt markets, irrespective of underlying economic fundamentals, were at the heart of the Fund's analysis of Europe from 2009 onwards (Blanchard 2012c: xv–xvi; 2014b: xiii; IMF 2011n: 36; IMF 2012c: 4). Distinguishing between 'good' and 'bad' sovereign debt equilibria became central to Fund commentary on the Eurozone crisis. This New Keynesian understanding of multiple possible equilibria highlights the role for institutions in stabilizing expectations in conditions of uncertainty. In this worldview, central banks, national fiscal institutions, and bodies like the Fund, need to provide reassurance to financial market participants about countries' fiscal positions. They do this partly through interventions in bond markets, and also through medium-term fiscal frameworks and 'sound' fiscal institutions (IMF 2013j). The construction of effective backstops and firewalls are central to efforts to prevent contagion and limit herd behaviour.

Appreciation of the non-self-correcting pathologies of markets, and their potential to deliver socially suboptimal outcomes is also at the heart of a wider range of 'non-linear' (self-aggravating) threats identified which endanger macroeconomic stability. Blanchard terms these 'diabolical loops' (2014). These vicious cycles are increasingly prevalent within post-crash Fund commentary and surveillance (see IMF 2015g: xiii). Demand deficiency at the root of the prolonged post-crash recession is linked directly to deflation (Decressin & Laxton 2009), hysteresis[15] effects (IMF 2013j: 21, 29–30), and secular stagnation

[15] Hysteresis is a New Keynesian idea, a process whereby substantial persistence of higher unemployment leads to loss of skills, human capital degradation, and insider/outsider effects

(Summers 2013) or 'lowflation' (Moghadam et al. 2014), as leading Fund figures articulated it in the European context. Another prominent vicious cycle within Fund commentary is the 'sovereign-bank feedback loops [which] have amplified sovereign debt crises' (IMF 2013j: 1, 5; 13–14). Hysteresis and secular stagnation are products of thinking about the economy where aggregate demand matters and plays a crucial role in determining the level of output. Both are at odds with Say's law and the neo-classical economic views of markets tending towards equilibrium of their own accord. In these circumstances, non-linear risks of vicious cycles of low activity and low growth threatened to become entrenched, locking advanced economies in a suboptimal equilibrium, falling further behind potential growth rates and paths.

The stability dimension of the Fund's mandate takes on greater significance in this light. It can and has been mobilized as a call to greater activism in a range of policy spheres, from unconventional monetary policy, to revived advocacy of capital controls (IMF 2012m; Chwieroth 2014; Gallagher 2015; Moschella 2015; Grabel 2015), to macro-prudential regulation (Baker 2013a & b; Baker & Widmaier 2014; IMF 2011b & m; IMF 2013i), and counter-cyclical fiscal policy (Spilimbergo et al. 2008; Freedman et al. 2009; Lagarde 2011b; IMF 2013j). The view that crises are the norm, rather than the exception, including for advanced economies, has gained much wider acceptance within the IMF. Not just financial market stability, but macroeconomic stability more broadly is recognized as something that has to be actively pursued, and reinforced through policy activism, and supported by oversight and surveillance (Blanchard et al. 2010; IMF 2015b: xv–xvi). Fund views on both the scale of the task of economic stabilization which is at the core of its mandate, and the range of policy tools, both monetary and fiscal, which can and should be used in its pursuit, expanded markedly after 2008.

Following the GFC, there was an innovative reinterpretation of the IMF's mandate, wherein the concern with growth and stability has been extended. Specifically, the Fund directly linked inequality and iniquitous outcomes from macroeconomic policy to instability and to lower growth. Research found that higher inequality reduces the size and duration of growth spells (Berg & Ostry 2011; Berg et al. 2012). Senior Fund figures from the last two Managing Directors down identified inequality as 'a macro-critical social indicator' (IMF 2011l). As Ostry put it,

> I made the point (to DSK) that a core objective of the Fund is to come up with policy advice that underpins macro-financial stability. So if we can show that avoiding excessive inequality is in fact essential for strong, healthy and sustainable

within the labour market. The enduring scarring effect on productive capacity then leads to a permanent ratcheting up of the unemployment rate and reduction of the growth potential of the economy. See Blanchard and Summers (1986).

> growth (which I believe the research I have been engaged in does show), then indeed there is a direct link between issues of inequality and distribution and issues that lie at the core of the IMF's mandate.[16]

Mainstream economics argues that the market determines the distributional outcomes of economic activity, and does not focus on the iniquitous effects of economic policy. Economists' default eschewal of political or ethical commentary on questions of inequality only began to be countered some years after the GFC when Piketty (2014, 2015) and Stiglitz (2012, 2015) directly addressed this issue. The Fund under Strauss-Kahn and then Lagarde shifted significantly to make tackling inequality a priority in terms of its commentary, research, and contributions to the international economic policy debate (Lagarde 2012d). The work of Ostry and others has demonstrated that

> avoiding excessive levels of inequality can actually help economies grow more strongly and more sustainability, a point we have developed in a series of research and policy papers. Fiscal redistribution, unless you do it in an extreme fashion, can bring about both greater equality and stronger, more healthy growth. The efficiency losses from redistributive fiscal policies, moreover, appear to be small, unless redistribution is extreme.[17]

This is another manifestation of the idea that some form of public action is required to temper the iniquitous outcomes of the most unfettered markets.

On inequality, as with market instability, the Fund is camped out on unconventional territory. Most mainstream economists would leave distributional questions to the market, comforted by the presumption that 'a rising tide floats all boats'. The Fund, however, has deployed significant resources in recent years working to address equity and inequality through the design of economic policy. This accentuated focus on inequality had a very specific relevance to the politics of austerity and the post-GFC fiscal policy debate in advanced economies. A standard mantra of Lagarde as IMF Managing Director, like Strauss-Kahn before her, emphasized how fiscal policy needed to focus 'not only on efficiency, but also on equity, particularly on fairness in sharing the burden of adjustment, and on protecting the weak and vulnerable' (Lagarde 2012c). It is, implicitly at least, a critique of how fiscal consolidation has been pursued in certain advanced economies. This dovetails with work on fiscal multipliers to reinforce the case for targeting spending on lower earners, to get the greatest bang for buck in supporting economic activity in the face of a severe downturn. More broadly, it indicates a role for macroeconomic policy in managing aggregate demand to sustain a high level of employment in the

16 Interview with IMF Research Department Deputy Director Jonathan Ostry, June 2013.
17 Interview with IMF Research Department Deputy Director Jonathan Ostry, June 2013.

economy, and is further testament to the renewed influence of Keynesian thinking (IMF 2013d: 4).

As the Fund's own research has recognized, fiscal consolidation leads to increased inequality (Ball et al. 2013; Furcedi & Loungani 2013: 25–7; Woo et al. 2013). Thus, the benefits of fiscal consolidation for the public finances need to be weighed against the costs in terms of iniquitous economic and social outcomes, and potential damage to long-term growth. Moreover, leading Fund figures underlined that equity and equality considerations were important for gaining social and political acceptance for fiscal adjustment measures, which will take many years (Lipton 2013a). Although couched in the technocratic terms of the 'optimal composition' of fiscal consolidation, this was the IMF engaged in the politics of economic ideas. Key players at the Fund sought to shift approaches to austerity, endeavouring to convince governments with fiscal space to alter the pace of adjustment to limit adverse effects on demand and growth. These were all part of the Fund's contribution to the central economic policy debate of the post-crash era for advanced economies.

Outline of the Book

Chapter 2 advances in depth the case for a Constructivist Institutionalist (CI) approach to the analysis of ideational change in general, and within IOs in particular. The explanatory framework developed here foregrounds the cognitive and ideational filters through which actors make sense of their institutional environment and indeed their interests. We underline the importance of how Fund staff see themselves and their role as a means to operationalizing these constructivist insights. This requires understanding of the institutional, organizational, and ideational context in which economic ideas are produced and deployed—hence the analysis charts key facets of the Fund's internal workings, including its hierarchical nature, internal review processes, and how internal interactions are evolving. It then goes on to spell out four mechanisms of ideational change within the IMF—reconciliation, operationalization, corroboration, and authoritative recognition, revealing how ideas need to be framed and packaged to jump through the hoops of internal social recognition. 'Feedback loops' are identified within Fund practices which act as transmission mechanisms through which reflexive actors respond to their environment, perceive the boundaries of socially acceptable policy ideas within the IMF, and reshape their institutional context. This chapter sets out the case for 'bricolage' (Campbell 2004: 69) rather than paradigm shifts as a framework for understanding Fund ideational evolution, due to the complexities of institutional mediation, and the sedimented but ongoing influence of multiple ideas from different paradigmatic homes.

Chapter 3 places the IMF's recent and longer term evolution within the context of evolving prevailing approaches in the economics profession to macroeconomic and fiscal policy. As such, it maps the landscape on which the politics of austerity debates about fiscal consolidation, debts, and deficits have played out. Rooting the analysis and prescriptions contained in Fund flagship publications within prevailing thinking in academic economics is an important dimension of the IMF's intellectual authority. Scholars and schools of economic thought are evoked to provide a 'seal of approval' for Fund economic knowledge, analogous to how the Fund endorses a country's economic policy settings. Eminent academic economists revisited their policy thinking post-GFC, and the chapter charts how parallel re-evaluations were helpful to those within the Fund seeking to shift positions and priorities. It then sets out the Fund's pre-crisis stance and thinking, before charting what has changed since the GFC within the Fund's approach to fiscal policy. It calibrates claims about the repertoire of fiscal policy ideas the Fund draws on, noting the enduring role of Keynesian insights. Counter-posing 'time 1' and 'time 2' throws into relief the highly distinctive characteristics of post-crash Fund fiscal policy thinking. A key finding is the breadth, along a wide continuum, of the policy approaches reconcilable to mainstream economic thinking post-GFC. Provided certain *form* conditions (distilled in the four mechanisms specified in Chapter 2) are met, the *content* of acceptable new economic thinking within the Fund is surprisingly open. This gives authoritative commentators such as the IMF scope to select, prioritize, and choose within this menu of respectable economic thinking. In this, it is guided by views on the principles of political economy about, amongst other things, the market's propensity to equilibrium, and the efficacy of policy interventions in a given context and conjuncture.

Chapter 4 locates the Fund within the wider context of world politics to develop a framework for understanding of IMF influence over advanced economies, and explores the sources and limits of the IMF's authority and autonomy. The interests of powerful members and power relations at board level delimit the range of IMF policy ideas. That said, within the parameters of 'thinkable' policy (Seabrooke 2010: 141), there is scope for Fund leadership and staff to use their agenda-setting capacity to strategically promote, advocate, and corroborate particular approaches to economic policy. It then sets out the conditions of possibility for the Fund's exercising intellectual authority. IMF influence is contingent upon its ability to frame policy advice in a way which resonates with policymakers, as well as its ability to mobilize its scientific expertise, knowledge bank, and mandate in a given policy context. Non-borrowing advanced economies constitute a less likely case for Fund influence to prevail, since the institution lacks leverage mechanisms. The IMF surveillance regime contains no means of enforcement, and given competing authoritative claims, the socially recognized expertise of economists does not work solely in the Fund's favour. Thus, the IMF's reach often exceeds its grasp.

Chapter 5 drills down into IMF/advanced economy government interactions and Fund efforts to influence the international economic policy debate. It provides fresh insights into the sources, scope, and limits of IMF intellectual authority during the Great Recession. It situates the Fund's evolving thinking within the wider politics of austerity, and charts how the Fund's post-crash views on fiscal policy efficacy and the conduct of economic stabilization were increasingly at odds with major European players over the key battleground of what constitutes 'sound' and 'unsound' fiscal policy. It examines the IMF role within the Troika, and the failure of Fund views on prior debt restructuring and limiting the scale of fiscal consolidation to prevail in European programmes. Building on its self-appointed role as a font of economic policy knowledge, the IMF mobilized its knowledge bank and scientific reputation to attempt to correct what key Fund figures saw as mistaken premises of austerity policies, and the shortcomings of attempts to create Eurozone backstops. The Fund's empirically backed policy advice advocated a 'less now, more later' approach to consolidation by countries with fiscal space. Yet the Fund had limited impact on the austerity-centric policy settings of European authorities and governments, and its calls for systemic risk-reducing strengthened fiscal and financial backstops for the Eurozone went largely unanswered.

Attention then turns to the two detailed case studies. The rationale behind the selection of the UK and France is to focus on two broadly similar advanced economies with large deficits—with comparable role and status within the IMF. Both are non-borrowers as this is the key lacuna in the literature my book addresses. Overall it is a 'most similar systems' design, but the key point of difference is to analyse one country within the Eurozone, and one outside it. This is partly because textbook economics would suggest different fiscal policy dynamics and effects for a country inside a currency union as compared to outside. It is also salient because of how central to the crisis the euro and Eurozone architecture have been—and how much efforts to resolve the European crisis have focused on the fiscal policy issues at the heart of this book. Chapter 6, the first of the two detailed case studies exploring IMF surveillance and commentary seeking to inflect and influence national policymaking, focuses on the UK policy debate.

The central assumption of the coalition government's construction of fiscal rectitude was that Britain faced a 'crisis of debt' (Hay 2013a & b), yet the IMF did not share this view. As a result, there were sharp dissonances between IMF recommendations and UK policy under the coalition government, especially between 2010 and 2013. Fund work on fiscal multipliers being higher during recessions, and on the adverse effects of fiscal consolidation on growth all had pointed relevance for UK policy. George Osborne, David Cameron, and

Nick Clegg's understanding of the UK economic position saw very little potential for activist fiscal policy in support of growth, and paid little attention to aggregate demand or the distributive impact of fiscal policy. In 2013 Blanchard accused the UK authorities of 'playing with fire' by pursuing an excessively harsh programme of austerity, which threatened a prolonged and deep recession.

Chapter 7's case study provides the first account of IMF commentary on and interventions in the French economic policy debate following the crash. It analyses how the Fund sought to inflect French policy settings and policy approaches, and worked to influence wider reforms to the Eurozone's architecture. The research reveals shared interpretations of the crisis and appropriate responses between IMF and French policy experts. It demonstrates how the French government, alongside the IMF, sought a less pro-cyclical approach and to open up 'fiscal space' for growth-oriented policies within European economic and monetary arrangements. However, key centres of power, notably the German government, the European Commission, and the European Central Bank prioritized 'moral hazard' and the 'crisis of debt' narratives, whose policy corollaries were ever-tighter fiscal discipline and ramped up austerity.

The Conclusion draws together the themes of the book to reflect on how the IMF's post-crash rethink has sought to alter the contours of 'sound' economic policy. It reflects on the implications of the argument of the book as a whole about the malleability of economic orthodoxy, and considers the scope and limits of IMF authority in its dealings with advanced economies.

2

Ideational Change at the IMF after the Crash

Introduction

Before delving into the evolution of Fund thinking on fiscal policy thinking later in the book, this chapter advances the case for a Constructivist Institutionalist (CI) approach, developing a novel theory of ideational change in international organizations (IOs) in general and the IMF in particular. CI understands institutions in non-deterministic terms, recognizing the enactment of rules by autonomous actors able to reinterpret and recreate their environment. It also foregrounds the cognitive and ideational filters through which actors make sense of their institutional environment and indeed their interests (Hay 2008, 2011a; Schmidt 2010; Clift 2014a: 145–54). We underline the importance of how Fund staff see themselves and their role as a means to operationalize these constructivist insights (see also Clegg 2013).

Analysing ideational change from a CI perspective requires understanding the institutional, organizational, and ideational context in which economic ideas are produced and deployed (see Clift & Tomlinson 2004, 2008b, 2012; Clift 2012, 2014a; Baker 2015; Campbell 2004, 2010; Blyth 2002a & b; Woll 2008, 2010). Thus, this chapter charts key facets of the Fund's internal workings, including its hierarchical nature, internal review processes, and how internal interactions are evolving. It builds on a tradition of scholarship interested in opening up the black box of the Fund (Chwieroth 2010; Momani 2005a & b, 2007, 2010; Nelson 2014, 2017; Park & Vetterlein 2010). The IMF and other IOs are not unitary actors with a single homogenized viewpoint, but sites of 'persuasive struggles' (Baker 2015; Checkel 1998, 2001; Widmaier 2003b) between actors seeking to effect ideational change.[1] These inter-subjective struggles over economic ideas between different 'subcultures' involve 'battles over norm interpretation and application' (Chwieroth 2010: 2),

[1] A view corroborated by many Fund interviewees including Senior IMF economist Paolo Mauro, a senior fellow at the Peterson Institute for International Economics at the time of the interview in 2014.

shaped by hierarchical power relations. Institutionally constituted and mediated cognitive filters, such as those operating within the Fund's scientific and technocratic culture and its existing body of economic policy knowledge, present constraints and opportunities for ideational change. These elements inform a novel theory of ideational change, which specifies a series of mechanisms of incremental evolution at the IMF. Identifying these enables us to discern the permissive conditions necessary for key actors to navigate these internal constraints and opportunities to effect ideational change. In the process, it reveals the internal workings of the Fund's ideational evolution, and this helps explain which ideas come to prevail within internal persuasive struggles, why, and how.

The mutual constitution of socially acceptable understandings of 'sound' policy *within* the IMF detailed in this chapter involves an internal politics of economic ideas. This politics is difficult to research, partly because the Fund's scientific and technocratic self-image assumes it away, and Fund editorial practices tend to conceal it. The tortuous writing style of Fund documents, its 'Delphic' language as Pauly terms it (1997), evokes different policy positions and includes differences of view, whilst papering over cracks (or chasms) between them. The caveats, rejoinders, and 'on the other hand' statements which pepper Fund publications are the footprints of persuasive struggles, revealing the dissonances and disagreements which emerge in the internal review process. The internal politics of economic ideas is revealed through a research strategy combining careful content analysis of Fund intellectual output combined with numerous searching background interviews with Fund staff. Countering what some see as an excessive textualism in constructivist analysis, this enables the researcher to cut through the Fund's dry drafting style to access the 'lived in' space of IMF debates.

As mentioned in the Introduction (and explored in depth in Chapter 4), the interests of powerful members and power relations at Executive Board level delimit what kinds of policy ideas are 'thinkable' within the Fund (Seabrooke 2010: 141). The argument here is that the IMF possesses significant autonomy (Barnett & Finnemore 2004, 2005), and actors are understood as creative agents able to revisit and revise pre-existing thinking and practice. Hence, within the parameters of 'thinkable' policy, there is a great deal of scope for Fund staff to use their agenda-setting capacity (Momani 2010: 30–1; Martin 2006) to exert their autonomy and strategically promote and corroborate particular understandings of economic policy. These understandings are used to inform surveillance and commentary and to craft its prescriptive discourse on economic policy. The research has unearthed 'feedback loops' within Fund practices which act as transmission mechanisms through which reflexive actors respond to their operating environment and reshape their institutional context. The politics of economic ideas in the Fund entails discursive struggles between competing authoritative claims about economic policy, wherein the support of powerful backers, and packaging ideas to pass through the internal review process and secure social recognition are vitally important.

Along the way, the analysis calibrates claims about what degree and what kind of ideational change can be anticipated from an institution like the Fund with its particular mandate, make-up, history, and characteristics. The parameters of change are delimited by institutional context, but significant scope remains for incremental change. We make the case for 'bricolage'—the crafting of new institutional solutions by actors through innovative recombining of elements in their repertoire (Campbell 2004: 69), rather than paradigm shifts as a framework for understanding changing economic ideas within the Fund. Bricolage is selected due to its superior ability to incorporate the complexities of institutional mediation, and the sedimented but ongoing influence of multiple economic ideas from different paradigmatic homes.

After introducing the CI theoretical framework for the book, and how to apply it, this chapter sets out the Fund as an institutional and ideational context, focusing on internal knowledge production practices and how they are evolving. It then goes on to spell out four mechanisms of ideational change—reconciliation, operationalization, corroboration, and authoritative recognition—and how their operation in the particular context of the GFC and Eurozone crises and their aftermath opened up scope to redefine 'sound' economic policy. Recent scholarship on IO ideational change has highlighted the importance of what Park and Vetterlein call 'norm advocates' (2010; see also Finnemore & Sikkink 1998; Chwieroth 2010: 14, 55; 2014; Moschella 2015). First and second tier management at the Fund, including Managing Director, Deputy Managing Director, but also Department and Division heads played an especially important role in the mutual constitution of socially acceptable 'sound' economic policy. Here we term them IMF 'bricoleurs' (see Campbell 2004; Carstensen 2011a & b; 2015a). Their ability and scope to draw selectively on and emphasize particular elements within the Fund's repertoire of economic ideas (see Chapter 3) shaped the Fund's post-crash policy thinking and practice.

Ideational Change but *not* Paradigm Change

The global financial crisis at first heralded an anticipation that everything in the realms of economic ideas would change, and perhaps that resurgent Keynesian insights might redefine post-crisis economic orthodoxy (Skidelsky 2009). Shortly afterwards, this was superseded by waves of studies decrying that nothing had, in fact, changed and that the old economic orthodoxy remained intact (Crouch 2011; Quiggin 2012; Farrell & Quiggin 2012; Schmidt & Thatcher 2013; Helleiner 2014). Still others claim, perhaps tongue in cheek, that everything did change, but not for long; 'we all became Keynesians for about eight months from October 2008 to June 2009' (Blyth 2013b: 208). This book finds that none of these narratives is wholly persuasive. Each takes a problematic view of economic ideas, their institutional mediation, and the dynamics and politics of their evolution in IOs, amongst policy elites, and beyond.

The default expectation of political scientists and international relations scholars, when faced with discussion of ideational change, is to think in terms of policy paradigms and either paradigm change or maintenance (see e.g. Hall 1993; McNamara 1998; Blyth 2002a, 2013b; Wade 1996). Paradigms are ideational structures of relatively internally consistent and coherent understandings of the world and how it works. Within a paradigm, cohesion is provided by a set of underlying assumptions leading to a widely shared approach to explanation, and to policy. Analysis in terms of policy paradigms focuses attention on how these 'normative structures restrict the set of policy ideas that political elites find acceptable' (Campbell 1998: 378). Policy paradigms provide 'cognitive templates through which policymakers come to understand the[ir] environment', notably as paradigms 'become institutionally embedded in norms, conventions and standard operating procedures' (Hay 2004b: 504–5; see also Campbell 1998: 389–92; Clift 2014a: 157–68). One much studied example is the displacement of Keynesian macroeconomic thinking with monetarism with UK economic policymaking in the 1970s and 1980s (Hall 1993; Oliver & Pemberton 2004; Hay 2001; Clift & Tomlinson 2007).

The Kuhnian framework which many political scientists distil via Hall's influential article (1993: 279–80) sets out a clear hierarchical scale of paradigm change. At its zenith is '3rd order' change, a clean break with prior causal assumptions, understandings of how the world works, and the thinking and premises about economic policy—this amounts to a paradigm shift. As Baker notes, only third-order change, or 'gestalt flip', entails the embrace of a 'diametrically opposed set of assumptions about how things are actually constituted' (Baker 2015: 349). Much work on the economic ideas in the Fund accepts and operates within the paradigm framework. Momani, in focusing on IMF recruitment practices, denotes 'the Fund's economic paradigm' as a singular intellectual edifice (2005a: 183; see also Evans & Finnemore 2001: 9; Barnett & Finnemore 2004; Broome 2015; Nelson 2014). Pre-crisis work on Fund ideas, even in volumes focused on the politics of economic ideas (Grabel 2003, Blyth 2003b), imparts more singularity and homogeneity to 'Fund thinking' and the Fund's intellectual framework than is accurate. Whilst this is an understandable shorthand, it is problematic for grasping the nature of Fund economic thought. Empirically, this search for and anticipation of paradigmatic change is at odds with the fact that the Fund, either in the post-war era or in the contemporary period, is never wholly in thrall to one set of economic ideas drawn from a single paradigmatic home. Theoretically, the paradigm change view sits uncomfortably with the institutionally mediated nature of ideational change in IOs, and the contingency which characterizes how Fund economists draw on particular economic ideas from different theoretical homes as conjuncture and policy context dictates. Section 2.3 sets out a CI approach which develops this last point.

Constructivist Institutionalism and Ideational Change at the IMF

The analysis presented here generates an ideationally attuned account of institutionally mediated change. As such it connects with debates in international and comparative political economy about the mechanisms of incremental change (see Streeck & Thelen 2005b: 11; Campbell 2004; Campbell & Pedersen 2001b; Crouch 2005: 19; Mahoney & Thelen 2010: 11–14; Clift 2014a: 101–22, 142–67; Bell 2011). Not all embrace constructivist insights (see Hay 2011: 65–9), but most underline how actors' interpretation of the rules, norms and shared beliefs which give life to the institution imparts their agential input into the structure, and they are united by a desire to explain institutional change better. Rather than rehearsing the 'my institutionalism is better than yours' debate (see e.g. Bell 2011; Schmidt 2008, 2010, 2011; Hay 2008, 2011a), this account recognizes how different approaches to institutionalist analysis are helpful in addressing different kinds of questions (see Campbell & Pedersen 2001a & b), and highlights scope for cross-fertilization.

Historical institutionalism (HI) constitutes the often implicit default methodological position or starting point for analysis in interpretive political science. At its most elemental, historical institutionalism highlights how historically developed institutions matter politically and have enduring effects (see Peters 1999: 19, 63–77; Fioretos 2011b; Farrell & Newman 2010). Its focus on path dependency underscores how initial choices early in the history of any policy field or system have an enduring impact as they shape both the strategies and goals pursued by political actors in ways which are instructive for other kinds of institutional analysis. The likes of Campbell, Thelen, Streeck, and Mahoney seek to reinvigorate HI analyses. They understand institutional evolution and reproduction as 'a dynamic political process' (Streeck & Thelen 2005b: 6; Thelen 2010; Campbell 2010), and highlight agents' reinterpretive scope in ways not so far removed from CI scholarship. The approach here notes the distinctive advantages of a CI perspective, emphasizing as it does the contingent and open-ended nature of institutional change, and the crucial role of its ideational mediation.

Sociological institutionalist (SI) approaches explore the means by which values impact upon behaviour through the generation of norms, rules, understandings and routines that 'define appropriate actions' (March & Olsen 1984: 741; 1989: 21–6). This 'logic of appropriateness' can constrain and shape the behaviour of actors. Actors consider whether behaviour is consistent with the internal norms or value structure of the institution. Thus choice is constrained by what Peters calls 'the parameters established by the dominant institutional values' (1999: 29). SI explorations of institutionally constituted 'systems of meaning' draw attention to the environment within which ideas are produced in IOs (Barnett & Finnemore 1999, 2004), identifying prevailing norms. In doing so, they highlight cogent reasons to anticipate ideational continuity (for a discussion see Weaver 2008). Findings from these SI studies are, as Schmidt notes (2008, 2010), important starting points for CI analysis.

Notwithstanding some important differences between HI, SI, and CI, attempts to debunk CI from other institutionalist perspectives (see e.g. Bell 2011) often share more common foundations with CI than they care to admit. Many scholars view institutional reproduction, innovation, and evolution as processes of struggle and political contestation (Hay 2008, 2015; see also Steinmo & Thelen 1992: 17; Bell 2011: 892; Thelen 2010; Campbell 2010). This analysis also finds itself in relatively close alignment with many insights developed within much HI work (Steinmo & Thelen 1992; Campbell 1998, 2001, 2004, 2010; Fioretos 2011a & b; Hall 1986, 1989, 1993).

The insistence upon 'play' between institutional context and actors' conduct, rooted for some in ambiguity about the meaning and interpretation of institutional rules, infuses a welcome degree of agency and dynamism into the analysis of political struggles wherein certain institutional settlements win out over alternative possibilities (Campbell 2004: 41; Streeck & Thelen 2005b). The actors animating these processes are not drones, their actions are not wholly determined by their institutional context. Thus, in our case Fund staff are not slaves to their institutional mandate or prior standard operating procedures, nor simply the bearers of institutional logics following pre-programmed scripts. The preferences of Fund actors are by no means wholly determined by material conditions. Attuned to the politics of institutional change, Campbell has developed two useful concepts, 'translation' and 'bricolage'. Translation involves 'the combination of locally available principles and practices with new ones originating elsewhere', whereas bricolage entails actors 'recombin[ing] locally available institutional principles and practices in ways that yield... path dependent evolutionary change' (Campbell 2004: 65; see also Engelen et al. 2011: 51–2). Campbell argues that actors 'craft new institutional solutions' through recombinative bricolage 'whereby new institutions differ from but resemble old ones' (2004: 69). The work of Thelen, Streeck, Mahoney and others has identified other institutionally mediated, incremental processes of change, notably the 'layering' of new rules on top of existing ones (Streeck & Thelen 2005a & b; Mahoney & Thelen 2010). These useful mechanisms have enhanced our ability to understand and explain institutional and ideational change.

Yet whilst CI analysis can draw on HI-inspired analysis, concepts, and mechanisms, and its conception of agency bears passing resemblance to theirs, important differences remain. The approach of, say, Streeck and Thelen (2005a & b), built on materialist foundations, sees preferences as shaped by material conditions, and ambiguity as confined to institutional rules. So whilst Thelen and co-authors rightly underline institutions as sites of the political struggle over change, they understand that politics in terms of given interests derived from material conditions. Resorting solely to material conditions along these lines to account for why and how actors seek to reshape institutions misses the central point of CI (see Hay 2011a: 65–9). CI underlines the ideationally mediated and contingent nature of the inter-relationships between actors, institutions, and their social context. Actors' 'ideas about interests' matter, since 'agents do not monotonically decode the material world around them and act uniformly' (Blyth 2007: 774; see also Blyth 2003a). Rather, in order to appreciate this ideational mediation, CI foregrounds the cognitive and ideational filters through which actors make sense of their environments, institutions, and interests. These are inherently social, inter-subjective processes (Ruggie 1998: 4; Campbell 1998, 2004; Woll 2008, 2010; Schmidt 2008; Clift 2012, 2014a: 152).

Materialist accounts tend to see actor behaviour in primarily 'rational' or norm-driven terms (Streeck & Thelen 2005b; Mahoney & Thelen 2010b). CI scholarship, by contrast, conceives of a more open-ended politics characterized by the contingent processes of institutional change and/or reproduction (Hay 2011a, 2015). Rather than deriving fixed interests and preferences from given material conditions, CI underlines how actors' interests are social constructions. They are emergent, in formation, and based on partial information, forged by actors understood as reflexive, sentient beings (Blyth 2003a; Hay 2011a: 67–8, 2015). For CI, 'rationalities (*plural*) cannot be "read off" from a given set of material conditions', because 'mental frames of reference and interpretive leeway enter the picture and give actors a degree of autonomy in terms of how they respond to (and indeed how they perceive and interpret) a given set of material conditions' (Clift 2014a: 145; see also Béland & Cox 2011: 12). Ambiguity for CI, then, extends beyond how actors interpret institutional rules to encompass material structures more widely, and indeed actors' interests. This makes for a more open-ended account 'profoundly wedded to the inherent contingency of social, political and economic change' (Hay 2015: 1).

Are efficient and stabilizing paths chosen in institutional evolution? For materialist accounts, the default answer seems to be yes. The change agents appear like super-human figures who cut through manifold complexities and uncertainties of social life to perceive the equilibrating and efficient paths of change and act accordingly (see e.g. Mahoney & Thelen 2010b; Bell 2011). Within CI, uncertainty is seen to be more pervasive, agents are not presumed to be so well-informed, and the paths of institutional evolution they craft are not presumed to tend necessarily towards efficiency and stability. For CI, path-dependent dynamics are 'no more likely to prove self-equilibrating than they are cumulatively destabilising' (Hay 2015: 1; Hay 2011a). From CI's perspective on the political process of institutional reconstitution, whether or not changes prove efficient or equilibrating constitutes a research question, not a prior assumption.

Ideational and mental frames are at the heart of the inter-subjective processes of social construction which animate CI accounts. One way to understand these cognitive filters, and acts of social construction central to CI approach is through Searle's account of social facts. These social facts are not objective in the sense that what makes them 'true' or 'false' is 'independent of anybody's attitudes or feelings about them' (Searle 1995: 8). Instead, social facts rest upon particular understandings and assumptions which, CI insists, are contingent and potentially autonomous from underlying material conditions. When particular shared understandings become sufficiently embedded they develop the quality of 'social facts' (Searle 1995: 24–5; Ruggie 1998: 13, 20–1; Sinclair 2005: 5, 12, 53–4; Hay 2015; Schmidt 2008). These inter-subjective processes are similar to Keynes' account of conventions (1937). Salient examples include prevailing political economic orthodoxies, views of 'sound' economic policy, and 'acceptable' debt and deficit levels.

Searle makes another useful distinction for constructivist accounts of institutions—between regulative and constitutive rules. Regulative rules (like driving on the left) regulate inter-subjective interactions which exist independently of the rule, whereas constitutive rules (like how to play chess) create or define new forms of behaviour (Searle 1969: 33; 1995: 27). Searle's constitutive rules point towards institutional facts as an important subset of social facts. For CI, institutions are understood as 'genuinely constitutive of the social practices they institutionalise' (Hay 2015: 8; see also Farrell & Newman 2010). These social and institutional facts reflect what Searle calls 'the primacy of process' (1995), reproduced as they are through socially and politically contingent, inter-subjective practices. CI foregrounds a focus on 'practice' and 'process', specifically 'ongoing processes of constitution and re-constitution in and through which institutional practices both reaffirm and, at the same, contribute to the evolution of institutions' (Hay 2015: 15).

Whilst the Fund's institutional structures and standard operating procedures (discussed in sections 2.4 and 2.5) establish certain parameters of possible ideational evolution, CI scholars recognize how institutional facts are contingent. Thus, there is scope for the reconstitution of Fund thinking and practice. For example, in relation to the Fund's mandate, its wording may not change, but what 'growth' and 'stability' mean, and their policy corollaries, are open to interpretation and reinterpretation by leading Fund figures. Their implications, and what they entail in terms of how the Fund works to secure them within the world economy, are equally 'up for grabs'. For example, in the economic liberalization era of the 1980s (Boughton 2001: 3–4, 25–8; Babb & Buira 2005) the Fund saw low inflation and austerity policies as necessary preconditions for growth; fiscal policy was relevant to growth primarily through its role in ensuring budgetary discipline and debt sustainability. By contrast, the post-crash Fund adopts a more activist and Keynesian approach, which identifies supporting aggregate demand through counter-cyclical policy, infrastructure investment, and tackling inequality as key macroeconomic components of securing growth in advanced economies.

These inter-subjective processes, conventional understandings, and social facts play an especially significant role in the wake of economic crisis which destabilizes prior conventional wisdoms. Many political economists noted how, under conditions of Knightian uncertainty (Blyth 2002a; Schmidt 2008), ideas about 'sound' economic policy are more likely to shift (Widmaier 2003a & b, 2004; Widmaier et al. 2007). The post-crash 'new normal' provided just such a context (Gamble 2009; Hay 2011b, 2013a & b; Blanchard et al. 2010, 2013). That said, any ideational innovation is institutionally mediated. Such change takes place within the parameters of change set by the Fund's history and structure. CI foregrounds 'the simultaneously enabling and constraining qualities of institutions' (Hay 2015: 7; 2008; Schmidt 2008, 2010; Béland & Cox 2011).

Putting the CI Approach into Practice: Mechanisms of Ideational Change in the Fund

This study aligns with CI, but it draws directly on 'discursive institutionalist' (DI) insights and approaches as well (Schmidt 2002, 2008, 2010, 2011; Campbell & Pedersen 2001a & b). DI pays attention to what level an idea operates at (policy, programmatic, and philosophical), and what type it is (cognitive and normative) (Schmidt 2008; Campbell 1998, 2002, 2004). One of Schmidt's most telling insights is that ideas matter for the form in which they are expressed as well as their content. Thus, making form distinctions helps explain 'why certain ideas succeed and others fail because of the ways in which they are projected to whom and where' (Schmidt 2008: 309). Schmidt's 'causal beliefs'—directly policy-relevant ideas about the efficacy of a given policy—'matter' and play a role within the institution. The role and significance of this form of idea is distinct from what Schmidt terms principled beliefs—broader economic theoretical insights such as multiple equilibria, or Knightian uncertainty. The variety of forms ideas can take is important, as is the context, or 'where, when, how, and why it was said'. Taking account of these elements is integral to putting 'ideas into their "meaning context"' (Schmidt 2008: 304, 305), and grasping ideational change as an inter-subjective process.

CI and DI are best seen as 'fellow travellers' on a road to a more ideationally attuned form of institutional analysis. Both embrace a contingent and open-ended understanding of change, and both share a frustration with materialist accounts. There are also similarities in terms of research strategy and process. DI highlights the role of cognitive framing, and this dovetails with CI's highlighting of the 'cognitive filters' actors use to help them interpret ideas and orient themselves towards their environment. These are crucial to how actors 'make sense' of their role, institutional practices, and their interests within a 'meaning context' (see Hay 2015: 13–14; 2001, 2008; Béland 2010; Béland & Cox 2011; Schmidt 2008, 2010).

CI favours 'an inductive approach to process tracing', which at its most ambitious approaches what Hay terms 'a political anthropology of institutionally-situated action and change' (2015: 14). Schmidt's desire to situate actors within a 'meaning context' is equally well-suited to this kind of process tracing (Schmidt 2008; see also Campbell & Pedersen 2001a & b). We underline the importance of how Fund staff see themselves and their role as a means to operationalizing constructivist insights about how actors 'make sense' of their environment in a given meaning context (Hay 2008, 2011a, 2015; Schmidt 2008, 2010). As Clegg puts it, 'what practitioners do and how they understand their environment' is crucial to understanding the dynamics and practices of the Fund. This forms an important part of the 'intersubjective frameworks used by actors to navigate their social environments' (Clegg 2013: 3; see also Adler & Pouliot 2011). This is best unearthed through numerous lengthy background interviews with a variety of Fund actors as a complement to close content analysis of IMF intellectual production.

Within international organizations like the IMF, the internal culture and standard operating practices provide a set of cognitive filters which bring the Fund's 'meaning context' into sharp focus. IMF bricoleurs have to be mindful of this social realm of Fund thinking, these internal cultural conditions, and how they limit the ideational parameters of the possible. For new insights to gain broader acceptance, 'win out' in the internal battle of ideas at the Fund, and constitute 'usable' doctrine, they require certain qualities. Ideas need to be presented in a particular form to stand a chance of gaining acceptance within the IMF's internal 'meaning context'. This book proposes analysing economic ideas and Fund meaning context in terms of four mechanisms of ideational change. These reveal how ideational change is refracted through the Fund institutional structures, and mediated by its internal intellectual culture.

Firstly, reconciliation—new ideas have to be introduced in a manner capable of being reconciled to existing Fund thinking and practice. Secondly, operationalization—new ideas have to be introduced in a form that can be operationalized and put into practice. Thirdly, corroboration—ideas need to be supported by methodological and empirical corroboration—to retain conformity with the Fund technocratic and scientific culture. Fund staff combine technical and scientific elements with 'causal stories' (Blyth 2002a; Schmidt 2008, 2010) about economic policy effects. Fourthly, authoritative recognition—ideas need to find authoritative endorsement from the socially recognized expertise of economists through referencing and citing from leading scholars and state-of-the-art research published in economics journals.

Reconciliation conveys how, in order to gain social recognition within the Fund, new thinking must be capable of being made compatible at some level to Fund standard operating procedures, and pre-existing frameworks. In one of the earliest post-crisis empirical reassessments of fiscal policy as a counter-cyclical policy tool by the Research Department, published in the *World Economic Outlook* in October 2008 (IMF 2008b: ch. 5), the *pre-crisis* fiscal policy record indicated it to be more effective than its reputation shaped by anti-Keynesian thinking inspired by New Classical Macroeconomics (see Chapter 3). This point was restated and reinforced at various points thereafter, including by the Fiscal Affairs Department in 2015 (IMF 2015a: 21–48). Thus, there could have been scope to revisit the antipathy towards fiscal policy along the lines that, *under normal conditions*, activist fiscal policy is more effective than mainstream economists had given it credit for of late.

This line would be harder to swallow for those accepting much of the standard case *against* fiscal policy as it had been assimilated in economics, and within the Fund, since the 1970s. Contradicting this conventional wisdom directly jarred too much with the cognitive filters through which Fund staff viewed economic policy issues. Instead, in an episode that illustrates the importance of the 'framing' of policy issues and economic ideas (Béland 2009: 704–7; Blyth 2007: 775–6; Campbell 1998; Widmaier et al. 2007), the fiscal policy rehabilitation was couched in terms of a special case argument. There is a historical parallel with the incorporation of Keynes' seminal *General Theory* into mainstream academic economics in the 1930s and 1940s. One reading of Keynes' work suggested that the market's failure to balance supply and demand at full employment was an endemic, intrinsic problem of the market economy. One pertinent analogy is of a lift getting stuck at the wrong floor, with no in-built mechanism returning it to the right one. Keynes viewed this as an inherent feature of market economies (Skidelsky 2009; Eatwell & Milgate 2011; cf. Patinkin 1990). In the process of translating some insights from the *General Theory* into the economic models of the day, as Hicks (1937) and Hansen (1949) did, Keynes' radical insights about uncertainty, herd behaviour, confidence, aggregate demand, and market failure were largely lost. The formalization morphed into an equilibrium model of the economy, with the kinds of market failure identified by Keynes rendered as a special case, and not the general condition of the economy.

The upwards re-evaluation of fiscal multipliers by the Fund between 2008 and 2012 (see Chapter 5) indicated a more Keynesian understanding of greater fiscal policy efficacy as a counter-cyclical tool. This crucial element within post-crash Fund understandings of economic policy was also packaged as a special case, contingent upon the state of the economic cycle and other conjunctural conditions including the 'zero lower bound' constraining monetary policy. It also applies specifically and only to advanced economies, rather than emerging economies (Scott 2008; IMF 2013d). Making the rehabilitation of fiscal policy contingent on the specific post-GFC economic conjuncture, and only applying it to certain countries, serves to *perpetuate* the assumption that the economy tends towards a market-clearing equilibrium under normal conditions. This view, rooted in the neo-classical synthesis, remains in the foundation of how lots of Fund economists think about the economy and economic policy (see Chapter 3). Reconciliation proceeded via the 'special case' framing which dovetailed with this centre of gravity of prior Fund thinking. The disjuncture between prior practice and new thinking cannot be too great. As Olivier Blanchard characterized his efforts to change Fund economic ideas 'this is a supertanker analogy—and I think of myself as a tugboat... if it tries to pull a supertanker with too much angle the chain will break' 'so you have to choose your angle and you have to admit that it is going to take a long time'.[2]

The second mechanism of internal ideational change at the Fund is operationalization. Numerous interviewees highlighted the importance of this translation process from abstract economic notions to operational concepts.[3] In order to gain 'traction' internally, new or revised thinking must be presented to desks in a format they can use; 'whenever there's a big policy paper, for example, on capital flows... we usually follow it up with a guidance note which boils down the principles that the board has largely endorsed into

[2] Interview with IMF Chief Economist Olivier Blanchard, June 2013.

[3] Interviews with senior Fund economists, June and September 2013, September 2014.

specific steps that country teams need to take into account.'[4] For the new ideas to become 'usable' doctrine, it is necessary that 'the policy lines... ideally should be baked into guidance somehow so that it gets solidified', as one insider put it.[5] Feeding the assumptions into 'cheat sheets', or into elementary spreadsheets, enables hard-pressed staff to put the insights into practice in their policy work. At the more bureaucratized and official level, technical guidance notes get developed, approved, and disseminated. The 'even-handed' treatment of all member states, although never a standard it fully meets, is nevertheless an important norm for the Fund's legitimacy and authority. This 'even-handed' approach is one means to tackle the Fund's 'legitimacy gap' (Seabrooke 2010), and it became increasingly institutionalized since the later 1960s and was nurtured by consistent internal use of normalized agreed guidance notes to facilitate approaching policy issues in a more or less consistent manner across countries.

A salient example is the 'bucket approach' to the upwards re-evaluation of fiscal multipliers, spurred on by Blanchard and Leigh's work recognizing the Fund's prior understating of fiscal policy effects in the October 2012 *World Economic Outlook* (IMF 2012j: 41–8). The bucket approach began life as a working paper (Batini et al. 2014a; see also Eyraud & Weber 2013), and was later developed into a guidance note prepared and approved by FAD and circulated to all desks distilling the essence of the more Keynesian account of heightened fiscal policy efficacy in a downturn (Batini et al. 2014b). It provided a rule of thumb approach for calibrating fiscal multiplier assessments, incorporating, for example, how if fiscal stimulus is not offset by counter-acting monetary policy, its impact is much stronger and longer. The updated operational guidance on fiscal policy efficacy disseminated in 2014 'baked' new fiscal policy thinking into guidance, transforming it into what Weaver calls 'theory in use' (Weaver 2008). This enabled hard-pressed staff to quickly and easily operationalize the higher fiscal multiplier assessments prevalent within the Fund. Here again though, subjective judgements play an important role. As Research Department economist Daniel Leigh notes, 'Is the fiscal multiplier normally operationalized as just one number plugged into an Excel spreadsheet?.... No. My experience is that desks typically use a combination of models and judgement when it comes to the effects of fiscal policy.'[6]

The third mechanism of internal ideational change is the methodological and empirical corroboration of new thinking. Couched in technocratic terms

[4] Interview with Vivek Arora, then Deputy Director of the Strategy, Policy and Review Department, September 2013.

[5] Interview with Vivek Arora, then Deputy Director of the Strategy, Policy and Review Department, September 2013.

[6] Interview with IMF Research Department economist Daniel Leigh, September 2013.

and aligned successfully with Fund scientific norms, particular economic ideas come to be seen as 'socially appropriate' and 'culturally valid' (Park & Vetterlein 2010a: 5, 6; Momani 2010: 45). The internal review process discussed in section 2.5 is an important part of this corroboration process. To pass muster within the Fund's internal scientific culture, economic ideas need to be substantiated both by state-of-the-art methodological techniques in the academic literature, and be solidly supported by the Fund's own evidence base. Fund scientific norms differ slightly from academic economics. The Fund as a system of knowledge production bears distinct, somewhat more methodologically pluralistic, traits when compared to twenty-first-century academic economics as practised in North America and Europe. By comparison to academic economics, a wider range of methodological techniques and approaches are considered scientifically valid, including historical and narrative methods as well as case studies (see IMF 2011o: 138–45; Ball et al. 2011). Accordingly, it improves the idea's chance of gaining ascendancy within the Fund if its validity can be further corroborated by analysis using a range of different methodological techniques and approaches.

A fourth mechanism of internal ideational change, also linked to Fund scientific norms, is authoritative recognition. The logic and rationale of new ideas needs authoritative support from leading economists. Chwieroth has identified the economics profession as agent of social construction, and underlined the 'productive power' of economics (2010: 33), shaping understandings of the behaviour of actors, the properties of markets, and economic policy dynamics and outcomes. The Fund is to some extent swayed by the centre of gravity of mainstream economic thinking. The symbiosis with academic economics, and evolutions within its mainstream thinking, are important for the intellectual authority of the IMF (see Chapter 3). The increasing connection to and interaction with the economics profession, including Fund staff publishing in respected journals, fosters deeper engagement with a range of academic economic thinking. There is, in short, a range of 'usable' doctrine from the modestly sized but somewhat diverse community of highly respected economists, upon whom the Fund draws and repeatedly cites. This recourse to the contemporary economics canon can create openings for revisiting Fund ideas and positions, as well as new sources to draw on for intellectual corroboration and authoritative recognition.

Specifying these four mechanisms enables us to be systematic in discerning which ideas prevail and why, a key concern for ideational scholarship. New Fund thinking is more likely to prevail when tailored and framed to take account of reconciliation, operationalization, corroboration, and authoritative recognition. These four mechanisms, in particular 'reconciliation', help explain why bricolage (see Campbell & Pedersen 2001a; Campbell 2004; Carstensen 2011a & b, 2013; Engelen et al. 2011: 51–2), translation (Campbell 2004), and 'layering', or 'the introduction of new rules on top of or alongside existing ones' (Mahoney & Thelen 2010b: 15) are helpful ways to approach IMF ideational change. Ideas get recombined pragmatically according to policy context and economic conjuncture by Fund actors in search of 'traction', working to retain their relevance to policy thinking. As the ideas in question pass through these mechanisms, they evolve and change. Indeed, one corollary of understanding ideational change at the IMF in this way is that ideas are no longer seen as fixed, settled, or even wholly coherent in actors' minds (Carstensen 2011a & b), a theme returned to and developed in section 2.7.

Power Relations and Practices of IMF Economic Policy Knowledge Production

Below we detail some alterations in social interaction about economic ideas within the Fund since the crash, underscoring how these processes affect the path of ideational change. Proceeding to lower levels of abstraction allows us to operationalize CI insights and hone in on the politics of ideational change in the Fund and beyond. We highlight how careful framing of economic commentary is used by IMF bricoleurs to gain wider acceptance for novel insights and policy ideas. Choosing among different interpretations 'opens up space for politics' within dynamic and iterative processes of ideational evolution (Béland and Cox 2011: 4). Indeed, 'at the core of politics is the way ideas are packaged, disseminated, adopted, and embraced' (Béland and Cox 2011: 4, 13). This packaging and framing of new thinking in light of salient cognitive filters is the stuff of, as well as a major terrain for, the politics of economic ideas.

As constructivist scholars have pointed out, global finance is a social process, shaped by inter-subjective beliefs and shared understandings (Sinclair 1994, 2005; Seabrooke 2006; Clift & Tomlinson 2004; Hall 2008; Widmaier 2003a & b, 2004; Widmaier et al. 2007). The same goes for the construction of economic knowledge within international economic institutions (Barnett & Finnemore 2004, 2005; Best 2005; Nelson 2017). Within IOs and elsewhere, knowledge production is an inter-subjective and 'inherently social process' which is carried out in part 'through discussion' (Park and Vetterlein 2010a: 13). The process of reconstituting IMF orthodoxy through bricolage takes place in an institutionally constituted social setting, shaped by power relations. Fund staff are engaged in the mutual constitution of economic policy norms, developing and reproducing the approaches to and understandings of sound economic policy which are socially acceptable within the organization (Park & Vetterlein 2010a: 6; Weaver 2008: 13; Best 2010; Fourcade-Gourinchas & Babb 2002; Momani 2005a & b, 2007).

Earlier research situating evolutions in Fund economic ideas in their institutional context, focused on the 1960s, unearthed a 'feedback loop' between the Fund and member countries operating through stand-by arrangement agreements. These are a 'repeated game', wherein national authorities, politicians, and officials came to know what kinds of policy mechanisms and settings the Fund was likely to find favour with, and incorporated these insights into framing their negotiations (see Chapters 6 and 7; Clift & Tomlinson 2008a, 2012). This diachronic understanding of the politics of economic ideas brings to life how ideas are iterative and dynamic, and agents are reflexive and strategic. Interviews with Fund staff about post-crash evolutions in Fund economic policy thinking discovered similar feedback loop dynamics *within* the internal exchange of ideas amongst Fund staff. Shaped by hierarchical power relations at the Fund, these 'feedback loops' operate as staff discuss their ideas formally and informally, and as they submit their research for internal peer review. Feedback loops provide bricoleurs with information about how to package and frame new thinking in light of the mechanisms of ideational change to pass successfully through the cognitive filters represented by the Fund's internal scientific culture, standard operating procedures, and existing practices. They also operate as new Fund thinking moves towards being presented to the Executive Board. As a result of repeated interactions over time, Fund staff and departmental management have developed a keen sense of which kinds of initiatives and ideas are likely to receive a favourable hearing within the wider Fund, and at Board level.

There is a 'self-censoring' process, affecting not just which ideas get taken to the various levels, but also how they are packaged. Staff recommendations are tailored in view of what will fly higher up, and likely to survive the cut and thrust of internal review. Analysing successive phases of ideational innovation which followed the GFC reveals how ideas and insights get repackaged in light of their reception, and what happens to them as they pass through the cognitive filters of the IMF's internal scientific culture. Highlighting these 'feedback loop' dynamics is one helpful way to operationalize CI insight that staff need to be understood as reflexive, creative actors. New ideas get refined in reiterations to pass through the 'hoops': the four mechanisms of reconciliation, operationalization, corroboration, and authoritative recognition. In these ways, key Fund actors navigate the internal politics of economic ideas in exerting strategic doctrinal flexibility.

The remainder of this section fleshes out the institutional meditation of ideational change, setting out some of the key characteristics and working practices of the Fund as an institution, and how its practices of intellectual production are evolving. In doing so, it explores how the Fund is a social setting suffused with power relations wherein internal structures and procedures shape the conditions of possibility of ideational innovation. The first key characteristic is that all Fund interlocutors attest to the Fund being a very hierarchical organization (Momani 2005b, 2010; Woods 2006). Either explicitly or implicitly, every interview conducted illustrated the hierarchical nature of the Fund's internal structures and politics. It has been described as a 'command and control organisation'. IMF bricoleurs, as more senior staff, especially department heads, are crucial to the successful adoption of new ideas. Most obviously, those with editorial control over the 'flagship' publications have agenda-setting power to propose policy advice and analytical commentary themes. More generally, however, how *influential* any new ideas become depends on how gatekeepers in key departments react. They navigate the internal institutional and cultural environment to develop policy-relevant advice and insights pertinent to the economic conjuncture. They channel the institutional mediation of new thinking, and shape the Fund's evolving interpretive line.

The Fund's peer review processes for Fund flagship publications, Board papers, article IV reports, working papers, and so on are an important site for the mutual constitution of socially acceptable 'sound' economic policy. Legitimacy is conferred (or not) upon ideas through internal peer review, which is a site where the battle over which ideas get taken forward (and potentially taken up more widely) is won and lost. As in academia, ideas gain credence, corroboration, and credibility through peer review. If, ultimately, a difference of view cannot be reconciled within the peer review process, decisions about what gets published—especially in flagship publications—go up the hierarchy to be resolved by management. These formal peer review mechanisms are an important conduit for the 'social recognition' of Fund thinking (Park & Vetterlein 2010; Momani 2010). The intensity of the internal scrutiny varies for different kinds of Fund documents, with only a relatively small proportion requiring approval at Board level.

Key players in the internal review process, notably the Strategy, Policy and Review (SPR) department, have to sign off on a wide array of Fund documents, from article IV surveillance reports to Board papers and programme agreements. This is the successor to the Policy Development and Review Department, described by one staff member as the 'thought police' (Momani 2005a: 182). SPR sign-off 'is meant to indicate that the paper is consistent with fund policies and procedures, so when we sign off we are looking to make sure that the strategic priorities for surveillance are being reflected'.[7]

As a hierarchical bureaucracy, the IMF prizes being able to speak with a relatively coherent single voice. A variety of views are aired in a lively internal exchange as a new position is developed (Momani 2005a: 182). Once the line

[7] Interview with Vivek Arora, then Deputy Director of the Strategy, Policy and Review Department, September 2013.

is agreed, one goal of internal review and SPR sign-off procedures is to ensure a relatively consistent Fund 'line' emerging across the range of Fund outputs. The (normally very restricted) extent to which differing or dissenting Fund views are heard outside the institution is a function of Fund management. This consistency of the Fund's line is important for its intellectual authority on economic policy matters, and for gaining 'traction' for its policy thinking (see Chapter 6).

A second aspect of the institutional and ideational context shaping the evolution of the Fund's interpretive line is the IMF's developing reflexivity. Its staff are increasingly mindful of how their practice is viewed externally, particularly in times of economic crisis. The Fund has, since the late 1990s, been trying to actively learn the lessons of past crises and their mishandling—notably by creating the Independent Evaluation Office (IEO) in 2001, whose terms of reference includes enhancing 'the learning culture of the Fund' (Schwartz & Rist 2016: 2–5, 159).

Yet, as a well-developed critical literature on the IMF has pointed out of its operations in earlier periods, many poorer countries had previously suffered the effects of the Fund's prior harsh approach to fiscal adjustment (Taylor 1987; Peet 2009: ch. 3; Buira 2005; Killick 1995). In the 1980s and 1990s, these episodes had not led to a rethinking inside the Fund. What changed in the post-crash era was firstly, *which* countries were feeling the pain from harsh fiscal adjustment (and their power within the Fund). Secondly, the Fund of the early twenty-first century had been facing a multifaceted crisis of legitimacy (Seabrooke 2010: 138–44). Its intellectual authority since the East Asian crisis had come to depend on heightened reflexivity and a demonstrable ability to learn from past shortcomings as a means to shore up its legitimacy. 'When the facts change, we are prepared to change' has become something of mantra within the building (see e.g. Lagarde 2013), often evoked by interviewees. The IEO's prominent and highly critical evaluations of the Fund's failure to anticipate the 2008 crisis, and its shortcomings in responding to this and earlier crises (IEO 2011, 2014, 2016), are important aspects of the internal social milieu of a more reflexive Fund. The IEO and other Fund auto-critique resonate with more stinging criticism from within the academic literature on Fund past practice (Best 2003; Soederberg 2004; Wade 2001; Wade & Veneroso 1998).

This active learning process is an important part of the Fund's projected self-understanding in the contemporary period. In the realms of macroeconomic policy under the post-crash conditions dubbed 'the new normal', the IMF convened three conferences bringing Fund staff together with numerous leading economists on *Rethinking Macro Policy* as well as numerous seminars. These have led to books co-edited by the Chief economist entitled *What Have We Learned? Macroeconomic Policy after the Crisis* (Alerkof et al. 2014), another subtitled *Leading Economists Re-assess Economic Policy* (Blanchard et al. 2012), and one co-edited by the former FAD director entitled *Post-Crisis Fiscal Policy* (Cottarelli et al. 2014). Meanwhile, in an example of institutionalized, bureaucratized reflexivity, the SPR's oversight and sign-off remit covering all Fund intellectual production now includes ensuring that current Fund practice is not repeating the already identified shortcomings of the past. One dimension of SPR sign-off is also to check that Fund thinking and practice has learned from and addressed concerns raised about prior Fund activities. As Arora puts it,

> the whole point of reviewing our surveillance from time to time is to make sure that gaps are being filled, for example, a big gap in the past has been interconnections across countries.... appreciation of risks, making sure that we cover the financial sector competently and also recognize the linkages between the financial and the real sectors.[8]

The Fund has to walk a fine line, however. Being reflexive and open-minded is one thing, but Fund intellectual authority is compromised if the institution changes its mind or admits it was wrong too often. As Blanchard puts it, 'there is a sense in which you build credibility by admitting mistakes, but there is a short run and a long run effect' involving some short-term damage to your reputation by recognizing the Fund got something wrong. Nevertheless, 'when the mistake exposed turns out to be important to correct you just swallow hard and correct it.'[9]

Numerous interviewees identified a third aspect of the Fund as an institutional and ideational context, describing it as an 'intellectually live' place, where there are 'big battles' and 'lots of back and forth'.[10] Others characterized the most important evolution within the Fund since 2008 as a more 'open-minded' approach to economic thinking with 'much more intellectual freedom'.[11] These claims are not to be taken at face value. IMF hierarchy and the need to conform to agreed Fund positions as discussed above places limits on this 'open-mindedness'. Nevertheless, taking such self-understandings seriously is part of a CI approach to the political economy. Many Fund staff, in giving life to the work of the Fund, 'make sense' of the institution as open-minded and intellectually live. These interpretive frames and cognitive filters intervene between actors and their institutional context and shape practices, how they perform their roles, and remake their environment.

[8] Interview with Vivek Arora, then Deputy Director of the Strategy, Policy and Review Department, September 2013.

[9] Interview with IMF Chief Economist Olivier Blanchard, June 2013.

[10] Interview with Senior IMF economist Paolo Mauro, a senior fellow at the Peterson Institute for International Economics at the time of the interview in 2014.

[11] Interview with IMF Research Department Deputy Director Jonathan Ostry, June 2013.

Furthermore, some new practices have been introduced since the crash, with an increasing variety in the way debate occurs. This creates a more receptive context for this 'open-minded' approach to economic policy thinking. Talking in 2013, Arora noted: 'We have a lot of collaboration on research, and we have seminars so there's a lot of informal interaction . . . Before that we used to be completely in a written word world. We exchanged memos but you didn't verbally debate a lot of things.'[12] Formerly, the peer review interactions discussed above were largely or exclusively written, but in recent years it has become a much more social interaction. The internal review process continues to play its important formal role, but it now exists alongside a wider array of less formal exchanges through which champions of new thinking gauge the likelihood of ideas being taken up more broadly within the Fund.

The IEO has critiqued how the Fund 'tends to operate in silos' which limits 'cross-fertilization of ideas, and "out-of-the-box" thinking' (IEO 2015: 5). These new practices are an attempt to tackle recognized problems with past Fund practice. Interviewees noted that evolutions in internal Fund dissemination and discussion practices, some introduced following Blanchard's arrival, involved more face-to-face 'back and forth' exchanges. Viñals and Blanchard hosted weekly 'brown bag' seminars, with an open invitation to Fund economists for any of them to share new thinking and research; 'The lively intellectual atmosphere is there both informally and formally. I think the informal interactions probably are more lively where we have these so-called surveillance issues meetings on Tuesdays chaired by Olivier Blanchard and José Viñals, where economists present their new thinking and ideas.'[13]

These new ways in which economic ideas are 'intersubjectively shared, collectively legitimated' (Park and Vetterlein 2010a: 14) alter the dynamics of ideational development within the Fund. The shift from purely written feedback to much more direct social interaction has an effect on the mutual constitution of norms. The development and legitimation of socially acceptable economic policy ideas became a more overtly social process as a result, providing additional feedback loops for proponents of new thinking to take the temperature of their reception. As anyone who has conducted a PhD viva and also refereed a journal article by providing written comments can attest, providing face-to-face as opposed to written feedback constitutes a very different mode of sharing and critiquing knowledge. Within these intersubjective interactions, both formal and informal, those seeking to move Fund positions on important policy issues also become aware of limits of the

[12] Interview with Vivek Arora, then Deputy Director of the Strategy, Policy and Review Department, September 2013.

[13] Interview with Vivek Arora, then Deputy Director of the Strategy, Policy and Review Department, September 2013.

possible in shifting the boundaries of legitimate policy. This modus operandi of exchanging economic ideas potentially expands the scope for the social reconstruction of policy norms.

A fourth facet of the post-GFC Fund, linked to open-mindedness and learning the lessons of the past themes, is some limited evolution in Fund recruitment practices since the 1980s and 1990s. The Fund of the late twentieth century was engaged in what Momani calls the 'selective recruitment of conservative macroeconomists' (Momani 2010: 31; 2005a, 2007; see also Chwieroth 2007a & b, 2010). The limited staff diversity was one reason given for the failings in the response to earlier crises (Group of Independent Experts 1999: 71–2; IEO 2003), and the need to broaden the educational background and skill mix of Fund staff was again re-emphasized following the GFC (IEO 2011: 21, 42, 45), needed not least to tackle IMF 'groupthink' (IEO 2011: 1, 17, 36). To the extent that the Board has taken on board staff diversity issues, it has been more focused around the gender dimension and geographical origins of Fund staff. Diversity of educational background has not been to the fore in how the IMF has attempted to change its recruitment practices. There have been only limited attempts within hiring patterns to broaden slightly the 'gene pool' in terms of the kinds of economists and where in the world they were trained. So Fund recruitment includes both New Classical 'freshwater' and New Keynesian 'saltwater' economists, as Krugman terms them (2009, 2012). The Fund of the twenty-first century, whilst still staffed by mainstream economists, is something of a broader church, drawn from a wider array of institutions. This includes economics departments with a slightly wider range of theoretical orientations, and from more parts of the world as compared to their recruitment practices of the 1980s identified by Chwieroth (2010). Lagarde's speech to the Executive Board in June 2011 when she was bidding to become the Managing Director highlighted the importance of 'ensuring equal opportunities and diversity in all its facets, genderwise, academic and geographic'. This was because 'In-breeding leads to groupthinking and "silo mentality" leads to underperformance, as the report from the IEO (Independent Evaluation Office) pointed out. Diversity will strengthen legitimacy, but will also reinforce effectiveness. This is an area where progress will be achieved, should I be elected' (Lagarde 2011a).

This shift towards slightly more diversity in staff composition was remarked on favourably by numerous interviewees. They spoke of the modestly more heterogeneous feel to the Fund staff profile, and identified it as one source of the Fund's more open-minded approach to economic policy questions. This idea of a broader range of economists should be treated with some caution, since this is still within a fairly narrow range of mainstream economic thinking. Of course, this probably tells us more about how *narrow* thinking and recruitment practices were in the 1980s (see Chwieroth 2010) than how broad they became subsequently. IMF recruitment still operates within the confines of recruiting an overwhelming majority of economics PhDs, and only very small numbers of other social scientists (see Momani 2005a; Vetterlein 2010: 99). Nevertheless, the Fund of today is not quite such an intellectual monoculture. The academic background of the large numbers of Fund economists covered in Cornel Ban's dataset of IMF staff and their background indicates recruitment patterns have broadened somewhat, drawing from a wider range of North American and European universities, including some not-so-conservative economics departments (Ban 2016). These evolutions in hiring practices help explain the increased visibility of the somewhat more market-sceptical, Keynesian, 'subcultures' identified previously by Chwieroth (2010) in Fund intellectual production since 2008. This chimes with the increased prevalence identified by Ban of 'revisionist' economic policy thinking alongside 'orthodox' ideas in the work cited in Fund publications (2015a & b; Seabrooke et al. 2015).

Hierarchy and Path-Contingent Change in IMF Economic Ideas after the Crash

Combined with Fund hierarchical norms, the feedback loops, and internal review processes would normally be expected to act as informal constraining mechanisms on ideational innovation (IEO 2011: 1, 17, 36). However, in the specific conditions of 2008–9, the institutional mediation of ideas through the Fund's hierarchical structures generated opening, not closure. Integral to this was Strauss-Kahn's encouragement of new, and the revisiting of old, economic policy thinking. This chimes with findings of the CPE and IPE literature on crises, and on the conditions of Knightian uncertainty being conducive environments for ideational change (Blyth 2002a; Hay 2011a, 2015; Schmidt 2008, 2010). One thing which all staff economists and management at the IMF agreed on and volunteered unprompted during interviews was how pivotal Dominique Strauss-Kahn was to reviving the Fund's fortunes and relevance. From 2008 onwards, Fund leadership were encouraging the staff to revisit the premises of their policy thinking. The appointment of Blanchard, an open-minded and somewhat heterodox mainstream economist, as Chief Economist was also important. As he noted in September 2014, reflecting on the implications for future research of the crash of 2008, 'the message should be to let a hundred flowers bloom. Now that we are more aware of nonlinearities [revealed by the financial crisis and its aftermath] and the dangers they pose, we should explore them further theoretically and empirically—and in all sorts of models' (Blanchard 2014a: 28).

The feedback loop mechanisms which affect how staff make sense of their environment and seek to reshape it operated differently in light of Strauss-Kahn's call to 'think outside the box'. This entreaty, coming from the highest authority within the deeply hierarchical Fund, effectively neutralized their normally constraining effects. Suddenly, in 2008, the overweening need to articulate new economic thinking in a manner consistent with a conservative understanding of mainstream economic thought evaporated amidst an economic policy orthodoxy profoundly destabilized by the crisis. Rethinking the premises of policy thinking, perhaps even revisiting prior Fund policy stances, was actively sanctioned. This top-down encouragement of eclecticism further built up the conducive environment for ideational change. IMF bricoleurs had a following wind as they set their sails to undertake a reconstruction and adjustment of IMF prescriptive policy thinking, using as source material many insights already found within the Fund's repertoire, and post-crash rethinking in academic economics. This post-crash thinking drew inspiration from a range of economic perspectives including more market-sceptical ones. The 'top-down' entreaty to think outside the box offered scope for 'bottom-up' research and working papers to feed into the rethink (see also Chwieroth 2010; Vetterlein 2010: 111); as Paolo Mauro notes: 'There is a process where you go top down and bottom up, and the management and the department directors have ideas and request that people work on them and sometimes people (staff economists) have ideas—they feed them through the machinery.'[14]

As the Deputy Director of the Research Department characterized the Fund since 2008, 'I think there has been a fundamental rethinking on fiscal policy, on monetary policy, on managing capital flows, and on inequality... much more questioning of conventional wisdom.'[15] Indeed, instead of ideas being prioritized because they fell within the Fund's established practices and modes of thought, this presented a mirror image where ideas were likely to gain momentum *only if*, or at least *especially if* they came from outside the pre-crash comfort zone of economic thinking. Citing less conventional economists under these unusual conditions became a way to get thinking 'mainstreamed' rather than marginalized, and could enhance rather than impede career development prospects. These were novel inter-subjective conditions for the mutual constitution of socially acceptable economic policy thinking in the Fund. The evolving forms of internal interaction played a supporting role. So, too, was an open-minded self-understanding amongst Fund staff, and a view of the institution as reflective and willing to learn from shortcomings

[14] Interview with Senior IMF economist Paolo Mauro, a senior fellow at the Peterson Institute for International Economics at the time of the interview in 2014.

[15] Interview with Jonathan Ostry, Deputy Director of IMF Research Department, June 2013.

in its responses to previous economic crises. These factors, together with the entreaty to rethink from on high, provided a conducive environment for ideational evolution.

On its own, however, having powerful internal backers was not sufficient for fiscal revisionism to carry the day. Changing ideas and emphases in academic economics are a necessary but not a sufficient condition for shifting Fund economic policy positions. For changes in economic thinking to succeed, they must take account of and strategically engage with the Fund internal bureaucratic and scientific culture (Clegg 2013: 17; Leiteritz 2005). Ideas need to be rendered compatible with the Fund's 'internal belief system and organizational culture' if they are to achieve 'social recognition'. They have to be 'adopted in a way that was socially and implicitly congruent with common practice' (Momani 2010: 32). At first glance this may suggest a very high degree of ideational path dependence, but that would be to underestimate the creativity and reflexivity of actors. The social recognition for new ideas was secured through processes of bricolage, characterized by Carstensen as 'kneading or moulding an idea to try to get it to hang together and gain the acceptance of other actors', wherein 'ideas are actively and oftentimes creatively used by actors' (2011b: 157, 163).

The four mechanisms of internal ideational change at the Fund developed in this chapter not only highlight just how institutionally mediated the process is, but also address a key concern for CI and ideational scholarship more broadly—explaining *which* ideas are likely to get taken up and why. Fund power relations matter, and new ideas require influential support from 'gatekeepers'—but equally important is the form the new ideas take (Schmidt 2008, 2010). This kind of ideational change is better understood as 'path contingent' (Johnson 2003; Bell 2011: 896), rather than path dependent. With sufficient backing and support, a variety of different ideas could potentially pass through the four mechanisms of ideational change and prevail within the internal politics of economic ideas. Both 'corroboration' and 'authoritative recognition' require, at different levels and in different ways, new thinking to be placed in the context of mainstream economics research and methods. The post-GFC re-evaluation of economic thinking revealed that quite a range of different policy ideas and positions could be reconciled to that mainstream, and find champions amongst leading economists (see Chapter 3).

IMF Bricolage and the 'New Normal'

As set out at the beginning of this chapter, paradigm change frameworks struggle to capture the dynamics of ideational change within the IMF.

Through its long history, economic ideas drawn from different paradigmatic homes became, to varying degrees, influential within Fund thinking and practice (see e.g. Boughton 2004). There is an amalgamation of different elements within useable Fund doctrine. This range of ideas, and cognitive frameworks which are in part institutionally constituted, have been sedimented into Fund practices over many decades. Fund economic thinking gets incorporated into its models (Rajan et al. 2004; Laxton 2008; Botman et al. 2007; Kumhof et al. 2010), and bureaucratized through policy frameworks, standard operating procedures, and guidance notes. Subcultures of different economic thinking coexist at the Fund (Chwieroth 2010; Ban 2015a & b), their insights informing Fund operational work to varying degrees and in combinations which evolve pragmatically over time according to policy context. The theoretical underpinnings of the Fund's approach to policy are 'eclectic' and 'by no means monolithic' (David 1985: 5, 7), but an amalgam of these varied elements.

How Fund staff see themselves, and their use of economic doctrine, is also instructive. It again sits uncomfortably with the paradigm framework. In lengthy interviews it comes across that Fund economists think of themselves as non-doctrinaire, 'practical', and policy-oriented economists. They feel uncomfortable identifying with what they see as 'philosophical' labels of theoretical schools such as Keynesian, New Keynesian, Neo-Classical, or New Classical. As Deputy Managing Director David Lipton put it, 'I don't think you'd find that many people here think of themselves as adherents to some school of thought.'[16] A standard reaction is that these are not terribly helpful for organizing thinking about or approaches to their policy work; 'we in essence approach policy recommendations from the standpoint of empiricism; of trying to figure out what makes sense in a given setting and make sure it's right.'[17]

Many draw a distinction between their 'policy' or 'operational' work, the latter seen as largely atheoretical, and qualitatively different from more theoretical understandings of the economy built up from first principles, such as done by the Fund's modelling team. Even there, Fund modeller in chief Doug Laxton notes, 'it's not a question of philosophy. It's a question of what the empirical evidence suggests.'[18] That 'non doctrinaire' self-understanding should not be accepted at face value. It is at odds with the argument made in the book's Introduction that all economic analysis is inevitably underpinned by ideology (see also Blyth 2003b: 244–51; Best & Widmaier 2006).

[16] Interview with IMF Deputy Managing Director David Lipton, September 2013.

[17] Interview with IMF Deputy Managing Director David Lipton, September 2013.

[18] Interview with Doug Laxton, Division Chief of the Economic Modelling Division, IMF Research Department, September 2013.

Nevertheless, there is ample evidence that IMF Staff economists *are* willing to draw on economic ideas from different paradigmatic homes according to context, conditions, and conjunctures. Fund flagship publications, technical notes, Board papers, and working papers reflect a diversity of economic views, frequently referencing New Keynesian ideas, 'Real Business Cycle' models (inspired by New Classical economics), as well as traditional Keynesian ideas.

The reality of differing economic viewpoints, from varied theoretical positions, coexisting within the Fund's repertoire of operational economic thinking does not fit the paradigm framework. Furthermore, ideational change at the Fund is more incremental, additive, and pragmatic than many renderings of paradigm change admit. Accordingly, 'bricolage' (Campbell 2004; Campbell & Pedersen 2001a; Carstensen 2011b, 2015a), 'layering' (Streeck & Thelen 2005a & b; Mahoney and Thelen 2010b; Chwieroth 2014), and 're-combination' (Quack & Djelic 2005; Crouch 2005) are more helpful frameworks for analysing Fund ideational change. The appeal of these alternative models of ideational change is reinforced by problems not just for the notion of paradigm *change*, but the very notion of paradigms themselves.

The eschewal of the paradigm framework in this analysis reflects a broader and deeper point. Economic ideas in the minds of policy elites are varied and composite, and are not as fixed, settled, coherent, or perhaps even commensurable as the paradigm framing indicates (Carstensen 2015a & b). We should not assume a priori an idea has 'conceptual coherence' and need to be alive to 'tensions and inconsistencies' within ideas, and to their 'relative malleability' (Carstensen 2011a: 599). Ideas, in this view, 'are not closed systems of fixed meaning' and are shaped by 'social practices' rather than 'logical necessity' (Carstensen 2011a: 602; see also Bevir 2002). This pragmatism of IMF bricoleurs—adapting economic policy thinking to policy context and economic conjuncture—also aligns with thinking in terms of bricolage; unlike 'paradigm man [or woman]' the 'bricoleur is... above all pragmatic... the bricoleur takes stock of his existing set of ideas, policies and instruments and reinterprets them in the light of concrete circumstances' (Carstensen 2011b: 155–6).

The limits to the coherence and even the commensurability of economic ideas identified by critiques of the paradigm framework (Carstensen 2011a) are recognized and accommodated by IMF bricoleurs as they work with economic ideas. Multiple different ways of thinking about the economy are embraced, within different departments, but also within a single staff member. Policy-oriented Fund economists are keenly aware of uncertainty, convention-driven financial market behaviour, and multiple possible belief-driven equilibria. The linearity which is a necessary feature of the Fund's 'dynamic stochastic general equilibrium' (DSGE) models coexists with greater attentiveness to and appreciation of potential non-linear policy and expectational dynamics, be it hysteresis, secular stagnation, deflation, 'sudden stops', or 'bad debt' spirals. The rational expectations assumed at the heart of DSGE type modelling coexist with more convention-driven ideational understandings—where individuals' expectations need to be stabilized. Appreciation of these notions and insights colour how Fund staff calibrate their surveillance commentaries. Fund Missions, for example, take great care in drafting reports because they are aware that slightly negative assessments can have disproportionate effects on bond market participants already nervous about a particular economy's credibility. IMF economists can readily reconcile this grasp of the relative autonomy of convention-driven understandings of an economy from underlying economic conditions to working within mainstream economics, built on very different understandings of agents.

Fund modellers, for example, do not see their thinking about the economy as reducible to those models, and highlight the importance of the caveats attached to the use of models. IMF modellers are careful to clarify what they can and cannot explain and predict, and mindful to incorporate 'additional judgement that they think is appropriate for the current context of deleveraging or an economy that has been hit with a very large shock'.[19] Modelling is not ideally attuned to address all the salient dynamics of the post-crash world economy, the linear foundations of models struggling to accommodate hysteresis, for example; 'the foundations of hysteresis are non-linearities and multiple equilibria, and the problem is that, when you write those models down, they are extremely sensitive to detailed modelling assumptions . . . small differences in parameter values can result in dramatic differences in their implications.'[20] Models, although vitally important to Fund work, do not reflect the sum total of Fund economists' thinking about the economy and policy (see also Seabrooke et al. 2015).

More important than models are Fund frameworks such as financial programming (Babb 2007; De Vries 1987; Clift & Tomlinson 2012), which operate as cognitive filters through which IMF staff make sense of their working environment. After all, the modelling team is small within the Fund—and the day-to-day operational workings and practices of most Fund staff are quite far removed from what Matthew Watson calls 'the model world' of economics (2014). Fund economists work with models, but also with their intuitions and subjective judgements (Nelson 2017). Their decision-making practices and operational work are informed by all three. As Arora puts it, 'at the end of the day a lot of [IMF decision-making] is based on the judgement of the review

[19] Interview with Doug Laxton, Division Chief of the Economic Modelling Division, IMF Research Department, September 2013.

[20] Interview with Doug Laxton, Division Chief of the Economic Modelling Division, IMF Research Department, September 2013.

officer and the mission chief, ... the judgement is based on the guidance notes for the broad principle, the multi-lateral products, the discussion and debate among mission chiefs and reviewers.'[21]

This multiplicity of renderings of the economy, coexisting in how Fund economists approach and think about policy issues, is revealed best through face-to-face discussions with a large number of Fund staff. It cannot be 'read off' or gleaned from solely engaging in textual analysis of working papers or other Fund publications. Indeed, it comes across in interviews that some are inclined to make mental separation in their minds between their empirical and policy work, and theoretical modelling of the economy built up from first principles.

Conclusion

The Fund's bureaucratic nature, large size, internal scientific culture, and reputation for conservativism and steadfast commitment to the 'Washington Consensus' (Soederberg 2004; Babb 2013) might lead us to expect little or no substantial ideational change in the wake of the GFC. Yet, within the parameters of 'thinkable' policy set by powerful members, the focus on Fund autonomy and the agency of Fund staff in this chapter unearths scope the Fund enjoys to reshape understandings of sound economic policy. The post-crash scenario provided particularly and unusually propitious conditions for the Fund to revisit conventional wisdom.

The approach adopted here sees Fund actors as reflexive agents, able within limits to recreate their environment. CI's appreciation of cognitive filters, the differential appeal of the varied forms ideas take, and how processes of social interaction about ideas matter lead us towards a more fine-grained analysis of the mechanisms of ideational change. The 'feedback loops' are the means by which reflexive Fund actors navigate sources of resistance to present ideas in palatable fashion within iterative processes of pragmatic and contingent ideational evolution. Those involved in moving the lines of economic policy thinking were mindful of the mutual constitution of socially acceptable Fund doctrine, the need for new thinking to become legitimated, and the difficulties in the shifting of 'legitimate' policy space.

The Fund's authority rests on its credentials for scientific and technocratic economic policy expertise. It wishes to avoid the perception of it being a political institution, or engaged directly in political debate and discussion. The forces of ideational path dependency appear strong at first glance.

[21] Interview with Vivek Arora, then Deputy Director of the Strategy, Policy and Review Department, September 2013.

Nevertheless, there is a politics of economic ideas within the Fund, and struggles over the relatively broad repertoire of economic thinking upon which the Fund draws. The unexpected finding of this research is that, provided the *form* conditions distilled in the four mechanisms of change—reconciliation, corroboration, operationalization, and authoritative recognition—are met, what constitutes the acceptable *content* of new economic thinking is surprisingly open.

An array of plausibly 'authoritative' claims can be mobilized, from competing sources of intellectual authority, to justify different policy stances in any given context. The sedimentation of economic ideas through bureaucratization into Fund practices over many decades, and the institutional mediation of ideational change at the Fund detailed above leads to the coexistence of a variety of economic doctrine, from different paradigmatic homes, underpinning Fund thought and practice. This means that the idea of paradigmatic change is not a helpful lens or framework for approaching evolving economic ideas and thinking within the Fund. The internal politics of economic ideas is shaped by social, power-infused processes wherein IMF bricoleurs select amongst the range of acceptable doctrine, and then frame policies to garner support within internal persuasive struggles. They use the building blocks of a range of economic perspectives to maintain a pragmatic relevance to current policy debates, packaging new ideas so as to channel them through Fund cognitive filters. In Chapter 3, we explore how the ebb and flow of theoretical and policy debates in academic economics shapes the contours of the landscape on which IMF thinking and practice evolves.

3

The IMF, Economic Schools of Thought, and Their Normative Underpinnings

Introduction

In this chapter the evolution and maintenance of the Fund's interpretive framework for thinking about economic policy is explored against a backdrop of evolving prevailing approaches in the economics profession. Scholars and schools of thought within academic economics are evoked to provide a 'seal of approval' for Fund economic knowledge, analogous to how the Fund endorses a country's economic policy settings. Debates within mainstream academic economics thus form important parts of the social world within which the IMF seeks to exert intellectual authority. Hence the focus here is on the relationship between the IMF and what J. K. Galbraith termed the 'conventional wisdom' of the economics profession (1958: 6–17). These familiar understandings, deemed acceptable without being reflected upon, rather than embraced due to their intrinsic merit, are understood following Keynes' insights into 'conventions' as important inter-subjective structures (see Baker & Widmaier 2014; Keynes 1937).

Chapter 2 highlighted the need to analyse the internal structures, politics, and culture of the Fund to understand how they influenced the social process of knowledge production (see Weaver 2008: 13; Watts 2001; Broome 2008). Previous work on IMF economic ideas has highlighted the significance of 'shared beliefs' of IMF economists and the production of economic policy knowledge by the Fund as a social process (Chwieroth 2010; Nelson 2014, 2017). Consistent with the broader arguments of this book, the development and maintenance of economic policy orthodoxies is here understood as a social, inter-subjective process carried out amongst academic and policy economists. The scientific nature of Fund knowledge production, as indicated in the mechanisms of corroboration and authoritative recognition developed in Chapter 2, requires connecting Fund thinking to academic economics.

Whilst the work of the Fund is clearly distinct from academic economics, an issue we explore in section 3.2, the Fund's attempt to wield intellectual authority requires couching its commentary, advice, and interventions in the economic policy debate as backed up by current mainstream economics. As such, the conventional wisdoms of the economics profession are important parameters of the Fund's intellectual authority. They influence how the content and framing of Fund advice and policy recommendations towards advanced economies have changed in recent years. This chapter places the IMF's recent and longer-term evolution within the context of the development of economic thinking on macroeconomic and fiscal policy. The aim is not to unpack all these economic ideas in detail, but to briefly outline them, to underline their role and their coexistence alongside each other within Fund thinking and practice.

In his path-breaking survey of the economic ideas which proved influential within the Fund since the 1980s, Chwieroth identifies eight different schools of economic thought, from traditional Keynesianism to various positions along the 'neo-liberal continuum', each finding advocates over the Fund's evolution, many drawn on by pockets of Fund staff (2010: 16–22, 61–86). Chwieroth highlights generational change whereby the Keynesian economists, who dominated the Fund in its first three decades, began to retire and be replaced by various kinds of neo-liberal economists in the 1980s (2010). Focusing on the 1990s and early to mid 2000s, he noted the limits of the traction of Keynesian thinking highlighting market failures within both mainstream economics and the Fund.

What was arresting exploring the lived-in debates at the Fund some years after the crash was just how far the default faith in the market's self-correcting propensities had been shaken. Rather than assuming that economic stability and growth would arise out of free market operations, the pre-supposition of the post-crash Fund is that the stability and growth at the core of its mandate needs to be actively nurtured and maintained through a wide range of policy and regulatory activism. This helps explain the shift in institutional view on capital controls (Gallagher 2015; Chwieroth 2014; Moschella 2015), but also the embrace of macro-prudential economic governance with its focus on counter-cyclical regulation and policies (Viñals 2011, 2016). As IMF Research Department Deputy Director Jonathan Ostry describes the Fund post-crash stabilization efforts, 'an essential part of the rethink is the realization that we have multiple policy instruments, and—economics being the science of concavity—it makes sense not to put everything on one instrument, but instead to use all the available instruments.'[1] The risk of vulnerability and

[1] Interview with IMF Research Department Deputy Director Jonathan Ostry, June 2013.

instability spreading from the financial sector to the real economy, and the need to understand these interactions better, is underlined as core to the Fund's research agenda (Blanchard 2008b, 2012b, 2014a; Blanchard et al. 2010, 2013). These lessons were assimilated by key leadership in major policy departments of the Fund such as Research (Blanchard), Fiscal Affairs (FAD) (Cottarelli), and the IMF's Financial Counsellor and Head of the Monetary and Capital Markets (Viñals). Post-2008, there has been a revival of more market-sceptical 'subcultures' linked to Keynesian ideas within the Fund. Some recent and some more long-standing variants of Keynesian thinking have been used by Fund staff to identify shortcomings and suboptimal pathologies of markets under certain carefully specified conditions. These, Fund flagship publications and speeches repeatedly point out, have important implications for the post-crash conduct of macroeconomic policy.

Our analysis highlights how economic ideas and insights have been taken up within the Fund, and how IMF bricoleurs operate within the parameters of mainstream economic thinking, and paint from a palette of the extensive repertoire of IMF economic ideas. Fund thinking about economic policy is composite, drawing on different theoretical influences. It is also highly contingent on national institutional context and circumstances, and on the economic conjuncture. This in turn reveals the wide range of economic insights and policy positions reconcilable to the economic orthodoxy. Such a scenario affords key actors within the IMF scope to select, prioritize and choose within this menu of respectable economic thinking. The increasing prominence of 'fiscal space' (see Chapters 1 and 4) underscores how the Fund seeks to offer differentiated economic policy, specific to national economic conditions and economic conjuncture.

This contingency, combined with the Fund's repertoire, increases the interpretive latitude enjoyed by Fund policy commentators. *Which* economic ideas and insights are afforded primacy in authoritative economic policy commentary is a highly significant and a deeply political process. The differentiation and variegation within Fund economic thought and the more Keynesian tone of Fund policy commentary since the crash has hitherto gone under-reported and appreciated by many IMF scholars. After distinguishing the key characteristics of the IMF and academic economics as systems of knowledge production, this chapter underlines the normative underpinnings of bodies of economic thought. It then charts the evolution of prevailing macroeconomic ideas over the life of the Fund, from Keynesianism, to the Neo-Classical Synthesis, to New Classical, New Keynesian (NKM), and finally New Consensus Macroeconomics (NCM). This forms the backdrop to an exploration of how the repertoire of Fund economic ideas has been recombined since the crash in ways which increase the scope for Keynesian thinking *within* mainstream economics.

The Fund's Repertoire of Economic Ideas and Academic Economics

Fund economists feel the need to find corroboration for their economic policy thinking within academic economics. The IMF's intellectual authority rests in part on what Chwieroth terms the 'socially recognized expertise' of economists and the 'productive power' of economics as a profession (Chwieroth 2010: 12, 40–7). The connection between academic economics and Fund Staff's research and work has become closer since the 1990s, a shift some credit Stanley Fischer with initiating when he was IMF Chief Economist. Fund staff increasingly seek to publish in academic journals, which many interviewees reported has become a progressively more salient consideration within internal Fund career progression. Citations from and corroborating references to the academic literature, and to schools of economic thought or key concepts and arguments within it, are important sources of intellectual justification for Fund ideas and advice. These practices reflect the mechanisms of authoritative recognition and corroboration identified in Chapter 2. Interviewees also noted how the extent and depth of referencing in Fund publications has increased in recent decades.

In order to understand how economic ideas and insights get incorporated into Fund work, we need to say a bit about the similarities and differences between the Fund and academe. The two are related—often quite closely—but they are not the same thing. This distinction is important and should not be overlooked. Best's otherwise excellent account of how Fund economic ideas evolve, for example, talks at a general level about 'mainstream economic theory and practice' (2005: 111). This fails to draw sufficient distinction between evolutions in academic economics and evolutions in Fund thinking and practice, and significant differences between these systems of knowledge production. The twists and turns of the academic economic debate were followed with interest by the Fund, and some ideas originating in academic economics attracted widespread influence within the Fund and its practices, such as inflation targeting. There is always, however, a distinction to be made between the more policy-oriented, practical work of the Fund and academic economic theorizing—with some ideas more likely to get taken up by the Fund than others (see e.g. Boughton 2004; Blanchard et al. 2010).

Four aspects of the Fund's internal intellectual universe mark it out from academic economics. Firstly, by dint of its mandate and operational remit, IMF staff have a more policy-oriented approach and focus than academic economists. As economics PhDs, Fund staff bring into the organization the insights they gleaned in graduate school (Klamer & Colander 1990; Colander 2005, 2007), yet their day-to-day operational work is more policy and empirically grounded and alive to the practical and pragmatic considerations of policymaking than much academic economic research. As Deputy Managing Director David Lipton puts it,

> the Fund works on what's happening and academics are interested in the same set of subjects. I think there has been a very good synergy between the two. We are clinical economists, in the sense that we have to act... I think we can be better clinical economists by talking to academics and reading what they say.[2]

Secondly, the range of theoretical positions routinely evoked in flagship publications and working papers is testament to a greater degree of theoretical pluralism within the IMF. Fund flagship publications, Staff Position Notes, Staff Discussion Notes, working papers, and so on seek to incorporate different schools of thought—from the New Classical-inspired Real Business Cycle (RBC) theory to traditional Keynesianism. They do so in ways which tend to find some merit on all sides, and which paper over the cracks of ontological incommensurability between, for example, RBC and New Keynesian thought.

There is thus a broader range of economic ideas, drawn from a wider array of theoretical homes, and a more pluralistic approach to the merits of those various positions than the more monotheistic tendencies in academic economics. Fund use of economic theories involves some 'macroeconomic pragmatism (the rejection of doctrinaire approaches to economic management)' (Annesley and Gamble 2003). As regards the Fund's approach to economic modelling, Doug Laxton, its chief modeller, notes 'for policy modellers it is always a question of a synthesis. You are taking the best ideas from different schools or camps.'[3] This drawing of inspiration from more than one macroeconomic policy tradition is arguably the consequence of being 'clinical economists', whose work goes beyond the purely theoretical (see Sachs 2005). IMF staff see themselves as 'simply trying to figure out what we think is the right policy recommendation', an issue they approach 'from the standpoint of empiricism, of trying to figure out what makes sense in a given setting'.[4] Fund surveillance and economic policy advice has to deal with institutional arrangements that are never fully captured by economic theory. The influence of economic theory upon actual policy advice is always mediated, both by events, and by recognition of the material and ideational constraints under which Fund Missions and government economic policymakers operate.

Peter Heller, a long-serving senior figure in the IMF's Fiscal Affairs department, charted the evolution of IMF's positions on fiscal policy over recent decades (Heller 2002). Heller's approach, rather than emphasizing theoretical underpinnings, was strongly inductive, summarizing the Fund's stance by

[2] Interview with IMF Deputy Managing Director David Lipton, September 2013.

[3] Interview with Doug Laxton, Division Chief of the Economic Modelling Division, IMF Research Department, September 2013.

[4] Interview with IMF Deputy Managing Director David Lipton, September 2013.

drawing on the positions taken in its discussions and negotiations with members. This chimes with the consistent self-identification of Fund staff as non-doctrinaire, pragmatic policy economists, which came across in all interviews. This is one reason why the term 'IMF bricoleurs' is favoured here to capture how somewhat diverse economic ideas can be recombined and brought together. The degree of openness to heterodox ideas should not be overstated. After all, Post-Keynesian economics, feminist economics, Marxian economics, or Austrian economics are largely or totally unrepresented in the Fund's intellectual production. Nevertheless, *relative to economics as practised in academe*, the IMF constitutes a more pluralistic environment for discussing economic ideas from varied theoretical homes.

Thirdly, there is greater methodological pluralism within the Fund compared to academic economics. Importance is attached, as elsewhere in the economics profession, to mainstream econometric techniques, catchily termed dynamic stochastic general equilibrium (DSGE) modelling, which make linear assumptions about self-correcting markets. Whilst in academic economics there are those who keep the faith and see no need to revise DSGE models, many at the IMF, notably its Modeller in Chief Doug Laxton and Chief Economist Olivier Blanchard, see scope for necessary innovations and improvements within its use of DSGE models. There is a debate about whether ad hoc amendments do enough in practice to counter the proclivities of NCM-inspired DSGE models which retain the same consumption function as their pre-crash versions. That said, Fund efforts managed to introduce banks, unemployment, and even concepts like hysteresis, into some of its DSGE models following the crash.[5]

Partly because some limitations to modelling, notably the absence of the financial system from the DSGE approach to the macroeconomy, are keenly recognized within the Fund, it is seen as far from the only credible approach. Narrative approaches, case studies, and historical methods, for example, are seen as having some scientific validity within the Fund, whereas they are more marginal at best to academic economics. Once again, the methodological pluralism should not be overstated. There remains a prioritization of DSGE modelling and quantitative corroboration of claims, but the modelling team is relatively small. The point is that the range of alternative techniques considered respectable extends much further within the Fund by comparison to the narrow methodological strictures of mainstream academic economics. As Senior IMF Economist Paolo Mauro put it, extolling the virtues of historical methods,

[5] Interviews with IMF Chief Economist Olivier Blanchard in June 2013 and with Doug Laxton, Division Chief of the Economic Modelling Division, IMF Research Department, in September 2013.

> I've spent the last couple of years putting together a data set with fiscal variables going back to the 1800s for a very large group of countries—to me that is maybe more descriptive, but its more doable. I do believe that for macro, history is very important. For macro—you just have to look at history.[6]

Finally, the importance of compatibility of new economic thinking with pre-existing Fund operational frameworks and approaches, the need for reconciliation as detailed in Chapter 2, marks the Fund out as a distinctive ideational environment. The Fund is a bureaucratic institution which has been engaged in economic policy issues through surveillance and programmes for many decades. This longevity of the Fund's involvement in applied economic policy research, advice, lending, and programme operations means that the Fund's work has spanned different waves of dominant economic thinking in academe. Along the way, particular approaches, concepts, and frameworks, such as its financial programming practices built on the Polak model (see e.g. Babb 2003; Polak 1957, 1997, 2001), have become sedimented into Fund staff mindsets and activities. These accreted practices get reproduced in how the Fund approaches its operational economic policy work. They become the standard operating procedures through which this economic thinking gets bureaucratized. The premises on which this operational edifice is built affect how far new thinking in academic economics gains influence within the Fund. Compatibility with these characteristics of the Fund as knowledge production regime is important if new ideas are to gain ground within the organization. New economic ideas have to be picked up in a certain way, and operationalized and corroborated using a range of methodological techniques including those considered state-of-the-art within academic economics. It is against this backdrop that this book, as noted in Chapter 2, advances a CI-inspired account of institutionally mediated incremental ideational change (Hay 2008; Schmidt 2008).

The Fund's limited methodological and theoretical pluralism, combined with an institutional memory and set of standard operating procedures which incorporate insights from a range of perspectives, help account for the repertoire of Fund economic ideas, from different economic theoretical schools within the IMF. As Chwieroth rightly highlights (2010), there is significant diversity of views on economic policy issues within the Fund, composed as it is of different 'subcultures' of economic thinking. Such a variety often goes under-appreciated within the literature on the IMF (although see Ban 2015a & b; Boughton 2004). This diversity of economic thought chimes with the findings of extensive fieldwork, conducted through dozens of searching interviews

[6] Interview with Senior IMF Economist Paolo Mauro, a senior fellow at the Peterson Institute for International Economics at the time of the interview in 2014.

with Fund Staff. These revealed a diversity, breadth, and variety of economic thinking underpinning the Fund's work. There is never one view, uniformly endorsed to the same degree within the building.

It thus makes sense to disaggregate the Fund's economic thinking in a fine-grained manner, made up of numerous different schools and positions. This variegation, which partly reflects the footprints of the protracted theoretical evolution of the discipline through waves of dominant orthodoxies discussed in sections 3.4 to 3.8, has been incorporated into Fund thinking and practice over decades. A repertoire of economic ideas, from different paradigmatic homes, is deemed respectable within the organization. As set out in Chapter 2, internal review and sign-off procedures, and the Fund's hierarchical structure, place limits on how far the differences of view are visible or audible from outside the building. As Vivek Arora puts it,

> If there are issues that are new and evolving... like for example the fiscal multipliers or the appropriate pace of fiscal consolidation in a downturn, then I think there is usually a staff view that emerges through this whole process of debate and review. Often it will be expressed in our flagship publications so the WEO and Fiscal Monitor... and we [in SPR] take those into account as well.[7]

Settling upon and falling in behind an agreed line can be very important for the 'traction' of Fund ideas (see Chapter 6). The evolution of fiscal policy thinking within the IMF both during the 2008 crash and subsequently needs to be understood against the backdrop of the fairly broad repertoire of Fund economic policy thinking.

Schools of Thought in Economics and Their Normative Underpinnings

Best notes how one aspect of the Fund's approach to economic theorizing, which she terms the 'hollowing out' of Keynesianism, was that economic policy came to be seen as a wholly 'technical' pursuit, abstracted from any 'ideological' discussion (2005). The technocratic approach to economic policy issues has over the subsequent decades come to be central to Fund internal culture (Momani 2007; Barnett & Finnemore 2004). Fund economists, when interviewed, see themselves as apolitical, non-doctrinaire technocrats. They self-identify as practical, policy-oriented economists taking a pragmatic approach to which ideas prove useful for policy in different conditions. It

[7] Interview with Vivek Arora, then Deputy Director of the Strategy, Policy and Review Department, September 2013.

reflects a commitment to 'open-minded'-ness, an empirical bent, and how Fund advice needs to reflect the conjuncture and the policy context.[8]

The self-affirmation of Fund Staff as non-doctrinaire is a conspicuous feature of discussions with them. Some interviewees equate 'theoretical' work with the modelling, as built up from first principles. This they differentiate from their 'empirical' work, the implication being that in their minds their 'empirical' work is atheoretical. One sense in which this non-doctrinaire claim rings true is the range of theoretical perspectives they are in the habit of alluding to and drawing from in discussion of any economic policy issue. The spirit of theoretical pluralism, and the policy-oriented focus characterizes how different schools of thought are evoked and drawn upon. This array of economic ideas and concepts is utilized in a contingent manner when pertinent to the economic conjuncture or circumstances, and at other times may lie dormant.

The 'non-doctrinaire' self-understanding is not disingenuous, but neglects how there are always normative underpinnings in any economic analysis (Klamer & Colander 1990; Colander 2005, 2007). We noted in the Introduction to this book how economic ideas, even if they appear technical, are rooted in underlying ideological assumptions—in understandings of the principles of political economy (see e.g. Best & Widmaier 2006; Dow 2015). Such claims to pragmatism cannot be taken purely at face value, since such a standpoint underplays how any position on economic policy is informed and underpinned by taking a stance on underlying a priori theoretical issues. The scientific and technocratic presentation of Fund economic thinking is of necessity a façade. Fund staff, as economists, cannot escape the ideological foundations of economic theorizing and analysis (see e.g. Blaug 1996: 698–700).

Nelson notes how Fund staff's economic ideas have been broadly 'neo-liberal' in character from the 1980s to the 2000s, as gleaned from their training in particular economics departments, primarily in the US (2014, 2017). This chapter reveals the pay-off of disaggregating further between different variants of economic thinking to paint in the more fine-grained contours of Fund ideas. In this it builds on Chwieroth, who, as noted above, differentiates within and extends beyond 'neo-liberalism' to present a richer, more fine-grained picture composed of eight schools of thought. Three of Chwieroth's eight schools—the Keynesian, post-Keynesian, and New Keynesian—highlight the shortcomings and failings of markets (Chwieroth 2010: 16–17). The specific critiques of, and scepticism towards markets offered by each are significantly different (see e.g. Colander 1992, 1996) but they are

[8] Interviews with Olivier Blanchard, Jonathan Ostry, and Paolo Mauro, June 213; interviews with David Lipton, Doug Laxton, and Daniel Leigh, September 2013.

united in emphasizing that markets cannot be relied upon to consistently deliver economic stability.

Each of the economic theoretical approaches to policy which have been and to some extent remain influential within the Fund is built up from a priori premises about how the economy works. Each is rooted in an account of the principles of political economy—about to what extent the market can be relied upon to deliver optimal outcomes, or about the relative merits of economic policy interventions. Are markets viewed as inherently self-correcting or, to use the terminology of economics, 'Walrasian', or are they subject to shortcomings? Even for empirically oriented Fund economists, at some level, sets of assumptions are informing how they approach their data. As we shall see, drawing out the Keynesian understandings of the economy and policy, and counterposing them with the also influential orthodox, neo-classical inspired understandings of the market highlights some starkly different views of the economy and policy.

Keynesianism

Attempting to define Keynesianism is to enter a 'semantic minefield' (Hay 2004a: 40). In the early twenty-first century Keynesianism, with qualifying adjectives, has become a church so broad that its doctrinal limits are difficult to delineate. At the core of a Keynesian position is a perception of the inherent instability of a capitalist economy such that the market, left to its own devices, cannot safely be relied upon to deliver stability and full employment. One important theoretical premise underpinning a Keynesian view of the economy is the rejection of Say's law—or the idea that supply calls forth demand (Keynes 1936 [1964]: 23–34). The Keynesian conception of national economic management is built upon insights in Keynes' *General Theory* about the potential role for fiscal policy and interest rates in managing aggregate demand to increase or reduce output. The essence of a Keynesian view is 'the perception of the role of aggregate demand in setting the level of economic activity and the lack of automatic forces leading a market economy to full employment' (Arestis & Sawyer 1998: 181).

Unlike neo-classical economic thought, in a Keynesian understanding of the economy, markets do not contain an inexorable propensity or tendency for supply and demand to balance. This provides the rationale and role for public power intervening through economic policy levers to guide the economy towards a full employment equilibrium (Hall 1989: 6–7). Colander notes: 'Keynes set out to justify a government activist policy for affecting the aggregate economy. It is reasonable to conclude that models that do that are Keynesian' (1992: 438). Key features of Keynesianism include the pursuit of low unemployment, which in an unstable world requires, *in principle*, the use of all possible policy instruments. Active counter-cyclical fiscal policy raises the possibility of fiscal deficits. While deficit spending is by no means the *sine qua non* of Keynesian policy, the possibility of running deficits is crucial to the counter-cyclical policy approach of Keynesianism. This is another point of contrast with neo-classical economic thinking, which holds fiscal discipline and balanced budgets very dear.

Keynesian thinking foregrounds relevance of this short-run economic stabilization, and within that highlights fiscal policy's efficacy. Fiscal multipliers refer to assumptions plugged into economic models about how much effect on economic activity increasing (or reducing) government spending has. The notion of 'multipliers' associated with public spending is derived from Richard Kahn (1931) and closely associated with the classical Keynesian position as set out in the *General Theory* (Keynes 1936 [1964]: 113–31). Kahn and Keynes assumed that expenditure multipliers were greater than one, which meant that 'a rise in investment or government spending would produce a rise in income that was larger than the initial increase in spending' (Backhouse 2006: 32; see also Blaug 1990). The ability of Keynesian economics to calculate the precise value of the income multiplier 'placed the case for demand management on an entirely new footing by making it seem incontrovertible' (Blaug 1996: 648). This recognition of the potentially beneficial consequences of increased public spending through positive spillover effects is important for the politics of fiscal policy. Identifying how the aggregate demand boost has favourable knock-on effects on consumption, economic activity, and confidence in this way strengthens the case for a focus on demand and the need to sustain it, and for increased public spending and activist, expansionary fiscal policy in a recession, and when monetary policy is already accommodating.

Economic stabilization is in the Keynesian worldview a legitimate, necessary, and indeed unavoidable short- to medium-term goal of macroeconomic policy. Counter-cyclical 'stabilization policy' is justified theoretically, and pursued using both fiscal and monetary policy. Its goal is securing a sufficiently buoyant level of aggregate demand to maintain full employment. The efficacy of counter-cyclical macroeconomic policy, therefore, is an important element of the Keynesian view of the economy and economic policy.

The Neo-Classical Synthesis

It is helpful to differentiate between 'traditional' Keynesian ideas and the 'neo-classical synthesis' (NCS)—a composite doctrine partly inspired by Keynesian thinking but also by more orthodox neo-classical economics. The NCS variant of Keynesian thinking, following on the foundations laid by Hicks (1937) and

Hansen (1949), sees the market's failure to 'clear' as a special case, not a core ongoing feature of free market economies (Braun 2014). The IS-LM model[9] which set out the relationship between aggregate demand, interest rates, and output is widely seen as a Keynesian construct. It is a product of the NCS, specifically Hicks and Hansen, and it in fact left out important elements of Keynes's thinking, notably those concerning dynamics and expectations (Backhouse 2002: 232–6; Blaug 1996: 669–73). Colander (1992) charts a dramatic narrowing of the debate—traceable largely to the Hicks article (1937) which introduced and formalized what has subsequently been called the short-run Keynesian and long-run neo-classical dichotomy (see Romer 1993; Stockhammer 2011: 150; Tanzi & Zee 1997).

The NCS took hold within academic economics in the 1950s and 1960s through the influential writings of Samuelson, Solow, Hicks, Tobin, and others (Colander 1992; Backhouse 2002: 232–6; Eatwell & Milgate 2011; Samuelson 1997). Coddington used the term 'hydraulic Keynesianism' (1976; 1984) to capture the mechanistic approach to macroeconomic demand management. This alluded to work by Phillips, of Phillips curve fame, who developed a hydraulic machine to model the functioning of the economy (Backhouse 2002: 293). The Phillips curve (1958) was 'grafted on to Keynesian economics' and revealed 'the amazing fertility of the Keynesian system' (Blaug 1996: 651). It posited and modelled a trade-off between unemployment and inflation, such that a predictable additional amount of inflation was a price to be paid for lower unemployment achieved through demand management. This relationship was integral to the fine-tuning demand management of the Keynesian approach to macroeconomic policy. In treating the economy as a plumbing system, and levers of monetary and fiscal policy as sluice gates, national economic managers are deemed capable of manipulating consumer and investor behaviour, and thereby aggregate demand and confidence in the economy. Keynesian fine-tuning was inspired by such thinking, though how far policymakers and theorists took seriously the mechanistic understanding of the economy and policy varied. In the US, the MIT Keynesians Samuelson and Solow promoted the use of the curve and suggested that it could be used to guide fiscal fine-tuning (see Samuelson & Solow 1960). It entailed a focus on short-run demand in determining output and employment levels and was compatible with the idea of government-managed economic recovery through counter-cyclical policy.

Mainstream NCS-inspired economics from Hicks onwards already makes assumptions akin to Say's law about economies tending towards full employment equilibrium in the long term. This, of course, was Keynes' principle objection to neo-classical economics in *General Theory*. By reaching its

[9] This is the 'Hicks–Hansen' Keynesian macroeconomic model setting out in two curves the relationship between interest rates, investment and savings, and output income and employment.

accommodation with more mainstream economic thinking of the time in these ways, the NCS stripped away some of the more radical elements of the original Keynesian analysis contained in the *General Theory*. As Patinkin put it, 'the main message of Keynesian economics' is that 'the automatic adjustment process of the market... is too unreliable to serve as a practical basis of full-employment policy' (1959: 582). Yet the NCS focused attention on very specific and delimited market failures, notably wage rigidities and fixed nominal wages, to the exclusion of most of the broader issues raised in Keynes's work.

After all, Keynes argued in his *General Theory* that wage and price flexibility was not the issue in debate (Colander 1992: 445). Economists of a more Keynesian bent noted how, apart from recognizing that nominal wages were slow to adjust, 'the remainder of the neoclassical synthesis was Walrasian. Markets for goods and labour were competitive, externalities were absent, and information was perfect' (Romer 1993: 5). Radicals such as Joan Robinson saw this synthesis as creating a 'bastard Keynesianism' which drained Keynes ideas of their revolutionary economic theoretical potential in relation to uncertainty, and the nature and extent of market failures (Robinson 1974, 1978; see also Best 2005; Braun 2014; Blaug 1996; Davidson 2007). The assumption that markets tend to clear at full employment (implied by the need for intervention being a special case), limits the extent and degree to which activist counter-cyclical stabilization macro policy is pursued and emphasized.

New Classical Macroeconomics

Scepticism about the 'hydraulic' Keynesian approach to fiscal policy associated with 'fine-tuning' and demand management grew, especially within academic economics, in the 1960s and 1970s. New Classical Macroeconomics challenged the Keynesian and NCS vision of the economy and economic policy. In a more fully-fledged rehabilitation of Say's law, New Classical economists such as Lucas, Sargent, and others rejected core Keynesian insights about market failure (Lucas and Sargent 1978, 1981; Lucas 1980). The New Classical reassertion of a strong belief in the Walrasian market-clearing model denied the possibility that economies can operate below full capacity for protracted periods due to endogenous features of markets.

This recovery of an older, neo-classical faith in markets and the price mechanism generated 'models with no role for aggregate demand' (Alesina & Giavazzi 2013a: 2), wherein supply is deemed to call forth demand. The economy was conceptualized as a self-equilibriating system, within which individuals were understood to be rational. A central methodological goal of New Classical economics was to provide rigorous micro-foundations for macroeconomic models, rooted in its highly distinctive and extremely exacting conception of rational expectations (Quiggin 2012: 94–9). Both the economy and the rationality of the individual were conceptualized in such a way that market self-correction was assumed a priori. Hence, economic stabilization through interventionist macroeconomic policy was deemed unnecessary and counterproductive. This is what Blaug terms 'the policy-ineffectiveness proposition of new classical macroeconomics' (Blaug 1996: 686; see also Prescott 1986: 21; Lucas 1977; Barro 1974, 1989).

New Classical economics is based on a moral and ethical worldview, under-acknowledged within economics, which perceives public action and intervention in markets as deeply suspect (Best & Widmaier 2006). Operating within that understanding of the economy, the fiscal policy discussion takes on a very different complexion. The premises of New Classical thinking engendered deep scepticism towards macroeconomic policy activism; 'if one does not believe that downturns can be caused by insufficient aggregate demand, and, conversely that stimulation of aggregate demand can facilitate the end of recessions, asking about spending multipliers is meaningless' (Alesina & Giavazzi 2013a: 2–3). The Real Business Cycle model, one of the fruits of New Classical economics, posited that any fluctuations in demand and employment of the observed business cycle were socially optimal equilibrium responses to exogenous shocks (Quiggin 2012: 99–101). This attempt to deny Keynesian market failure continues to be a standard reference point in literature review sections of Fund working papers alongside approaches drawn from Keynesian and other theoretical schools.

New Classical economics entailed changing the theoretical premises for understanding the economy and policy to make the case against 'fine-tuning', demand management, and the efficacy of fiscal policy. Samuelson and Solow's refinement of the Phillips curve (1960) provided the target for Monetarist and New Classical assaults on Keynesianism. Friedman's adaptive expectations approach dismissed the idea that there was a long run Phillips curve trade-off between inflation and unemployment, and put the case that lower unemployment could only be 'bought' at the price of accelerating unemployment (see e.g. Thompson 1990: 48). This theoretical challenge to the Phillips curve trade-off (Phelps 1967; Friedman 1968), although in Friedman's version built on different theoretical foundations from the New Classical view (Laidler 1981; Hoover 1984), was helpfully anti-Keynesian.

New Classical versions of rational expectations went further than Friedman's adaptive expectations, contending that 'the long-run Phillips curve is vertical and there is no short-run Phillips curve' (Blaug 1996: 686; Quiggin 2012: 98). This removed the 'Keynesian' connection between aggregate demand and macroeconomic policy on the one hand, and the level of employment on the other. Another New Classical application of rational expectations insights in the realms of fiscal policy, the notion of 'Ricardian equivalence', was still more anti-Keynesian (Barro 1989). The core a priori assumption is that forward-looking agents will anticipate fully any future tax rises (which will have to pay for higher debts, deficits, and public spending in the present). Their adjustment in behaviour, spending or consuming less, will offset fully and nullify any boost to economic activity or demand that a fiscal stimulus was designed to initiate. This further challenged the rationale for counter-cyclical fiscal policy.

New Classical economics sought new foundations for economic modelling—built on rigorous microeconomic foundations of 'rational choice and market equilibrium' (Quiggin 2012: 99). This, amongst other things, effectively assumed away the financial system which had been so central to the macro-economy for Keynesianism and the NCS. Individuals must be assumed to be rational and possessed of perfect information, and the market must be assumed to be in equilibrium, with demand balancing supply. Lucas's dramatic assumptions about rational expectations and continuous market clearing, both a world away from a Keynesian worldview, transformed the face of macroeconomics. New Classical economics rejected the idea of involuntary unemployment or sub-optimal market outcomes, and in so doing undermined the case for policy intervention (Backhouse 2002: 298–301; Quiggin 2012: 94–101).

New Keynesian Macroeconomics

New Keynesian macroeconomics (NKM) constitutes a spectrum of economic thinking which gained prominence in the 1980s and 1990s. A number of leading New Keynesians played important roles within the Fund, either as Chief Economist (Stanley Fischer, Olivier Blanchard, Maurice Obstfeld), or as visiting academics working at the Fund (George Akerlof, David Romer, Larry Ball). One of the central themes of NKM is the recognition that markets do not always clear. NKM underlines and explores the prevalence of non-Walrasian phenomena within the economy, notably information asymmetries, imperfect competition, and externalities. None of these, it should be noted, were the primary sources of market failure identified in Keynes' *General Theory*. In what constitutes a watered-down version of the Keynesian critique of markets' ability to deliver full employment equilibrium, NKM explores how each of these insights undermine Walrasian market clearing assumptions. NKM focuses on institutional factors and imperfections in capital and labour markets as a potential means to explain the price and wage rigidities which had been assumed within the NCS.

NKM is more oriented towards micro-economic analytical endeavours, trying to explain the rigidities which the earlier NCS assumed on the premise that 'correct description of the microeconomy would give rise to the phenomena that they believed characterized the macroeconomy' (Romer 1993: 6). Some of the more orthodox versions (Mankiw & Romer 1991) accept many of the central tenets of the New Classical counter-revolution in economic thought outlined above. It thus in some ways continues the trend of integrating Keynesian ideas into the mainstream of economics in a way which is counter to the spirit of Keynes' critique of neo-classical economics. NKM encompasses a variety of positions, embracing non-Walrasian assumptions to varying degrees at macro and micro levels, with some proponents adhering to traditional Keynesian insights regarding the merits of fiscal activism (Colander 1992). Those closer in spirit to older Keynesian notions retained the desire to explain 'how changes on the demand side—like shifts in government purchases and investment demand—could have substantial real effects' (Romer 1993: 6). 'New Keynesian' ideas like hysteresis recognize how a demand shock can end up, through the skill depletion of the long-term unemployed and problems with price adjustment, having permanent adverse effects (Blanchard & Summers 1986; Blinder 1988). This kind of analysis retained the link between macroeconomic policy, demand side phenomena, and unemployment reminiscent of 'no-prefix' Keynesianism.

The New Classical approach to rational expectations assumes perfect information, costlessly and uniformly distributed, which determines the beliefs individuals entertain about the behaviour of other agents, and results in a single, socially optimal equilibrium. NKM also operates with a version of rational expectations, but the spanner which New Keynesian insights about imperfect information and uncertainty throws into this tidy Walrasian mechanism is the possibility of *multiple equilibria*; 'there are a number of expectations any *one* of which will prove to be a rational expectation if expected and acted upon by *all* agents, and any *one* of which will *not* prove to be rational if held in isolation' (Hargreaves Heap 1994: 39). Multiple equilibria are the product of a worldview where markets do not tend inexorably towards efficient outcomes. New Keynesians readily recognize the possibility of 'underemployment equilibria' which may persist because the 'forces acting to return output to its initial level are weak' (Romer 1993: 16). NKM envisages a possible conjuncture where 'individuals believe there will be low demand and in expectation of that low demand, they produce little and there is low output' (Colander 1992: 445). The NKM world is not linear, and it 'challenges the conception of the production function and the conclusions that an economy with perfectly flexible prices will be operating at the socially optimal equilibrium' (Colander 1992: 446). That sub-optimal employment equilibrium scenario is perfectly compatible with New Keynesian 'rational' micro-foundations of macroeconomic thinking, but admitting the possibility of such a market failure is anathema to New Classical thought.

The New Keynesian idea of 'multiple equilibria', although based on a different understanding of rationality and expectations than Keynes, nevertheless links back to ideas initially associated with *General Theory* about herd behaviour and irrational exuberance of financial market, swayed by waves of pessimism and optimism through the inter-subjective mechanism of economic conventions. Central to Keynes' account of the economy was the prevalence of uncertainty, and how economic actors were operating on incomplete information in a world characterized by uncertainty and guided by convention (See Keynes 1936, 1937; Klaes 2006; Blyth 2002a; Nelson & Katzenstein 2014; Widmaier 2003a). These are important insights for thinking about financial markets and their potential instability, its causes and consequences. The non-linear New Keynesian world of multiple equilibria denies any inherent self-correcting tendency of the economy, and is attuned to the possibility of markets delivering socially sub-optimal outcomes. This creates both space for critical reflection upon market outcomes and greater potential for macroeconomic policy to tackle instability.

New Consensus Macroeconomics

Since the mid-to-late 1990s, New Keynesian thinking has been partially reconciled to insights from New Classical economics within the development of what has been widely termed 'New Consensus Macroeconomics' (NCM) (Arestis & Sawyer 2008; Arestis 2007). What New Classical and New Keynesian economists could agree on was that microfoundations were important, and some version of rational expectations applied to the micro level would, in an ideal world, underpin economic models developed to explain the macroeconomy. This commonality of purpose, though limited, was sufficient to harness the two camps to an approach to economics using 'assumptions that were also acceptable to the old Neoclassical Synthesis proponents' (Arestis 2011: 89).

The financial system, so central within Keynesianism, was marginal to the NCM approach, effectively assumed and modelled away by Lucas, rational expectations, and DSGE models. Banks, and the financial system more broadly, were conspicuous by their absence from the DSGE modelling heavily relied upon with NCM. Partly this reflected a default (if unrealistic) assumption of perfect capital markets, but more fundamentally it is because it has proved very difficult to model default in general equilibrium models (Braun 2014: 69; Tovar 2009; Goodhart 2009: 299). This was one factor contributing to the ever narrower focus on consumer price inflation for monetary policymaking, to the exclusion of wider financial system variables.

The Taylor rule (Taylor 1993) exemplifies a macroeconomic policy approach built on New Consensus foundations, seeing inflation as a monetary phenomenon, controllable via interest rate manipulation (Arestis 2011: 89; Goodfriend 2007: 59). The approach to macroeconomic policy centred on using monetary policy to target and control inflation, justified along the lines that keeping inflation under control would also maintain output around its optimal level. This assumption, termed the 'divine coincidence' by Blanchard and Gali (2007; Blanchard 2003), was another under-reflected-upon conventional wisdom. It assumed that there was a limited role for fiscal policy in economic stabilization. As Blanchard et al. summarized the pre-crash position in 2010, 'we thought of monetary policy as having one target, inflation, and one instrument, the policy rate. So long as inflation was stable, the output gap was likely to be small and stable and monetary policy did its job' (Blanchard et al. 2010: 3). This chimed with Lucas's hubristic claim to the American Economic Association in 2003 that 'the central problem of depression prevention has been solved', a view based on the NCM-inspired assumption that monetary policy is all you need for economic stabilization (Lucas 2003).

The case for monetary policy as a primary economic stabilization tool, and the case *against* fiscal policy, were both integral to and fruits of NCM thinking. The New Consensus builds on New Keynesian thinking (e.g. Woodford 2003, 2009; Arestis 2011), yet is a relatively broad church. As Arestis and Sawyer (2006) have noted, some versions of the NCM drew from Real Business Cycle and other New Classical thinking. There was scope within NCM to incorporate some of the more extreme anti-Keynesian assumptions and ideas about fiscal policy inefficacy, notably Ricardian equivalence. Whilst such ideas could be made compatible with NCM, they were not necessarily part of its core identity. Another aspect of the NCM was a general acceptance of the vertical long-run Phillips curve (Woodford 2009; Arestis 2011). This is another way of saying that it makes sense to assume a 'natural' rate of employment exists. In the long run, monetary and fiscal policy 'could not influence the level of employment that is "ground out by the Walrasian system of general equilibrium equations"' (Friedman 1968: 87; Eatwell & Milgate 2011: xv). Whilst this in principle left open the possibility of a short-run trade-off, for many working in the NCM frame, they tended to reproduce the short-run Keynesian/long-run neo-classical dichotomy in such a way as to reinforce the case against fiscal policy.

NCM's theoretical edifice had similar policy implications to more 'commonsense' thinking about the limitations of fiscal policy. Reservations about fiscal policy were both practical and a priori theoretical. This combination explains NCM's relegation of fiscal policy as an active policy tool (see Arestis 2011: 88–9), albeit retaining some residual role for automatic stabilizers (Arestis &

Sawyer 2003: 5). Since the 1960s, academic economics has drifted away from the idea that macroeconomic policy and aggregate demand have real impacts on the unemployment rate. Focal points like demand management, fiscal multipliers, and governments using counter-cyclical macro policy to steer an economy towards a higher employment equilibrium were no longer central to how NCM-inspired economists thought about economic management in open economies during 'normal' times.

The IMF's Repertoire of Fiscal Policy Thinking before the Crash

Having covered the schools of economic thought that have influenced Fund thinking in the decades since its inception, it is now possible to summarize the contours of the Fund pre-crisis fiscal policy stance. Setting out how the Fund drew on its repertoire of ideas to underpin its fiscal policy advice in the pre-crash era enables us to calibrate and refine claims about what has changed following the GFC within the Fund's approach to fiscal policy, and throw into relief highly distinctive characteristics of post-crash Fund fiscal policy thinking.

As regards the Fund's relationship with Keynesianism, Boughton claims 'the IMF was conceived basically as a Keynesian institution' (2012: lv; 2004), and this characterized its thinking and practice up to the 1960s and 1970s (Boughton 1997: 8–9, 2004: 13–16; De Vries 1987). The Keynesian training of the economists who joined the Fund in the 1940s and 1950s continued to shape IMF approaches until their retirement in the 1980s (Chwieroth 2007a: 14–18; 2010). Keynesian elements of Fund thinking and practice include the emphasis on and use of monetary aggregates in IMF surveillance and conditionality. This has Keynesian roots in the 'absorption' approach to the balance of payments (Alexander 1952; De Vries 1987: 16–19), the Polak model (1957, 2001; see Joyce 2012: 20–34), and the Mundell/Fleming approach to economic adjustment seeking full employment and balance of payments equilibrium using fiscal and monetary policy (Fleming 1962; Mundell 1961, 1962; see James 1996: 82–3). The financial programming of the Fund, developed in the 1950s and which provides the Fund's framework for approaching economic adjustment issues (Babb 2003) has evolved but it remains rooted in Keynesian practices developed in the post-war era (Clift & Tomlinson 2008a).

The accretion of economic knowledge and understanding which underpins and informs the Fund's mindset includes certain Keynesian characteristics, rooted in the IS-LM model, and seeing the roots of balance of payments problems reflecting imbalances in expenditure and output within a national economy. Fund policy and surveillance tools were built on a worldview which recognized the importance of activist macroeconomic policy to pursue demand management and maintain full employment (Clift & Tomlinson 2012: 486). The premises of Fund policy are shaped in part by its operational frameworks. As Heller noted in 2002, IMF economists 'certainly start with the standard macroeconomic policy framework which emerged with Keynes and which was elaborated by Mundell and Fleming in addressing the role of aggregate fiscal policy in an open economy' (2002: 8).

Fund interviewees refer to a 'more or less Keynesian working model', or to a 'meta-Keynesian' mindset at the Fund, wherein 'in the short run it is aggregate demand which determines outcomes'.[10] Partly, no doubt, due to its Keynesian heritage and the enduring influence, insights about the potential role for fiscal policy in managing aggregate demand to increase or reduce output have their place within Fund fiscal policy thought (Heller 2002). The concept of the structural fiscal balance which anchors the Fund's fiscal thinking contains the essentially Keynesian notion that fiscal policy has an important impact on overall output. The goal to determine the structural balance also comes from a mental universe where fiscal policy has an impact on output. This element of Keynesian-ness and its relevance for short-run economic stabilization is taken for granted within the IMF. For example, as Paolo Mauro recalls,

> there was a lot of scepticism about fiscal policy efficacy in the 80s and 90s but the Fund, and the OECD were still among those within the profession who believed in the concept of the output gap—which you never hear about in American academia on economics. So the notion that fiscal policy has an impact on output was always there.[11]

It resembles what Campbell terms a 'background' idea, an underlying, taken for granted, unthinking script, akin to habit of thought which actors 'rarely subscribe to... self-consciously or deliberately', such ideas being 'virtually invisible to the actors themselves' (Campbell 1998: 378–82; 2004).

What continues to get evoked within the Fund today as the Keynesian bedrock on which its edifice of economic policy knowledge is based (Jahan et al. 2014) is not primarily the Keynes of the *General Theory*, but some variant of the NCS (see Best 2005: 114; Colander 1992; Chwieroth 2010; Clift & Tomlinson 2012). As Blanchard put it, 'I think the Fund has always been in the short term Keynesian—it's kind of Samuelson's neo-classical synthesis'.[12] It is this NCS *à la* Samuelson that remained part and parcel of the repertoire of economic theorizing that Fund economists draw on when circumstances dictate. The NCS recognized the possibility of the economy finding an equilibrium

[10] Interview with Olivier Blanchard, June 2013.

[11] Interview with Senior IMF Economist Paolo Mauro, a senior fellow at the Peterson Institute for International Economics at the time of the interview in 2014.

[12] Interview with Olivier Blanchard, June 2013.

below full employment, and in this sense retained what Best terms 'the basic Keynesian belief in the central role of public economic policy' (2005: 96). A focus on short-run demand in determining output and employment levels in the economy informed the idea of government-managed economic recovery, and FAD thinking specified a role for counter-cyclical policy (Heller 2002).

The importance of using macroeconomic policy tools to achieve the goal of economic stabilization which is central to the Keynesian approach to the economy is reflected in the Fund's attachment to automatic stabilizers. Allowing their 'free play' in both directions played a prominent counter-cyclical role in IMF pre-crash policy thinking, commentary, and advice for advanced economies (see Heller 2002). As former IMF Mission Chief Alessandro Leipold put it, 'I think the Fund has been sort of a bit Keynesian throughout in a way, not favouring fine-tuning but in their understanding of the way that fiscal policy matters, the way fiscal policy has an impact on the real economy...It's been let the multipliers, the automatic stabilizers play.'[13] Whilst apparently a reflection of even-handed treatment—in fact many emerging and less developed economies have weak or no automatic stabilizers. Seeing counter-cyclical fiscal policy in this way in effect closed off stabilization policy options for many economies. Thus, it reflects an intuition at the Fund that some countries and their institutions can be more trusted to pursue counter-cyclical fiscal policy than others. As Heller pointed out in 2002, 'Rare is the IMF Article IV document *for an industrial country* that does not accept the fact that in a period of economic slowdown, one should accommodate the higher fiscal deficit and not seek to achieve annual balance budget targets' (Heller 2002: 9, emphasis added).

Assumptions about the size of fiscal multipliers are one important proxy for the strength of attachment to Keynesian thinking about fiscal policy efficacy. This, Fund staff recognized, would be more moderate under floating exchange rates, and where monetary policy is not accommodating, and in open economies due to potential leakages. All of these, received Fund wisdom indicates, 'influence the size of the likely Keynesian multipliers one would observe' (Heller 2002: 8). Fund reviews of the literature attached caveats and noted the difficulties of precisely gauging fiscal multipliers. Nevertheless, its assessment placed the figure towards the middle-to-low end of the spectrum at about 0.5, indicating a modest effect of fiscal policy on output (Hemming et al. 2002a). The take-home point was that 'despite Keynesian orthodoxy, fiscal policy is only marginally effective in countering economic downturns' (Hemming et al. 2002b: 237). Multipliers were not zero or negative, so this was

[13] Interview with Alessandro Leipold, former Deputy Director of the IMF European Department, September 2013.

not an embrace of the fiscal policy ineffectiveness proposition. Nevertheless, the 0.5 figure attested to a pre-crash Fund lukewarm on fiscal policy's potency.

Modest multipliers, a focus on automatic stabilizers, and a pre-supposition that advanced economies could be more trusted to enact fiscal policy efficiently than others were notable facets of pre-crash fiscal policy thinking. Partly this reflected a default Fund scepticism about encouraging government spending, especially discretionary spending. The IMF's goal of encouraging fiscal sustainability amongst their members led Fund economists to prioritize fiscal discipline very highly. 'Deficit bias' concerns that governments always spend more than they raise in revenues are never far from Fund staff 's minds. The aversion of Fund economists to encouraging government spending were described by experienced insiders variously as 'innate' and 'congenital'. One analogy evoked by a staff member to critique the Fund's overly-cautious approach compared governments seeking to retain fiscal credibility as akin to walking by the shore in the fog. It is hard for governments to know exactly when they are going to get their feet wet—or see their borrowing costs rise. In such a scenario, how serious an issue this is depends significantly on whether one is walking along a beach, or at the top of a cliff. Fund instincts have been to presume that countries are always on the verge of tumbling off a cliff (see also Goldsbrough 2007: 12–24, 53–4).

Fund economists were always keen to (over)emphasize the risks of not doing enough to tackle debt, but perhaps under-cognisant of not doing enough through fiscal policy to support economic activity. This gives a flavour of the pre-crash balance of prioritization around fiscal policy. In practice, the primary focus on fiscal discipline and deficit bias in FAD under Vito Tanzi (1981–2000) and then Teresa Ter Minassian (2001–8) was reflected in IMF surveillance and conditionality. Within this pre-crash Fund position, fiscal policy was not seen as a motor of growth. The role of fiscal policy was to ensure 'sustainable public finances', placing emphasis on building up fiscal buffers. Doing that was, many in the pre-crash Fund thought, all that fiscal policy could do to contribute to growth and stability (see Daniel et al. 2006; Ter Minassian & Schwartz 1997; Fiscal Affairs Department 1995). The Fund has always had an aversion to high taxation, which it considers distortionary. There was also very limited support in the pre-crash Fund for using progressive income tax as a fiscal policy tool to achieve fiscal sustainability and equity goals (Tanzi & Zee 2000: 308–11; Daniel et al. 2006: 35–6).

The roots of this reticence towards fiscal policy were not just Fund intuitions, but also conventional wisdom in the economic profession from the 1980s onwards. The New Keynesian centre of gravity of Fund staff thinking in the pre-crisis period had come to see monetary policy, not fiscal policy, as the main tool for stabilization. The reasons were both practical and theoretical. Fund economists acknowledged some of the New Classical critique of traditional

Keynesian fiscal policy. As Blanchard put it in 2010, reflecting on pre-crash Fund doctrine, 'We thought of fiscal policy as playing a secondary role, with political constraints sharply limiting its de facto usefulness' (Blanchard et al. 2010: 3). The prevailing view of the case against fiscal policy as a tool for counter-cyclical economic stabilization in normal times was that due to implementation lags, expansionary fiscal policy was not sufficiently 'timely' as a policy tool. This combined with a general Fund wariness of the tendency of governments to run up deficits. Furthermore, due to 'political economy' constraints, fiscal policy had difficulties in normal times of being 'credibly temporary'. These shortcomings of fiscal policy are more readily associated with discretionary as opposed to rules-based fiscal policy, and thus this thinking reinforced the Fund's emphasis on automatic stabilizers.

Fund economists summarized the pre-crisis practical considerations of policymakers, that fiscal policy can be hard to do well, recognizing implementation lags, difficulties of timing, and turning off fiscal stimulus (Hemming, Kell & Mahfouz 2002a). These coexisted with more strident a priori assumptions that fiscal policy cannot be effective within stabilization. In this book, the amalgamation of Fund thinking over many decades is understood not as a single cohesive paradigm, but as a more complex composite. The Fund's repertoire was influenced in the 1980s and 1990s by changing prevailing wisdoms in academic economics outlined above. Many note the importance of IMF staff being trained at neo-liberal economics departments at US universities (Leiteritz & Moschella 2010: 164; Chwieroth 2007a, 2010; Nelson 2017). Thus, the Fund's approach was shaped to a significant degree by the reformulation of the microfoundations of macroeconomics around ideas of rational expectations within 'New Classical macroeconomics' (Boughton 2004: 17; Chwieroth 2007b).

One of the main goals of New Classical thinking, and the monetarist insights of Friedman et al., was to critique Keynesian stabilization and demand management using fiscal policy. Blanchard et al. summarized the pre-2008 position in *Rethinking Macro Policy*: 'fiscal policy took a backseat to monetary policy. The reasons were many: first was wide scepticism about the effects of fiscal policy, itself largely based on Ricardian equivalence arguments' (2010, 5–6). This is revealing as to the economic theoretical 'home' of the opposition to fiscal policy, and its acceptance. Whilst full Ricardian equivalence was by no means a default assumption, notions about limits of fiscal policy inefficacy gained adherents among Fund staff. This added a theoretical dimension to the practical concerns about the timeliness of fiscal policy as a stabilization tool, and how 'credibly temporary' new spending could be.

According to the Fund's official historian, New Classical thinking never fully took hold within the Fund (Boughton 2004). Arguments were never completely officially bought into inside the organization. The ideas like Ricardian equivalence were highly influential in many quarters, but held more sway in academia than amongst policymaking economists (Blanchard et al. 2010). The decidedly anti-Keynesian New Classical Ricardo/Barro view (a variant of Ricardian equivalence) that fiscal policy is ineffective because private economic agents adjust their behaviour to neutralize changes in such policy (Barro 1989), was explicitly dismissed as insignificant in Heller's overview of fiscal policy thinking (Heller 2002: 11). Similarly, Hemming et al. noted in an IMF working paper, 'There is little evidence of direct crowding out or crowding out through interest rates and the exchange rate. Nor does full Ricardian equivalence or a significant partial Ricardian offset get much support from the evidence' (Hemming et al. 2002: 5). This period is usually seen as the peak of neo-liberal economic ideas and the 'Washington Consensus', and some Fund staff were doubtless more sympathetic than others to such views. The impact of New Classical economics on Fund fiscal policy thinking was more to engender a deepened and generalized scepticism about fiscal policy efficacy, rather than to entrench a particular a priori view on it.

Overall, Fund staff did tend to operate within the parameters of the NCS and the synthesis of New Keynesian and New Classical thought developed within the mainstream of academic economics in the 1990s and 2000s. Attempts were made to incorporate rational expectations insights within a Keynesian framework, notably with the creation of the Fund's MULTIMOD model in the late 1980s (Masson, Symansky and Meredith 1990; Rajan et al. 2004: 4–7). Thereafter, the IMF Research department constructed some RBC models (see e.g. Mendoza 1991), although these were not widely used because their assumptions 'left little room for the analysis of macroeconomic policies' (Rajan 2004: 7). The Fund later developed DSGE models such as GEM which integrated supply and demand responses through microeconomic theory—as was *de rigueur* in New Consensus thinking (Rajan 2004 et al.: 8–12).

A Fund staff discussion note summarizes the prevailing wisdom in the decades before the GFC thus: 'a widespread consensus identified low and stable inflation as the primary (sometimes sole) mandate of monetary policy. New Keynesian models (with nominal rigidities as the main, or only, friction) provided the intellectual foundation for this approach' (Woodford 2003; Bayoumi et al. 2014: 5). Yet much hinges, in terms of the ideological character of those models, on *what kind* of rational expectation assumptions are made. Ideas about rational expectations were influential, though not necessarily the anti-Keynesian conception of rational expectations (such as Ricardian equivalence) at the heart of New Classical economics. The Fund's models, even before the crisis, were based on non-Ricardian assumptions about economic actors (Laxton 2008; Botman et al. 2007; Freedman et al. 2009: 11).[14]

[14] Interview with Doug Laxton, Division Chief of the Economic Modelling Division, IMF Research Department, September 2013.

Rather than the specific theoretical propositions, it was the broader insights and pre-sentiments about the economy which, through the changing content of graduate training in economics, came to shape the sensibilities of incoming Fund staff. This engendered more scepticism about the possibilities of fine-tuning, and decreased confidence in discretionary fiscal and monetary policies (Chwieroth 2010; Clift & Tomlinson 2012). There was an instinctive preference for fiscal discipline, and a default faith—during Great Moderation—in the self-equilibrating properties of market forces. The short-term Keynesian/long-term neo-classical dichotomy (see e.g. Romer 1993), which forms a background idea about the economy for many Fund economists, sees a role for Keynesian counter-cyclical insights in the short run. Yet such instability as might arise could, most Fund staff were confident, be managed through stabilizing monetary policy. For practical reasons, especially where countries with weak fiscal policy institutions are concerned, fiscal policy was not seen as either an engine of economic growth, nor as a front-line counter-cyclical policy tool. Keynesian-inspired demand management ideas were sedimented into Fund fiscal policy thought over a long and formative period and never entirely lost their influence (see e.g. Heller 2002). Yet in practice they were, in the 1980s, 1990s, and early 2000s, for the most part overshadowed in the judgements and intuitions informing IMF decision-making by deficit bias, aversion to distortionary taxation, fiscal discipline considerations, and an instinctive preference to use monetary policy.

The Fund and its Post-Crisis Fiscal Policy Rethink

Signalling the radically changed context of economic policy for advanced economies, much IMF discussion referred to the conduct of post-crash macroeconomic policy as 'navigating the new normal' (El-Erian 2010; see also Bayoumi et al. 2014). As Mauro puts it, 'I don't think that the economics has changed very much, its just that the situation has changed dramatically, and the emphasis has changed dramatically.' Prior concerns about the timing and time lags of fiscal policy did not arise because 'in this case it was obvious to everybody from the beginning that this was going to be a prolonged recession so there was going to be plenty of time for fiscal policy to act.'[15] The scale of the crisis prompted a re-evaluation of Fund policy thinking. As part of this, some influential Fund figures began to question some elements of the NCM approach, its linear assumptions about self-correcting markets, and its attendant DSGE models (Blanchard et al. 2010, 2013; Blanchard et al. (eds.) 2012;

[15] Interview with Senior IMF Economist Paolo Mauro, a senior fellow at the Peterson Institute for International Economics at the time of the interview in 2014.

Cottarelli et al. 2014). Blanchard noted the changing climate of economic ideas, and the questioning of old orthodoxies in February 2010: 'economists and policymakers alike were lulled into a false sense of security by the apparent success of economic policy ahead of the crisis—a period known as the "Great Moderation"...The crisis has taught us a lot and we want to proactively draw lessons from the "Great Recession"' (Blanchard 2010a).

The crisis, and the crucial role that fiscal policy was playing in responding to it, sparked a revitalization of interest in fiscal policy within academic economics, some of the work being done from a New Keynesian and even an old Keynesian perspective. Indeed, a revived interest in fiscal policy had been prevalent in sections of the economics profession since the early 2000s, notably Blanchard when professor and chairman of the Economics department at MIT. Blanchard's arrival as IMF Chief Economist in September 2008 strengthened the Keynesian-sympathetic subculture, and helped expand the space for policy rethinking within the Fund. Strauss-Kahn began to bring in like-minded and highly talented individuals broadly sympathetic to a more Keynesian interpretation of the crisis to senior positions within the Fund, notably David Romer from Berkeley, who headed up work on fiscal multipliers and on fiscal policy which fed into key chapters of the *World Economic Outlook*.

Leadership of FAD was also changing at that time. Carlo Cottarelli, a Fund insider who had not previously demonstrated a taste for more activist fiscal policy, took over FAD in autumn 2008 and turned out to be 'on the same page' as Blanchard. One significant feature of the early post-crash period was a 'duet' between the heads of the Research Department and FAD on appropriate post-crisis fiscal policy (Blanchard & Cottarelli 2010). As Carlo Cottarelli put it in 2013, 'it happens also that on macro fiscal issues, we (FAD) fall fully in line with the Research Department—and the WEO obviously also deals with fiscal issues—and there was no disagreement, there has never been any disagreement between them and us on what to say'.[16] David Lipton, brought in as Deputy Managing Director in 2011, was an activist fiscal policy enthusiast (2013a), moving from the White House, where he had worked with one of the architects of the US fiscal stimulus Larry Summers. Research Department Deputy Director Jonathan Ostry noted the Fund's heightened appreciation that

> fiscal policy is a more potent counter-cyclical tool in periods of deep recession, and so when you get into the kind of soup that we have been in for the past several years—where monetary policy loses potency, the credit channels are undermined because the financial sector is dysfunctional—then you need to rely more on fiscal policy as a counter-cyclical tool. But the thing you need to be wary of also is that

[16] Interview with Carlo Cottarelli, the Director of FAD, June 2013.

> you want to have sufficient room for manoeuvre so that when you do avail yourself of this instrument, markets don't end up penalizing you because they see you running closer to your debt limit.[17]

Lower down the organization, Blanchard found like-minded junior researchers within the Fund, such as Daniel Leigh, and began to work with his former PhD students already within the Fund, such as Antonio Spilimbergo (whose PhD was supervised by Blanchard and Krugman). Given the Fund's hierarchical nature (see Chapters 1 and 2), the explicit encouragement from Strauss-Kahn as Managing Director that Fund economists should 'think outside the box' on fiscal policy was a crucial condition of possibility for the 2008 and 2009 work, for example, on fiscal multipliers (Spilimbergo et al. 2008; Spilimbergo et al. 2009). The Fund was emboldened to make strategically important interventions on fiscal policy efficacy. IMF thinking shifted towards more endorsement of activist fiscal policy to address deficient demand in the specific post-GFC conjuncture. From the bottom up and the top down, the Keynesian subculture had some success in effecting change within the Fund's prevailing fiscal policy norms. In interviews, many Fund economists recognized, implicitly or explicitly, the pertinence of the short-run Keynesian, long-run neo-classical dichotomy. They did this in ways which highlighted a more activist role for fiscal policy within stabilization. Fiscal policy activism also extended to advocacy of progressive taxation, and redistributive fiscal policy on grounds of higher marginal propensity to spend, and hence fiscal multipliers, associated with liquidity constrained households. For Ostry, 'Fiscal policy, fortuitously, is more potent in periods of economic slack such as the aftermath of the global financial crisis, so it makes sense to use it. And to use it not only for counter-cyclical purposes, but also to facilitate redistribution, which itself can help to spur economic growth.'[18]

As Cottarelli et al. noted on the first page of their IMF volume *Post-Crisis Fiscal Policy,* the crash 'soon evolved into a demand-deficiency recession. Lack of demand, abetted by uncertainty and rising unemployment, was driving output further and further down. Keynes' *General Theory* was the relevant textbook' (Cottarelli et al. 2014: 1). During the 'Great Moderation' in the decade or so prior to the crisis, the fairly strong assumption of a return to steady state contained in the DSGE models looked like a not too outlandish approximation of how these economies were actually operating. Obviously, that looked like a less defensible position when the crisis hit and was followed by a long drawn-out downturn in the advanced economies (Blanchard 2014a).

[17] Interview with IMF Research Department Deputy Director Jonathan Ostry, June 2013.
[18] Interview with IMF Research Department Deputy Director Jonathan Ostry, June 2013.

There was some explicit questioning in Fund publications of how useful NCM models had proved (Romer 2012). All the models developed by New Classical, New Keynesian, and New Consensus economists, after all, 'presume that the economy has a tendency to operate at a position in which all markets clear at full employment' (Eatwell & Milgate 2011: xvi). This assumption, which also underpinned orthodox renderings of the NCS of the post-war period, was not a helpful starting point to understand the profoundly destabilizing financial crisis of 2008–9, or engage in policy recommendations to navigate the long protracted downturn which followed. Both were on a scale not seen in the advanced economies for decades.

Integral to the rehabilitation of fiscal policy was greater recognition by Fund economists that economic policy potency varies according to the position in the economic cycle. Yet as Corsetti, Meier, and Muller note, 'the simple linear structure of standard VARs [a prevalent modelling methodology] severely constrains any analysis of conditional dynamics in fiscal policy transmission' (Corsetti, Meier, & Muller 2012: 9). Conditional, that is, upon the state of the economic cycle. This was important because the linear assumptions of a return to equilibrium built into IMF and other modelling could not admit or account for the fact that the potency of macroeconomic policy levers pulled by governments in pursuit of economic stabilization was greater during recessionary conditions. Post-crash macroeconomic policy had demonstrated dynamics that could not be captured by IMF models because of their assumptive foundations and construction (Parker 2011). For this reason, and also because the economy can get 'stuck' below potential output levels for a prolonged period, it was important for the Fund not to assume away the cycle in its thinking, for example, through over-reliance on DSGE modelling.

Fund unease with linear assumptions of the economy's inbuilt propensity to return to a socially optimal equilibrium chimed with New Keynesian and Post-Keynesian academic reservations about the construction of NCM models. The building blocks of the NCM have been subjected to extensive interrogation and critique since the GFC—both within the Fund and beyond. NCM makes some fairly heroic assumptions about how to operationalize rational expectations—choosing a 'representative agent' or what Solow calls 'a single immortal consumer-worker-owner' who 'maximizes a perfectly conventional time additive utility function over an infinite horizon under perfect foresight' (2008: 243). Interestingly, the lines of Keynesian critique of NCM (Arestis 2011) align closely with the Fund's own post-GFC rethink. Both the 'representative agent' and the fact that banks and the financial system were absent from its models were identified as problems with NCM by critics from a post-Keynesian or traditional Keynesian perspective (Arestis 2009a & b, 2011: 90–2). These have been focal points for Fund revisions to its models, and the premises of its policy thinking.

Behind the absence of banks, money, and a financial sector in the NCM universe is an assumption of a 'perfect capital market' (Arestis 2011: 96). The infamous efficient market hypothesis (Fama 1970, 1991) is used to obviate the need for incorporation of banks and the financial sector. The idea that some individuals might be credit constrained is 'excluded by assumption' (Arestis 2011: 96). Stiglitz, in an IMF volume of leading economists reassessing economic policy in the wake of the crisis, noted how problematic the competitive equilibrium assumptions underpinning pre-crisis mainstream thinking and modelling were, notably efficient-market hypothesis assumptions denying the possibility of financial bubbles (2012: 32–4).

Keynesian critics of NCM questioned the exclusive focus on the supply-side of the economy to explain unemployment, which assumes that the 'NAIRU is unaffected by aggregate demand and economic policy' (Arestis 2009a: 7; Arestis (ed.) 2007). This was subsequently an important axis of Fund thinking about advanced economies after 2008, with ideas like hysteresis gaining prominence (see e.g. IMF 2013j; Blanchard & Summers 1986; Stiglitz 1997: 8). This reaffirms the recognition, long present within Fund thinking, of an important if context-dependent role for aggregate demand in determining unemployment and output. The Fund's Modeller in Chief noted how Fund models, in their 'DSGE' construction, contained too many Ricardian features to capture fiscal policy issues: 'there is a literature where people dispute whether or not the world really is Ricardian or not. I don't really think a policy modeller would ever take that literature seriously. The world is non-Ricardian'[19] (Laxton 2008; Botman et al. 2007). Blanchard pointed out in 2013 how the Fund's models had improved since 2008, but that there was still more to do; 'we have made progress. We have models which do not necessarily converge, where there is unemployment, which have a banking system, even some in which there is hysteresis... Whether they have all the bells and whistles which are relevant for the fiscal discussion? No they don't.'[20]

The idea that economic agents betrayed Ricardian behaviour patterns was decisively rejected following the crash. IMF models evolved to accommodate more non-Ricardian features, including hand-to-mouth households (Freedman et al. 2009: 11). As Carlo Cottarelli, Director of FAD, put it in 2013, 'nobody is a Ricardian in the Fund any more. I don't know how long it will last, but for the moment.... it's not that the world will never be Ricardian again, it's that at the moment it is not.'[21] This indicates just how

[19] Interview with Doug Laxton, Division Chief of the Economic Modelling Division, IMF Research Department, September 2013.

[20] Interview with IMF Chief economist Olivier Blanchard, June 2013.

[21] Interview with former FAD Director Carlo Cottarelli, June 2013.

contingent upon context and economic conjuncture the attachment to particular economic ideas by Fund economists can be.

The Scope for Keynesian Thinking *within* the New Consensus

One under-reported facet of contemporary NCM economic thinking is the breadth of acceptable views of fiscal policy which can be accommodated within it (although see Ban 2015a & b). This had been masked by conventional wisdoms presuming the inefficacy of fiscal policy within stabilization. What only became fully apparent in the wake of the post-crisis rethink was that this antipathy was not a necessary or necessarily integral part of NCM thinking. In the unusual post-GFC conjuncture, the normally agreed economic policy tool for economic stabilization—monetary policy—was hamstrung by the Zero Lower Bound and hence ineffectual.

Part of the standard NCM case against fiscal policy efficacy depends on central bank response, the idea being that central bankers with an ideological aversion to big government will raise interest rates as deficits rise. Thus, significantly, the causal mechanisms are identified as central bank policy preferences, not as a direct result of market operations (Arestis & Sawyer 2003). As Mauro puts it, 'if you do fiscal expansion through tax cuts it's somehow better than doing it through more spending—but the fact that you get this finding is actually driven by how central banks respond to each; because apparently central banks would respond more aggressively when they saw an increase in spending.'[22] This is especially important in a Zero Lower Bound recessionary context, such as that following the crash, where interest rates were kept very low. Under these monetary policy conditions, central banks responding to fiscal stimulus were not likely to undermine the efficacy of less restrictive fiscal policy. This weakened the argument against using fiscal policy.

Following the crash, it soon became apparent that policy positions could be reconciled to the New Consensus mainstream that takes vastly differing views of the viability and desirability of fiscal policy as a stabilization tool (see Seabrooke et al. 2015). Indeed, within the mainstream could be found almost diametrically opposing views, from the decidedly anti-Keynesian 'expansionary fiscal contraction' (see Chapter 5) exponent Alesina to the Keynesian leanings of Auerbach and Gorodnichenko (2012, 2013a & b), who identified high fiscal multipliers under recessionary conditions (see Alesina & Giavazzi (ed.) 2013a). At one extreme, some used Ricardian assumptions to assert a

[22] Interview with Senior IMF Economist Paolo Mauro, a senior fellow at the Peterson Institute for International Economics at the time of the interview in 2014.

priori that fiscal policy is ineffectual as a stabilization tool (see e.g. Barro 1974). At the other end of the spectrum, David and Christy Romer see a potent and important role for fiscal policy in macroeconomic stabilization, with fiscal multipliers as high as three under certain conditions (Romer & Romer 2007, 2010). This was a particularly stark example of what Kirschner calls 'the indeterminacy of economic theory as a guide to policy' (Kirschner 2003a: 7). Those seeking to adopt positions anywhere along this spectrum could find corroboration from holders of Nobel prizes—be it Robert Lucas or Paul Krugman. This breadth of respectable assessments was important because the Fund's claims to technical and scientific expertise rest on being able to corroborate its economic policy analysis with reference to eminent highly respected economists.

This spectrum of reputable economic opinion on fiscal policy offered latitude to IMF bricoleurs to draw selectively from this variety of economic thought, both within the economics profession, but also within the Fund. In doing so, the Fund reconnected with long-standing insights about fiscal policy which have been part of the IMF mindset, one element within the repertoire of economic ideas it deploys according to economic conjuncture and policy circumstances. This ideational sedimentation meant the Fund could draw readily on ideas and insights from a range of different economic theoretical homes without compromising its intellectual authority or scientific norms.

Conclusion

The IMF, before and after the crash, continued to operate within the mainstream of a New Consensus in Macroeconomics which combines New Keynesian economic thinking with some element of New Classical economics. This builds on, and remains reconcilable to earlier NCS, which was the variant of Keynesian economics that forms a bedrock of Fund economic policy thinking and practice from the 1940s to at least the 1980s. Compatibility with this broad economic worldview is important for ideas to get a chance to rise to prominence. Yet there was scope within these parameters for the contours of Fund prescriptive discourse to evolve. The bottom line for Fund staff developing their policy recommendations is that, to be taken seriously internally and externally, economic ideas need backing within the Fund hierarchy, and to pass through the mechanisms of reconciliation, operationalization, corroboration, and authoritative recognition. The pre-crash Fund eschewed progressive taxation and prioritized fiscal discipline to the extent that it did not see fiscal policy as an engine of growth and recovery. After the crash, key IMF figures embraced a thorough-going rehabilitation of counter-cyclical fiscal policy.

Significant here is that, in each phase of the development of these successive 'conventional wisdoms' in economics, there are a variety of positions which form part of the mainstream. This broadens the repertoire of the Fund's economic thinking. The interaction between NCM and the crash brought a wider array of policy positions into the realms of the respectable. The Zero Lower Bound conditions and their implications for stabilization policy conduct revealed NCM to be less narrow, less conservative, and less inimical to fiscal policy activism than it had appeared during the 'non-inflationary continuous expansion' (NICE) decade.

IMF bricoleurs found they had surprisingly large latitude to remain compatible with NCM whilst having recourse to heterodox positions. The key lines of critique of NCM from a 'Keynesian' direction were taken up within the Fund rethink, notably by the Research department and by the modelling team. These included critique of the a priori assumption of an efficient financial market, and the recognition that earlier NCM thinking had been excessively dismissive of fiscal policy. The New Keynesian inspired thinking about multiple equilibria, and the broader Keynesian thinking about the limitations of markets and their lack of inherent self-correcting properties became important points of reference in Fund discussions of post-GFC economic policy.

The breadth of fiscal thinking found within the Fund, combined with the particular special case conditions of the post-GFC economic conjuncture, afforded significant room to manoeuvre for IMF bricoleurs enabling the centre of gravity of Fund thinking and recommendations on fiscal policy to evolve in a more traditional 'Keynesian' direction. Since 2008, the Keynesian subculture within the Fund, identified as relatively marginal in recent decades (Chwieroth 2010), saw its fortunes revived. It became clear that there was intellectual space within the parameters of NCM to both question significant pre-crisis assumptions about efficient markets and to endorse 'short-run Keynesianism'. The crisis, its aftermath, and the rethinking of economic policy premises both within the Fund and in academic economics created the policy space for Fund bricoleurs to reshape understandings of 'sound' fiscal policy in the post-crash context. We explore the ramifications of this in the next chapters.

4

Analysing the IMF Surveillance of Advanced Economies

The Social Construction of Fiscal Space

Introduction

The Fund is a significant actor within world politics, but its importance is often misconstrued—either overstated by those critics who see the IMF as imposing its will on poorer borrowing countries (see e.g. Peet 2009), or understated by those seeing the IMF as simply a conduit of the interests of its powerful rich members who sit on its Board (see e.g. Killick 1995). This chapter locates the Fund within the wider context of world politics to develop a theory of IMF influence over advanced economies, and explores the sources and limits of the IMF's authority and autonomy. Focusing on advanced economies not borrowing from the Fund, it explores how the Fund has, throughout its history and by a variety of means, used its intellectual authority and resources to mould the international climate of opinion on economic policy (Barnett & Finnemore 2004: 52–5; James 1996; Pauly 1997, 2008, 2009; Park & Vetterlein 2010a & b). The Fund derives significant intellectual authority from its mandated role as guarantor of stability in the international monetary system. The IMF's role within the world economy changed substantially following the collapse of Bretton Woods in the 1970s, but it continued to play an important role as a source of information and economic knowledge for advanced and emerging economies alike. This rationale for Fund operations has remained, through all the changes in the global political economy.

The Fund's articles of agreement specify its purpose as 'a permanent institution which provides the machinery for consultation and collaboration on international monetary problems' (IMF 1993: 2). It is tasked with providing some level of international accountability and coordination for countries' economic policies. Following Pauly, we understand Fund surveillance as 'a process of regular consultations, analysis, and consensus-building in a nearly universal forum' (Pauly 1997: 139). It is conceived here as a mechanism by which the Fund disseminates its intellectual framework for approaching economic policy. Through multilateral and bilateral surveillance, the IMF can shape the policy possibilities for all countries, rich and poor, facing financing constraints or not.

Attempts to shape understandings of sound economic policy through Fund surveillance receive much less attention in the academic literature than IMF loan conditionality. There is a blind spot in the literature on IMF relations with advanced countries not borrowing from the Fund. Much research on the Fund focuses on conditionality in developing economies in receipt of Fund loans (Copelovitch 2010; Woods 2006; Stone 2011; Boughton & Lombardi 2009; Broome 2010a; Breen 2013; Williamson 1983). To the extent the advanced economies' relations with the Fund are considered, the focus is normally on the power of these countries within the Fund, and how far the organization is an agent of their foreign economic policies (Copelovitch 2010; Thacker 1999; Lavelle 2011). In the wake of the crash, as patterns of Fund lending have changed, studies of the IMF's role in world politics have focused on conditionality and programmes (see Rogers 2012: 174–98; Ban 2016; Nelson 2017; Kentikelenis, Stubbs, & King 2016). They have explored demands for adjustment and restructuring of economies facing market pressure and lacking policy space in the Eurozone periphery and Central and Eastern Europe (see e.g. Lutz & Kranke 2014; Gabor 2010). The upshot of the focal points of the IMF literature is that little attention has been paid to IMF interactions with those advanced economies not facing immediate financing constraints, and IMF views on their conduct of macroeconomic policy. Yet surveillance, rather than loan programmes, is what the Fund spends most of its time doing.

As a range of 'principal/agent'-oriented scholarship on the IMF has underlined (Hawkins et al. 2006b), the interests of powerful members and power relations at board level delimit what kinds of policy ideas are 'thinkable' within the Fund (Seabrooke 2010). Set against that backdrop, the argument here is that the IMF possesses significant autonomy, and its staff and management are creative agents able to revisit and revise pre-existing thinking and practice. Instead of being understood and defined solely in terms of its powerful members' interests, the Fund is an actor in its own right, possessed of a mandate, significant resources, and its own intellectual agenda. Hence, within the parameters of 'thinkable' policy, there is scope for Fund leadership and staff to use their agenda-setting capacity to strategically promote, advocate, and corroborate particular approaches to economic policy.

What the Fund says matters not because it must be heeded, but in the way it contributes to understandings of appropriate economic policy (see Best 2010; Barnett & Finnemore 2004, 2005). The IMF's intellectual framework for understanding economic policy is an important site of ideational power (see Chapter 1). Fund staff's self-understanding of their role, and the institution's role in pursuit of its surveillance mandate is that they can and should subtly work to change how national authorities think, and spread Fund understandings of what constitutes sound and legitimate economic policy. After all, as Clegg puts it, 'these dominant frameworks... in essence *are* the very norms that IOs disseminate' (2013: 13). This chapter explores a crucial but under-explored connection between Fund economic ideas and room to manoeuvre for advanced economy governments, between Fund prescriptive discourse on 'sound economic policy' and advanced economy policy space. Fund actors use the strategic doctrinal flexibility of the IMF in constructing the increasingly prevalent notion of 'fiscal space' in ways that prioritize particular policy options. The Fund uses fiscal space to encourage a rethink of the premises of policy settings, and to create the conditions of possibility for particular policies. It enables Fund counsel to reconcile medium-term entreaties for a country to get its fiscal house in order to short-term calls for counter-cyclical activism.

Non-borrowing advanced economies constitute a less likely case for Fund influence to prevail, since the institution lacks leverage mechanisms, and these governments have their own well-honed economic policy expertise. After addressing the scope and limits of Fund autonomy, this chapter identifies the sources of the IMF's power to speak with intellectual authority about economic policy. It then analyses to what extent the Fund can exert influence over advanced economies, and the conditions of possibility for the Fund's exercising ideational power. It finds that the institution's ability to achieve this goal ebbs and flows. The level and kind of influence the Fund enjoys is contingent upon the Fund's ability to frame policy advice in a way which resonates with policymakers, as well as its ability to mobilize its scientific expertise, knowledge bank, and mandate in a given policy context.

Between 2007 and 2009, the Fund's crisis (and crisis legacy) narrative resonated widely with national authorities, its efforts at shaping policy responses and stabilizing expectations saw Fund influence expand beyond its material resources. Yet from 2010 onwards, the Fund proved something of an outlier on fiscal policy thinking. Many advanced economies chose not to take up the growth-supporting fiscal policy opportunities, or exploit the policy space the Fund sought to carve out. The IMF surveillance regime contains no means of enforcement, and given competing authoritative claims, the socially recognized expertise of economists does not work solely in the Fund's favour. Thus, the IMF's reach at times exceeds its grasp.

The IMF as an Actor in World Politics: Conceptions of Fund Autonomy and Agency

The case has been convincingly made that powerful states can exert significant influence over Fund activities. The Fund is a hierarchical organization, and its larger shareholders enjoy formal influence through their permanent membership of and voting rights on the Executive Board. Indeed, the IMF ultimately depends on these rich and powerful nations for the financial support vital to its continued existence (Lavelle 2011). Within this, the US as the major shareholder is widely recognized as especially powerful, seen by some as imposing relatively tight limits on what the Fund thinks and does (Wade 2002, 2003a; Breen 2014; Broz & Hawes 2006; Woods 2006; Momani 2004; Reynaud & Vauday 2009; Thacker 1999; Wade & Veneroso 1998; Pop-Eleches 2008; Gould 2006). Indeed, Randall Stone sees evidence of the IMF acting as a conduit for US foreign policy interests (2008; 2011; see also Oatley & Yackee 2004; Dreher & Jensen 2007). Copelovitch identifies a slightly wider cast of characters, seeing the G5 of UK, France, Germany, and Japan, as well as the US as being of crucial importance (2010: 5–6, 45–57). Joyce sees a broader array of powerful actors with the shift from the G7 to the G20 (2013: 2,4).

It is important to take account of powerful member states' concerns and policy priorities in analysing the IMF. A range of scholarship on Fund interactions with its powerful members approaches the issue in terms of 'principal/agent' (PA) relations. IOs are seen within this literature as constructed by states to resolve coordination problems within 'the anarchic international system' (Hawkins et al. 2006a: 6). Much PA analysis takes as read US power at the heart of the international system within which authority and tasks are delegated to the IMF on a conditional basis. PA research questions then explore 'agency slack' through 'shirking' or 'slippage', as well as discretion and authority enjoyed by agents to identify instances where the principals' wishes are contravened by agents, and how mechanisms can be designed to limit this (2006a: 8–9).

Focused as it is mostly on principals' (powerful states') efforts to control troublesome agents, PA 'contains a remarkably thin view of agent behaviour' (Hawkins & Jacoby 2006: 199; see also Clegg 2013: 9–11), of the Fund, and the nature of its agency. As a result, whilst agent autonomy is recognized within the PA framework, it is largely confined to attempts to hide action or information from the principal. Such approaches to IO analysis understand the IMF more or less exclusively in terms of the extent to which they reflect major country preferences. This recalls how pluralist theory understands the state as a straightforward conduit of societal interests (see Barnett & Finnemore 2005: 162).

Given the intellectual goals of PA analysis, this kind of work struggles to conceive of IMF actions or activity *except in terms of major shareholder interests*. Furthermore, the focus on certain given structural conditions of world order on which PA analysis is often based can neglect how levels of influence, and dynamics of power relations, can evolve on a contingent basis. As set out in Chapter 2, this book's CI approach aligns with constructivist accounts of IOs in advancing a broader and more encompassing understanding of the potential for IMF agency and autonomy. The starting point is a recognition that the IMF and other IOs are independent actors in world politics, and not reducible to conduits of state interests or preferences. The corollary of the CI view of Fund staff as creative, reflexive agents who 'make sense' of their interests and are able to reinterpret and recreate their environment is significant autonomy for the managing director, senior management, and other staff within the recognized limits imposed by major shareholder positions.

IOs are not 'mere tools' of states, but also 'autonomous actors', enjoying—within limits—some 'ontological independence' (Barnett & Finnemore 1999: 704, 705; 2004; 2005: 161). The IMF is imbricated in the inter-subjective processes where understandings of economic policy are constituted and reconstituted. As such, it has scope and leeway to advance its interpretation and garner support for its priorities. This continues a tradition of work recognizing that IOs such as the IMF, with their expertise and their resources, are independent actors enjoying a degree of autonomy as a source of economic policy knowledge (Chwieroth 2010, 2013, 2014; Ban 2015a & b; Clegg 2013; Hawkins & Jacoby 2006; Woods 2006; Nelson 2017). This point of departure makes possible a different understanding of the relationship between the Fund, its powerful members, and their economic policies. Whilst PA analysis can admit the possibility that agents 'may use theoretical autonomy to influence future decisions by principals' or even 'utilize their resources and knowledge to influence principals' preferences or strategies' (Hawkins et al. 2006a: 31), these instances are marginal to PA research programme. They are, by contrast, at the heart of how constructivists approach IOs and their relations with members (see e.g. Barnett & Finnemore 2004; Best 2010; Broome & Seabrooke 2012), revealing the differing intellectual goals of the two research programmes.

Different aspects of Fund activity can enjoy more or less autonomy, with surveillance towards the more autonomous end of the scale. Importantly, the 'flagships' like WEO are viewed externally as the voice of the Fund, and understood internally as the voice of the Fund *staff*. Senior IMF economist Vivek Arora summarizes their role:

> If there are issues that are new and evolving... like for example the fiscal multipliers or the appropriate pace of fiscal consolidation in a downturn, then there is

> usually a staff view that emerges through this whole process of debate and review. Often it will be expressed in our flagship publications namely the *WEO* and *Fiscal Monitor*.[1]

Indeed, the section in each *WEO* which briefly reports Board discussion of the latest issue can at times reveal dissonances between the Fund staff position as distilled in the *WEO* and the views of some board members. In Fund flagship publications, as in economic policy commentary more broadly, IMF staff enjoy significant agenda-setting power (Martin 2006: 149). IMF thinking and commentary can and does evolve along lines not predetermined by or wholly consonant with the preferences of major powers on the board. The analysis in the chapter sets out how the Fund's ability to speak with its own voice evolves depending on economic conjuncture, Fund/member relations, and internal developments within the Fund.

The CI approach of this book entails a different focal point for the analysis (as compared to PA oriented studies), and a different understanding of the Fund as an actor. This study takes heed of those focused on US power within the IMF (Lavelle 2011; Woods 2003), and insights about how major shareholders set parameters on the limits of the possible for the Fund. Interviews with Fund staff indicate a keen awareness of Board level and 'major shareholder' dynamics, but equally reveal effort and abilities to navigate and overcome such constraints. IMF management and staff recognize the need to be mindful of these power relationships, but there remains scope within those parameters for these reflexive actors to select which economic ideas and insights to prioritize.

Fund Authority, its Surveillance Mandate, and Advanced Economies

The IMF's capacity to speak with authority about economic policy is an important source of its ideational power and autonomy. In this section we explore where that authority comes from, finding these sources to be both institutional and intellectual. The institutional sources of Fund authority are numerous, linked to its central role in enacting the IMF's ongoing surveillance and oversight function laid down in the 1978 rewriting of Article IV of its Articles of Agreement. These define the Fund's purpose as 'to promote international monetary cooperation', and to provide 'the machinery for consultation and collaboration on international monetary problems'. The Keynesian

[1] Interview with Vivek Arora, then Deputy Director of the Strategy, Policy and Review Department, September 2013.

spirit of the Articles, first drafted in 1944, task the Fund with facilitating 'the expansion and balanced growth of international trade' and 'the promotion and maintenance of high levels of income and employment' as 'primary objectives of economic policy' (IMF 1993: 2). Surveillance of all members, rich and poor alike, has been a very large part of what many Fund staff spend their time doing. Surveillance benefits, as Pauly notes, from 'substantial financial, intellectual and political resources' and is 'at the very core of the institution' (1997: 41). As Carlo Cottarelli puts it, regarding Fund surveillance activities 'our voice is what matters.'[2]

At the core of the Fund's role in the world economy is what Pauly has termed 'the principle of international oversight' over economic policies (1997: 38). This multilateral accountability for their domestic economic policies is, importantly, enacted through the IMF. It has to deliver coordination of economic policies, and render its members 'accountable to one another for the external effects of their domestic economic policies' (Pauly 1997: 39). The IMF's surveillance mandate places a legal obligation on all member states reinforcing what Pauly calls 'the basic principle of Bretton Woods: they were accountable to one another for the external effects of their policies' (Pauly 1997: 137). This crucial source of Fund authority also provides 'an institutionalized mechanism for sharing and learning' (James 1996: 275). As James wrote of the Fund in the 1970s, 'supplying information and ideas—as well as funds—now became the major means by which the IMF would seek to guide the evolution of economic policymaking' (1996: 275). Since the late 1960s the Fund has developed and refined its forecasting framework and economic policy analysis as published in *World Economic Outlook*. This long experience and institutional memory, along with the energy and resources the institution expends on surveillance, are important elements of the IMF seeking ideational influence over its members and their economic policies (Pauly 1997: xi).

The execution of its surveillance mandate ascribes the IMF a role as guarantor of international economic stability. No other body is mandated to act as conduit of this accountability, as agent of this oversight, or as source of coordination. The IMF's institutional memory has developed as it has sought to carry out these roles. All these reinforce Fund authority as it seeks to feed 'conventional' wisdoms into the process whereby particular understandings of economic policy become stabilized. The impression gained from interviewing numerous members of Fund staff is that the Fund sees itself as dispassionately policing, or at least pronouncing upon the imperceptible but important boundaries of 'legitimate' or 'sound' economic policy.

[2] Interview with Carlo Cottarelli, then Director of FAD, June 2013.

The purchase the IMF enjoys over the international economic policy debate is nevertheless limited, partly by the requirements of the surveillance function and the nature of relations with member countries the mandate generates. The Fund must be at once trusted advisor and independent auditor of a country's policy settings, fiscal stance, debt sustainability, and so on (IEO 2013). Whilst it can seek to impress its view, Fund missions are mindful not to overstep their brief and respect the national sovereignty and the constitutional niceties of the surveillance relationship. As Cottarelli notes, 'it's always difficult for us under surveillance to take views that are very much different from the views of the authorities'.[3] Fund staff can prioritize certain economic policy approaches, but these acts of persuasion within surveillance interactions must operate within the confines of a surveillance relationship which, as IMF Articles of Agreement state, 'shall respect the domestic social and political policies of members' (1993: 6). Fund surveillance interactions with advanced economies ultimately 'rest on no practical power to enforce sanctions' and Fund advice has been 'frequently ignored' (Pauly 1997: 40). This can have an adverse effect on Fund authority. Mission advice, therefore, uses the feedback loops from repeated interactions with national policy elites (see Chapter 2) to carefully tailor and edit recommendations to reduce the prospects of Fund counsel being obviously ignored.

The Fund's authority has intellectual, as well as institutional origins. Harold James' IMF-sanctioned history of international monetary cooperation concludes that the IMF's influence has shifted within the world economy since the 1970s. He characterizes the evolution in how authority is configured in international monetary relations as an earlier 'dollar standard' being replaced by the IMF's 'information standard' (1996: 612). In similar vein, Fund official historian James Boughton notes in self-congratulatory fashion that 'throughout the Fund's history', 'the staff has relied primarily on the power of its economic analysis to bring about welfare-enhancing policy changes' (2012: lxii). Each of these IMF-centred views overstates the 'traction' enjoyed by the Fund over member governments' economic policy thinking. They underplay the role of other sources of authoritative information on economic policy, from other IOs such as the World Bank, OECD, bond rating agencies, and other bodies. Nevertheless, the IMF remains an important source of respected information and authoritative knowledge claims about economic policy.

The dynamics of Fund staff interactions with national authorities are rather different for Fund-advanced economy interactions as compared to emerging markets or low income countries. Fund institutional power in this regard as linked partly to its 'technical capacities' and Fund staff 'expertise'

[3] Interview with Carlo Cottarelli, then Director of FAD, June 2013.

(Best 2010: 197). Yet in advanced economies, national authorities have highly trained and well-resourced finance ministries and central banks, so the socially recognized expertise of economists does not work solely in the Fund's favour. Under these conditions, the Fund cannot rely on an asymmetry of expertise and technical capacities. Fund surveillance missions enjoy a wealth of comparative data and knowledge, whereas national authorities have superior familiarity with the domestic conjuncture and institutional context.

Fund ideational authority to enact its self-appointed role as an arbiter of sound economic policy also derives from its technical expertise, with the Fund operating as a leading economics research institution in its own right. Fund hiring practices, recruiting its 800+ economists from well-regarded economics PhD programmes (Chwieroth 2010; Ban 2015a & b), marks the Fund out as a distinctive combination of research and operational work, and a uniquely resourced actor in developing economic policy wisdom. As noted in Chapter 2 when discussing 'authoritative recognition' as a mechanism of ideational change, IMF surveillance cites carefully selected parts of the academic literature extensively, and its flagship publications contribute to a set of policy-relevant debates within the profession. The ability to present Fund research as contributing to, consistent with, and drawing upon the latest research and ongoing debates at the cutting edge of economics bolsters the authority of Fund policy recommendations (see Chapter 3).

The IMF's unique selling point is its unparalleled knowledge bank, built up over decades by Fund staff's day-to-day activities executing its mandate for multilateral surveillance, and conditional lending. This accretion of economic policy knowledge, programme, and technical assistance work is crucial to the Fund's power to speak with authority on economic policy matters. So too is the way this operational work is underpinned by the analysis of the Research Department. The IMF's comparative advantage in cross-country evidence on economic policy and economic developments reinforces its credibility. These are all ways of reinforcing and reproducing the IMF's ideational authority and productive power through what Chwieroth terms the 'socially recognized expertise' of economics and economists (Chwieroth 2010: 12, 40–7; see also Fourcade 2009).

A key facet of the Fund's intellectual authority and importance within the world economy as the provider of an 'information standard' is the 'intellectual framework' that Fund staff develop, operationalize, and disseminate in assessing economic policy (James 1996: 612–13; David 1985: 5–11). The fact that it is the Fund's own, distinctive intellectual framework, developed incrementally over many decades of Fund activities, is a manifestation of the Fund's agency and autonomy. The IMF, like other IOs, exercises authority by developing and spreading norms (Barnett & Finnemore 1999, 2004, 2005; Clegg 2013; Park & Vetterlein 2010b; Weaver 2008). This highlights the 'productive power' of international organizations to shape 'systems of knowledge' which 'works through diffuse constitutive relations to produce the situated subjectivities of actors' (Barnett & Duvall 2005: 9, 11–15). This Fund 'productive' power operates through attempts to 'set and fix meanings' (Barnett & Duvall 2005: 21–2; Chwieroth 2010; Broome & Seabrooke 2012; Nelson 2014). The IMF intellectual framework provides 'guideposts for interpreting economic actions', the goal being 'redefining the terms of sound economic behaviour' (Best 2010: 203; see also Barnett & Finnemore 2004: 52–5). The Fund works to develop 'a new grammar of economic perception, providing market actors with new definitions of economic soundness' (Best 2010: 209). At its most ambitious, the Fund seeks to codify 'normal economic behaviour'. Through the role of norms, and the 'constitutive nature of these new rules and practices', the IMF seeks not only to 'make certain actors change their behaviour' but also actively working 'to constitute them in new ways' (Best 2010: 196).

The IMF's influence, according to James, 'depends largely on its ability to provide speedy, accurate, and persuasive economic analysis' (James 1996: 612). A manifestation of its ideational power is how the Fund routinely produces, teaches, and diffuses economic norms 'from standards for the collection of economic data to analytical categories for thinking about economic questions and courses of action regarding economic policy' (Fourcade-Gourinchas & Babb 2002: 535–6; Broome & Seabrooke 2012). These mental frames mediate how the appropriateness (or otherwise) of fiscal policy strategies, settings, and positions are perceived. As Clegg recognizes, this is a distillation of the norms of economic policy conduct and interpretation the IMF seeks to propagate through its surveillance and other activities (2013: 13). Interviews with Fund staff support this view of their self-understanding of efforts to disseminate Fund views and constitute shared beliefs about fiscal policy matters.

Where emerging market economies are concerned, the IMF's shaping of understandings of sound economic policy happens in concrete form through its training programmes for developing economy policymakers, notably at the Joint Vienna Institute (see Broome 2010a), and through its provision of technical assistance. The Fund flagship publication *WEO*, and the understandings of economic policy contained therein, provides the syllabus for Fund economic policymaker training. Its efforts to shape the thinking of advanced economy policymakers are channelled through Article IV consultations with national authorities, the IMF Spring and Autumn meetings, and the *WEO* and other flagships. Cottarelli highlights the role of *Fiscal Monitor* as the 'tool for the communication of our voice on certain fiscal policy issues'.[4] These are the

[4] Interview with Carlo Cottarelli, then Director of FAD, June 2013.

mechanisms through which the Fund develops and propagates its intellectual framework for understanding economic policy. This is all part of the IMF's 'preaching of "sound economics"' (James 1996: 612).

Powerful Members, Fund Autonomy, and the Moveable Limits of 'Thinkable' Policy

This book's CI approach entails a different conception of agents and their interests (see also Clegg 2013: ch. 1) as compared to PA analysis discussed above. Thus, whilst our analysis begins from the premise that 'the basic voting structure has a disciplining effect on what range of policies are "thinkable"' (Seabrooke 2010: 141; see also Pauly 1997: 113), the limits of thinkable policy are not set in stone. Here, ideas and interests are seen as socially constructed, malleable, and emergent, rather than fixed and given (Blyth 2003a, 2007; Campbell 1998). Fund staff and management retain significant autonomy from those powerful members, and the interests of powerful member states are always in the making, especially in times of crisis, instability, and upheaval.

During 2008 and 2009, the conjuncture offered latitude to Fund Staff to inflect fiscal policy thinking. The advanced economies, notably the US and UK, were at the heart of the storm. Before long, all other major European economies were drawn in. Given the scale of the threats to economic stability, these traditionally powerful members of the Fund were exploring policy responses (including coordinated fiscal stimulus) which lay beyond the parameters of pre-crisis economic orthodoxy (IMF 2008f). The realms of Seabrooke's 'thinkable' macroeconomic policy (2010) had accordingly expanded by common consent. As Cottarelli characterized fiscal policy thinking in 2013,

> for the normal ups and downs of the economy, I think it will still be OK just to let the automatic stabilizers operate. I think there is still a risk of a deficit bias that would discourage use of discretionary fiscal expansion in normal circumstances... But—we are not in normal circumstances.[5]

The crisis context reduced constraints on Fund thinking sometimes imposed by powerful Board members. The permissive conditions were improved to shape post-crash thinking in that Fund ideas about crisis response were evolving along similar lines to a number of key major powers.

As the Fund's fiscal policy rethink was in progress, the US government was unveiling its Troubled Asset Relief Program and, on an equally large scale, its fiscal stimulus package. Ben Bernanke at the Federal Reserve was a distinguished

[5] Interview with Carlo Cottarelli, the Director of FAD, June 2013.

historian of the economic policy mistakes of the Great Depression, while Larry Summers at the White House was a New Keynesian sympathetic to prioritizing demand and active fiscal policy. He had, along with Blanchard, developed influential theories about hysteresis in the 1980s (Blanchard & Summers 1986). Gordon Brown as Prime Minister and Alistair Darling as Chancellor in the UK were similarly thinking along these lines of the need for fiscal stimulus to stave off a deeper crisis. In this they were joined at an early stage by President Sarkozy of France and Christine Lagarde, who was then Finance Minister (see Chapters 6 and 7).

In the context of the crash, economic policy thinking in the US and elsewhere was gravitating towards a more fiscally active and market-sceptical position. The signals coming from the feedback loops of surveillance interactions with national authorities were encouraging. This environment encouraged the Keynesian-sympathetic subculture within the IMF, which enjoyed revived prominence within the macro policy discussion, in advancing their interpretation of the crisis and appropriate policy responses. Pursuing their counter-cyclical stabilization research agenda rethinking within the Fund was worth the effort because, in the 2008–9 period, there was little prospect of new activist fiscal policy thinking being 'shot down' by the Fund's Executive Board.

The stock of fiscally activist New Keynesian thinking was rising within economic policy circles. The recruitment of two influential New Keynesian economists to new posts in Washington DC in late 2008, Christy and David Romer, gives a flavour of a somewhat symbiotic relationship between US Treasury and the Fund. They had produced work highlighting large fiscal multipliers, and the efficacy of fiscal policy as a counter-cyclical tool in the US case (Romer & Romer 2007, 2010). Christy Romer arrived to serve on the Council of Economic Advisors, while David Romer became a senior visiting researcher at the Fund. There he directed some of the key early post-crash work on fiscal policy efficacy, leading to the landmark *Will it Hurt? WEO* chapter that debunked the expansionary austerity thesis (IMF 2010g: 93–124). That this power couple of New Keynesian economics simultaneously took up key posts within the US administration and inside the IMF was an indicator that the thinking of the two institutions on the crisis and appropriate responses was evolving in cognate directions. There was a following wind behind the IMF economic policy rethink from 2008 onwards, increasing the receptiveness and resonance of its ideas amongst key economic policymaking elites.

This commonality of view was one of the conditions of possibility for the Fund to push further in a Keynesian direction. As other Fund scholars have noted, the Fund's power is enhanced when its policy thinking finds a favourable audience amongst national authorities, what Woods calls 'sympathetic interlocutors' (2006: ch. 3; see also Nelson 2017; Moschella 2010a & b). Relatedly,

Pop-Eleches identifies as the alignment (or not) between 'IMF-style economic reforms' and the ideological persuasion of domestic governments, and powerful domestic economic interests as a crucial intervening variable affecting the extent of IMF influence (2008). Our findings broadly align with theirs—with the Fund's 'traction' at its zenith when national authorities, faced with a pressing crisis, were persuadable around Keynesian policy responses (see Chapters 5, 6, and 7).[6] Furthermore, key national policy elites were pulling in the same direction. These sympathetic audiences, and the crisis context of interests in flux, as in the autumn of 2008, enhanced the possibilities of the Fund's policy ideas gaining traction.

Fund Influence over Advanced Economy Policies and Its Limits

A wide array of historians and analysts of the Fund concur about the Fund's attempt to wield ideational influence through its surveillance and other activities (James 1996; Boughton 2012; De Vries 1985; Best 2010; Chwieroth 2010; Broome 2008, 2010b). The IMF works, through its research, operational work, and policy advice to influence both domestic policy elites' understandings and their policy actions, and the climate of opinion within which economic and fiscal policy rectitude is assessed (Pauly 2008; Broome & Seabrooke 2007, 2012; Woods 2006; Lombardi & Woods 2008). Fund staff see this as essential to the Fund fulfilling its role in the world economy. The extent to which these attempts are successful is hard to gauge and therefore more contested. There is ongoing anxiety, including at high levels within the Fund, about the extent to which its counsel is being heeded. How to increase the 'traction' for Fund policy thinking is a constant topic of discussion and reflection within the organization. This concern arose again and again in interviews with staff members.

As discussed above, there are limits to Fund influence rooted in the nature of the surveillance mandate and relationship, and the Fund is also constrained by power relations with its powerful members. Particularly where non-borrowing advanced economies are concerned, the IMF lacks the monopoly on 'sound' ideas, and the requisite resources and leverage to fully prevail within this battle of economic ideas, or of interpretations of economic policy. This is a less likely case for Fund influence to prevail entirely, or perhaps at all. The IMF can hope for modest influence, which might at most lead to subtle

[6] Interviews with Olivier Blanchard and Carlo Cottarelli, at the IMF, and with Philippe Gudin, former director for macroeconomic policies and European affairs at the directorate general of the treasury in the French Ministry of Economy.

alterations in economic policy prioritization. As such, its aim to become an 'information standard' for the world economy is never fully realized.

The account developed here contributes to debates about the IMF's role in world politics by setting out the conditions under which the Fund can shape domestic economic policymaking of advanced economies not borrowing from the Fund. The CI approach, focused on how Fund staff make sense of their role, provides fresh insights into the sources, scope, and limits of IMF intellectual authority in the Great Recession. Fund staff are reflexive, creative actors who adjust their persuasive efforts to take account of national authorities' positions and priorities. There is appreciation of the need to find subtle means to inflect the policy debate and the thinking of economic policymakers in the advanced economies. It becomes clear when interviewing Fund staff about their surveillance activities that they realize they have limited sway and therefore pick their battles. They choose to deploy their persuasive efforts where they stand the greatest chance of securing the 'traction' which is all important to Fund staff in their dealings with policymakers.[7]

What this analysis underscores, furthermore, is that the IMF's level of influence is not fixed or structurally given, but rather contingent upon context and economic conjuncture. Fund chances of success in shaping the thinking of advanced economy governments depend on the economic conjuncture (in particular economic crisis), and how it frames its interventions. The efficacy of Fund acts of moral suasion around fiscal policy was contingent upon the policy message connecting with the thinking and fears of advanced economic policymakers. Certain economic ideas 'resonate' (Moschella 2009: 857–61; 2010a: 11) at particular moments in time. This affects the ability of the Fund to gain the 'traction' it seeks in international policy debates. This depends to a significant degree on the Fund's ability to alight on and promote economic ideas which enjoy this resonance. Hence, as Moschella notes, 'explaining the variation of the influence of economic ideas over time requires understanding their co-evolution with the economic environment in which they are floated' (Moschella 2010a: 9).

Notions of inter-elite persuasion (Blyth 2007; Checkel 2001; Baker 2015; Widmaier 2003a; Widmaier et al. 2007) are helpful for analysing how Fund staff use these interactions to try and induce shifts of policy settings, and shape understandings of sound policy. Blyth discusses 'the politics of "inter-elite" persuasion' as a 'distinct and important mechanism of social construction in moments of economic crisis', affected by 'the inherent ambiguity of economic ideas in moments of uncertainty'. Crucially, up for grabs within this contingent inter-elite persuasion process is 'what a crisis means, and how it

[7] This view came across in many interviews at the Fund.

should be institutionally resolved' (2007: 761; see also 1996; Widmaier 2003b, 2004; Gamble 2009, 2014).

IMF surveillance and commentary after the GFC through Article IVs, *WEO*, and later *Fiscal Monitor*, as well as the supporting and corroborating research undertaken by Fund economists, are here understood as acts of 'inter-elite persuasion'. In the autumn of 2008, with the crisis deepening by the day, governments and policy elites were casting about for 'what is to be done?'. Blanchard, together with Strauss-Kahn and others, seized the opportunity to advance a distinctive IMF leadership line on crisis response and necessary measures to avoid another Great Depression. As time wore on, the Fund also sought to advance its interpretation of the crisis *legacy* (see Chapter 1), and its implications for economic policy conduct. Fund staff and leadership worked to use these crisis and crisis legacy interpretations to shift the boundaries of legitimate economic policy.

In a highly unstable world, pervaded by what Blanchard characterized as 'Knightian' uncertainty (2009; 2012c), some coordinating mechanism is needed to stabilize expectations—and hopefully thereafter, markets. Amidst economic uncertainty, actors rely on social conventions, looking for cues and other 'mental models' to stabilize their expectations (see Nelson & Katzenstein 2014: 363–7; Blyth 2007; Widmaier 2003a & b, 2004). Just as central banks seek to construct market expectations under conditions of uncertainty (Nelson & Katzenstein 2014: 380; Hall 2008; Braun 2014), so too the IMF seeks to play a similar role—shaping the conventional understandings through its Keynesian account of the crisis and appropriate policy responses. The Fund was central to the internationally coordinated fiscal stimulus. It worked to construct economic credibility, shape investor and public expectations, and stabilize expectations in a way that Fund staff saw as crucial to staving off deeper crisis.

The November 2008 G20 action plan bore the hallmarks of the Fund's distinctive interpretation of the crisis. In early November 2008, Strauss-Kahn noted how

> the financial crisis has created a sharp fall in demand, what economists call a Keynesian recession ... To help confidence revive, there is no alternative but to use macroeconomic tools to boost demand and sustain output ... Fiscal policy must, therefore, play a central role. Fiscal expansion is always risky, as it adds to debt and raises dangers later. But, given where we are, the benefits exceed the costs in countries with sustainable debt (Strauss-Kahn 2008b).

The rapidity with which this Fund line was developed by Blanchard and Strauss-Kahn helped the Keynesian-sympathetic subculture within the Fund overcome any objections of more fiscally conservative internal voices. Accordingly, Fund commentary gave prominence to problems of weak aggregate demand, lack of confidence, and the need for monetary and fiscal policies in support of growth to counter such tendencies. It highlighted the instability of markets, especially financial markets and the 'non-linear' threats of deepening and potentially self-aggravating economic pathologies the crisis posed (Spilimbergo et al. 2008; IMF 2008c & d).

Maximizing Traction? IMF Bricolage and Framing Policy Advice

The conducive context of the crisis played a highly significant role in the Fund's thoroughgoing, if contingent, rehabilitation of counter-cyclical fiscal policy as a crisis response and an economic stabilization tool. Yet the mere fact of crisis was not sufficient to ensure the Fund would get its message heard. To increase the chances of getting its ideas across through surveillance and other interactions with national authorities, self-aware Fund bricoleurs carefully crafted and framed their prescriptive policy discourse. In this section we identify four aspects of Fund advice which increased the chances of gaining traction.

Firstly, where its policy advice can be justified and framed around the central Fund mandate, notably with reference to one or more of international coordination, economic stability, and growth—this enhances the legitimacy and leverage of Fund policy advice. The external effects of internal policies, central to the Fund's surveillance mandate, become especially salient issues in times of certain kinds of economic crisis. The global financial crisis which began in 2007, and spread rapidly from the debt securities originating in the US sub-prime mortgages to engulf much of the wider global financial system, was a case in point. Thus, the crisis not only had the advanced economies at its heart, but furthermore it was triggered and aggravated by precisely the kinds of adverse external effects of internal policies which Fund multilateral economic surveillance is designed to monitor and hopefully counter.

The aggravating 'spillovers' identified by the Fund entailed cross-border contagion. An additional spillover dimension underscored the spreading economic dysfunctionalities from the financial sector into the heart of the real economy. These particularities bolstered the Fund's authority and brought enhanced salience to Fund surveillance activities. Policymakers seeking to understand and address the deepening fragilities, vulnerabilities, and instability which bedevilled advanced economies were apt to take note. This created the intellectual and policy space for the Fund to advocate various forms of counter-cyclical macroeconomic policy alongside measures to repair the financial system.

Secondly, the Fund can attempt (albeit imperfectly) to provide international public goods. As the crisis erupted, advanced economy policymakers were casting about for policy direction, and recognized in particular the need to collaborate and work together in developing crisis responses. Reinforcing its mandated role, Fund commentary underlined the need for *international coordination* of economic policies. Received Keynesian economic wisdom, after all, indicates that fiscal stimulus is more effective and successful if it can be on an international scale (Spilimbergo et al. 2008). Policymakers knew the merits of fiscal stimulus being coordinated internationally, but had no means to effect this.

This underscored a core element of the IMF's mandate and function, and the Fund found itself uniquely well-placed to contribute, delivering the international synchronization required to maximize the chances of policy success. Its mandate for surveillance delivered frequent interactions with policymakers providing scope for 'consensus-building' (Pauly 1997; James 1996). The Fund also exerted influence through the G20 by providing the background papers underpinning research for policy recommendations for G20 crisis meetings and summits. One mechanism where the IMF's renewed role as a font of economic knowledge became formalized was through the Fund's G20 'secretariat' role, which was an important means for IMF thinking to inform crisis-defining and crisis legacy-defining ideas amongst advanced economy policymakers. For example, an IMF staff note prepared for the G20 meetings in London in March 2009 (IMF 2009a: 17–22) set out a variety of fiscal multiplier assessments to guide fiscal stimulus efforts (Spilimbergo et al. 2009: 3). One focus and conduit for Fund influence was the 'mutual assessment process', designed to monitor imbalances and promote sustainable balanced growth, introduced at the Pittsburgh G20 in 2009. This created a framework through which Fund staff discussed with national authorities medium-term policy frameworks, policy options to deliver objectives, and the development of 'more specific policy recommendations for the G20 leaders' (IMF 2009i: 2–3; Blanchard 2010c).

Thirdly, the chances of gaining traction are enhanced by focusing on policy questions where *the Fund itself* is in the vanguard of doing the policy-oriented research work. Where the Fund can itself provide corroboration of claims, and is doing the cutting-edge research, this can shift the asymmetry of knowledge (between Fund and national authorities) back in the Fund's favour. IMF bricoleurs in key places of authority, notably leadership within the Research Department and FAD, had from 2008 onwards deployed their troops working on these crucial fiscal policy issues, and the fruits of these labours were finding expression in Fund flagship publications, *WEO* and *Fiscal Monitor*, as well as through multilateral and bilateral surveillance more broadly. Key themes included the need to support aggregate demand using macroeconomic policy, the need to avoid all countries consolidating at once, and fiscal multipliers were likely higher during a downturn following a financial crisis—and hence the case for delaying fiscal consolidation until the recovery was well entrenched and stronger. To gain maximum traction, Fund policy advice ideally requires a combination of theoretical argument, and also qualitative *and* quantitative evidence, drawing on the IMF's wealth of cross-country experience (the corroboration and authoritative recognition mechanisms identified in Chapter 2). The Fund sought to insinuate its fiscal policy thinking and prioritization into the international economic policy debate, and in this it was aided and abetted by the institutional and intellectual sources of its authority discussed above.

Fourthly, the nature of Fund influence is not primarily about impressing upon national authorities policy ideas that had not occurred to them. Rather, the Fund can inflect policy thinking by playing ideas (like fiscal stimulus) 'onside' (see Chapter 7). As one senior French Treasury economist noted, French authorities had already been considering fiscal stimulus, but

> the Fund participates and makes it possible, because the Fund, usually, is not the one that advocates for fiscal stimulus. So, when you have the Fund saying we should do one, everybody listens more. You could say, if even these guys say that we need to do something, it means that we have to do something.[8]

Expansionary fiscal policy was outside the realms of respectable economic policy at the time, implying as it does higher deficits which might provoke adverse market reaction. By relying on the IMF's independence and scientific, technocratic reputation, Fund staff can use the institution's 'seal of approval' to provide intellectual legitimacy for economic ideas. This can be particularly important where national authorities embrace ideas not hitherto within the day-to-day economic management toolkit. The Fund can also, in building stronger corroboration behind policies national authorities were already contemplating, shape their operationalization.

The final insight about the conditions under which the Fund can gain influence, flowing from the CI approach of this book, is the recognition that ideas matter for the form they take, not just their content (see Schmidt 2008, 2010). Particular ideas, presented in carefully crafted forms, can act as the conduits of Fund influence. The notion of fiscal space, developed in section 4.7, is the most salient case in point in the realms of post-crash IMF fiscal policy advice.

All interviewees within the Fund noted with approval how, under these specific conditions, Strauss-Kahn's political acumen enabled the Fund to wield influence beyond its material resources or its direct leverage capabilities vis-à-vis powerful members. In this phase the Fund's definition of the crisis,

[8] Interview with Anne Epaulard, former Deputy Assistant Director at the Treasury Department at the French Ministry of Finance, September 2013.

crisis legacy, and recommended policy responses resonated widely with national authorities. The conjuncture combined with careful framing of its counsel maximized Fund 'traction'. This moment more than any other secured the revival in fortunes of the Fund as a key economic policy advisor—to the advanced as well as other economies. The crash saw the Fund transformed from an institution enacting significant staff cuts and engaged in soul-searching about its role (Kaya 2012: 24–5; Woods 2010: 51) to premier global fiscal policy advisor, with increased resources and enhanced global authority on increasingly crucial fiscal matters in and through fora such as European summits and the G20. The crisis jolted Fund economists to recognize that, contrary to received wisdom in pre-crisis macroeconomics, it was not safe to make 'linear' assumptions about a natural return to something approximating an optimal equilibrium (see Chapter 3; Blanchard 2014a). As Fund speeches and *Staff Position Notes* subsequently set out, such international coordination would increase the size of the fiscal multipliers, and thus the beneficial output effect of expansionary fiscal policy. IMF research, speeches, and publications provided a compelling analysis of why the specific autumn 2008 crisis conditions necessitated fiscal stimulus (IMF 2008d).

The Politics of Austerity and the Social Construction of Fiscal Space

Within the politics of austerity, the Fund used its concept of fiscal space which it had been developing since the mid-2000s to couch and frame its policy narrative (Heller 2005; Ostry et al. 2010). Its imprecision notwithstanding, fiscal space was crucially important in enabling the Fund to differentiate its policy message according to national conditions, trajectories, and debt structures and maturities. The Fund's social construction of 'sound' economic policy was refracted through this prism. The increased degree of differentiation is a key evolution of the post-GFC Fund. The fiscal space framing offered licence for Fund staff and missions to adjust how, and how far, debt and deficit reduction should be prioritized over other objectives, such as boosting aggregate demand, and supporting economic growth. This provided scope to counter the myopic focus on deficit and debt reduction prevalent in some European capitals, notably Berlin and London. In short, the strategic doctrinal flexibility of key players within the Fund was enacted and operationalized through the concept of fiscal space.

Notions of fiscal credibility and rectitude are social constructions, arising intersubjectively out of shared understandings amongst a variety of actors in the world economy, notably financial market participants. As Rodney Bruce Hall puts it, 'credibility is a social relationship as much as (or rather more than) an economic relationship' (2008: 2); its assessment is mediated by intersubjective processes through which market participants take cues about how to gauge a country's fiscal sustainability and economic health. Keynes' beauty contest analogy illustrated how credibility with financial markets is shaped by conventions and arises out of actor expectations about the expectations of others (Keynes 1936: 156, 1937: 114–18; Blyth 2002a: 42; Kirshner 2003b: 264–5; Widmaier 2003a & b, 2004). These dynamics mean that the Fund's surveillance and publication machinery, and its track record, constituted considerable convention-creating and convention-shaping resources as the IMF sought to edit post-crash understandings of fiscal rectitude. The Fund, given its knowledge base and long experience assisting countries facing economic crises in restoring their fiscal position and creditworthiness, was well placed to act as arbiter of fiscal credibility (Broome 2008; Clift & Tomlinson 2008a).

What matters for fiscal credibility is not just the raw data on public finances, but the lens through which the data is interpreted—how actors 'make sense' of fiscal issues. The foundations of shared understandings about fiscal credibility are underlying economic ideas, which are shaped and reshaped intersubjectively. The Fund's 'productive power' and ability to 'set and fix' meanings can come into its own under such conditions (Barnett & Duvall 2005; Best 2010). The Fund's intellectual framework for analysing fiscal credibility and sustainability issues is the manifestation of the economic policy norms it seeks to disseminate. This could—Fund actors hoped—provide a template for how to make sense of fiscal issues in the wake of the crash. This intellectual framework has been evolving in recent times in ways which illustrate and underscore the heightened contingency and differentiation of Fund fiscal policy advice. The content and emphasis of fiscal advice shifted under the post-crash 'new normal'. For years, IMF fiscal thinking had emphasized 'prudent fiscal policy', foregrounding deficit bias and fiscal sustainability concerns, with staff advising countries to build up fiscal buffers (Fischer 2001a; IMF 1995a & b; Daniel et al. 2006). The crash provided a conjuncture where (some) advanced economies were counselled that they ought to *use* their fiscal buffers to boost demand.

Created by the Fund, but only sparingly theorized and specified (Ostry et al. 2010; IMF 2012c: 4–7), the definition of fiscal space is somewhat elusive, and gets used in different ways within the Fund (contrast Heller 2005 with Ostry et al. 2010). Although initially developed in 2005–6 by former FAD Deputy Director Peter Heller, the concept really gained prominence in the Fund only after 2008–9, when articulated by Deputy Director of the Research Department Jonathan Ostry and others. It became central to the intellectual framework the Fund put forward to frame fiscal policy discussions and commentary. The days of 'one-size-fits-all', so maligned by critics of the Fund, were gone. Fiscal space underscored how the levels of policy space open to advanced economies vary widely depending on debt structure and maturity, revenue-raising capacity, financial market access conditions, and perceptions of creditworthiness. These national specificities affect 'the degree to which each country has fiscal space' (Spilimbergo et al. 2008: 11; IMF 2010b: 5–6). In short, given the diverse positions which advanced economies faced, some countries had much more leeway than others to delay fiscal adjustment in order to support economic recovery.

Fiscal space involves the assessment of a debt limit, a point at which debt servicing costs exceed a government's ability to raise revenue through taxation, or cutting expenditure; 'fiscal space is basically just the arithmetic that follows from that... a country's distance from its debt limit. It's the gap between your current or your projected debt and the point at which markets cut you off.'[9] It involves a prudential approach to debt and fiscal policy given the 'sharp discontinuity' in borrowing costs as countries approach their debt limit; 'you're going to be able to borrow at something close to the risk-free rate—almost right up to the point where you fall off the edge and markets cut you off completely' and therefore it makes sense to keep well away from a country's debt limit, and preserve significant fiscal space.[10] To an extent, entreaties to keep well away from one's debt limit chimes with long-standing Fund risk aversion where fiscal sustainability is concerned. Yet for countries with fiscal positions well away from their debt limits, fiscal space potentially offers much more leeway.

The luxury of 'fiscal space' is thus conditional upon national specific trajectories, factors, legacies, and institutional contexts. This is a recognition of 'heightening market sensitivity to variations in fiscal performance across countries', and 'increased attention being paid by markets to differences in underlying fiscal conditions across countries' (IMF 2010b: 5; IMF 2009h: 18–19). This is one reason why the post-GFC Fund has not developed new policy norms or new 'associational templates' (Broome & Seabrooke 2007) for fiscal policy which could be applied to all Fund members. Moreover, new policy templates for fiscal policy did not lend themselves to the Fund's more contingent, differentiated persuasive efforts amidst the politics of austerity. Instead of hard and fast new templates or targets, IMF efforts focused on attempts to shape the climate of fiscal policy opinion more broadly. The Fund used fiscal space to reshape views of what fiscal rectitude looked like in the post-crash environment.

Fiscal space is a judgement call,[11] enabling Fund staff to weave qualitative evaluations of a government's reputation and track record into assessments of

[9] Interview with IMF Research Department Deputy Director Jonathan Ostry, June 2013.
[10] Interview with IMF Research Department Deputy Director Jonathan Ostry, June 2013.
[11] A term used by numerous Fund staff interviewees when discussing the concept of fiscal space.

quantitative fiscal policy data. It is another instance of how important, yet under-reported, subjective judgements are in IMF decision-making (see Nelson 2014, 2017). There is not a 'formulaic approach', but rather 'a lot of judgement involved' which is 'informed by expertise, on-going experience, and by the multilateral work [of the Fund]'.[12] Fiscal space comes down to a rule-of-thumb assessment taking into account the various national historical and contextual factors, along with intangible reputational aspects, in gauging fiscal policy credibility. The shift in Fund fiscal policy thinking outlined in this book is contingent upon the Fund deeming countries to enjoy fiscal space. Crucially, fiscal space can be used to navigate around perennial Fund deficit bias concerns to open up room to manoeuvre and access a more fiscally active counter-cyclical policy agenda.

The non-quantifiable and not directly measurable quality of the fiscal space concept provides latitude for Fund staff to define what constitutes economic policy virtue for particular economies. Evocations of fiscal space are built upon views about what the policy priorities for particular governments should be. For all countries, the Fund medium-term goal is to get their public finances in order—targeting a structural fiscal balance and encouraging the building up of fiscal buffers in good times. Fund counsel involves countries ensuring they have 'a decently sized buffer (and so you have debt well below your debt limit)'[13] and aiming 'for structural rather than nominal targets'.[14] At the same time, a key lesson the Fund drew from the crisis, reinforced by its post-crash research, was that fiscal policy was a more powerful counter-cyclical tool than had hitherto been appreciated. Fund surveillance, couched in terms of fiscal space, sought to encourage those countries not under fiscal strain to keep sight of that. In tandem with the rehabilitation of fiscal policy as a tool of economic stabilization, fiscal space brought to the fore a broader range of economic policy levers and options for national economic policy-makers to use.

The Fund enjoyed some success in gaining 'traction' for its views on fiscal policy. Its concept of fiscal space was, for example, taken up and used by Fitch in their ratings process.[15] This is an example of how, following the crisis, for advanced economies, the IMF became more relevant as an assessor of (and source of credibility for) advanced economy government policies than had been the case in previous decades (Moschella 2010b: 431–2; Lutz & Kranke 2014; Broome 2010b; Joyce 2012). It demonstrates how the IMF is one of a

[12] Interview with Vivek Arora, then Deputy Director of the Strategy, Policy and Review Department, September 2013.

[13] Interview with IMF Research Department Deputy Director Jonathan Ostry, June 2013.

[14] Interview with former IMF European Department Deputy Director Alessandro Leipold, September 2013.

[15] Interview with IMF Research Department Deputy Director Jonathan Ostry, June 2013.

very small number of actors or institutions in the world economy that can shape and even generate these conventional understandings about sound fiscal positions and legitimate or credible economic policies.

The Wax and Wane of Fund Influence over Advanced Economy Fiscal Policy Debates

The framing of Fund economic policy counsel, then, can influence the likelihood of IMF advice gaining 'traction'. The distinction made earlier in the book between 'what's going on?' and 'what is to be done?' is important here. It helps throw into relief the ebb and flow, and the limits of Fund influence over advanced economies. The IMF can more confidently advance its interpretation of 'what is going on?', since that falls within its surveillance mandate and does not require any particular response from its members. It is thus less evident when Fund interpretation of the economic situation goes unheeded. On the other hand, the Fund has to be circumspect in pressing for 'what is to be done?' because the latter requires buy-in from member governments. Fund staff are mindful of the adverse effect on IMF credibility of direct and explicit economic policy advice or recommendations being ignored.

The IMF's initial success in 2008 and early 2009 in garnering support for its interpretations of what's going on and what is to be done, and orchestrating crisis responses was built on contingent foundations. After initial consensus around crisis response, where all advanced economies seemed to embrace fiscal activism and the need for coordinated stimulus, fiscal policy opinion began to fracture. As the Great Recession drew on, daylight began to emerge between Fund thinking and the priorities of many advanced economy governments about the conduct of economic policy. From mid-2009 onwards, as public finances deteriorated, and it seemed that another Great Depression *had* been averted, fiscal consolidation became increasingly centre stage. In the second half of 2009, disputes emerged over the pace of exit from fiscal stimulus (see Chapter 5). This provoked intense debates as to 'how far?' and 'how fast?', around the politics of austerity (Blyth 2013a; Streeck & Schafer 2013; Hall 2012). The Fund agreed that fiscal adjustment was necessary, but was convinced it could and should wait until the economic recovery had been strengthened further by macroeconomic policies in support of demand. Views of many advanced economy governments on the appropriate balance of prioritization between fiscal consolidation (debt and deficit reduction) and supporting growth and the very fragile recovery began to drift away from the IMF's position.

One indicator of the contingency of Fund influence was the status of the G20 MAP process. Key Fund figures noted that as the conditions which fostered remarkable levels of international coordination waned, the policy coordination capacities of the MAP were called into question (Faruqee & Srinivasan 2012). The Fund continued to provide research notes for G20 (see e.g. IMF 2012l), and used them to promote its agenda, notably by bringing threats of 'secular stagnation' to policymakers' attention (IMF 2014e). These did not garner such widespread acclaim as Fund advice had done in the immediate post-crash period.

The IMF continued to confidently proclaim its account of the crisis, and its legacy—'what's going on', but became more circumspect in advancing its prescriptive discourse on 'what is to be done?' This revealed the limits of Fund influence within the surveillance relationship in a context from 2010 onwards where many advanced economies not facing financing constraints saw the Fund as something of an 'outlier' in its enthusiasm for rehabilitating fiscal policy activism. Many advanced economies wanted to proceed further and faster with fiscal consolidation than the Fund thought wise. More qualifiers were inserted into its policy advice, and a wider range of scenarios were set out in its forecasting. Fund flagship publications and surveillance reports even included boxes presenting the cases for and against front-loaded as opposed to slower paced fiscal consolidation (IMF 2010l: 11, IMF 2010k: 28). A gap emerged between the policy settings the Fund was recommending, and the more austerity-oriented instincts of the governments of major countries such as Germany and the UK. Under these conditions, the IMF's capacity to shape the post-crash debate about fiscal policy conduct and the politics of austerity was reduced. Chapters 5 to 7 of this book chart the ebb and flow of Fund influence over the international fiscal policy debate in more detail.

Conclusion

The Fund has a potentially significant coordination and information sharing role to play for advanced economies in pursuit of stability and growth. It comes across in lengthy interviews that the surveillance function, seeking to live up to the role of guarantors of stability in international monetary relations, is the larger part of Fund staff's self-understanding of their purpose, and the IMF's role in the world economy. As has been shown in this chapter, the interpretive framework through which economic policy is assessed and evaluated crucially underpins the Fund's surveillance functions through which the Fund works to impress its interpretation upon member countries. These efforts are not always successful—especially where advanced economies are concerned. Yet Fund views on economic policy matter because they shape the international climate of opinion, even if they are not directly heeded.

In 2008, in pursuit of its mandate to bolster stability in international monetary affairs, the Fund thus enjoyed some legitimacy and authority in calling for advanced economies to engage in coordinated global fiscal stimulus. In a kind of Keynesian praxis, the Fund's key economic policy thinkers were operating in a world where they perceived what economists call multiple possible equilibria (see Chapter 3). The Keynesian-sympathetic subculture—including in very high places within the Fund—gained succour from their alignment with key economic policy figures in the US administration. The range of possibilities included damaging downward spirals—the impending threat of another 'Great Depression' facing all the advanced economies. Under conditions where all were motivated to act together to counter this threat, the Fund provided the ideal tools, in its knowledge bank, intellectual authority, and its capacity to facilitate international coordination through its seat at the table.

Thereafter, through its surveillance and other interactions with policymakers, Fund actors sought to subtly reshape how fiscal issues were understood in the 'new normal' for advanced economies. Influential Fund figures sought to revisit prevailing understandings of 'sound' fiscal policy using their new concept of fiscal space, a framing device for policy recommendations which vary markedly for different countries. This is in part the result of a reflexive Fund keen to learn, and be seen to learn, from its performance in past crises, and accusations of 'one-size-fits-all' or 'cookie cutter' approach to economic policy advice (IEO 2014). As this chapter has underlined, Fund influence over non-borrowing advanced economies is contingent upon careful framing of its advice, and permissive conditions which obtained in the immediate post-crash period. From 2010 onwards, Fund called for advanced economies to coordinate fiscal adjustment to prevent all countries consolidating at once, for surplus countries to invest more to boost demand, and for 'backloading' to limit the adverse effect on growth proved less successful.

Fiscal space is a social construct, containing the value judgements which, as pointed out in the Introduction to this book, are inextricably part of economic policy assessment (see also Best & Widmaier 2006). The careful construction of fiscal space allowed the Fund to critique the overriding prioritization of deficit and debt reduction of some advanced economy governments, without seeming to get drawn into a political argument. Yet the Fund sails close to the wind in using fiscal space to critique the austerity-oriented approach of advanced economies, such as Germany and the UK. In advocating a different policy prioritization, the Fund lets its 'technocratic' and 'scientific' façade slip. The focal points of IMF research and policy commentary and recommendation entail the institution getting involved in the politics of austerity. We explore how that fiscal policy line has evolved, and how IMF bricoleurs have looked for openings to make pointed interventions in the politics of austerity debate, in Chapter 5.

5

The Fund's Fiscal Policy Views and the Politics of Austerity

Introduction

This chapter charts the Fund's extensive revisiting since 2008 of pre-crisis assumptions about fiscal policy efficacy and conduct, and economic stabilization. It examines how the IMF sought to influence the international economic policy debate and the politics of austerity. Blyth (2013b: 206–10) and Gamble (2014: 64) see the IMF as falling in step with the austerity prescriptions which, from 2010 onwards, came to dominate much advanced economy discussion around the nature of the crisis and its aftermath, and appropriate policy responses. Rather, as this chapter demonstrates, the Fund's role within the politics of austerity debate builds on its self-appointed role as a font of economic knowledge and arbiter of sound policy within the world economy. IMF bricoleurs such as Strauss-Kahn, Lagarde, Blanchard, Ostry, Cotarelli, and many others rethought the appropriate underpinnings of and settings for post-crash economic policy. Leveraging its mandate for pursuing international coordination and economic stability, as well as its knowledge bank and scientific reputation (see Chapter 4), the Fund's prescriptive policy discourse sought to counter and correct certain premises of austerity policies which it saw as mistaken.

Fund staff recognize that there are always trade-offs, for example between short-term and longer-term goals, in economic policy recommendation. Thus, using fiscal policy more can support growth and recovery but can also have future implications for the health of public finances, economic credibility, and borrowing costs. Arguably, the whole 'politics of austerity' debate has been about how to approach such trade-offs. Those favouring austerity policies have been overwhelmingly of the view that the long-term public finances considerations trump all. The Fund used the social construction of fiscal space (see Chapter 4) to escape the singular fixation upon debt and deficit reduction, favouring instead medium-term fiscal frameworks credibly committing to fiscal sustainability, combined with short-term macroeconomic activism to boost demand and growth.

The IMF advanced the case, on a contingent basis, for a very different approach to that trade off—prioritizing more macroeconomic policy activism to support demand and foster growth, and indeed to tackle inequality. The Fund challenged the view that fiscal consolidation would be expansionary, and counselled against a focus on debt reduction to the exclusion of supporting growth (Ban & Gallagher 2015). Fiscal consolidation, the Fund underlined, can be self-defeating and lead to *increased* debt to GDP ratios through its adverse effects on growth. They have also called for international coordination, urging pointedly that advanced economies should not all consolidate at once. Surplus countries, and Germany in particular, were called upon to do more to boost global demand (Decressin 2012; IMF 2014d: 20; Lagarde 2017). More fundamentally, the IMF has called relentlessly for the use of public power, and central bank actions, to build firewalls powerful enough to effectively limit financial market contagion (Lagarde 2012a). In so doing, it sought to increase fiscal space and expand the macroeconomic policy options of advanced economies facing the crisis.

One of the Fund's more pointed interventions was in repeatedly raising inequality concerns about which societal groups bear the burden of adjustment. A consistent theme of surveillance of advanced economies is that fiscal adjustment must be 'fair' if consolidation efforts are to be sustained, and socially and politically accepted (Lipton 2013a). The Fund has paid very close attention since 2008 to the distributive consequences of post-crash macroeconomic policies in the advanced economies, much more so than in the East Asian crisis of the 1990s (on which see Chwieroth 2010). This prioritization of equity considerations, including *within* fiscal adjustment, and the need for macroeconomic policy to tackle inequality has been a clear hallmark of Fund commentary under both Strauss-Kahn and Lagarde. This is perhaps the most dramatic shift in the yardsticks by which the Fund assesses the success or failure of economic policy. As Ostry has pointed out, 'the period of great moderation was only great for a small portion of the population, and so it was not delivering broad-based benefits (as seen for example in the stagnation of median wages in a number of countries).'[1] This has been one of the angles from which the Fund policy recommendations have advanced a measured yet powerful critique of austerity policies. Ostry continues, 'Fiscal policy, fortuitously, is more potent in periods of economic slack such as the aftermath of the global financial crisis, so it makes sense to use it. And to use it

[1] Interview with Deputy Director of the IMF Research department Jonathan Ostry, June 2013.

not only for counter-cyclical purposes, but also to facilitate redistribution, which itself can help to spur economic growth.'[2] Fund work by Ostry and others demonstrated how avoiding excessive levels of inequality can actually help economies grow more strongly and more sustainably (Berg & Ostry 2011; Ostry et al. 2014), such that fiscal redistribution, calibrated correctly, can improve equality and deliver stronger, as well as more inclusive, growth (Lagarde 2014a).

The analysis below charts how a Keynesian-sympathetic interpretation of the crisis, and crisis legacy, won out within the Fund's internal battle of economic ideas. It situates the Fund's evolving thinking within the wider politics of austerity, and charts how the Fund's post-crash views on fiscal policy efficacy and the conduct of economic stabilization were increasingly at odds with other key European players. A key battleground in the Eurozone crisis has been over what constitutes 'sound' and 'unsound' fiscal policy, with ECB Governor Trichet, the German and Dutch Finance Ministers and others calling for more powers to enforce budgetary austerity and fiscal soundness. For the Fund, by contrast, the central lesson of the Eurozone crisis was the need to complete construction of effective fiscal backstops to limit contagion. The Fund continuously called for expanded and more muscular lender and spender of last resort functionality for the European Central bank (ECB) and European Stability Mechanism (ESM). More generally, the Fund's empirically backed policy advice advocated a 'less now, more later' approach to consolidation by countries with fiscal space.

The Fund's Re-Evaluation of Fiscal Policy Potency and Efficacy for Advanced Economies

The crisis had begun in July 2007, and as 2008 wore on, Strauss-Kahn and others at the Fund became increasingly convinced that significant shifts in macroeconomic policy conduct and thinking were needed to avert an economic catastrophe. Notably, Strauss-Kahn argued for a global fiscal stimulus at the January 2008 Davos world economic forum. This contradicted pre-crisis received wisdom that fiscal policy was a problematic stabilization tool due to implementation lags, and question marks surrounding its efficacy and whether spending could be 'credibly temporary'. Thereafter, in the April 2008 *WEO* the Fund urged the ECB to pursue a more accommodating monetary policy to counter the looming crisis (IMF 2008a: 77), but its July Euro Area Mission received short shrift from an ECB with a very different reading of the

[2] Interview with Deputy Director of the IMF Research department Jonathan Ostry, June 2013.

economic situation. The Fund saw—presciently as it turned out—the deflationary risks posed by the increasing turmoil in financial markets, and hence argued for no change in interest rates, or a cut (IMF 2008b). The ECB, by contrast, was fixated upon higher inflationary pressures and chose to raise rates despite growing evidence of deteriorating credit channels and financial conditions.

Although the niceties of IMF communication cloaked this, the Fund saw key economic policy authorities as making the wrong policy choices in response to the looming crisis. The Fund's research, surveillance, and commentary efforts focused on trying to encourage policymakers to rethink their understanding of the economic conjuncture. The first intervention fleshing out the fiscal stimulus agenda was delivered before the worst effects of the crisis had yet been felt. The April 2008 *WEO* contained a discussion entitled 'Can fiscal stimulus be effective' amidst a discussion of whether Europe could avoid a sharp slowdown, with the answer in the affirmative (2008a: 70–8). This was followed by a chapter entitled 'Fiscal policy as a counter-cyclical tool', in the October 2008 *WEO*. This recognized some familiar potential pitfalls, such as the implications for government debt, and whether in an open economy, 'fiscal stimulus might simply "leak out"'. Nevertheless, the study found that the prevailing assumptions of fiscal policy's inefficacy were misguided. The chapter found considerable support for the 'Keynesian position' where 'output is highly responsive to changes in fiscal policy', concluding 'empirical evidence suggests that discretionary fiscal stimulus has a moderately positive effect on output growth in advanced economies' (IMF 2008c: 160–3).

Earlier in this book we noted the importance of mechanisms of ideational change within the Fund, notably 'reconciliation' of new thinking with preexisting Fund doctrine (see Chapter 2). In this vein, the *WEO* chapter criticizes the failures of all governments to build up fiscal buffers in good times (IMF 2008c: 163). This more fiscally conservative reiteration of deficit bias concerns is a hardy perennial of IMF commentary on fiscal policy throughout the ages. As 'the voice of the Fund', *WEO* chapters need to command broad assent from across the different departments. If earlier drafts fail to pay sufficient attention to fiscal sustainability considerations, the internal peer review process offers scope to reassert them. What is more surprising is the *WEO* chapter's combination of familiar fiscal prudence themes with a confident assertion that fiscal stimulus *can* be timed right, delivered quickly enough, and well-targeted. The take-home point at the heart of the chapter is a thorough rehabilitation of 'the role of fiscal policy in stabilizing output'. This extends beyond automatic stabilizers to include discretionary fiscal policy (IMF 2008c: 160–2).

As noted in Chapter 2, crucial to the fiscal policy rethink was that influential senior figures—including Strauss-Kahn as Managing Director and Blanchard as incoming Chief Economist—were on board and encouraged a questioning of pre-crash orthodoxy (see Blanchard 2008b; Blanchard & Cottarelli 2008; Strauss-Kahn 2008a & b; IMF Research Department 2008). This more Keynesian thinking from 2008–9 onwards extended beyond fiscal policy to include financial markets and capital controls (see Chwieroth 2014: 461–2; 2010; Moschella 2015). This social process of recalibrating the Fund's line also involved informal, ad hoc advocacy, by mid-range officials to build up a groundswell of support. Another key figure was Carlo Cottarelli, the incoming Director of FAD in September 2008. He noted that, faced with the GFC conditions of 'a demand deficiency recession... abetted by uncertainty and rising unemployment' and collapsing output, 'Keynes's *General Theory* was the relevant textbook' (Cottarelli et al. 2014: 1). The power and resources at the disposal of department leadership, combined with the Fund's hierarchical norms, is important in mobilizing analytical effort to pursue particular research agendas, designed to feed into the wider policy debate. FAD was normally a bastion of fiscal conservatism—so Cottarelli was important in winning the internal battle of ideas in 2008.

With these *WEO* chapters, fiscal policy as an active tool of economic stabilization began its brisk post-crash march to renewed respectability within the Fund. The analysis is contingent and contextual, applying only to certain countries. Senior Fund figures underlined how the Fund's theory and evidence suggests fiscal policy is *particularly* effective for advanced economies in the specific conditions of economic downturn following a financial crisis which prevailed after 2008.[3] There is explicit differentiation between advanced economies and others, with the former deemed more likely and able to pursue effective economic stabilization through fiscal policy (Scott 2008).

Fiscal Policy for the Crisis

As the global financial crisis deepened in the autumn of 2008, the Fund took centre stage in efforts to coordinate international policy responses. At the pre-meeting in Sao Paulo of the International Monetary and Financial Committee (IMFC), the policy-setting body representing the IMF's 185 member countries, the IMF was asked to take the lead in preparations for the G7 in October 2008 (IMF 2008e). With Strauss-Kahn at the helm, the IMF was again advocating monetary easing, more vociferously than earlier that summer, and urging global action to support financial markets. Strauss-Kahn and Blanchard called for global fiscal stimulus in a bid to prop up demand, restore some confidence, and avert another Great Depression. Continuing the theme of a differentiated

[3] Interviews with Blanchard, Cottarelli, Mauro, Ostry, June 2013–September 2014.

approach to policy advice, Jorg Decressin, Editor-in-Chief of *WEO*, pinpointed in the press conference accompanying publication of the flagship, that the US, Germany, and China could and should pursue additional fiscal stimulus (IMF 2008d). As noted in Chapter 4, international coordination in pursuit of stability in the world economy is at the core of its legal mandate, and this bolstered the authority of Fund actions. Fund speeches and publications underscored how (Keynesian) economic theory indicated that fiscal stimulus would be much more effective if internationally coordinated (IMF Research Department 2008; Blanchard 2008b; Spilimbergo et al. 2008).

This all paved the way, in November 2008, for the 2 per cent global fiscal stimulus target agreed as the centrepiece of the G20 action plan brokered by Strauss-Kahn and the Fund. The significant but somewhat 'back of the envelope' intervention was finessed in the context of a G20 summit, the headline figure arrived at to secure maximum international assent. As Blanchard put it, 'why don't we have a call for fiscal stimulus, we thought of numbers, 1 was too small, 3 was too big, 2 seemed about right . . . it was still a number out of a hat', 'more would have scared the fiscal conservatives, less really didn't seem to be enough'.[4] The final 2 per cent figure, which emerged through the feedback loops from discussions with advanced economy leaders, reflected the fruits of a 'Goldilocks approach' to international economic policy diplomacy.[5] This was a particularly stark instance of a strategic Fund responding to the feedback loops to arrive at a policy recommendation which aligned with what they deemed the conjuncture required, but was also politically viable. The 2 per cent fiscal stimulus was both consistent with its view of what needed to be done, but also stood a good chance of gaining 'buy-in' from, and being implemented by, powerful member countries (see Chapter 4). Hence the Fund's investing of political capital in the proposal.

The Fund's high-profile endorsement of fiscal activism 'played onside' a whole set of fiscal policy options for governments which lay outside what had been the 'Great Moderation' policy mainstream. Under conditions where the pre-crash approaches offered no answers to the pressing economic policy questions of the hour, economic policy rectitude was up in the air, and markets were tumbling, there was a risk that sudden embrace of leftfield economic policy ideas could exacerbate credibility concerns and further fuel market instability. Yet if *even the IMF* was saying this, then it *must* constitute sound fiscal policy.

Calling for expansionary fiscal policy on this substantial scale, all but regardless of the state of the public finances, was a very unusual stance for the Fund. It had not gone through normal channels in terms of Fund internal

[4] Interview with IMF Chief Economist Olivier Blanchard, June 2013.

[5] This was a point made unprompted by numerous Fund interviewees.

review, and bypassed any opposition from more fiscally conservative voices. Instead, this new Fund position was experienced as a surprise by some inside the Fund. Nor was there scope—if a clear and bold statement was to be made to panicking politicians—to add the normal qualifiers which accompany Fund policy recommendations. Caveats about country public finances conditions were omitted in order to deliver a clear unambiguous, actionable message. Strauss-Kahn saw that this was a window of opportunity to seize and shape the international economic policy agenda. The extraordinary events called for an unambiguous and timely intervention which could garner widespread support and achieve the desired resonance.[6]

Once the 2 per cent global fiscal stimulus number was 'out there', Fund economists were tasked with providing the intellectual bulwark substantiating the case for global fiscal stimulus. As Blanchard put it, it was a case of 'there is a fire, we'll use the hose' and 'in a way the scientific work was done a bit ex post'.[7] The Staff Position Note *Fiscal Policy for the Crisis* published in December 2008 provided the rationale and justification. Significantly for the internal politics of ideational change within the institution, its authors included Blanchard and Cottarelli, the directors of two key departments, FAD and Research (Blanchard & Cottarelli 2008).

> The optimal fiscal package should be timely, large, lasting, diversified, contingent, collective, and sustainable: timely, because the need for action is immediate; large, because the current and expected decrease in private demand is exceptionally large; lasting because the downturn will last for some time; diversified because of the unusual degree of uncertainty associated with any single measure; contingent, because the need to reduce the perceived probability of another 'Great Depression' requires a commitment to do more, if needed; collective, since each country that has fiscal space should contribute; and sustainable, so as not to lead to a debt explosion and adverse reactions of financial markets. (Spilimbergo et al. 2008: 2)

Whilst the October 2008 *WEO* chapter had made the *general* case for using fiscal policy as a counter-cyclical tool, it was the special case element of the argument that prevailed subsequently. This was easier to reconcile to a wider breadth of economic policy opinion within the Fund (see Chapter 2). The Fund's rehabilitation of fiscal policy emphasized the particular conjuncture of recessionary conditions, broken credit channels, liquidity trap problems, and the Zero Lower Bound. The latter hamstrings monetary policy, the normal 'go-to' economic stabilization tool (Spilimbergo et al. 2008; IMF 2009c: 98, 103–30; IMF 2008c: ch. 5). The Fund's bid to shape crisis responses was an iterative process. In March 2009, the Staff Position Note entitled *The Case for*

[6] Interviews with numerous members of Fund staff, June 2013–September 2014.

[7] Interview with IMF Chief Economist Olivier Blanchard, June 2013.

Global Fiscal Stimulus urged redoubled efforts and additional stimulus measures by advanced economies, beyond those already taken (Freedman et al. 2009: 16).

The concepts which pepper the Fund post-crash commentary are revealing of how the IMF wanted policy elites to rethink their responses to the crisis. The size of the output gap is afforded priority in Fund assessments of the policy context (see e.g. IMF 2009a: 29). As Mauro notes, thinking about the economy in terms of an output gap is built upon the assumption 'that fiscal policy has an impact on output', a view which was 'always there' at the Fund, despite being out of favour in academic economics for many years; 'Within the profession, there was a lot of scepticism about fiscal policy efficacy in the 80s and 90s but the Fund, and the OECD, were still among those within the profession who believed in the concept of the output gap—which you never hear about in American academia on economics.'[8] In this context, the output gap seeks to capture how much the crisis has reduced economic activity compared to the prior trend, seeing macroeconomic policy and deficient demand as primary causes of the shortfall. As Blanchard notes, thinking about post-crash economic policy in terms of larger output gaps reveals the strength within the Fund mindset of 'the view that in the short run it is aggregate demand which determines outcomes, which I would define as kind of meta-Keynesian'.[9] Consumption is down due to crisis turbulence and a credit crunch, hence 'Global fiscal stimulus is essential now to support aggregate demand and restore economic growth' (Freedman et al. 2009: 2).

Perhaps the most salient concept, however, was the fiscal multiplier, which economists use to gauge the potency for stabilization of fiscal policy. These had been somewhat neglected by many in the pre-crash Fund, assumed to be a modest 0.5 per cent (Hemming, Kell et al. 2002). From 2008 onwards those persuaded by the Keynesian rethink at the Fund underlined how international coordination can increase multipliers, and also how certain policy interventions (such as transfers to low income households) have higher multipliers: 'in the current circumstances, spending increases, and targeted tax cuts and transfers, are likely to have the highest multipliers' (Spilimbergo et al. 2008: 2). The beneficial interaction of fiscal and monetary policy was also foregrounded: 'expansionary fiscal policy combined with accommodative monetary policy can have significant multiplier effects on the world economy' (Freedman et al. 2009: 5).

Fund commentary focused on the enormous 'downside risks' of another Great Depression if counter-cyclical fiscal policy were insufficiently bold.

[8] Interview with Senior IMF Economist Paolo Mauro, a senior fellow at the Peterson Institute for International Economics at the time of the interview in 2014.

[9] Interview with IMF Chief Economist Olivier Blanchard, June 2013.

The Fund interpretation and definition of the crash brought with it new appreciation of the vulnerabilities and instabilities facing advanced economies. Its commentary and policy advice foregrounded looming 'non-linear' or self-aggravating threats, especially 'a vicious cycle of deep recession and deflation' (Freedman et al. 2009: 3; Blanchard 2008b; Blanchard & Cottarelli 2008). Back in 2002, an earlier IMF deflation task force, whilst noting that the danger of a global deflation was small, advocated pre-emptive action, and unorthodox policy responses if the threat strengthened. These included the fairly radical suggestion of using monetary expansion to finance activist fiscal policy (Kumar et al. 2003: 30). A member of that task force, Jorg Decressin, had by 2008 risen to Deputy Director of the Research department and Editor of *WEO*. In 2009, along with IMF Modeller in Chief Doug Laxton, he reprised these ideas, along with coordinated fiscal stimulus and unconventional monetary policy including quantitative easing. This policy toolkit was likely to be needed 'to prevent a deflationary episode becoming entrenched'. Countering objections from fiscal conservatives, the Fund urged that 'policymakers should err on the side of acting too soon rather than too late in countering deflationary shocks' (Decressin & Laxton 2009: 3–4, 6–9, 18–23). These insights permeated 'voice of the Fund' flagship outputs (IMF 2009a: 22–3; IMF 2009c: 29–31, 34), indicating the internal ascendancy of these views.

In the immediate aftermath of the crash, the IMF's calls for counter-cyclical fiscal activism resonated with advanced economy governments. The then IMF FAD Director Carlo Cottarelli noted that national governments were a welcoming audience for the Fund's policy message: 'it's an easier life if as any Mission Chief you say what the authorities are doing is right. Clearly the consensus of work and views in the G20 in 2008–9 was to expand fiscal policy.'[10] The Fund again provided research and background papers for the pre-meetings for G20 deputies in January/February 2009, where the agenda of the London G20 were discussed. The world economy, the Fund pointed out, was not out of the woods yet. Indeed, 'advanced economies will experience their sharpest contraction in the post-war period'. The Fund focused on the 'adverse feedback loop between the real and financial sectors', calling for a broad range of internationally coordinated policy action to 'bolster demand to sustain a durable recovery in global activity'. The fiscal stimulus programme, the IMF staff insisted, 'should support demand for a prolonged period of time and be applied broadly across countries with policy space to minimize cross-border leakages' (IMF 2009a). In the build-up to the London G20 in April, the IMF message was an unambiguous 'New Keynesian' call for public action and state intervention to reshape conventional understandings,

[10] Interview with then FAD Director Carlo Cottarelli, June 2013.

counter adverse market pathologies, and set the economy on a superior equilibrium path. 'In effect, governments can break the negative feedback between the real economy and financial conditions by acting as "spender of last resort"' (IMF 2009c: 126).

The Fund's focus on aggregate demand and higher multipliers contrasted with views of the ECB and German government, in particular. They remained rooted in pre-crisis assumptions about low multipliers, and a less Keynesian view of fiscal policy efficacy. In November 2008, Peer Steinbruck, the SPD Finance Minister in Germany, vociferously criticized the 'crass Keynesianism' of the UK government's tax-cutting efforts to stimulate the economy (2008). Meanwhile, Angel Merkel boycotted a meeting between Brown, Sarkozy, and Barroso to plan for an EU-wide €200bn fiscal stimulus plan.[11] Ahead of the London G20, members of the German government, the German Economic Council, and the Bundesbank President warned of the inflationary risks posed by the looser monetary policy in the US and elsewhere. This reinforced Merkel's own concerns. Germany had undertaken significant stimulus measures, notably increasing in-work subsidies to prevent lay-offs (Vail 2014), but were encouraged by the IMF, US, and UK authorities to go further. Merkel steadfastly rejected calls for still more fiscal stimulus, arguing that Germany had done enough already.[12] The risks of not only loose monetary policy, but also excessive public debt, were consistently highlighted by the German authorities. This policy prioritization was echoed by the ECB, notably its Governor, Jean-Claude Trichet, referred to in some quarters as a member of 'the inflation Taliban' (ECB insider, quoted in Braun 2014: 165–6).

Barnett & Finnemore (2004) see efforts to 'fix meanings' as ways that IOs seek to exercise power (see Chapter 4). Fund interpretation of the fiscal politics of the crisis is a case in point. The Fund's interpretation of the crisis, as revealed in contributions from Blanchard and others, was motivated by a kind of short-run 'Keynesian' view that demand had collapsed, and must be revived. The difficult trade-offs and policy dilemmas between the short-term (getting growth going) and long-term (sustainable public finances) were constantly at the forefront of post-crash economic policy reflection, as revealed when interviewing numerous Fund staff members. IMF advice recognized fiscal sustainability concerns, calling for 'credible medium-term fiscal frameworks' (IMF 2009b), with scope to use counter-cyclical fiscal policy conditional upon 'the fiscal space available' (Freedman et al. 2009: 3). Nevertheless, 'aggressive monetary and particularly fiscal measures are needed to support aggregate demand in the short term' (IMF 2009a: 98). The Fund saw short-term potentially catastrophic consequences of not providing sufficient stimulus as outweighing

[11] *Financial Times*, 11 December 2008.

[12] *Financial Times*, 27 March 2009.

medium-term debt sustainability risks. Trichet, Schäuble, Merkel, and others saw things rather differently. These differing interpretations and policy prioritizations would anchor, in the following years, the austerity debate. What is instructive is how the IMF did *not* see cutting public expenditure as priority number one. Indeed, the Fund consistently offered a counterpoint and corrective to German and other voices, rejecting trenchant fiscal conservatism in its analysis, research, and commentary. As the crisis drew on, views on the nature and timing of crisis response began to diverge. A key focal point for this dissonance was over the timing of 'exit' from stimulus measures.

The Evolving Crisis Narrative: From Macroeconomic Stimulus to Exit Strategies

As early as the second half of 2009, the European authorities (EC, ECB) began to urge turning off the taps of fiscal stimulus (González-Páramo 2009). The German and Dutch governments and some others began to argue for a precipitate exit, and a move towards fiscal consolidation. What had in the first instance been identified as a crisis of growth was becoming more widely understood as a crisis of debt (see e.g. Hay 2011b, 2013a & b; Gamble 2014; Blyth 2013a). In essence, was the principal economic problem facing the advanced economies in the wake of the crash best understood as too little growth, or too much debt? Not only the German government and the ECB, but smaller fiscal hawk countries in Europe including the Finns, the Dutch, and the Austrians lined up behind the 'crisis of debt' interpretation which entailed a shift towards austerity policies. The UK coalition government elected in May 2010 took a similar line.

Meanwhile, the IMF, the US, UK (before May 2010), France, and others were much less inclined to think in those terms. Strauss-Kahn reiterated the case for sustaining aggregate demand through counter-cyclical stimulus policies at the September 2009 G20.[13] In similar vein, the October 2009 *WEO* warned against 'premature and incoherent exit' from stimulus measures—for it was these policy interventions, the Fund was convinced, that were propping up the recovery. The timing of exit strategies was a major discussion theme of the Ecofin meeting of Europe's finance ministers in Gothenburg in early October 2009 (Ecofin 2009). A few days later, ECB Governor Trichet highlighted the 'increasingly pressing' need for 'ambitious and realistic fiscal exit and

[13] Chris Giles, 'Fiscal Stimulus: Weaned off the stimulus', *Financial Times*, 23 September 2009.

consolidation strategies', in the context of discussing ECB plans (which in hindsight look rather premature) to wind down its monetary stimulus.[14]

In the background of these differing views were political economic assumptions about state/market interconnections (see Chapter 1): would public action deliver superior outcomes, or impede efficiency enhancing actions of the private sector? The ECB et al. were confident that the private sector would 'take up the slack' and be the motor of recovery, whilst more public spending was just building up future debt problems, hence advocacy of withdrawing state support. The IMF and others, on the other hand, saw public power as necessary to restore confidence, stimulate economic activity, repair the financial system, and nurture the advanced economies back towards recovery. This built into a terse exchange between Strauss-Kahn and Trichet over the ECB's exit strategy from looser monetary policy in November and December 2009 which played out in the pages of the *Financial Times*, which operates as a sounding board for such financial elites to air their views to a wider informed audience.[15] Strauss-Kahn urged erring 'on the side of caution, as exiting too early is costlier than exiting too late' (2009), but Trichet and the ECB took a different view.[16]

Blyth has convincingly argued that those seeing the post-crash scenario as a crisis of public debt neglected the root causes of the crisis, namely, excessive risk-taking in the private sector. Rather than recognizing that socialization of these immense risks to save the financial system caused much of the deterioration in public finances, 'crisis of debt' interpretations asserted that profligate public spending caused all post-crash economic woes (2013a: 71–4). This, as Blyth and others have pointed out, is erroneous on a range of counts (see also Newman 2015; Portes 2014). Yet putting the story together in this way was an important part of the justification behind more austerity policies (Schäuble 2010a). Revealing the very different model of how the economy worked of those persuaded by the 'crisis of debt' reading, reducing public spending and public sector involvement in the economy, cutting welfare, and flexibilizing labour and other markets were being championed as the best way to restore economic growth. Furthermore, in Germany, painful welfare and labour market reform since the late 1990s had heralded decline in German real wage levels and living standards which had coincided with a return to economic growth. This fuelled arguments that Eurozone periphery countries needed to put their own political economies in order in similar fashion, both in the interests of fairness, but also to restore competitiveness (see Newman 2015; Jacoby 2015). Yet this ignored what the Fund's more differentiated approach

[14] Ralph Atkins, 'ECB Presses for Fiscal Exit Plan', *Financial Times*, 8 October 2009.
[15] *Financial Times*, 23 November 2009.
[16] Ralph Atkins, 'ECB Starts to Unwind Bank Liquidity Steps', *Financial Times*, 4 December 2009.

to policy recommendation appreciated—that the same policy would not have the same impact in these very different political economic contexts.

The IMF, by contrast, saw the advanced economies as facing first and foremost a 'crisis of growth' caused by spillovers from the broken financial sector to the real economy, and fuelled by a collapse in demand and confidence (IMF Research Department 2008; Freedman et al. 2009; Blanchard and Cottarelli 2008, 2010; Blanchard 2012c: xv).[17] Increasing debts and soaring deficits, the Fund pointed out, were fuelled only in small part by the fiscal stimulus itself. A much larger part was due to lost fiscal revenues following the collapse in asset values and the protracted downturn, and bank bail-outs shifting huge financial institution liabilities onto the public debt book (IMF 2010b: 14; IMF 2011n: 23). The reason that catastrophe had been averted, Fund interpretations were keen to underscore, was the swift, coordinated macroeconomic policy responses which the IMF helped orchestrate. Strauss-Kahn noted in *Fiscal Monitor* in May 2010, 'A timely and simultaneous application of supportive fiscal and monetary policies prevented a far worse outcome' (2010: 4).

As advanced economy public finances deteriorated, the conditions were no longer ripe for the insouciant 'Keynesian' counter-cyclicality of October–December 2008. Fund forecasting hoped the economic recovery would germinate soon, nevertheless, the shift of emphasis towards restoring the public finances in the ongoing downturn amounted to a pro-cyclical fiscal policy stance. Some have interpreted the Fund around 2010 as falling back into line with the standard austerity-centric narrative (Blyth 2013b: 206–10; Baker 2010; Radice 2011; Gamble 2014: 64). However, this misreads the Fund's prioritization within its prescriptive fiscal policy advice. In important respects, the Fund interpretation of the crisis and its policy implications stood apart from the account offered by the ECB, the UK coalition government, the German authorities, and other European fiscal hawks. To understand the Fund's multi-faceted and nuanced stance, it is important to appreciate the limits imposed by a fiscally conservative constituency within the institution. FAD under Cottarelli shifted in the earlier post-crash period towards the Research department's more Keynesian focus on economic stabilization. FAD accepted and advanced the higher multipliers analysis, yet they retained a concern for deficit bias and fiscal sustainability. Many within FAD became more preoccupied by deteriorating public finances as the recession drew on. It is also necessary to appreciate how the disagreements with major powerful members over post-crash macro policy hemmed in the Fund. IMF norms avoid engaging in overt political disagreements over economic policy (see Chapter 4),

[17] Interviews with Carlo Cottarelli, Olivier Blanchard, Jonathan Ostry, June 2013.

added to which, Fund leadership keenly appreciate the costs to their intellectual authority of making policy recommendations, only for them to be ignored.

In this complicated context, the IMF worked to inflect the economic policy debate, noting that fiscal adjustment would clearly be necessary in the medium term, but it should be stepped up only *once the recovery was under way*. Supporting the recovery through boosting demand was a priority in the short term, with corroborating research to underpin the position (IMF 2009a & c: 42–3; IMF 2010a; 2010l: xi–x, 11). If growth disappoints, Fund advice consistently underlined, contingency plans should prepare further demand stimulus since the private sector cannot be relied upon to take up the slack. Mobilizing its mandated role as the guarantor of international economic policy coordination, the Fund repeatedly highlighted the need to avoid the damaging effects of all countries tightening their fiscal policies at once. As Cottarelli summarized the position, 'the Fund has become nicer, more expansionary, more worried about growth.... It all comes from the fact that there is a crisis and a growth problem—so how do we address it? Fiscal policy tools, more financing.'[18] The Fund's 'crisis of growth' interpretation was focused on the large output gap—which it anticipated would be persistent (Blanchard 2010b; IMF 2010a: 9, 20, 52–6). The lost growth the GFC portended was central to the Fund's interpretation of the crisis legacy. The IMF sought macroeconomic policy measures to claw back this 'lost' growth potential, seeing revived growth as central to any successful restoration of the public finances.

The Troika and the Politics of Austerity

Yet the beginnings of the Eurozone sovereign debt crisis, erupting via the unearthing of Greek fiscal profligacy and dishonesty in reporting its fiscal accounts, were not propitious conditions for advocating expansionary fiscal activism. This wounding episode did much to reinforce the 'crisis of debt' narrative. The Greek episode seemed to confirm 'deficit bias' fears that governments could not be trusted to spend public money wisely, nor to build up fiscal buffers. This view had its constituencies of support within the IMF, but was especially strong in certain European capitals. As Jacoby put it, 'if Greece did not exist... [Merkel's] CDU–FDP coalition would have had to invent it, as it plays *the* essential rhetorical purpose in their joint crisis narrative' (2015: 193). Newman notes how 'the central narrative coming out of Berlin as early as

[18] Interview with then FAD Director Carlo Cottarelli, June 2013.

2009 focused on the potential moral hazard to German taxpayers of throwing good money after bad in the periphery of Europe' (2015: 121; see Schäuble 2011a, 2012, 2013a & b). As one senior French official observed, 'the Germans thought that this crisis was due to the fact that we have not been serious enough with the SGP. Their solution was to strengthen the pact, and enforce fiscal consolidation to address debts and deficits.'[19] The European Council meeting in May 2010, held as the Greek programme developed, presaged what was in store for Troika programme counties, auguring fiscal consolidation and structural reform requirements which would 'be accelerating where warranted' (see European Council 2010; Dellepiane 2015: 401).

The Fund's involvement along with the ECB and EC in the 'Troika', which enacted its Greek bail-out programme in May 2010, limited the IMF's ability to speak with its own voice on Eurozone crisis matters (El-Erian 2015, Palaiologos 2015, Lutz & Kranke 2014). This and subsequent programmes for Ireland and Portugal required the IMF to find common cause with powerful European authorities whose interpretation of the crisis, as noted in section 5.3, it did not wholly share. The dissonance over debt restructuring was stark, but over fiscal adjustment it was limited. After all, the more growth-oriented approach to macroeconomic policy was an option, the Fund argued, *only* for those countries enjoying fiscal space. By definition, this did not include programme countries that no longer had access to financial markets for borrowing. The very different policy prescriptions for these countries reveal how consequential fiscal space is. Nevertheless, there were significant differences over the scale of adjustment that should be required in the Troika programmes. In the Ireland case, the ECB wanted budget cuts of €8bn up front, whilst the Fund recognized that fiscal profligacy had not been a cause of the Irish crisis, and favoured a figure of €4.5bn. The programme eventually settled on €6bn (Ahamed 2014: 114).

Crucially, the IMF agreed, given German 'moral hazard' concerns about letting the Greek authorities off the hook, and its own anxieties about contagion, to proceed *without* requiring the debt restructuring. Putting debt on a manageable path via restructuring would normally be a precondition if such a programme were authored by the IMF alone, rather than the Troika. As the minor partner (in terms of financing), brought in relatively late into the discussions about the nature of the programme, the Fund acquiesced to the absence of debt restructuring and the harder fiscal adjustment line taken by European Troika partners (Warner 2011; Taylor 2015). This fateful decision 'magnified the requirement of fiscal adjustment' and 'contributed to a large contraction in output' but 'left debt sustainability concerns unaddressed'

[19] Interview with Philippe Gudin, former head of macroeconomic policy and European affairs in the *direction générale du Trésor*, Paris, November 2013.

(IEO 2016: 15). As the IMF's own analysis later reflected, the absence of early debt restructuring had hugely damaging long-term consequences for prospects of Greek recovery (IMF 2013e).

The Fund subsequently defended how social spending was protected to some degree within these European programmes (Roaf 2011; Arora 2016). Yet the overriding characteristic of the Greek programme was harsh pro-cyclical fiscal adjustment. In the end, the Greek experience provided a grim policy laboratory. The Fund's own painful experience of the fiscal consolidation's economic effects within the Greek programme was an important catalyst for, and focal point within, the IMF's ongoing fiscal policy rethink.[20] Ajai Chopra, then Deputy Director of the IMF European department, and who negotiated the Irish programme, reflected, 'Right from the get-go the Fund said that it could not state that there was high probability of debt being sustainable. But this also led to a lot of reflection on how rudimentary our debt sustainability analysis was.'[21] As the IEO subsequently pointed out, the programme contained unrealistic growth forecasts, born out of underestimating the adverse effects on growth of the fiscal contraction (i.e. the size of fiscal multipliers) (IEO 2016: viii, 3–4, 27–8, 29–30, 49; Moschella 2016). The disappointing growth outcomes from the Greek programmes, along with the self-professed learning culture in the institution, and the rethink already underway in the Research department in particular, meant that the Greek experience was an important driver of the Fund's upwards re-evaluations of fiscal multipliers by 2012.

Growth Friendly Fiscal Consolidation?

With the growing Eurozone crisis as a backdrop, the Toronto G20 in June 2010 saw the positions in the international economic policy debate crystallize (IMF 2010d). One view, building on the ideas of Trichet, Schäuble, and others, saw rising public debt and potentially inflationary pressures unleashed by unconventional monetary policy as the key policy concerns. Excessive public spending and interventionist economic policies were part of the problem; they were undermining confidence and crowding out a private sector which alone, they felt, could lead the recovery. This chimed with the German 'moral hazard' concerns discussed earlier—of profligate governments getting off the hook despite their overspending.

[20] A point made by numerous Fund economists in interview.

[21] Interview with Ajai Chopra, by then Senior Research Fellow at the Peterson Institute for International Economics, September 2014.

It was at this point that the 'expansionary fiscal contraction thesis' enjoyed renewed prominence, and arguably anchored the politics of austerity debate. 'Expansionary austerity' (EA), as it became known, asserts expansionary effects, via improved confidence and reduced borrowing costs, of cutting public spending. Propagated by an influential group of Italian economists termed by Blyth the 'Bocconi boys', it played a significant role in the international economic policy debate (2013a: 165–77; Dellepiane 2015). In this view, the spending cuts and public sector reforms associated with austerity were, Merkel, Schäuble et al. argued, vital preconditions to restoring economic competitiveness. Schäuble claimed that 'restoring confidence in our ability to cut the deficit is a prerequisite for balanced and sustainable growth' (Schäuble 2010b). EA owed its salience to its apparent ability to offer an intellectual rationale for pursuing harsh consolidation at the earliest opportunity, and was seized upon by those favouring such a course of action. It was evoked by ECB head Jean-Claude Trichet, and the German and UK governments (see Chapter 6), amongst others, in justifying their policy stances. At its root is a stridently anti-Keynesian view of political economy—reminiscent of Say's law (see Chapter 3) which sees the private, not the public sector, as the sole agent of sustainable economic recovery. At this time, Alesina and Perotti published a blog arguing that increasing German levels of public spending was not the answer to the crisis (Alesina and Perotti 2010; Schäuble 2010b, 2011a). By contrast, entreaties for surplus countries such as Germany and China to do more to boost global demand, including by increasing public spending, were a continuous theme of Fund crisis commentary (see e.g. Decressin 2012; IMF 2014d: 20; Lagarde 2017).

The Toronto G20 communiqué alluded to the EA idea in its espousal of 'growth-friendly fiscal consolidation'. This almost oxymoronic term can admit widely divergent interpretations. *Either* it could mean that, when pursuing necessary consolidation—do so in a manner which limits the adverse effects on growth. *Or* it could imply that cutting spending is in and of itself favourable to growth. The term 'Growth-friendly fiscal consolidation' papers over the enormous chasm between these two positions. For Blanchard, who more or less eradicated the term from Fund publications soon after it rose to prominence, 'for most people it is somehow the implicit assumption that fiscal consolidation is good for growth. One can see why this looks like a marvellous phrase, but I thought it was hypocritical, and so you've seen less of it.'[22]

Fund intellectual leadership were unconvinced that 'expansionary fiscal contraction' insights were germane to the specific post-crash conditions facing most advanced economies. The Fund's Research department and FAD

[22] Interview with IMF Chief Economist Olivier Blanchard, June 2013.

trained their intellectual guns on the underlying assumptions and applicability of the 'expansionary austerity' thesis (Alesina & Giavazzi 2013a & b; Giavazzi & Pagano 1990, 1996). As Carlo Cottarelli noted, 'others have argued that if you do the fiscal adjustment with the right tools—in particular spending cuts rather than revenue increases—they say you get a boost. We don't think that this is true.'[23] Blanchard and Cottarelli, keen to establish an IMF line to feed debate about fiscal consolidation, produced a blog containing '10 commandments' for fiscal policy in the days preceding the Toronto G20. Its central aim was to challenge and debunk the notion—implicit in some renderings of the oxymoronic term 'growth-friendly fiscal consolidation'—that fiscal consolidation may in and of itself be helpful for growth. Blanchard and Cottarelli's '10 commandments' noted in their first paragraph there was a paramount need to avoid 'undermining the still fragile recovery', after all 'too much adjustment could also hamper growth, and this is not a trivial risk'. They emphasized the need for credible medium-term plans to restore public finances but took a clear stand *against* front-loading fiscal consolidation. One commandment encouraged a 'focus on fiscal consolidation tools that are conducive to strong potential growth', for example, shifting from universal to targeted social transfers. They also emphasized healthcare and pension reforms which could bring down *future* costs, but would not take spending out of the economy in the present. Such forms of fiscal adjustment had the merit of bolstering long-term fiscal credibility without taking public spending in support of demand out of the economy in the short term—thus avoiding hurting the recovery (Blanchard & Cottarelli 2010).

Thereafter, further Fund work undertaken by Daniel Leigh, who became a close collaborator with Olivier Blanchard, supported and advised by celebrated New Keynesian economist David Romer, interrogated the effects of fiscal consolidation. This culminated in the landmark 'Will it Hurt?' chapter in the October 2010 *WEO*, which directly took on and critiqued the 'expansionary fiscal contraction' thesis. Their reason for publishing the research debunking this thesis was, as Daniel Leigh recalled, 'we wanted to be on the right side of history'.[24] Alesina claimed, as Leigh et al. put it, that 'positive "non-Keynesian" confidence effects offset the negative "Keynesian" impact on aggregate demand' (2010: 104). Questioning their techniques for identifying and measuring fiscal consolidation episodes, Leigh and others developed an alternative method rooted in the policy intentions and actions (2010: 93–9; 104–7). On closer inspection the 'poster child' examples of successful EA in the 1980s—Ireland and Denmark—did not stand up to scrutiny. Thus, 'typically, fiscal consolidation in advanced economies has

[23] Interview with the FAD Director Carlo Cottarelli, June 2013.
[24] Interview with IMF Research department Economist Daniel Leigh, September 2013.

been contractionary. And even in the special cases, there's very little evidence of expansionary effects. That's something you shouldn't count on...you shouldn't kid yourself that fiscal consolidation's going to be expansionary. It's going to be contractionary.'[25]

'Will it Hurt?' found that, for advanced economies, 'The idea that fiscal austerity triggers faster growth in the short term finds little support in the data', rather, it has 'contractionary short-term effects on economic activity, with lower output and higher unemployment' (2010: 113). Fiscal consolidations are contractionary, a conclusion which 'reverses earlier suggestions in the literature that cutting the budget deficit can spur growth in the short term' (Ball et al. 2011). Moreover, 'Will it Hurt?' found that, in the post-GFC context, the pain was going to be greater:

> The painkillers that monetary policy typically provides were not available. And indeed the *WEO* chapter found that, in those situations, fiscal multipliers—the effects of fiscal consolidation—could be larger than they would have been, typically, in the past. That was an important conclusion of the chapter... that this time is probably going to be more painful than you're used to.[26]

With the Blanchard and Cottarelli '10 commandments' blog, and then the more in-depth 'Will it Hurt?' intervention, the Fund put down an important intellectual marker in the politics of austerity debate. The Fund took on EA-inspired renderings of the Toronto G20 nostrum of 'growth friendly fiscal consolidation'. The *WEO* chapter reprised the likelihood of higher fiscal multipliers during a recession (2010: 108–9), and pointed out that, under the conditions faced by advanced economies, 'expansionary fiscal contraction' effects were unlikely to materialize (see also Perotti 2011). Numerous interviewees noted that theirs was not a theoretical objection to the possibility of expansionary fiscal contraction effects. Mauro noted that

> most Fund thinking and attention in the 1990s was devoted to emerging markets where I believe expansionary fiscal contractions were more relevant exactly because spreads were large. If you move into the situation of the UK, US—countries that don't have those spreads, that channel of spreads going up—then forget about expansionary fiscal contractions.[27]

Thus, it was a pragmatic and contingent objection that, with most advanced economy interest rates at or approaching the Zero Lower Bound, it was hard to see how confidence effects could take hold. As Deputy Managing Director David Lipton recalled, 'there certainly was a fair amount of thinking in

[25] Interview with IMF Research department Economist Daniel Leigh, September 2013.

[26] Interview with IMF Research department Economist Daniel Leigh, September 2013.

[27] Interview with Senior IMF Economist Paolo Mauro, a senior fellow at the Peterson Institute for International Economics at the time of the interview in 2014.

European circles, academic as well as some official circles, that said that fiscal contraction would so enhance confidence that it would be expansionary'.[28] In fact, the Fund's analysis found that 'countries that face a higher perceived sovereign default risk tends to be less contractionary. But *expansionary* effects of consolidation are unusual even for this group' (2010: 113). As Blanchard put it, within the Fund, the expansionary fiscal contraction thesis

> was killed, fairly quickly... expansionary fiscal [contraction] can happen, if the consolidation convinces markets that the government was losing its grip, but now it has fiscal policy under control. Risk spreads and interest rates decrease, people and firms suddenly become much more optimistic. But this was not the situation then.[29]

'Will it Hurt?' was a frontal assault on the likes of Trichet, Schäuble, Cameron, Osborne, and others (see Chapter 6; Blyth 2013a: 59–61; Dellepiane 2015; Schäuble 2010b, 2011a; Trichet 2010), revealing the dubious intellectual grounds upon which austerity was being justified. Its take-home point was to make the case for cutting spending less compelling. As Lipton characterizes the Fund contribution on EA, 'the academic work that the Fund did has helped everyone who is interested in this subject rethink the premises of their policy thinking, and that's been useful.'[30]

The goal of 'Will it Hurt?' and other similar interventions was to shape perceptions of 'sound' fiscal policy under the post-crash conditions faced by the advanced economies. It sought to counter the myopic focus of ECB leadership and the German and Dutch governments, amongst others on fiscal consolidation, shifting the balance of prioritization by increasing emphasis on supporting the recovery by boosting aggregate demand. Whilst there were reasons to countenance fiscal consolidation, it was, Fund bricoleurs felt, simply disingenuous to pretend that such retrenchment would foster growth. The Fund was using its scientific prowess, knowledge bank, and modelling expertise to fulfil its role as arbiter of sound economic policy. In this instance, this entailed countering what key Fund figures saw as wrong-headed approaches to and premises for fiscal policy.

Fiscal Policy Efficacy and Consolidation in Recessionary Conditions

IMF endorsement of the move towards fiscal consolidation from 2010 to 2011 was based on the premise—indicated in earlier forecasts—that growth was

28 Interview with IMF Deputy Managing Director David Lipton, September 2013.
29 Interview with Olivier Blanchard, June 2013.
30 Interview with IMF Deputy Managing Director David Lipton, September 2013.

returning to advanced economies. However, in 2011 and 2012, the over-zealous pursuit of austerity triggered a renewed downturn (Gamble 2014: 51, 66–7; IMF 2011o: 1–31). These adverse growth effects revealed precisely the kinds of interaction between austerity policy prescriptions and activity in the real economy which the Fund's revived fiscal policy research from 2008 onwards was unearthing.

The international economic policy debate was in thrall to what was later termed 'deficit fetishism' (Rosamond & Hopkin 2015), with powerful voices in Europe such as Trichet, Merkel, and Schäuble, but also Dutch Prime Minister Mark Rutte, and successive Dutch Finance Ministers Jan Kees de Jager and Jeroen Dijsselbloem, arguing for drastic immediate necessary spending reductions and other austerity measures to reduce deficits (Merkel 2009; Trichet 2010, 2011; Schäuble 2010a & b, 2011a & b). Increased fiscal consolidation reinforced the need, identified by the Fund since 2008, to accurately gauge fiscal multipliers which Fund research reaffirmed were the 'key parameters in the nexus between fiscal consolidation, growth, and debt reduction' (Eyraud & Weber 2013: 2). It also brought the policy trade-offs between macroeconomic activism in pursuit of growth, and fiscal adjustment to restore public finances into sharp focus. Navigating the charged politics of austerity, the IMF sought to shape views on the timing and composition of fiscal consolidation. The Fund endorsed what it termed an 'easy does it' approach (IMF 2012c: 12–15)—deeming fiscal adjustment to be necessary *but not yet* in countries enjoying fiscal space. The Fund was tailoring its line to increase the chances of traction given what noises it was hearing through the feedback loops of its interactions with advanced economy governments. Fiscal space, the prism through which Fund fiscal policy advice is refracted, reveals again its significance in opening up policy space and policy options for certain governments.

As noted above, one important source of the new work on fiscal multipliers pursued by Blanchard, Leigh, and others was the disappointments felt at the IMF about the performance of the initial Greek programme (IEO 2016). Many interviewees alluded to the surprise within the Fund at how far the Greek economy contracted as the austerity measures associated with the initial Troika programme were imposed. Salient policy-oriented work continued at the Fund on how fiscal policy effects on output were affected by recessionary conditions, and by different mechanisms of fiscal adjustment, comparing spending cuts vs revenue-raising, and different kinds of expenditures (Baum et al. 2012; Baunsgaard et al. 2012; Mineshima et al. 2014; IMF 2012c: 33–9). This led the increasingly reflexive Fund to re-evaluate the premises of its fiscal multiplier assumptions when modelling fiscal adjustment, culminating with the high-profile publication of the Fund's upwards re-evaluation of fiscal multipliers in *WEO* in October 2012. Blanchard and Leigh created a quasi-natural experiment, by 'regressing the forecast error for real GDP growth on forecasts of fiscal consolidation' from 2010 onwards (2013a: 3). They asked 'whether the kind of growth disappointments that we'd seen could be linked to assumptions about multipliers', and they 'found that there was a systematic correlation between growth forecasters...disappointment on the growth front and how much consolidation had been planned'.[31]

Blanchard and Leigh unearthed a 'systematic relationship between fiscal consolidation and growth', and more pointedly that 'multipliers used in generating growth forecasts' [around 0.5] had been 'systematically too low since the start of the Great Recession, by 0.4 to 1.2' (IMF 2012e: 41). Continuing from 'Will it Hurt?' this was another landmark intervention which sought to alter perceptions of fiscal consolidation's effects, and with it change the politics of fiscal policy. Mindful that IMF commentary should not appear to critique the policies of member states, Blanchard and Leigh noted that their findings of underestimated multipliers did 'not have mechanical implications for the conduct of fiscal policy' (2013a: 6). Nevertheless, the findings clearly shifted the Fund's balance of prioritization between supporting growth and reducing deficits.

Fund research asked whether fiscal consolidation would improve current account balances of advanced economies. The unsurprising finding was that it would struggle to do so if all countries were consolidating at once (IMF *WEO* Sept 2011: ch. 4). Fund work underlined how fiscal multipliers are contingent on the state of the economy (IMF 2012c: ix, 15, 33–9; Batini et al. 2012: 7–8; Müller et al. 2012; IMF 2013j; Baum et al. 2012; Eyraud & Weber 2013; Batini et al. 2014a & b; IMF 2014d), and indicates that cutting during a recession is much more damaging than doing so once the recovery is clearly under way. This all re-enforced the Fund's 'less now, more later' stance, urging those countries enjoying 'fiscal space' to 'backload' their fiscal consolidation efforts (IMF 2012c: 12–15; Blanchard & Leigh 2013b).

The October 2012 *WEO* noted that 'fiscal multipliers are large' (Blanchard 2012c: xv; IMF 2012j: 41), highlighting 'supportive demand management' as an important element of economic policies to address and resolve the Eurozone crisis. Automatic stabilizers and other fiscal policy measures were, it argued, required to complement unconventional monetary policy interventions (IMF 2012j: xvii–xviii, 21–2, 67). Surplus countries (notably China and Germany) were once more entreated to introduce reforms which boost demand. The Fund assessment of the crisis legacy—large and persistent output gaps—were propitious conditions for short-run Keynesian policies. The proposed structural reforms in the Eurozone were justified in terms of their ability

[31] Interview with IMF Research department Economist Daniel Leigh, September 2013.

to 'promote aggregate demand, particularly investment, over time' (IMF 2012j: 26–7). For David Lipton,

> The point that multipliers really depend on a country's particular circumstances and the point in the cycle distinguishing in empirical terms for different cases what the situation is, I think that was a contribution that we made, again for the broader economic world but also in giving advice to individual countries.[32]

Drawing on Fund research and insights into which fiscal policy measures offer the best 'bang for your buck', Fund advice was that countries should take more counter-cyclical action if growth disappoints, such that 'contingency plans should be ready, prioritizing temporary revenue and expenditure measures with the highest payoffs in terms of economic activity' (IMF 2012c: 7). Counter-cyclical fiscal policy is understood as 'a stabilizing factor against short-term downturns or booms. Clear analogies can be drawn with the practice of successful monetary policy' (IMF 2012j: 21–2, 67). Blanchard and other senior Fund figures reflected that the fiscal multipliers work had reshaped the fiscal policy debate:

> it's a combination of message and opportunity...I have a sense that the papers made a difference. If you have a clear message then you have some effect, and you clearly have more effect if it fits the agenda...I think you can move the compass a little bit.[33]

The Eurozone Crisis and the Politics of Fiscal Rectitude

The Eurozone crisis was a constant backdrop to fiscal policy discussions from mid-2010 onwards. This provided a focal point for policy discussion, and also shaped the lens through which the IMF saw economic policy issues in its interactions with European authorities and member governments. The German, UK, and Dutch as well as the Finnish and Austrian governments used the threat of more Greek-style crises erupting to keep European policymakers focused on reducing debts and deficits to avoid adverse market reactions. The focus of the ECB and EC was also on harnessing the disciplining effects of financial market pressure to induce spending cuts and 'supply-side' structural and market reforms. The ECB, EC, and Germans were confident that such reforms would, in the long run, increase economic competitiveness.

Yet there were, the IMF consistently underlined, other ways to mitigate financial market pressure. The Fund sought policy interventions to bolster fiscal credibility *other than* retrenchment. Furthermore, the IMF saw that fiscal

[32] Interview with IMF Deputy Managing Director David Lipton, September 2013.
[33] Interview with IMF Chief economist Olivier Blanchard, June 2013.

discipline and supply side reform was not, in and of itself, going to resolve the crisis. As former IMF European department Deputy Director Ajai Chopra noted of the contrast between the German/ECB account of the Eurozone crisis, and the Fund's,

> the narrative up until Draghi's Jackson Hole speech was that we need structural reforms to get a revival in growth. I call this the search for golden unicorns, the belief that structural reforms will handle the growth problem even in the short term. There are a number of problems with that argument, it ignores that there is a demand problem... putting all that emphasis on structural issues swept the demand problem under the rug.[34]

A central policy recommendation—for countries enjoying fiscal space—was advocating *future* commitment to entitlement reform (notably pensions and healthcare), which could improve the fiscal position without taking spending and social transfers out of the economy (IMF 2011c: 1, 20, 56, 63–4: vii; Blanchard & Cottarelli 2010; Blanchard 2011b; see also IMF 2010b: 6; IMF 2010g: 113; Ball et al. 2011: 20). For the IMF, however, by far the most important way to secure fiscal credibility, preserve policy space, and to reduce the systemic risks posed by the financial crisis was to use public power and institutions to create 'backstops' to shore up the Eurozone. IMF concerns centred on

> the particular multiple equilibrium question in the European setting and the Eurozone setting was around doubts about the future of the Eurozone itself. If there were negative expectations those could be self-fulfilling in leading to a circumstance in which sustainability of the sovereign and hence their membership in the zone could come into question.

In order to mitigate such risk, Lipton recalls, the IMF 'gave a lot of thought to that question, and as a result of seeing that issue recommended the creation and deployment of financial backstops that would help anchor expectations and overcome the multiple equilibria risks'.[35] In this way, Eurozone architecture reforms could restore confidence in the creditworthiness of troubled sovereigns and fragile banks and limit financial market contagion. Part of the justification for advocacy of these policy responses to the Eurozone crisis, on the Fund's part, was that such measures could expand macroeconomic room to manoeuvre in pursuit of restoring growth to the European economies.

Meanwhile, higher public indebtedness and the implications for public finances of increased financial system fragility, both central themes of the

[34] Interview with Ajai Chopra, by then Senior Research Fellow at the Peterson Institute for International Economics, September 2014.

[35] Interview with IMF Deputy Managing Director David Lipton, September 2013.

banking and sovereign debt crisis in Europe, were affecting a Fund rethink of fiscal sustainability for advanced economies. The April 2011 *Fiscal Monitor*'s headline message deemed that 'steady annual progress, starting now, toward bringing debt ratios to prudent levels' was 'essential' (IMF 2011c: ix). To evaluate what 'prudent levels' might look like in the post-GFC context which the IMF now termed 'the new normal' (see e.g. Lipton 2014), FAD, SPR, and other departments developed a new debt sustainability analysis (DSA) framework (IMF 2011k). This important tool was another conduit of increasingly differentiated Fund macroeconomic policy prescription. The DSA operationalized the Fund's more sceptical view of financial markets, and its appreciation of adverse feedback from the financial sector to the real economy and to sovereign creditworthiness. It sought to gauge the degree and scale of advanced economy fiscal risks under post-crash conditions of increased uncertainty by assessing the probable impacts of future financial crises. As part of the broader Fund rethink of markets, such crises were now considered to be more frequent and likely events than pre-crash orthodoxy recognized (Viñals 2010, 2016; Blanchard et al. 2010, 2013; Blanchard 2014a; see Chapter 8).[36] The key innovation was attempting to account for large contingent liabilities (for example, of 'too big to fail' financial institutions) which, 2007–9 demonstrated, could unexpectedly become part of public debt and dramatically worsen a country's fiscal position (IMF 2011c: 8, 43, 48–9, 57–8). The major policy corollary of this was that advanced economies with large financial sectors needed larger buffers to mitigate systemic risk, and should target a sustainable debt level significantly *below* its pre-crisis level.

How did the Fund's new public debt evaluation affect its view of policy space for advanced economies? The IMF's increasing recognition of damaging speculative activity in the financial sector generating systemic risk dovetailed with its embrace of public power as a spender and lender of last resort. Avoiding further Lehman-like collapses in financial market confidence, especially ones which targeted sovereigns as well as financial institutions, was a central goal of the institution. It perceived that the contagion threats and spillovers from further financial turmoil were so serious and so sizeable that—in the interest of the economic stability it is mandated to pursue—all possible avenues should be explored by European authorities and EU governments. The search was on for ways to deal with systemic risk arising from financial sector fragility and instability that did not undermine growth, nor foreclose on scope for counter-cyclical macroeconomic stabilization.

In the second half of 2011, market sentiment turned against Italy and Spain, drawing them deeper into the crisis. The threat that the collapsing values of

[36] Interviews with Olivier Blanchard, Carlo Cottarelli, Jonathan Ostry, June 2013.

European periphery sovereign debt securities, held in huge quantities by the banks of France and Germany amongst others, meant the adverse feedback from the financial sector threatened the core Eurozone countries (see Blyth 2013a; Varoufakis 2017). Investors became increasingly uneasy about the health and sustainability of each economy individually, and the Eurozone as a whole. This threw into sharp relief the costs of not having a credible firewall or 'fiscal backstop' for the Eurozone, something Fund commentary called for consistently (IMF 2011c: 50; IMF 2011n: 36; IMF 2012g: 1–3, 8–9). Widening Italian bond spreads indicated declining creditworthiness of a 'too big to bail' Eurozone state. This raised the spectre of self-fulfilling adverse financial market dynamics which could threaten the viability of the Eurozone. The Fund conceptualized this as 'bad debt equilibrium', to be countered by stabilizing expectations around a more preferable path via a range of policy interventions. It urged more bond purchasing by the ECB in the secondary market (2011f: 9), and by the ESM in the primary market (IMF 2011c: 60).

The Fund argued that the ECB needed to act as lender of last resort for the Eurozone, and consistently called upon the ECB to embrace and expand its quantitative easing-style monetary policy and government bond-buying actions via first the Securities Market Programme and later Outright Monetary Transactions. At each stage when European authorities came together to seek crisis resolution measures, the Fund urged hesitant European policymakers and authorities to go further and faster to restore confidence and limit contagion, and to deliver more fully on previously agreed measures (IMF 2012j: xvii–xviii, 20–1). The IMF pushed for delivery on the 'strong policy response' agreed by European leaders at the 21 July 2011 European summit. This had promised direct recapitalization of banks using the nascent EU firewall initiatives (EFSF and ESM), and the buying of government bonds in the secondary market, acting on a precautionary basis. Meanwhile, the Fund urged the ECB to continue 'to intervene strongly to maintain orderly conditions in sovereign debt markets' (code for bond-buying) (IMF 2011o: xv), and to reduce interest rates to tackle deflationary concerns.

These mooted firewalls, and their political economic consequences, were a battleground in the politics of austerity—especially in the period before Draghi's 'whatever it takes' speech at Jackson Hole in July 2012 diffused the pressure. For the IMF, the scale of the systemic risks of new kinds of damaging financial market spillovers and vulnerabilities justified building powerful effective firewalls and financial backstops fast. The ESM, the Fund argued, needed to be empowered to limit financial market contagion (IMF 2011c: 60; IMF 2012j: xvii–xviii, 20–1). One of the central imperatives of resolving the European banking and sovereign debt crisis, Lagarde noted to a Berlin audience in January 2012, was 'larger firewalls' (Lagarde 2012a). By contrast, fiscal hawks at the ECB—Schäuble, Merkel—and in the Dutch, Austrian, and Finnish governments did not want to let the crisis go to waste. They saw the market pressure which underdeveloped firewalls prolonged as a necessary spur to competitiveness-enhancing reforms and fiscal discipline. Dissipating bond market pressure ran the risk of allowing under-reforming governments who might be soft-pedalling on fiscal adjustment off the hook. This undermined EU-wide efforts to put in place effective measures muscular enough to limit financial market contagion.

As dark clouds gathered over Europe's financial landscape in the summer of 2011, ECB Governor Trichet presented the battleground as one between 'sound' and 'unsound' fiscal policy in the Eurozone, arguing that the latter was fuelling and prolonging the crisis. He called for 'strengthening rules to prevent unsound policies', including an EU Financial Minister with powers to override and veto domestic fiscal policy decisions to institutionalize fiscal restraint and enforce 'individual responsibility' of governments for fiscal soundness, potentially even taking fiscal and structural reform decision out of national governments' hands (Trichet 2011). The Dutch Prime Minister Mark Rutte and Finance Minister Jan Kees de Jager toed a similar line, arguing that 'countries that systematically infringe the rules must gradually face tougher sanctions and be allowed less freedom in their budgetary policy', calling for an EU 'commissioner for budget discipline' as enforcer (Rutte & Kees de Jager 2011). For Schäuble, too, high debts and deficits rather than underdeveloped firewalls were the cause of the crisis: 'The main reason for the lack of demand is the lack of confidence; the main reason for the lack of confidence is the deficits and public debts which are seen as unsustainable' (2011b).

The Fund highlighted slowing growth and recessionary risks and saw the potentially cataclysmic market contagion effects as by far the more serious economic problem. In contrast to Schäuble's order of priorities, the Fund was concerned that the new debt benchmarks incorporated into the Six Pack (reducing debt by 1/20th a year to get back to 60 per cent of GDP) threatened to be damagingly pro-cyclical, and ignored the fact the debt does not depend solely on fiscal policy. The Fund underscored how new debt benchmarks within the excessive deficit procedure needed to be 'sufficiently flexible to avoid endangering growth through too much austerity' both in principle and in practice (IMF 2012a: 6).

Blanchard noted how lower growth exacerbated debt sustainability problems, and thus made the case for more macroeconomic activism to boost growth on the grounds that this was the best way to reduce debt levels. Lower growth 'leads markets to worry even more about fiscal stability' concerns, and more pointedly still 'front-loaded fiscal consolidation in turn may lead to even lower growth', so 'fiscal consolidation cannot be too fast or it will kill growth' (IMF 2011o: xiii, xiv, 2012a; see also Cottarelli 2011, 2012a;

Eyraud & Weber 2013). Outside the programmes to Greece, Ireland, and Portugal, the central and sustained focus of Fund prescriptions for Eurozone crisis resolution were innovating with public power to find ways of breaking the Gordian knot between failing banks (and massive contingent liabilities in the financial sector) and already overburdened sovereigns (see e.g. IMF 2011a: 5; 2011c: 7, 36). Such measures, along with decisive activism by the ECB and other European authorities, the Fund counselled, could alter the politics of fiscal rectitude in Europe—creating much more room to manoeuvre for the kinds of macroeconomic policy activism needed to restore growth (see e.g. IMF 2012j: 21–2).

One prominent initiative, harked back to in every Fund discussion of the Eurozone subsequently, was the proposed advent of an EU 'Banking Union' championed by François Hollande and others at the June 2012 European Summit. The IMF had consistently called for progress on EU-wide bank resolution mechanisms because 'the adverse feedback loop between weak sovereign and financial institution needs to be broken' (IMF 2011o: xvi). The 'doom loop', as the Fund would come to christen it (Blanchard 2014a), entailed vast liabilities of fragile dangerously over-exposed banks morphing into massively increased public debt for already over-burdened European governments. Although still a work in progress when announced, banking union promised a move towards a 'single resolution mechanism', and enabling the ESM to recapitalize banks directly, shielding sovereign states from bank crisis management costs. The Fund had been in the forefront of developing this crucial aspect of these financial sector firewalls since 2007, and their vision 'played a role in the euro area decision of mid-2012' (IEO: 2016: 24; Veron 2016). The potential for a fully realized banking union to reduce contagion risks, and open up 'fiscal space' for growth-oriented macroeconomic policies to invigorate the sluggish European recovery, was considerable.

However, this and other Eurozone architecture proposals had to navigate the tortured European politics or crisis response. None emerged unscathed—emasculated by resistance from a German government, ECB and others focused on their particular rendering of 'moral hazard', and were keen that financial market pressure should induce more structural economic reforms in Eurozone periphery countries (Newman 2015). The Fund favoured the development of Eurobonds as an effective fiscal backstop to bolster the credibility and future of the euro (IMF 2011g; Lagarde 2012a; IMF 2012g: 9; Claessens et al. 2012), but German government opposition prevented their emergence. Crucial elements at the heart of banking union were also very slow to see the light of day, with ECB banking crisis management and resolution only becoming a reality in 2016. Other Fund aspirations—such as a European deposit insurance scheme—remained elusive. As Chopra lamented, 'although the banking union plans included several good steps forward, the greatest disappointment was that it did not break the sovereign bank link.'[37]

What *did* reduce contagion risks, shortly after the euro area summit which promised the banking union, was the ECB belatedly answering the IMF's call to intervene strongly to calm bond markets. The Fund had long called for what it often termed 'further unconventional policy measures', meaning extending its bond-buying in the secondary market extensions of the Securities Market Programme (begun in May 2010), (see e.g. 2011f: 9). The ECB could and should, the Fund felt, play a greater and more central market-calming backstop role. In a familiar refrain, Lagarde in a speech in Germany said 'Central banks, in particular the ECB, should further loosen monetary conditions, and remain ready to use unconventional tools to ease tensions and provide funding to address liquidity constraints' (Lagarde 2012c; see also Lagarde 2012a). In July 2012, with Draghi's 'whatever it takes' comments, the ECB at last began to exercise the Eurozone backstop role the Fund had been willing upon it since 2010. This episode exemplified a 'neo-Keynesian' view of monetary relations and understanding of financial market sentiment. The key role for authorities and institutions like the ECB and the Fund, in the IMF's reading of how to resolve the Eurozone crisis, is to stabilize expectations (Widmaier 2004: 433), and shape conventional understandings about sound and sustainable fiscal policy. The ECB intervention steered market sentiment away from the 'bad debt' equilibrium. The Fund also credits itself, via involvement in European programmes, with countering bad equilibria.

The Fund consistently advocated European authorities going further, through measures such as Eurobonds, larger firewalls, and more unconventional policy interventions, as well as calls for fiscal union. Fund calls for institutional infrastructure-building of this kind to shape expectations and orient them towards a 'good debt' equilibrium largely went unanswered (see Chapter 7). Indeed, Chopra links this directly to Draghi's intervention: 'In July [2012] Draghi made his "whatever it takes" statement. My argument has been that the moral hazard went the other way in the sense that Draghi's statement took the pressure off European policy makers from devising a deeper banking union.'[38] The limited achievements of Eurozone infrastructure-building is due in large part to how these measures would transform the fiscal space for European governments, and the politics of fiscal rectitude in Europe. The Fund urged more activist counter-cyclical

[37] Interview with Ajai Chopra, by then Senior Research Fellow at the Peterson Institute for International Economics, September 2014.

[38] Interview with Ajai Chopra, by then Senior Research Fellow at the Peterson Institute for International Economics, September 2014.

fiscal and monetary policy to boost a European recovery. The fiscal hawks in the ECB and German authorities instead wanted austerity policies to bring debts and deficits down.

Both *Too Much* and *Too Little Fiscal Consolidation Can Be Dangerous*

As the hoped-for European recovery failed to materialize in 2011–12, the Fund's commentary took a new tack. The IMF sought to rebalance the economic policy debate away from a singular focus on debt and deficit levels and immediate fiscal consolidation by consistently highlighting the damaging, 'non-linear', and self-aggravating effects associated with *both* too much *and* too little fiscal consolidation. In May 2013, the then FAD Director Cottarelli highlighted the 'nonlinearities that arise from taking extreme positions' in the austerity debate (Cottarelli 2012a & b, 2013; Blanchard 2011a & b, 2012a).

The Fund's underlining of the dangers for demand and growth should fiscal consolidation proceed too fast was designed to reframe the debate, and shift its centre of gravity. Fund intellectual output sought to shape the climate of opinion by emphasizing a number of themes. The Fund's compromised faith in markets' inherent self-correcting abilities attuned the institution to threats of self-aggravating cycles of deflation (Decressin & Laxton 2009; Blanchard 2014b: xiii; IMF 2014d: 11, 13–15, 20; IMF 2015b) and hysteresis (Ball et al. 2011: 22; Cottarelli 2013; IMF 2013j: 21, 29–30; IMF 2014d: xvi, 20) to create equally serious risks to economic stability. Highlighting these vicious circles, and 'diabolical loops' (Blanchard 2014a) associated with absent growth pervaded commentary in Fund flagships. From the Fund's perspective, the central policy problems were 'the nonlinear costs of excessive frontloading or delay'. Hence those countries not facing market pressure should 'proceed with fiscal adjustment at a moderate pace' (IMF 2013j: 1).

Secondly, work by Cottarelli and Jaramillo (2012) on the drivers of market sentiment in 2011 found a close correlation between spreads and short-term growth, not long-term debt. This chimed with the ongoing desire to prioritize supporting economic recovery. The recognition that financial markets can be 'schizophrenic' (Blanchard 2011b), responding positively to fiscal tightening, but then negatively to resultant lower growth rates, was part of this heightened appreciation of the fallibility and unreliability of market sentiment (IMF 2012c; IMF 2013j: 11–14). As Cottarelli put it,

> unfortunately, we in the Fund are still a bit too afraid of telling markets openly that they are wrong. We have used fiscal monitor in this way—e.g. in 2012 you can read in fiscal monitor statements about how spreads in Europe were well above

> fundamentals and that they were not justified . . . but I felt that the institution was a bit afraid of saying this too loudly.[39]

Austerity policies might do more harm than good, since any positive credibility effects arising from markets giving governments credit for putting their fiscal houses in order are more than offset by the adverse reactions financial markets have to heavily indebted governments being faced with very low or no growth (Blanchard 2011b; IMF 2012a; IMF 2012b: 4–6; Cottarelli 2011, 2012a & b). Thus, for financial market confidence and credibility reasons, there were grounds to seek to support growth to the extent possible within fiscal consolidation.

The third Fund theme was that the pursuit of fiscal consolidation, especially if all countries were consolidating at once, can for a variety of reasons prove self-defeating; it can, for example, increase the debt ratio in an economy (see e.g. Lagarde 2012b; Cottarelli 2011; IMF 2012b: 6; Eyraud & Weber 2013; Ostry et al. 2015: 1–2). Countries with fiscal space should delay adjustment or reduce the pace of consolidation to avoid the drag on growth of all cutting at once. Not only the impact of fiscal consolidation on fickle market sentiment noted above, but also its impact on underlying growth rates can be a source of 'self-defeating' dynamics. The Fund became more trenchant about the damaging pro-cyclical effects of ramping up fiscal consolidation during the prolonged downturn, insisting in October 2014 that 'large negative growth surprises in euro area countries should not trigger additional consolidation efforts, which would be self-defeating' (IMF 2014e: 20). The fruits of the programme of fiscal policy research indicated fiscal multipliers to be higher during recessions (IMF 2013j: 18–19); this supported the 'less now, more later' approach to fiscal consolidation for countries with fiscal space (Blanchard & Leigh 2013a & b).

Fourthly, the effect of spending cuts on equity, as well as growth, was becoming increasingly important in Fund economic policy thinking (see chapters 1 and 8). Influential figures within the Fund's research department including Jonathan Ostry, Prakash Loungani, Daniel Leigh, and Larry Ball began to publish work on this theme. In a subtle but important reinterpretation of the IMF's mandate, inequality was construed, through its link to shorter growth spells (Berg & Ostry 2011), as a 'macro critical social indicator' and as such part of the Fund's mandate and remit (IMF 2011l). This chimed with the work of the 'Jobs and Growth' working group, founded at Strauss-Kahn's behest. Chopra noted where the Fund 'has actually been influential and important' on the 'bigger picture issues, not the country specific matters

[39] Interview with then FAD Director Carlo Cottarelli, June 2013.

but rather the broader macro implications of inequality'.[40] Fund research analysing the distributional consequences of fiscal consolidation found that making lower earners bear the brunt undermines growth more (Ball et al. 2011: 23; Furcedi & Loungani 2013; Ball et al. 2013). The inequality focus foregrounded the need for fiscal tightening to be 'fair', a goal defended on grounds of securing social and political acceptance of unpopular and drawn-out austerity measures (Lipton 2013a). It was also justified in terms of the beneficial effects for economic performance of more equity. This drew on and dovetailed with work on fiscal multipliers, bolstering the case for supporting liquidity-constrained households. The Fund's unusual policy recommendations here include the rich paying more through higher taxes and 'better targeted spending' to 'achieve equity objectives' (IMF 2013j: 34).

The Second Revival of Counter-Cyclical Policy

This book has highlighted the importance of crisis defining ideas in shaping policy responses. By 2013–14, the Fund was also seeking to mobilize particular crisis *legacy* defining ideas. In his foreword to the October 2014 *WEO*, Blanchard noted how substantially lower potential growth rates and weak demand were still the key legacies of the crisis (IMF 2014e; see also IMF 2012g; IMF 2015b: 1). The Fund highlighted the threatened onset of 'secular stagnation' (Hansen 1934; Summers 2013, 2014; IMF 2014b; IMF 2014d: xvi, 13, 16, 18–19; Blanchard 2015b), wherein 'economies would not be able to generate the demand needed to restore full employment through regular self-correcting forces' (IMF 2014c: 16). Persistent low inflation, and stagnation weighing down on confidence and demand, were consistently flagged as key policy problems facing advanced European economies (Moghadam et al. 2014; IMF 2015a: 1, 21–4, 45–50). The persistent slack and large output gaps in European economies, and the weak pace of the global recovery, were all evoked to frame Fund policy advice. IMF flagships made the case that 'raising actual and potential growth must remain a priority' (IMF 2014e: xvi; IMF 2015a: 1), with demand management and other macroeconomic and structural polices identified as the key policy tools.

These two elements—the crisis legacy of lower potential and actual growth rates, and the prospect of secular stagnation—were combined to inform the 'need for action on two fronts: continued support to domestic demand and the adoption of policies and reforms that can boost supply' (IMF 2014e: 13–19; 46, 75; Summers 2013; IMF 2014c & d). This framing was harnessed

[40] Interview with Ajai Chopra, by then Senior Research Fellow at the Peterson Institute for International Economics, September 2014.

to a bold shift back towards counter-cyclical spending for advanced economies. The Fund's perennial aversion to deteriorating public finances, which remained a preoccupation for an important constituency of Fund economists, combined with the policy preferences of powerful governments committed to fiscal adjustment (see Chapter 6), kept counter-cyclical policy largely off the agenda after 2010. For all the emphasis on timing to limit the adverse effect on growth, and despite the entreaties to protect the poor, the Fund's overall fiscal policy stance towards advanced economies remained broadly pro-cyclical. As the absence of recovery, or the sluggish recovery dragged on in many European countries, this pro-cyclical Fund stance changed in the summer of 2014. As Daniel Leigh put it in September 2014,

> the debate is shifting. It's also about boosting the supply side. The *WEO* has analysis showing how a regulated increase in infrastructure investment could in some settings pay for itself by boosting output in both the short and long term and avoiding an increase in the debt-to-GDP ratio. This is related to the work by Ball, DeLong, and Summers.[41]

Fund flagships made a series of carefully crafted interventions, designed to justify counter-cyclical increases in public investment in ways which circumvented fiscal sustainability concerns (see also Gaspar, Obstfeld, & Sahay 2016).

The work on composition of adjustment (IMF 2012k; 2013a) had re-enforced the view that government expenditure, especially in public investment infrastructure, has some of the highest multipliers (Mineshima et al. 2014; Abiad et al. 2015; Ganelli & Tervala 2016). This informed the Fund's innovative advocacy of counter-cyclical fiscal policy in an economic conjuncture of threatening secular stagnation. The very low interest rate environment, combined with recognition of many decades of public under-investment in infrastructure, created counter-cyclical policy opportunities. Fund research underlined the likelihood of lots of low hanging fruit in the form of efficiency-enhancing infrastructural projects, which could be funded at very low borrowing costs and would, the Fund advised, boost the long-term growth potential of advanced economies. Crucially, for the politics of fiscal rectitude, in boosting GDP, these public investments would *pay for themselves* through their positive effects on productive capacity and growth, not adding to public debt. This was a case for counter-cyclical fiscal expansion designed specifically for the post-GFC conditions, pre-emptively insulated against the standard objections that public expenditure increases debt. Advocates noted some differences of view within the Fund and internal resistance to the embrace of this line. Nevertheless, it prevailed within internal wrangling over the politics of economic ideas, and emerged as the centrepiece of the

[41] Interview with IUMF Research department Economist Daniel Leigh, September 2014.

October 2014 *WEO*, entitled 'Is it Time for An Infrastructure Push? The Macroeconomic Effects of Public Investment' (IMF 2014e: 75–114). It was reiterated in 2015 (IMF 2015b: 22).

Blanchard argued of the high debt context of advanced economy fiscal policy in the October 2014 *WEO*, 'this does not imply that there is no scope to use fiscal policy to help sustain the recovery'. Notably, he emphasized the scope for debt-financed infrastructure investment which 'may be justified and can help spur demand in the short term and supply in the medium term. And should the recovery stall, being ready to do more would be important' (Blanchard 2014b: xiii–xiv). Public infrastructure investment plans offered advanced economy governments struggling with the prolonged post-crash downturn 'one of the few remaining policy levers available to support growth' (IMF 2014e: 75–6; see also Gaspar, Obstfeld, & Sahay 2016: 11–14). It connected to a longer-standing thread running through Fund thinking, accentuated post-crash, of the potentially positive role of public investment. Continuing the theme that surplus countries should do more to boost demand, Germany, the Fund noted pointedly, 'could afford to finance much-needed public investment in infrastructure (primarily for maintenance and modernization), without violating fiscal rules' (IMF 2014e: 20). Infrastructure investment recommendations made their way into the IMF surveillance note prepared for the Brisbane G20 and infrastructure investment commitments were part of the communiqué from the meeting (IMF 2014d & f).

A counterpart to this Fund fiscal policy rethink was a re-evaluation of the pace at which debts should be brought down. A Fund Staff Discussion Note co-authored by Deputy Director of the Research department Jonathan Ostry sought to shift the emphasis in the public debate over debt levels in advanced economies. It questioned what 'safe' levels of debt are for countries with ample fiscal space, and what role public power and public spending should play in restoring economic growth (2015). Blanchard noted it 'has become clear that there is no magic debt-to-GDP number. Depending on the distribution of future growth rates and interest rates, on the extent of implicit and explicit contingent liabilities, one country's high debt may well be sustainable, while another's low debt may not' (Blanchard 2015a). More fundamentally, Ostry in particular questioned whether it made economic sense for debt reduction to be a policy objective. This was a direct counter to the 'crisis of debt' narrative, and the policy prioritizations which flowed from that influential interpretation.

Some countries facing market pressure have no option but to work to bring down the debt promptly. As regards other countries with more fiscal space, Ostry et al. questioned whether paying down the debt should be the highest economic policy priority. A viable alternative, they argued, is 'to live with high debt while allowing the debt ratio to decline organically through growth'. In a reiteration of the claim that fiscal consolidation can be self-defeating, they argue that 'the distortive cost of policies to deliberately pay down the debt is likely to exceed the crisis-insurance benefit from lower debt' (Ostry et al. 2015: 1–2). Part of the problem is that the idea of 'cutting productive public investment or raising taxes in order to bring the public debt down' lacks 'strong theoretical backing—such policies may actually make things worse rather than better, in terms of the welfare and growth outturns'.[42] Whilst accepting the insight that debt can adversely affect growth, the analysis rejects the view that debt should be paid down to restore growth: 'the cure would seem to be worse than the disease—the taxation needed to pay down the debt will be more harmful to growth than living with the debt' (2015: 5–6). The Fund identified a possible sweet spot 'if debt-financed public investment spending actually lowered the debt ratio, as can occur if Keynesian effects are large, the interest burden is minuscule, and investment is super-efficient', which may prevail in a small number of countries (Ostry et al. 2015: 2, 5; IMF 2014e; IMF 2015b). Similarly, in 2016 the IMF Chief Economist and Head of FAD and Deputy Director of the Monetary and Capital Markets Department noted, following Larry Summer's analysis, that a well-targeted fiscal stimulus which 'raises nominal GDP sufficiently' can 'improve the debt ratio . . . in the long term, and even in the near term' (Gaspar, Obstfeld, & Sahay 2016: 10–11).

Conclusion

In the early phase of the crisis, the Fund deployed its intellectual authority and worked to bolster the credibility of an activist macroeconomic response that owed much to Keynesian and New Keynesian economic ideas (see Chapter 3). The Fund's interpretation of the crisis and its legacies, underpinned by its research, sought to influence the thinking and prioritization of advanced economy policymakers. Building on its self-appointed role as a font of economic policy knowledge, the IMF mobilized its knowledge bank and scientific reputation to correct what key Fund figures saw as mistaken premises of austerity policies.

IMF commentary and advice counselled against precipitate exit from fiscal stimulus, urging a variety of policy interventions to support the recovery. IMF bricoleurs made a series of carefully targeted interventions in the 'growth "versus" austerity' debate, deploying its intellectual authority and scientific reputation to advocate policies to escape threats of protracted deflation and 'secular stagnation'. Along the way, the IMF put down a series of intellectual

[42] Interview with Jonathan Ostry, June 2013.

markers, spelling out flaws in the 'expansionary fiscal contraction' thesis, highlighting the increased potency of expansionary fiscal policy and public investment under recessionary conditions, and underlining how fiscal consolidation can be self-defeating. The stabilizing role of counter-cyclical fiscal policy in mitigating deep recessions was a central focus for Fund policy advocacy. The *WEO* noted that 'Clear analogies can be drawn with the practice of successful monetary policy' (IMF 2012j: 21–2, 67). This restored faith in fiscal policy marked a shift from a pre-crisis emphasis on monetary policy alone.

The Eurozone crisis complicated the Fund's fiscal policy counsel, not least via its involvement in the Troika and the harsh fiscal adjustment contained in the European programmes. Some dissonance between the Fund, ECB, and EC was evident in the formulation of programmes, notably around debt restructuring and the scale of fiscal adjustment. On the fiscal substance of programmes, the absence of fiscal space meant the menu of more growth-supporting fiscal policy options was not open to Greece and others. Yet Greece did play a crucial role in the politics of fiscal policy at the Fund. The harsh fiscal adjustment contained in the programme, and the strength of its deleterious effects on growth, served as a grim laboratory experiment to test the relationship between fiscal consolidation and growth. It was a spur to the rethinking of the potency of fiscal policy which spawned, amongst other things, the upwards re-evaluation of fiscal multipliers in 2012.

As regards managing the wider Eurozone crisis, the IMF called relentlessly for the muscular use of public power, the Eurozone architecture, and central bank actions to limit financial market contagion. In so doing, it sought to increase fiscal space and expand the macroeconomic policy options of certain advanced economies. This stance reflected both the Fund's view of the positive role for macroeconomic policy in crisis resolution, and its appreciation of the huge risks to the system and economic stability that a 'bad debt equilibrium' arising from further financial turmoil posed. Yet in the ideational struggle to define what constitutes 'sound' and 'unsound' fiscal policy within the Eurozone crisis, the Fund faced opposition from powerful European players. The European authorities, and German and other fiscal hawks, called for more powers to enforce budgetary austerity and fiscal soundness. They saw the market pressure which underdeveloped 'backstops' prolonged as a spur to necessary competitiveness-enhancing reforms and fiscal discipline. Bail-outs, ECB bond-buying, and the building of firewalls were interpreted in 'moral hazard' terms of letting supposedly profligate governments off the hook and throwing good money after bad.

As lower and more sluggish growth continued in the European economies, the Fund mobilized its crisis legacy framing, highlighting this lower potential growth and the need to try and reclaim 'lost' output following the crash to advocate a second burst of counter-cyclical fiscal policy, from 2014. Centred on public infrastructure investment to both inject demand and confidence, as well as boost future supply, this fed into the Brisbane G20 Action Plan of 2014, but did not garner the same level of widespread support amongst advanced economy fiscal policymakers as the IMF-orchestrated actions of November 2008. This draws attention to the contingent nature of increased Fund traction in the early crisis period.

6

The IMF, the UK Policy Debate, and Debt and Deficit Discourse

Introduction

In the first of two detailed case studies of how IMF surveillance and commentary seek to inflect and influence national policymaking, this chapter focuses on the UK policy debate. It charts the changing character of the economic ideas informing fiscal policymaking in Britain, and Fund responses to them. Drawing on interviews with the Fund's UK Missions and UK authorities, it shows how, despite the IMF's prizing of its non-political, scientific image, its differing views of UK policy space and prioritization became the stuff of a contested politics. Fund work on fiscal multipliers being higher during recessions, and the adverse effects of fiscal consolidation on growth, all had pointed relevance for UK policy. In the summer of 2010, the incoming coalition government's understanding of the UK economic position saw very little potential for activist fiscal policy in support of growth.

The coalition presented staving off a Greek-style crisis as a pressing concern, whilst the Fund considered a loss of UK financial credibility and rising borrowing costs a low probability. Accordingly, the IMF urged a slower pace of cuts, and an altered composition to shift the burden of adjustment away from the poorest groups. The analysis presented here identifies two phases of post-crash debt and deficit discourse in Britain, New Labour's crisis response between 2008 and 2010, and then Cameron's coalition government May 2010–15, with Cameron's Conservative government 2015–16 continuing with the same fiscal stance. Each phase is interpreted here as a process of reconstruction of economic and fiscal rectitude (see also Hay 2013a & b; Gamble 2010, 2012).

Understandings of the relationship between debt, public spending, and growth were markedly different between Labour 2008–10 and the coalition government elected in 2010. There was a shift in the crisis narrative underpinning the construction of fiscal rectitude in Britain, from a 'crisis of growth' to a 'crisis of debt' (Hay 2013a & b; Osborne 2011a, b, & c). Crucially, the scale and speed of fiscal retrenchment presented as imperative (and without which a damaging loss of confidence and credibility becomes likely) differed appreciably between the two post-crisis narratives. The IMF did not share the coalition's 'crisis of debt' interpretation, and as a result, there were sharp dissonances between IMF recommendations and UK policy under the coalition. These became especially pronounced between 2012 and 2013, with Blanchard remarking the UK authorities were 'playing with fire' by pursuing an excessively harsh austerity programme which threatened a prolonged and deepened recession.

The IMF's nationally differentiated, contingent analysis of each country's fiscal situation, its reputation, and debt dynamics (see Chapter 4) saw more fiscal space for the UK authorities to exploit. The IMF thus encouraged the UK government to slow down fiscal consolidation and display more flexible, nimble fiscal and other macro policy responses to address demand deficit given weaker-than-hoped-for growth, especially as growth disappointed and the recovery failed to materialize. They noted the key role of public infrastructure investment, amongst other things, in tackling what they saw as a persistent demand deficit fuelling a large output gap. The UK government between 2010 and 2013, however, largely refused to exploit the fiscal policy space the IMF identified at its disposal. This was crucial, because the Fund's post-crash fiscal policy advice was that advanced economies should not frontload fiscal consolidation *unless* they face a credibility problem.

The focus here is on the IMF's commentary on UK fiscal policy and debt and deficit positions since the crisis, where we unearth a battle of economic ideas about fiscal policy. The coalition position assumed that the private sector would 'pick up the slack' as public spending was cut back. Although the Office for Budget Responsibility (OBR)'s baseline assumptions on which coalition policy was based assumed positive fiscal multipliers, these were at the modest to low end of the spectrum of assessments at around 0.5. Indeed, the coalition alluded to notions of 'Ricardian equivalence' (i.e. the assumption of negative multipliers), and the confidence effects of the enhanced fiscal credibility arising from the government sticking to its announced fiscal consolidation plans. These views contrasted sharply with the IMF's post-GFC fiscal policy thinking.

UK/IMF Relations: IMF Intellectual Authority and the Limits of 'Traction'

This case study sheds new light on the scope and limits of IMF ideational authority, and the limits of IMF 'traction'. The nature of IMF relations with national authorities is shaped by the constitutional limits of Fund authority as spelled out in its Articles of Agreement. Fund staff can prioritize certain economic policy approaches, but these acts of persuasion within surveillance interactions must operate within the confines of a surveillance relationship which 'shall respect the domestic social and political policies of members' (1993: 6). The Fund also has a mandated role as guarantor of international economic and monetary stability—and its staff are mindful of the potentially adverse effects upon credibility, market sentiment, and borrowing costs that trenchant Fund criticism of economic strategy could have. This can fuel precisely the kinds of instability the Fund is tasked with avoiding. Accordingly, Fund commentary, and any critique, will always be phrased in very diplomatic and guarded terms. These constitutional and credibility parameters of IMF/government interactions shape the nature of the discussion, and how it is presented to the outside world (see Chapter 4).

The norms of IMF/Member State relations (especially a major member like the UK) mean that, outside an extreme crisis situation, the Fund will *never* get itself into the position of publicly arbitrating between a national government and its political opponent's approach to economic policy. This is partly a recognition of the Fund's importance as a 'reputational intermediary' (Broome 2008) in the construction of economic rectitude. Interlocutors on both sides were keen to downplay the distance between the IMF and UK authorities, accepting that there were 'differences of view' but avoiding terms like 'dissonance' or 'disagreement' in characterizing their respective positions. Both IMF staff and UK officials underscored the broad commonality of view about how the economy works, and the shared language and tools used to analyse policy. There were differences of interpretation, with each side using some different metrics, and seeing policy issues through slightly different lenses.[1] This understatement of dissonances is partly to observe the niceties of Fund/Member State interactions noted above.

The surveillance functions central to Fund activities since the 1970s make for regular and frequent interactions between national authorities and the IMF. These relations are a 'repeated game', within which officials and politicians become familiar with IMF preferences and opinions in relation to particular policies. This 'feedback loop' makes it difficult to discern the precise degree of Fund influence. As one UK official noted of exchanges with the Fund in the 1950s,

> we knew what policies would be acceptable to [the Fund]; and when framing our policies we knew that we wished to make a drawing from the Fund. In these

[1] Interviews with various IMF UK Mission members, and UK officials, Washington, June 2013, September 2014; London, August 2014.

> circumstances the distinction is a little subtle between submitting our policies for the Fund's approval and choosing policies we knew the Fund would approve.
>
> (quoted in Clift & Tomlinson 2008a: 549)

There are 'fund friendly policies' (Broome & Seabrooke 2007), whose status emerges through mutual learning and socialization within successive rounds of consultations and negotiations between IMF and policy elites (see also Lombardi & Woods 2008: 718–19; Barnett & Finnemore 1999, 2004).

In the absence of the leverage that comes with a lender/borrower relationship, the space for influence over policy is reduced. For advanced economies which are not borrowing from the Fund, the scope for the IMF shaping policymakers' understandings is less clear-cut than when doing their training or technical assistance work with policymakers in other countries. Unlike emerging economies, advanced economies already have highly trained technocratic experts in their treasuries and central banks. These highly capable economists are often well resourced, and have a very sophisticated and deep knowledge of the particulars of their economy. This puts any Article IV team at a disadvantage since the asymmetry of knowledge does not work in their favour. As Cottarelli notes, 'it's always difficult for us under surveillance to take views that are very much different from the views of the authorities . . . it's an easier life if as any Mission Chief you say what the authorities are doing is right'.[2] Fund surveillance interactions with advanced economies ultimately 'rest on no practical power to enforce sanctions' and Fund advice has been 'frequently ignored' (Pauly 1997: 40). We should be careful to calibrate claims about what constitutes influence, or in Fund parlance 'traction' in light of these dynamics. Many Missions visiting advanced economies see their role as working to induce changes of emphasis or prioritization at the margins.

Rather than telling policy elites what to do, Fund Missions provide alternative intellectual resources for policymakers to interpret both the economic crisis and appropriate macroeconomic policy responses to it. A case in point is the Fund's fiscal risk and debt sustainability analysis framework 2011 (IMF 2011k). The methodology for assessing contingent liabilities and their implications proved useful for national authorities. As Chopra put it, 'there was a lot of effort put into beefing up the debt sustainability analysis, not just the range of scenarios but also the sophistication of these scenarios . . . it gets summarized into a heat map that makes it quite visual.'[3] Governments took them up and incorporated this approach into their thinking. In this and other ways, the Fund and its Article IV Missions use their repeated interactions, and

[2] Interview with then FAD Director Carlo Cottarelli, June 2013.

[3] Interview with former UK Mission Chief and Deputy Director of the IMF European Department Ajai Chopra, by then Senior Research Fellow at the Peterson Institute for International Economics, September 2014.

the Fund's flagship publications, to contribute to the inter-subjective, social process of generating economic policy orthodoxies, by seeking to fix meanings about 'sound' fiscal policy.

In this UK case, interviews with its members revealed a self-aware Mission team, generating policy recommendations but well aware of the complexities and trade-offs faced by, for example, the UK Treasury team in piloting economic policy. Furthermore, there was also appreciation that their recommendations, forecasts, and scenarios, just like any others in economics, always hinge on the assumptions (about the size of multipliers, or the magnitude and persistence of the output gap) made to deal with multiple uncertainties. Some Fund economists noted anxiety, in pressing the case for a particular policy change, that they were seeking a level of precision in their recommendations that economic forecasting as a 'science' perhaps could not ultimately bear.

These uncertainties are factored into how forcefully the IMF pushes its policy line. After all, credibility and 'traction' would be lost if the Mission were to set too much store by a future development which then did not happen. One manifestation of this concern was increased use of a wider range of projections and alternative scenarios. These are included in part to underline the uncertainties which surround the forecasts. This is always a facet of economic forecasting, but especially so in the wake of an historically unusual crisis like the GFC which began in 2007. It echoes the intellectual underpinnings of the Fund's approach to the economy, a New Keynesian understanding alive to the 'multiple possible equilibria' which may be manifest in the economy. This less linear worldview refrains from bold assumptions about an economy's return to a prior steady state.

In suggesting policy changes, there is a limit to how much specificity the Mission can achieve given the modest size of the Mission and its resources. This places inevitable limits on the understanding and knowledge of all aspects of the policy context and process. Missions often encourage contingency planning, for example, that UK authorities should be prepared do more with macroeconomic policy to support demand if growth disappoints. Yet staff are fully aware that the UK authorities understand the mechanics and intricacies of the UK economic policymaking process more keenly than the small number of IMF economists in the UK Mission.

UK/IMF Relations, Fiscal Policy, and the 2008 Crash

When the initial crisis broke there was very close alignment between the Fund's view of appropriate crisis response and the UK government (see Chapter 5). The Treasury produced a working paper on fiscal stimulus (Treasury 2008) which struck the same chords as the IMF policy advice (IMF Research Department 2008; Blanchard 2008b; Spilimbergo et al. 2008; Strauss-Kahn 2008b). In the spring of 2009, the UK government's presentation of its fiscal argument was placed in the context of the international agreement made by the G20 countries and the European Council. This included a commitment to coordinated fiscal stimuli endorsed by the IMF (G20 2009). The Treasury underlined how the British stimulus efforts were in line with the G7 average (Treasury 2009: 15, 27–9).

The 2009 IMF's Article IV Mission endorsed the Government's 'forceful and wide-ranging' policy responses to the GFC, and anticipated a 'subdued and gradual' recovery (IMF Art IV UK 2009: 4). They focused also on the higher debt and deficits facing the UK economy. These were also of concern to the UK authorities (Ramsden 2012: 205–7), and this explained their shift to a neutral fiscal policy. Amidst the international debate about the timescale and pacing of exit from fiscal stimulus, there was agreement between UK authorities and IMF that fiscal consolidation would be needed but not yet.

The policies announced in the Labour government's last budget in March 2010 (Treasury 2010a) were stated to be 'fiscally neutral', with further loosening in 2010/11 followed by a more than offsetting tightening thereafter. There were signs of nascent recovery, and anticipation that this would strengthen informed the government's 2010 fiscal stance involving more fiscal retrenchment effort than the 2009 budget, stipulating a requirement that debt be falling in 2015/16 (Treasury 2010a: 15, 21, 29, 31). Nevertheless, New Labour was keen to retain scope for activist fiscal policy in support of growth. Although they had committed to this future fiscal consolidation, no concrete plans had been announced ahead of the May 2010 election.

The incoming coalition government had come in with a very clear fiscal stance—and divergence with Labour over fiscal policy had been the central focus of a divisive election campaign (Clift 2015). After the formation of the Conservative/Liberal Democrat coalition in May 2010, a new budget in June announced much larger spending cuts, and a much faster fiscal tightening than Labour had planned. The central claim of the coalition budget was that Labour's prior fiscal trajectory would 'put the recovery at risk' and undermine the possibility of sustained economic growth (Treasury 2010b: 1). Dave Ramsden, the Treasury Chief Economist, noted the 'accumulation of unsustainable levels of private-sector debt and rising public-sector debt', and the 'persistent' and 'dramatically widening' 'gap between spending and revenue in the pre-crisis years' which, in his view, reinforced 'the case for urgent action to put the UK's public finances back on a sustainable footing' (2012: 203, 205). In a highly selective reading of IMF advice, Ramsden also implied that the IMF viewed the UK's large financial sector as a source of high vulnerability to movements on sovereign debt markets (2012: 205).

The coalition's economic analysis made bold assumptions about the adverse effects of debt on future growth. Accordingly, its priority was fiscal retrenchment, with fewer concerns about balancing this with securing short-term growth (Treasury 2010b; Ramsden 2012). Hence the mooted need for a much more rapid fiscal tightening than Labour had put in place, composed of approximately 80 per cent spending cuts and 20 per cent tax increases. The ambitious aim of the new strategy was to achieve cyclically adjusted current balance by 2015/16.

The IMF Mission visited once the new coalition government had established itself. The Fund's view of the UK economic policy position in the autumn of 2010 was somewhat torn. On the one hand, they were keen to support the recovery. At the same time, their projections indicated growth was returning to the UK economy, and the Mission recognized that credible medium-term plans for fiscal adjustment were necessary. It was not clear how much fiscal credibility the UK had built up post-crisis, and the Mission saw the merit of taking additional steps to bolster market credibility. The Fund could not be seen to be entering the party political debate, or directly questioning the new government's fiscal consolidation plans. Furthermore, the Fund Mission were encouraged from on high within the Fund to give Osborne the benefit of any doubt.

For the Fund Mission, trying to pick a path through the highly politicized fiscal policy debate in the UK whilst retaining the IMF's prized technocratic and non-political reputation for scientific economic policy advice was not easy. As Mission Chief Chopra recalls, 'The question that we faced in 2010 was: do we support the new coalition government's fiscal plans? In the 2010 Article IV report, we had a box that went through the arguments and made the point that the government would need to be flexible.'[4] Unusually, the November 2010 UK Article IV report included discussion of debates for and against fiscal tightening, noting merit on both sides of the argument. In favour of the new government's line, they noted signs that growth was already returning to the economy, as well as the difficulties of assessing the size of the output gap, and the damaging inflationary consequence of underestimating the structural deficit. Finally, the Mission noted the need to secure political and financial credibility since a loss of market confidence—although not seen as probable—would be highly costly (IMF 2010k: 28).

The Mission also noted important criticisms of fiscal tightening which would come to play a central role in the Fund's counsel to the UK government in following years. Central to this was the effect of fiscal consolidation

[4] Interview with former UK Mission Chief and Deputy Director of the IMF European Department Ajai Chopra, by then Senior Research Fellow at the Peterson Institute for International Economics, September 2014.

undermining fragile growth—a view which hinged on scepticism about the private sector 'picking up the slack' as the public sector retrenched. Secondly, 'a bleak assessment of the UK's structural deficit could be self-fulfilling: because policymakers assume a large permanent drop in potential output, they tighten policies too early; this causes capital scrapping and human capital losses that a faster recovery would help prevent', and finally, 'the need to placate bond markets is overstated', they argued, given the evolution of long-term UK interest rates (IMF 2010k: 28). As former Mission Chief Chopra recognized later, 'we ended up endorsing the frontloaded fiscal tightening but emphasized contingency planning. Over time we slowly started pulling back from this endorsement.' In 2010, the Mission 'succumbed to the view that it might be worth taking the hit on growth to establish fiscal credibility. That hit on growth turned out to be larger, so we got that wrong.'[5]

The timing of the coalition's election meant that UK fiscal policy was at the heart of the wider international politics of austerity. This made the Conservatives' strident affirmation of their fiscal consolidation plans during the campaign and then in the coalition's 'emergency' budget all the more significant. In the Commons, Osborne couched coalition fiscal policy in terms of the Toronto G20 commitments to 'growth friendly fiscal consolidation' (Osborne 2010). Ahead of the G20, Blanchard and Cottarelli sought to frame the international fiscal discussion by issuing their '10 commandments for fiscal adjustment' (Blanchard and Cottarelli 2010). These argued against front-loading fiscal consolidation and reasserted the case for preserving short-term growth (see Chapter 5).

The coalition government self-identified with the more austerity-centric line agreed in Toronto. Allusion was made to expansionary fiscal contraction arguments in the first coalition Budget document. This noted that 'accelerated fiscal consolidation will help keep market interest rates lower for longer, supporting economic recovery' and also that the government's 'credible deficit reduction plan' should 'provide businesses with the confidence they need to plan and invest, supporting the necessary recovery in business investment' (Treasury 2010b: 9; see also Ramsden 2012: 208). In a box assessing the economic impact of fiscal consolidation, the June 2010 emergency budget highlighted 'wider economic effects' of fiscal consolidation, which 'will tend to boost demand growth, could improve underlying performance of the economy, and could even be sufficiently strong to outweigh the negative effects' (Treasury 2010b: 19).

Thus the expansionary austerity argument formed part of the rationale used to justify fiscal consolidation. The commitment to expansionary austerity was

[5] Interview with then Deputy Director of the IMF European Department and former UK Mission Chief Ajai Chopra, June 2013.

not full-blown. After all, the government's fiscal plans were rooted in OBR analysis assuming relatively small but nevertheless positive fiscal multipliers. More strident expansionary austerity arguments assume negative fiscal multipliers. Nevertheless, the degree of emphasis placed by the Chancellor and officials on 'confidence' effects arising from front-loaded deficit reduction as driving a private sector recovery owes much to the expansionary austerity worldview.

While they were pitched in general terms, Blanchard and Cottarelli's commandments contain at least an implicit critique of the UK coalition's ramping up of front-loaded fiscal retrenchment after May 2010. Questioned about Blanchard and Cottarelli's stance, the IMF's then UK mission chief Ajai Chopra compared Osborne's front-loading to 'buying insurance against risks of a costly loss of confidence in public finances, with the premium of this insurance being 30 basis points of growth in 2011', noting that he understood why the government chose to take out this insurance (IMF 2010h). Contained within Chopra's metaphor is a rejection of Osborne's assertion that fiscal consolidation on the scale he set out in June 2010 was a non-negotiable imperative of sustaining fiscal credibility.

In November 2010, the IMF Executive Board were, on balance, supportive of the UK stance on grounds of preserving confidence in debt sustainability, and restoring fiscal space. The Mission were prepared to accept that these benefits outweighed expected costs in dampening of near-term growth. Some Fund Executive Directors highlighted the need for the free operation of automatic stabilizers, and the need to retain the possibility of adjustment of the pace of fiscal consolidation (IMF 2010k). The IMF's endorsement of coalition policy was, it should be noted, contingent on the view that growth *was* already returning to the UK economy at this time, as set out in the Fund's own economic forecasts. As Chopra notes,

> we said that on balance, 'go ahead (with your fiscal adjustment)—but have a contingency plan.' We were very clear. The economy may not evolve as you think it will. At that point we just didn't know how the economy was going to evolve. Then the Bank of England launched QE [quantitative easing], and the basic line was that the first port of call is aggressive monetary policy.[6]

Assuming growth was returning to the UK economy in 2010 clearly affects the balance of prioritization in terms of how much macroeconomic policy settings need to be oriented towards supporting growth:

> The premise had been that the private balance sheets would recover faster; the external environment would get better, so external demand might grow; the banks

[6] Interview with then Deputy Director of the IMF European Department and former UK Mission Chief Ajai Chopra, June 2013.

> would get more healthy and be able to lend more—none of those things happened, and monetary policy did not have the traction that one hoped for.[7]

The Fund underlined that 'headwinds from fiscal consolidation could turn out to be more powerful than expected' (IMF 2010k: 42–3). In what became a recurrent theme, Fund endorsement included an important caveat: the need for contingency plans (for further policy action in support of growth) should the fiscal retrenchment choke off the economic recovery (IMF 2010i).

In the 2011 consultations, the staff team were somewhat puzzled by UK economic developments. Inflation had risen, but the UK team found it very tough to discern which way the UK economy was going to go. This was reflected in the broad range of scenarios they presented for the possible trajectory of the UK economy, from an output gap that was small and closing to one that was large and persistent, in which case fiscal policy would have to change. Thinking about the economy and macro policy in terms of the output gap evokes a 'Keynesian' understanding of the economy where activity is determined, at least in the short term, by aggregate demand.[8] The possibility of a persistent and large output gap is also counter to the New Classical notion of the economy of a self-equilibrating system (see Chapter 3). Thus, a negative output gap is seen as caused by weak demand, suggesting compensatory demand management through monetary and/or fiscal policy.

The 2011 Article IV report underlined serious 'downside risks', notably regarding 'the size of the output gap and fiscal multipliers', and the risk of 'prolonged weak growth' and the downturn becoming 'entrenched', which would require 'additional stimulus' (IMF 2011h: 46). Chopra recalled: 'we outlined different scenarios with different policy responses depending on how the economy might evolve. One of those scenarios was for a continued large output gap, and we laid down a marker already in 2011 that the course of fiscal policy might have to change.'[9] He spoke of the need for the British government to be 'nimble' in its policy response if growth failed to materialize. He recommended 'responding quickly with some combination of further quantitative easing by the Bank of England and temporary tax cuts' (IMF 2011c) targeted at low income households, investment, or job creation (2011h: 31–9, 46).

Fund calls for additional public infrastructure investment spending, or targeted, temporary social transfers or tax cuts for lower earners (see e.g. Chopra 2011a; IMF 2011h: 31–9, 46) went unheeded. The UK Chancellor

[7] Interview with then Deputy Director of the IMF European Department and former UK Mission Chief Ajai Chopra, June 2013.

[8] Interviews with Olivier Blanchard, June 2013; Paolo Mauro, December 2014.

[9] Interview with then Deputy Director of the IMF European Department and former UK Mission Chief Ajai Chopra, June 2013.

continued to flag the market credibility considerations in justifying his fiscal stance. As Chancellor Osborne put it in September 2011, countries with higher deficits 'are more exposed to a loss of market confidence' and they need to 'show they can live within their means' (Osborne 2011b, see also 2011a). Ramsden noted the need to 'move away' from 'unsustainably high government spending', and how 'it is essential to mitigate the downside risks from rising public debt' (2012: 206–7). Osborne said in November 2011 of the previous Labour government's fiscal adjustment plans, 'if we had pursued that path, we would now be in the centre of the sovereign debt storm' (2011c).

Although there were some marked differences of view on fiscal policy in this period, the Fund and UK authorities largely saw eye to eye on the need for unconventional monetary policy, QE, and various forms of credit easing, to do all it could to repair broken credit channels in the economy. This was an important pressure valve releasing some of the tension built up by the fiscal disagreement. The Fund, noted its Acting Director John Lipsky in London in June 2011, saw the UK's 'mix of tight fiscal and loose monetary policy' as 'appropriate' (Lipsky 2011: 1). The Bank of England's readiness to buy up hundreds of billions of pounds' worth of gilts (UK government securities) also played its role in insulating the government from market pressures.

In both 2011 and 2012, the IMF downgraded UK growth forecasts (IMF 2011d; 2012j). As it became clear that the purported return of growth forecast in 2010 was a mere chimera, the analysis and recommendation changed. The IMF Mission, while it was never going to criticize the British government's policies, reported a difference of view with the UK government over the proximity and scale of the risks entailed in fiscal consolidation plans (IMF 2011h: 39), as well as lower growth predictions than the UK authorities (IMF 2011h: 30). The IMF had become increasingly concerned about, even mildly critical of UK fiscal policy, focused on the inevitable adverse growth effects of the fiscal retrenchment as the UK economy fell back into recession.

2012: Stagnation . . . and Hysteresis?

By mid-2012, there was no longer any ambiguity, rather a bald recognition of the UK economy's 'stagnation since late 2010' (IMF 2012d: 5). The UK Mission chief noted 'we began to recognize—both through academic and IMF research, and through what we were seeing on the ground—that the consolidation was ending up being a huge drag on growth.'[10] The Fund Mission used its assessment of how far below potential the UK economy was to anchor its

[10] Interview with then Deputy Director of the IMF European Department and former UK Mission Chief Ajai Chopra, June 2013.

advice. The IMF was now clear that the UK economy had a large output gap and was suffering from demand deficiency. Extant policy settings were deemed 'insufficient to absorb significant slack in the economy, raising the risk of a permanent loss of productive capacity' (IMF 2012e: 1, 4–21). What was distinctive about 2012 was that the disagreement with the UK authorities was not just about contingency planning (doing more if growth disappoints) but also about the baseline assessment of the UK economy. IMF central scenario assessments for UK growth in 2012 and 2013 were 0.5 per cent lower than the OBR figures on which the 2012 budget was based. Similarly, the government and OBR assessment was that the output gap was smaller (–2.7 per cent), and would close quicker, than in the IMF's central scenario of a 4 per cent output gap (IMF 2012e: 5–10, 25, 36, 43).

The 'priority for UK policymakers', Chopra noted, should be 'more expansionary economic policies' to tackle weak demand, persistently slow growth, and high unemployment, all of which threatened to 'permanently damage the long-run capacity of the UK economy' (Chopra 2012). The self-fulfilling prophecy discussed in November 2010 (IMF 2010k: 28) was, in the Mission's eyes, threatening to become a reality. 'At that point,' recalls Chopra, 'we noted that the multipliers vary over the cycle, and by then there was the famous DeLong and Summers paper and work by a couple of people on our team . . . in 2012 we said, "If the economy hasn't picked up over the next year, then you do need to loosen."'[11] The Fund's central scenario foresaw the 'output gap' persisting until 2018, establishing 'this recovery episode as the weakest on record' (IMF 2012e: 24). The 'hit' that this lower growth path entailed for the UK's economic well-being saw 'output per capita a staggering 14 per cent below its pre-crisis trend', with unemployment at 8.2 per cent, and youth unemployment 21.9 per cent, though the Mission did note that the UK labour market was 'surprisingly resilient' (IMF 2012e: 5–10).

One primary explanation of the disappointing growth performance was that the anticipated 'hand-off from public to private demand-led growth' had 'not fully materialized', and this explained excessively high unemployment at 8.2 per cent, and an output gap of –4 per cent (IMF 2012d; IMF 2012e: 10–15, 24; see also 2011h: 8, 14). The Fund linked this 'weak and inadequate rebalancing of domestic demand' to increased uncertainties resulting from the Eurozone crisis, but also noted 'underlying private demand' has been 'insufficiently strong' such that domestic demand growth had been negative on average since 2010 (IMF 2012e: 10, 12, 24–5).

Whilst all aspects of the expansionary austerity thesis had not been at the core of UK policy, the UK government's faith in the private sector, buoyed by

[11] Interview with then Deputy Director of the IMF European Department and former UK Mission Chief Ajai Chopra, June 2013.

confidence effects, being the motor of economic recovery recalled this train of economic thought. The Fund had initially thought, back in 2010, that growth was returning, and the private sector could be relied upon to take up much of the slack. They recognized by 2012 that they had got this wrong.[12] The Fund Mission's increasingly candidly articulated view was that, since this 'hand off' had not happened, government needed to step in. Hence repeated calls for more fiscal activism: 'budget neutral reallocations should be undertaken to make room to increase government spending on items with higher multipliers' offering more support for growth, notably public investment (IMF 2012i: 1) and 'better targeting of transfers to those most in need' (IMF 2012e: 37, 39; see also IMF 2010k: 30; 2011h).

To make their point, the Mission hooked its advice around the threat of hysteresis—an adverse feedback loop where the enduring scarring effect on productive capacity via long-term unemployment becomes entrenched, thereby prolonging the downturn, and lowering the future growth path (IMF 2012e: 24–5, 54–61). IMF staff felt hysteresis was a non-trivial risk facing the UK economy in 2012, not least given the deficiency of demand. This was part of the Fund's increasing post-crash appreciation of non-linear economic dynamics—of the kind which cannot be readily reconciled to DSGE models[13] assuming a return to steady state equilibrium (Bayoumi et al. 2004; Botman et al. 2006, 2007). The Fund's attempts to wield influence over policy were often harnessed to an account of the crisis and its legacy. This was a case in point, with the UK Mission pressing the case that the crisis legacy for the UK was a risk of a new lower growth path.

The UK authorities thought demand, output, and employment were going to pick up anyway during 2012. Their strategy for boosting growth focused primarily on income and corporation tax reductions, removing regulation from business, and providing business with 'the confidence they need to invest' through bringing the public finances under control (Ramsden 2012: 213–14, 207). The protracted discussion of hysteresis in the report and its annex (IMF 2012e: 24–7, 54–61, 70–6) had as its goal not to point out an obvious policy solution but to clarify the key considerations, and raise some pointed questions for UK authorities to reflect upon. These included: How much did the UK authorities think that fiscal multipliers were time varying? Might they be a lot higher now than in the not too distant future when the fiscal consolidation will be implemented? How persistent is the output gap? The UK authorities argued that, if more needed to be done, it could better be

[12] Interview with then Deputy Director of the IMF European Department and former UK Mission Chief Ajai Chopra, June 2013.

[13] Interview with Doug Laxton, Division Chief of the Economic Modelling Division, IMF Research department, September 2013.

done on the monetary policy side with more credit easing, QE, and asset purchases. These, they felt, could offset the drag on growth which the fiscal consolidation strategy entailed. In the Mission's estimation, the UK output gap was *not* closing, and unconventional monetary policy—active though it had been—had not had the hoped-for traction.

Furthermore, indicating how asymmetries of expertise and knowledge about the specificities of the UK economy can limit the IMF's traction, the Treasury and OBR had access to a richer array of labour force participation data. This indicated, somewhat counter-intuitively, that amidst the high unemployment, levels of long-term unemployment were lower as compared to recessions in the 1990s and 1980s. The data showed strong labour market participation results, thus, people returning to labour market in good numbers. The Mission, too, had noted that the UK labour market was 'surprisingly resilient' (IMF 2012e 5, 8), but the UK authorities both had seen more evidence and attached more significance to it. These were some of the reasons why Steven Nickell, OBR Chief Economist, did not revise upwards the OBR's view of the equilibrium rate of unemployment in the UK—a point emphasized by the authorities in response to Fund concerns about hysteresis (2012e: 43). Whilst this *was* surprising, it made hysteresis seem less likely to be the explanation of what was happening. The view of the UK authorities was that the analysis of the IMF's UK Mission did not take full account of how the position of the UK was more complex and nuanced.[14]

There Is No Alternative . . . or Osborne's Switch to 'Plan B'?

Another possible element of explanation for the resilient labour market performance was that UK fiscal policy had, by early 2012, already changed course. The OBR had, in 2011, revised downwards, by quite a substantial margin, its assessment of trend output, or potential growth rate in the UK. Between November 2011 and March 2012, the OBR's downgraded output gap assessment—how far the UK economy was below potential—for 2010 was from –3.1 per cent to –0.1 per cent, with comparable adjustments for 2011 and 2012 (OBR 2012: 35–6, Table 3.1; OBR 2011: 35–9). These dramatic reductions were not due to better than expected economic performance, but instead were a recognition of the sizeable amount of permanent lost UK productive capacity arising from the crash and the prolonged downturn which had followed it (Ramsden 2012: 210).

[14] Interviews with UK officials in Washington, June 2013; London, August 2014.

The changed OBR assessment of UK trend growth altered how the fiscal stance should be gauged. Effectively, it rendered a greater part of the deficit structural, as opposed to cyclical. Thus, its corollary was that the assessment of the structural deficit was revised upwards. This indicated that more fiscal cutbacks would be needed to reach the 2010 stated goals of primary balance and eventually surplus. Chancellor Osborne conceded in his 2011 Autumn Statement the prolonged nature of the downturn, and that recovery was going to be slower than previously forecast, with fiscal deficits larger and more sustained (Osborne 2011c). The decision taken in the 2011 Autumn Statement, was *not* to add this further fiscal tightening onto existing consolidation plans. Instead, the Chancellor used the 'headroom' in UK fiscal plans—accepting a slower pace of return to balance. Indeed, subsequent analysis of OBR data on the UK government's cyclically adjusted borrowing from 2008 to 2015 indicated that the fiscal consolidation, pursued aggressively from 2010 to 2012, in effect stalled in 2012 (Portes 2014).

The central assumption of the construction of fiscal rectitude under the coalition was that Britain faced a 'crisis of debt' (Hay 2013a & b). As Ramsden put it, 'the Government has been clear that it is committed to delivering deficit reduction' to tackle 'unsustainable public finances' and 'to provide the right macroeconomic conditions to underpin a sustainable recovery' (2012: 208). Fiscal consolidation on the scale proposed was deemed an immediate imperative for UK macroeconomic policy to avoid increased borrowing costs since Britain did not enjoy the fiscal space to do otherwise. Appeals to adverse effects in bond markets were a consistent theme of the construction of its crisis narrative (2012: 206), particularly when asserting the necessity of staying the course of fiscal retrenchment. Osborne and Cameron repeatedly claimed that there was no alternative to the harsh fiscal consolidation of 'plan A'.

One reason why the UK authorities were reluctant when called upon by the IMF to shift policy, and also reluctant to acknowledge any shift in policy, was their view of what the anchor of fiscal credibility was. Here was another significant point of contrast on fiscal credibility between the IMF and UK authorities. For the IMF in general, and for the UK Mission, the cyclically adjusted primary balance was the key fiscal indicator. This is dependent upon the calculation of the output gap. By its nature, this can shift for reasons other than policy change. Indeed, the UK cyclically adjusted primary balance was on a completely different path by 2012–13 compared to what had been anticipated in 2010. The Fund's view, based on its chosen anchor of credibility, was that changes to announced fiscal policy were warranted. Provided these continued to plot a medium-term path to restore cyclically adjusted primary balance, they would not undermine credibility. Indeed, the Fund's large output gap assessment suggested very good reasons why changes in fiscal stance should be enacted.

For the Treasury, and especially the Chancellor, the anchor of UK fiscal credibility was the government sticking to its publicly announced, and oft-restated, fiscal plans. It was this, UK authorities claimed, which provided reassurance to financial market actors. IMF Mission members noted that they see the trade-off between policy flexibility and sustaining market credibility rather differently than the UK authorities. So much political capital was bound up with Osborne's 'there is no alternative' position that Treasury officials would have needed very strong evidence that there was a need to change course. This was why the differences of view between Mission and UK authorities were particularly pointed in 2012 and again in 2013. The headline fiscal consolidation plan as set out in June 2010 was retained. The calls for a 'plan B' were ostentatiously waved away by Osborne. Partly this was party political. The harsh fiscal consolidation, and its presentation as inexorable, played a key role in Cameron and Osborne's painting of the Labour opposition as fiscally profligate (Hay 2013a & b).

Although Osborne never admitted as much, the November 2011 use of 'headroom' was precisely the kind of fiscal policy shift called for by UK commentators arguing for a plan B. It was also what the Fund Mission had been urging the UK authorities to do with increasing fervour since 2010. The altered fiscal policy stance was supported by the UK IMF Mission (IMF 2012d). Challenged by the opposition in the Commons, Osborne—drawing selectively on IMF commentary—said, 'The IMF supports our deficit reduction plan. It explicitly asked itself the question, "Should Britain change course?", and said no' (Osborne 2011d).[15] This obfuscates the fact that Britain *had* changed course, and the IMF approved of the change.

The question remained as to whether the change of policy was sufficient in scale to address the UK's large output gap and claw back lost growth potential. As UK officials pointed out, UK automatic stabilizers are large and effective, and this informed a tendency to rely on them for economic stabilization. Faith in the efficacy of automatic stabilizers was another reason why the UK authorities were loath to embark on more discretionary fiscal actions, given the political and practical difficulties in rendering these 'timely', 'targeted', and especially 'temporary'. The use of fiscal 'headroom' was characterized by UK authorities as sticking to plan A, but allowing the automatic stabilizers to operate around it. It was, in their view, sufficient to achieve the economic stabilization task at hand.

[15] There were further attempts by both sides to evoke the IMF in support of their prognoses in the follow-up debate: House of Commons 6 December 2011, cols 184, 193–4.

In general terms, this policy line of allowing the full 'play' of automatic stabilizers around the fiscal plan, such that the deficit could be higher than planned when the economy performed less well, found favour with the Fund. In the post-GFC UK case, however, the Mission were concerned that, given the scale of the hit the UK economy had suffered in the wake of the GFC, more growth-supporting measures were needed. Underlying the Fund's view of how macro policy should become more supportive of the recovery in the 2012 Article IV report was that the UK government enjoyed credibility built up through the tightening in 2010 and 2011, and therefore the coalition government had fiscal space it could exploit. Indeed, the Fund thought there were good reasons to use the fiscal space and change fiscal policy. The UK government, by contrast, identified less room to manoeuvre—and thought that the slowing of the pace of fiscal consolidation in 2012 was change enough.

How Big Is the Output Gap? Supply Optimism/Pessimism and Its Policy Ramifications

An important consideration informing differing views between the Fund and UK government regarding how urgent or necessary fiscal policy changes were related to uncertainties surrounding how large was the UK output gap. This involved assessing how far the potential growth rate of the UK economy had been permanently reduced by the crisis. On the one hand, this had been a deep crisis. On the other, the historical trend growth rate of the UK economy had been remarkably stable and consistent over many decades, and previous major upheavals had not pushed it off that path.

Interpretation is rendered more complicated because there exists no single agreed and uncontested methodology for assessing output gaps or potential growth rates. This explains the debates surrounding its magnitude. The Fund and OBR used slightly different but comparable approaches. The complexities, difficulties, and unknowable factors bound up in output gap and potential growth rate assessment meant Fund economists recognized the limits of how far they could use their assessments to shape policy. The Fund UK Mission had earlier highlighted the sizeable margins of error when assessing output gaps due to 'measurement issues' and difficulties in 'identifying temporary demand factors'. They noted that the uncertainties surrounding output gap assessment were particularly pronounced in the post-GFC context. The Fund assessed three prominent methodologies and approaches to measuring output gaps. Each identified differing degrees of slack in the economy, but none escaped the measurement problems or margins for error associated with output gap evaluation. The difference between assessments could easily be in excess of

2 per cent of GDP, reflecting 'the large uncertainty about the lasting effects of the financial crisis on potential output' (IMF 2010j: 4–19).

These debates surrounding the size of the output gap, unresolvable as they were, had important implications for interpretations of appropriate fiscal policy. This difference in a hard-to-measure and always somewhat arbitrary economic statistic (how big is the output gap) was important for the politics of fiscal policy. All other things being equal, a context of large output gaps makes short-run Keynesian demand management policies more effective and powerful. The Fund's view that the output gap was larger implied that expansionary macroeconomic policy could do more good—addressing deficient demand and spurring the recovery in ways that would not create inflationary problems. The UK government's smaller figure implied such a 'free lunch' expansion was not available. Indeed, it may be that antipathy to active demand management type economic stabilization through fiscal policy is smuggled in through (excessively?) low estimates of potential growth, and a low output gap assessment (See Radice 2014; Wren-Lewis 2011). This is because of the fiscal policy corollaries that flow from this assessment, and how they inform the view taken of the optimal pace of fiscal consolidation depends on assumptions about the output gap.

The 2012 IMF Mission framed the debate about the UK's trend growth rate (and the size of its output gap) around three positions. Firstly, there were 'supply pessimists'—who see the post-crash drop in output as permanent (and therefore the output gap as small); secondly, 'supply optimists' who see no good account of why the crash would permanently reduce the long-term growth path of the UK economy—in their view the output gap is large, and a boost to demand would see productivity and the economy rebound. Thirdly, 'statistics sceptics' who suspected an underestimation of growth in the official figures (IMF 2012e: 5–10).

The Fund noted that all analysts concurred that the output gap was negative, and that 'the debate is about the magnitude'. The Fund's methodology yields a level of –4 per cent; the OBR's initial assessment in 2011 assessment (relying more on surveying business reports of spare capacity) was considerably lower at –2.7 per cent (IMF 2012e: 10). Once the OBR downgraded their output gap assessments to close to zero (OBR 2012: 35–6, Table 3.1; OBR 2011: 35–9) this put the UK authorities firmly in the 'supply pessimists' camp, leaving the IMF in the 'supply optimists' group. The UK government's 'supply pessimist' stance informed their view that a change of fiscal stance to impart more demand boost into the UK economy would not be advisable. The IMF team, with their more 'supply optimist' view of a large output gap, thought the risk of permanently lost productive potential could still be avoided if only policy became more expansionary. Therefore, measures over and above the stalling of fiscal consolidation could be warranted to boost UK growth.

Playing with Fire

The same lines of interpretation and disagreements were central to the IMF interactions with the UK authorities in 2013. The IMF's scepticism as to whether the UK authorities' policy stance was doing enough to support growth and prevent the danger of permanently lost productive capacity resurfaced at the IMF spring meetings. More UK public infrastructure investment was called for by the Fund as a particularly effective way to use public power both to boost demand, lead the recovery, and raise the productive capacity of the economy. Here Blanchard warned Osborne that the UK government was 'playing with fire', a view supported by Christine Lagarde (Elliot 2013).[16] The spectre of the UK's lost growth potential, the self-fulfilling bleak assessment of the structural deficit leading unnecessarily to permanently lost capacity first outlined in November 2010 (IMF 2010k: 28), and the idea it could still be averted through decisive policy action, loomed large in the minds of Fund actors. The April 2013 fiscal monitor provided general, not UK-specific, support for the Blanchard 'playing with fire' statement—citing evidence that fiscal multipliers were larger in the post-financial crisis recessionary conjuncture (IMF 2013a: 37).

First Deputy Managing Director Lipton noted that more planned infrastructure investment spending would have been desirable (Lipton 2013b). The UK authorities pointed out they had been 'shaking the tree' but it was hard for them to do more. There was a limited number of capital spending projects in the pipeline and ready to be brought forward. This was an important area of discord in the 2013 Article IV consultations. The meagre pipeline and the unavailability of large numbers of 'shovel ready' projects indicated a longstanding UK state tradition of relatively modest-to-low public infrastructure investment which could not, it seemed, be turned around rapidly when the conjuncture demanded. This was another indicator of the difficulties in making this kind of fiscal policy intervention 'timely'.

The discussion continued around whether the UK fiscal policy stance *had* changed since 2010, and also whether it should change further. Chancellor Osborne continued to stridently reject both calls for a plan B, and claims that he had already shifted to one. 'Britain must pay its way in the world', and financial market credibility would be put at risk by changing course, Osborne reasserted (2011c). For all the coalition government's deficit discourse insisting that there was no plan B, and that no change to its fiscal consolidation plans announced in June 2010 was possible, the truth was rather more complex. As assiduous observers had picked up, the rhetorical adherence to 'no

[16] See also <http://news.sky.com/story/imf-inflicts-double-blow-on-george-osborne-10448564>.

plan B' belied the reality of a more 'nimble' UK economic policy (IMF 2013f: 37; Chote & Riley 2014: 111–12). OBR forecasts indicated a public sector net borrowing requirement broadly plateauing between 2011 and 2014—7.7 per cent in 2011–12, 7.3 per cent in 2012–13, and 6.8 per cent in 2013–14, before beginning to come down again after that (OBR 2013: Chart 1.1). Robert Chote, director of OBR, noted that their evidence clearly demonstrated that the UK government *did* alter the pace of fiscal consolidation: 'deficit reduction slowed in 2012–13 as the recovery stalled' (Chote & Riley 2014: 111). This was all a far cry from the trajectory announced in June 2010. The coalition construction of fiscal rectitude was, in effect, being honoured in the breach.

Whether an alteration of the fiscal policy path could have been undertaken without damaging credibility remained a point of discussion between the Fund and the UK government. There is, however, every indication from the evolution of the bond markets both before and after June 2010 that the financial market had considerable faith in UK fiscal rectitude (Clift 2015). The actual evolution of bond market attitudes towards the UK remained overall extremely positive and benign, and rates very low, throughout the period (IMF 2010k: 14). There was no direct evidence from the market of loss of confidence in the UK, either under Labour or the coalition, as the IMF subsequently pointed out (IMF 2012e: 39). The nationally differentiated assessments of fiscal sustainability favoured by the IMF—and, it seems, bond market participants—put the UK in a very different category to the troubled Eurozone economies. For the Fund, financial markets seeing UK debt as lacking credibility, leading to rising borrowing costs à la Greece, Italy, or Spain, was deemed a very low probability. This was corroborated when the UK lost its AAA bond rating. There was barely a flicker in UK borrowing costs, and UK bonds retained a safe haven status.

The IMF's contingent, differentiated assessment of national debt conditions and dynamics appreciated how the UK government's strong revenue-raising capacities and powers, good track record on macroeconomic policy, and the structure and maturity of UK debt (Cottarelli et al. 2010: 6–7) all served to expand UK fiscal space. Furthermore, the UK government's construction of Britain's fiscal policy constraints arguably neglected or deliberately ignored the effects of the Bank of England's monetary activism, which was integral to the UK's overall policy mix. The appetite for 'unconventional' monetary policy interventions which all central banks had discovered following the GFC changed the debt dynamics of advanced economy governments enjoying credibility with financial markets. The Bank of England's Asset Purchase Facility (QE) entailed, amongst other things, large-scale purchases of gilts through the secondary market, and this contributed significantly to the low yields on Treasury bonds. This expansion of the central bank's balance sheet through very substantial interventions in the bond market was one cause of very low UK government borrowing costs. The Bank of England's ability to use their independent monetary policymaking powers for gilt purchases could facilitate a more expansionary fiscal policy.

In the press conference which concluded the 2013 Article IV consultations, First Deputy Director David Lipton highlighted the differing anchors of credibility between the UK government and the Fund. He called for greater flexibility, and to bring forward infrastructure investment, all of which could be reconciled to 'multiyear medium-term frame'. Underlining that the fiscal space was available, he pointed out that the Fund had supported other European countries making similar adjustments to their fiscal plans (Lipton 2013b). The credibility accrued from policies pursued since 2010 had, in the Fund's view, expanded UK fiscal space. That such a difference of view over what underpins fiscal policy credibility can exist and indeed persist between the UK government and the IMF is, of course, revealing of the differing constructions of economic rectitude that are possible. It also offers a glimpse as to the leeway governments have (within certain parameters) to choose their own yardsticks by which their credibility is judged.

The Politics of the UK Austerity Debate

The UK fiscal policy debate was deeply politicized—with Osborne having invested enormous political capital in the 'there is no alternative' stance he had taken since 2010. It was integral to coalition plans to defeat Labour at the 2015 general election on the grounds of Labour's mooted inferior fiscal credibility. This made performing its surveillance function particularly difficult for the IMF. As noted in this book, the Fund's prized intellectual authority is rooted in the technocratic, scientific, and apolitical veneer which coats all its economic policy advice and commentary.

This did not prevent Osborne, by proxy at least, drawing the IMF into a heated debate over the UK politics of austerity which agonized over the appropriate pace and trajectory of fiscal consolidation. The UK Chancellor consistently attacked what he termed the 'fiscalist' position of those calling for a fiscal policy more supportive of growth and economic recovery. His assaults were redoubled when signs began to emerge during 2013 that some modest growth was, at long last, returning to the UK economy. Calls for a shift in UK fiscal policy came not only from the IMF but also a range of highly respected economists and commentators—such as Jonathan Portes and the National Institute for Economic and Social Research (Portes 2012, 2013, 2014; Holland & Portes 2012), Simon Wren-Lewis (Professor at Oxford) (Wren-Lewis 2011, 2013, 2014b, 2015, 2016a), and John Van Reenen (Professor at LSE) (Van Reenen 2015; Portes & Van Reenen 2012).

Their central point was that what they saw as excessively harsh fiscal consolidation since 2010 had made the recession unnecessarily deep and prolonged, and was choking off and delaying the UK's economic recovery. This, they argued, was having an adverse effect on the strength of the recovery, and meant that the economy would not recover its pre-crash growth potential. This echoed the IMF Mission's warnings of November 2010 (IMF 2010k: 28). UK government policy settings, these commentators underlined, did not make sense in an economic conjuncture where the output gap was large and demand was clearly too weak. The UK government line after 2010 revealed, according to Simon Wren-Lewis, an ideological attachment to 'demand denial' (2011).

These scholars and commentators were willing to entertain the possibility that fiscal multipliers may be higher in the UK post-crash conjuncture of a protracted and deep downturn, along the lines set out by the October 2012 *WEO* (IMF 2012j: 41; Blanchard 2012c: xv). There was growing evidence from the IMF and others (Delong & Summers 2012; Baum et al. 2012; Batini et al. 2012) that fiscal multipliers vary across the cycle, and therefore would be higher at this point in a protracted recession. The UK Mission put the case for asymmetric fiscal multipliers (IMF 2012e: 38–9, 70–6), and used hysteresis threats to argue that permanent output gains could be made if the government changed the phasing of consolidation.[17] This was consistent with the Fund's 'less now, more later' advice on fiscal consolidation, allowing fiscal policy to play a greater demand management role for countries enjoying fiscal space (see Chapter 5).

The OBR and Treasury considered whether to revise upwards their assessment of UK multipliers. They decided not to for reasons of context, and economic conjuncture—linked to the UK's flexible exchange rate, its monetary policy autonomy, and its policy activism on credit easing and the 'funding for lending' scheme. They noted that for reasons related to the specificities of the UK economy, including its large and effective automatic stabilizers, the likelihood of the larger fiscal multipliers findings being pertinent to the UK case was limited.[18] In taking this line, Treasury officials also took succour from mixed messages emanating from different parts of the Fund on fiscal multipliers. Thus, for example, FAD's assessment in the spring 2012 *Fiscal Monitor* found little evidence of asymmetric fiscal multipliers in the UK case, although it did find evidence of them in Germany and some other countries (IMF 2012c: 36–9). Other Fund working papers exploring fiscal multipliers also offered somewhat lower assessments than the Blanchard–Leigh box in the October 2012 *WEO* (see e.g. Corsetti et al. 2012). Interestingly, OBR assessments

[17] Interviews with IMF UK Mission members, Washington, June 2013.
[18] Interviews with UK officials in Washington, June 2013; London, August 2014.

highlighted this variety of multiplier assessments: 'over recent months the International Monetary Fund alone has published a variety of estimates... some larger, some smaller and some broadly in line with those we have used to date' (Chote 2013).

The larger fiscal multipliers research fed into the UK policy debate. It accompanied and pushed a rebalancing of emphasis from an exclusive focus on austerity policies, tempering these concerns with the need to support growth (Holland and Portes 2012). Indicating their difference of view with the UK government over fiscal policy efficacy, the UK Mission team built their modelling and interpretation on 'higher and more asymmetric multipliers when the economy is weak'. On this basis, the Mission advocated changing fiscal policy settings in order to maximize multiplier effects. The Fund team identified 'permanent gains' which would ensue from such a slowing of fiscal tightening (Chopra 2012; IMF 2012e: 70–6). The rationale was that 'the benefits of delayed consolidation may increase during periods of weak growth due to larger multipliers' (2012e: 39; IMF 2012d). Yet assessments of fiscal multipliers—in the UK and beyond—continued to vary widely across and even within institutions. As Daniel Leigh points out,

> is the fiscal multiplier normally operationalized as just one number...? No. My experience is that desks typically use a combination of models and judgement when it comes to the effects of fiscal policy. They think about multipliers, but there is no such thing as a single multiplier. Every country is different, every instrument...There's no rigid approach to this, and there shouldn't be. It keeps evolving.[19]

These differences are significant because the size of the fiscal multiplier assumption plugged into economic models used to assess the impact of fiscal consolidation has a major impact on what the expected outcome of those economic policies will be.

Osborne derided a straw-man misrepresentation of what he termed, following Coddington (1976: 1264), 'the fiscalist position' and the views of Portes, Wren-Lewis, Van Reenen, and the IMF Mission. He claimed that their interpretation had been disproved by the fact that growth did eventually begin to return in 2013. Osborne asserted that those arguing that fiscal consolidation would hurt economic growth were wrong (Osborne 2013). This was disingenuous in more ways than one (Portes 2014; Wren-Lewis 2015). Firstly, those calling for a different UK fiscal policy stance 2010–13 did not claim that growth would never return—but rather that it was unnecessarily delayed and diminished by the fiscal policy stance. As Blanchard pointed out in October 2013 of the return of growth to the UK economy during 2013,

[19] Interview with IMF Research Department Economist Daniel Leigh, September 2013.

> I do not think this settles any of the debates that took place six months ago, or earlier. It does not tell us whether the pace of fiscal consolidation was the right one or not. It does not tell us whether growth could have come back earlier with a different fiscal framework.

Secondly, Osborne claimed that growth had returned while the government stuck to 'plan A'. In fact, as noted above, the fiscal stance had become more accommodating in 2012 as growth disappointed and growth prospects fell away.

Philip Gerson, the Deputy Director of the IMF's European Department and then Mission Chief for the UK, questioned the mooted causal linkages between fiscal consolidation and growth implied by Osborne's crowing dismissal of the 'fiscalist' position. In July 2014, when asked whether the increased growth rate in 2014 compared to earlier forecasts meant prior Fund thinking was flawed, he noted: 'it's difficult to say that growth has picked up because fiscal policy was tight' (Gerson 2014). This amounted to another high-profile Fund rejection of the expansionary austerity thesis, a line it had pursued consistently since publishing the 'Will It Hurt?' chapter in *WEO* in 2010.

Another strand of this highly politicized dispute over the conduct of fiscal policy and its effects surrounded disagreements over what was causing the UK's growth shortfall. All were agreed that two significant contributing factors to the UK's weak economic performance were the broken transmission mechanisms of the UK financial sector and credit system, and the ongoing Eurozone crisis and its damping effect on external demand. The way Osborne and Cameron sought to present the facts suggested that these were *the* causes of absent UK growth—to the exclusion of all other causes. This was another instance of the 'demand denial' identified by Wren-Lewis (2011). Cameron and Osborne's ideological refusal to admit the connection between fiscal policy and growth was revealed in the coalition government claim in early 2013 that disappointing growth in 2010–12 was unrelated to the fiscal consolidation effort. Cameron even claimed in March 2013 that the OBR had made it 'absolutely clear that the deficit reduction plan is not responsible' for depressed growth, even going so far as to evoke the expansionary austerity thesis again: 'in fact, quite the opposite. Tackling the deficit is the first essential step for growth and, if we don't do it, we'll end up facing even greater austerity' (Cameron 2013). The OBR Director promptly rebuked Cameron, pointing out that this was *not* the OBR's view. Whilst Eurozone crisis and other factors contributed significantly to disappointing growth, consistent with OBR assessment of the size of fiscal multipliers, fiscal consolidation in fact accounted for roughly 1.4 per cent of GDP in lower UK growth between 2011 and 2012 (Chote 2013).

The press conference at the end of the 2013 consultations involved, unusually, the Chancellor and the first Deputy Director of the Fund David Lipton. These atypically senior figures were presenting a reconciled and united front, perhaps publicly burying the hatchet following two years of disagreements. During the 2013 Article IV consultations, clear differences of view were again in evidence between the IMF Mission and UK authorities. For the UK authorities, as in earlier years, the emphasis on 'doing more' was on the monetary policy side, through additional credit-easing measures. Fiscal policy disagreement endured nevertheless, with the IMF still of the view that the UK output gap was large, and the Mission and Lipton advising 'in a range of policy areas the government should be more supportive of growth than it has been and than it plans to be'. In particular, the IMF Mission urged an additional £10bn on infrastructure investment. The prospect of a 'self-fulfilling' bleak assessment of the UK growth path and large permanent drop in potential output induced by 'supply pessimism' and excessively harsh and long fiscal consolidation—first outlined by the IMF UK Mission in 2010 (2010k: 28)—remained a significant concern and downside risk in the IMF's estimation. Fiscal policy was still central to averting this. The Fund Mission placed especially strong emphasis on infrastructure investment because it enjoys 'the best payoff' (IMF 2013b).

2012 and 2013 proved the high water marks of the IMF's difference of view with the UK authorities over policy settings. In the 2014 Article IV consultations, the Mission more or less doubled its anticipated growth level for 2014 as compared to the 2013 assessment. It also projected the UK to be the fastest growing advanced economy in 2014 and 2015. The eventual return of growth took considerable heat out of the exchanges. The IMF Mission identified concerns around productivity growth (not being strong enough) and house price rises fuelling further financial risks. The Fund were especially critical of the Help to Buy scheme, which they felt should be reined in to reduce threats of a housing price bubble. This was part of the Fund's enhanced appreciation of instabilities caused in the financial sector, and the dangers of spillovers from the financial to the real economy (see Chapters 1 and 8). With growth returned, the fiscal policy focus was more on deficit reduction and getting the debt ratio 'firmly on a downward path' (Gerson 2014). Gone were the entreaties to implement more expansionary policy actions should growth disappoint. The IMF came to view the slack in the economy in similar ways to the Bank of England (Gerson 2014).

Lagarde, in conciliatory mode, shared a platform with Osborne in June at the end of the 2014 Article IV consultations, and conceded that the IMF had underestimated UK growth in the previous year's forecasts. Their concerns had not been borne out by events (Lagarde 2014b). This was interpreted, not least by Chancellor Osborne, as an admission that the IMF had got it wrong—a point Lagarde conceded on UK TV.[20] Osborne claimed, 'Pessimistic

[20] <https://www.bloomberg.com/news/articles/2014-06-08/lagarde-says-imf-got-it-wrong-on-rallying-u-k-economy>.

predictions that fiscal consolidation was incompatible with economic recovery have been proved comprehensively wrong by events' (Osborne 2014). This, of course, deliberately misconstrued what the IMF had been saying since 2010. The former UK Mission Chief Ajai Chopra, who had by this time left the Fund for the Peterson Institute for International Economics, argued that the critique of front-loaded fiscal consolidation was that it unnecessarily delayed the UK recovery, not that there would not be one. Furthermore, 'underestimating the strength of the recovery does not mean that the government's path for fiscal policy was right, or that concerns expressed by the IMF and others were wrong'. The return of UK growth 'does not condone past policy errors'. In an unusually candid statement which is revealing about the nature of UK/IMF exchanges during his time as UK Mission Chief, Chopra notes: 'IMF surveillance and policy advice are more robust when they are well-grounded in economics and do not succumb to intimidation by country authorities' (Chopra 2014).

The Former UK Mission chief underlined once more the IMF characterization of the UK's 'dismal recovery' which ONS reports showed to be 'slowest in the G-7' and NIESR research indicated was 'the slowest in 90 years of UK economic history' (Chopra 2014; ONS 2014; NIESR 2014). The IMF's case was always that the pace of fiscal consolidation, in placing a substantial drag on economic activity, was a very significant cause of the depth of the recession. Their view was that the historically weak, and very protracted nature of the UK's recovery was unnecessary. Chopra—now outside the Fund—was defiant in insisting that the Fund had been on the right side of the earlier debate with Osborne et al. over fiscal policy and growth. Even using OBR estimates which—the Fund thought—may underestimate fiscal multipliers, the drag on growth imposed by fiscal tightening between 2010 and 2013 was calculated at 5 per cent of GDP. He also pointed out that the government's 'easing off the austerity brake' in 2013 contributed significantly to the recovery, as did Help to Buy. This he described as 'fiscal policy through the back door' (Chopra 2014). Furthermore, Chopra invoked a wide array of respected commentators and analysts (Wren-Lewis 2014b; Portes 2014; Skidelsky 2014; Krugman 2013; Wolf 2013; Delong & Summers 2012) in support of his and the Fund's interpretation that 'UK fiscal policy was too tight for the weak economy. With less fiscal austerity the recession would have been less severe and the recovery would have been faster' (Chopra 2014).

Conclusion

Consistent with the analysis in earlier chapters of this book, this case study has underscored the importance of crisis-defining economic ideas, and crisis *legacy* defining ideas in economic policy conduct, commentary, and analysis. The IMF had, in the *WEO* of October 2009, published a chapter on medium-term consequences of financial crisis (IMF 2009g: 121–52). This made the case that economies would not bounce back to trend swiftly. The IMF saw non-linearities such as deflation, hysteresis, and stagnation as key causes. The aim of this chapter was to anchor thinking internationally, and press the case for prompt and bold policy activism to boost demand and repair broken financial transmission mechanisms. The Fund's interpretation was that the UK faced a crisis of growth, centred on a large output gap, a deficiency of demand, and threats of adverse non-linear effects—notably hysteresis.

Competing constructions and interpretations of the crisis and its effects on the UK economy between the IMF and UK authorities prioritized different policy responses. For the IMF, the crisis of growth interpretation highlighted a crisis legacy narrative of lost potential UK growth. The deep and protracted recession which followed the crisis gave succour to its calls for a shift in fiscal policy approach between 2010 and 2013. The UK government articulated the 'crisis of debt' narrative centred on retaining market credibility and the UK's ability to 'pay its way in the world'. Its policy corollaries foregrounded deficit and debt reduction, with the mooted need to 'live within our means' used to justify the harsh fiscal consolidation from 2010 onwards. These constructions were mobilized to seek to promote certain fiscal policy responses, and rule out or marginalize others.

The IMF, playing its self-appointed role as arbiter of sound economic policy, viewed these positions as mistaken, and leading to bad policy under the conditions faced in the UK. The IMF view of 'what is to be done' restated the case for more public infrastructure investment if growth continued to disappoint. In this way, the Fund mobilized its research and multilateral surveillance outputs in an attempt to alter UK economic policy settings, and shift understandings of appropriate fiscal policy conduct in the wake of the crash.

The scale of the policy disagreement between the UK and the Fund between 2010 and 2013 should not be overstated. Both parties were agreed that fiscal adjustment must come—that the debt and deficit levels would require it, and that there was a UK structural deficit which needed to be addressed. The dispute between the UK and IMF was over the magnitude, pace and timing of adjustment. Secondly, UK authorities (albeit surreptitiously) did heed IMF calls to slow the pace of fiscal consolidation from 2011 onwards. The remaining dispute between the Fund and authorities was that the coalition government did not slow the pace of adjustment *enough*—delaying the recovery (IMF 2013f; Chopra 2014; Portes 2013, 2014; Wren-Lewis 2013, 2014a & b).

Two noteworthy limits to Fund traction emerged from this case study. Firstly, in 2012 when the debate about fiscal multipliers and fiscal consolidation's adverse effects on growth was at its height, UK officials and the OBR noted something of a plurality of views, and a variety of assessments, to be found in the Fund's intellectual production. They pointed out that they were quite closely aligned with what *some of* the Fund were saying. This issue of the Fund not speaking with one voice limited the ability of the Mission to impress on UK authorities the need to change fiscal policy settings. Secondly, the UK authorities' fuller picture of resilient UK labour market dynamics gave them grounds to question the scale of the hysteresis threat highlighted by the Fund (IMF 2012e). A self-aware Mission team were mindful of the capacity issues they faced, and that the UK authorities possessed a fuller understanding of the UK economy and the difficulties of policy implementation . In both instances, the Treasury made the case for a more country-specific approach, not an 'off the peg' recommendation from the Fund, illustrating how the asymmetry of information can limit Fund traction.

Another theme of the book is how economic ideas are always rooted in ideological assumptions about how the economy and policy work, about the efficacy and desirability of public spending and state intervention playing a major role in the market economy. So it was with the UK policy debate and the IMF's role within it. Behind Osborne and Cameron's 'paying our way in the world' and 'living within our means' justifications was steadfast 'demand denial' (Wren-Lewis 2011) and an ideological commitment to a smaller UK state intervening less in the economy, and a more minimal welfare settlement (see e.g. Gamble 2010). The UK authorities' confidence that the private sector would 'pick up the slack' drew inspiration from 'expansionary austerity'-type thinking wherein the private sector is always the motor of growth. In this view the market economy is a self-equilibrating system which, left to its own devices, tends towards optimal outcomes. This aligned with 'New Classical' economic ideas about 'Ricardian Equivalence' (Barro 1974, 1989) which saw fiscal policy as ineffective.

The IMF's more Keynesian working model takes a more positive view on the role of public power and fiscal policy. It sees a compelling case for governments to pursue stabilization policy and demand management. This chimes with New Keynesian thinking about multiple equilibria, which acknowledged the possibility of the 'elevator' getting stuck below full employment, and the absence of any inherent mechanism within the market economy to return it to full employment (see e.g. IMF 2012j: 61). State intervention, the Fund argued, especially through infrastructure investment, can and should play a central role to claw the UK economy back towards its prior growth path.

7

The IMF and French Fiscal Rectitude amidst the Eurozone Crisis

Introduction

This chapter looks at IMF relations and interactions with France as a non-borrowing advanced economy within the Eurozone. It provides the first account of IMF commentary on and interventions in the French economic policy debate following the crash to analyse how the Fund sought to inflect French policy settings and approaches. It also situates French macroeconomic policy developments in the context of the European policy debate to demonstrate how the IMF worked to influence reforms to the Eurozone's architecture. Drawing on interviews with French policy elites and advisors, as well as senior Fund economists and members of Fund missions to France, it demonstrates how the French government, alongside the IMF, sought a less pro-cyclical macroeconomic approach to the crisis of growth facing the French and European economies. As a former IMF Executive Director for France put it, 'the IMF to us is more helpful in terms of reining in the economy debate and putting the right questions and dialogue among policymakers.'[1] The Fund worked to open up 'fiscal space' for growth-oriented policies within European economic and monetary arrangements. However, the German and Dutch governments, the European Central Bank, and other European fiscal hawks prioritized 'moral hazard' and the 'crisis of debt' narratives, whose policy corollaries were ramped-up austerity and ever-tighter fiscal discipline through substantive and procedural tightening of the Stability and Growth Pact (SGP) in the form of the Fiscal Compact.

The Fund's interpretive line, and policy advice, evolved along Keynesian lines, advocating macroeconomic policy activism to boost demand in the

[1] Interview with Former IMF Executive Director for France, Ambroise Fayolle, Paris, September 2013.

short term, and fiscal adjustment to secure structural balance in the medium to long term. This contrasted with the German line, shared in most EU institutions, which focused overwhelmingly on fiscal sustainability considerations including in the short term. As one senior French official put it, the Germans showed 'a very strong bias towards explaining everything through insufficiently disciplined fiscal policy'.[2] The Fund's policy advice, and the intellectual authority it commanded, was a resource for French policymakers, officials, and advisors in aligning with their own thinking and fiscal policy priorities. French officials noted how the Fund's efforts to convince the Germans, the Commission, and the ECB could be built upon in their own exchanges with these powerful voices in the European economic policy debate.

As Former IMF Executive Director for France, Ambroise Fayolle, recalled,

> from my position at the IMF, what I think was clearly expressed by Olivier Blanchard—it's a combination of three things: a very clear medium-term objective, in terms of fiscal consolidation; sticking to the reduction in the *structural* [rather than nominal] deficit; and in the meantime, if you can keep the first two, 'don't over-consolidate'. I think the IMF has been really instrumental to put this debate at the table. At the time there were huge discussions among Europeans.[3]

In the absence of shifts in thinking in key European centres of power within the Eurozone, the expansion of French fiscal space was limited. The newly elected President Hollande in 2012 hoped to infuse Eurozone economic governance with more growth-oriented macroeconomic policy potential, notably through a Banking Union plan which built on Fund research and enjoyed fulsome Fund support. This could have broken the 'doom loop' between fragile financial institutions and overburdened sovereigns, transforming the scope for activist macroeconomic policy, but it foundered due to a lack of support from European partners, the European Commission, and the ECB.

The Fund's intellectual authority is considerable—their work, research, and commentary, and their leading lights such as Blanchard are held in high regard by policy elites in member states and European institutions. This can enable the Fund to set the agenda in policy discussions with French and European authorities, and it is in framing the policy debate that the IMF finds its influence. For example, in April 2009 the Fund's *Global Financial Stability Report* estimated overall write-downs of the global banking sector arising from the crash at $4.1 trillion (IMF 2009d: xi, 30). This arrestingly large figure was an important catalyst for French and other European banking authorities to recapitalize their banks. However, the IMF's direct power over

[2] Interview with Philippe Gudin, then Head of Macroeconomic Policy and European Affairs in the *direction générale du Trésor*, Paris, November 2013.

[3] Interview with Former IMF Executive Director for France, Ambroise Fayolle, Paris, September 2013.

non-borrowing advanced economies such as France is limited. French officials and policymakers were much more directly mindful of, and constrained by EU rules and obligations—which are a constant backdrop to discussions about policy settings. Ironically, however, they hold the Commission's policy thinking and underlying research in *less* high regard than the Fund's in terms of its intellectual calibre and quality, although they are more directly affected by it.

French Officials/Fund Relations and Article IV Consultations

The interactions between Fund Missions and the French officials and policymakers meeting with them have been built upon mutual respect over a long period. This flows partly from a broadly similar view of the economy shared between the Fund and French authorities. Significant here is which parts of the French state are to the fore in consultations. The French Treasury (Bercy, as it is known) and within it the Budget Ministry are those parts of the French administration historically charged with restraining and curtailing spending by other ministries. The Trésor's 'conservative liberal' instincts seek—not always successfully—to keep a lid on public expenditure (Howarth 2002; Dyson 1999; Bezes & Le Lidec 2015). As such not only do they share a broadly similar view of the economy, but there is a basic commonality of purpose between the French Treasury and the IMF Mission. Former Mission Chief for France Alessandro Leipold recalls fruitful exchanges with Bercy technical experts, as well as with the Conseil d'Analyse Economique—then headed by Jean Pisani-Ferry. As regards the Finance Ministry, Leipold notes, 'Bercy's own instincts were pretty close to ours. When you're talking to Bercy, it's much easier to be on the same wavelength or even more so to the actual budget minister. I don't recall substantive differences in point of view with Bercy.'[4]

The mutual respect also flows from the intellectual authority Fund commentary carries, rooted in the quality of the underpinning research, and the high calibre of key players such as Blanchard. That said, the view from both the Fund and French authorities sides was that, in the pre-crisis period, Fund Article IV consultations did not influence policy a great deal. French authorities found some of the Fund Mission's research useful, for example, on past French fiscal consolidation efforts (IMF 2010f: 18–31), but it did not lead directly to policy shifts. As one senior Bercy economist confided, 'When we want to sell a measure, and the IMF says this is the right thing to do, we are a little bit instrumental—"look, even the IMF says this". Whatever the IMF

[4] Interview with former IMF Mission Chief for France, Alessandro Leipold, September 2013.

publish, if it can be useful for us, we use it.'[5] On other occasions, French authorities shared with the Fund already formed plans for the reform of *taxe professionelle* and local government finance, and were happy to secure Fund endorsement of their strategy (IMF 2011e).

One source of limited traction was because French economic policy officials meeting with the Fund felt that they knew what the Fund was going to say before they arrived. Fund Missions trotted out familiar lines about reducing the size of the state, decreasing 'distortionary' taxation levels, and making labour, product, and services markets more competitive through structural supply-side reform. Year after year, these had been constant refrains of Fund Mission recommendations for France, with the same basic line also taken by the OECD. The limited resonance of this Fund advice is also explained by the high quality of the French authorities' own policy and research proficiency. The size of the French bureaucracy, combined with their high level of expertise and superior local knowledge of the specifics of the French policy situation and context, limited the 'traction' of the IMF Mission. Furthermore, from French policymakers' perspective, the policy debates in Brussels were a much more pressing concern. European Treaty obligations bound the French state to meet economic policy rules. These overshadowed the IMF's surveillance messages.

One of the things which *increased* the traction the IMF enjoyed after 2008 was that the Fund line began to change—and in ways which French authorities found more persuasive. This movement led to more substantive conversations. After the crash, for the first time in a long while the IMF Mission's line evolved in ways such that the French authorities did not necessarily know in advance what the IMF would say. Furthermore, the Fund's interpretation and policy advice changed in ways that were 'useful' and 'helpful' to the French administration in pursuing its fiscal policy agenda, notably vis-à-vis the European Commission and Germany.

French Fiscal Policy and the Crisis

France had struggled with its deficit levels, and had—along with Germany—loosened the strictures of the SGP in the early 2000s following a period of 'unrepentant sinning' and deficits over 3 per cent (see Clift 2006). French fiscal policy during the early Sarkozy presidency, in 2007 and 2008, continued established *dirigiste*[6] practices, prioritizing discretionary activist fiscal policy (his 'tax shield' capping higher income tax rates) over long-term fiscal

[5] Interview with Anne Epaulard, former Deputy Assistant Director at the Treasury Department at the French Ministry of Finance, Paris, September 2013.

[6] *Dirigisme* is the French tradition of directive state intervention in economic activity.

sustainability and rules-based economic policy. Summer 2007 saw Sarkozy's 'fiscal shock' delivering on his election tax reduction pledges, his fiscal profligacy attracting approbation from the German government.[7] France was, once again, overstepping SGP debt and deficit targets. Budget Minister Eric Woerth explicitly recognized the need for a 'pause' in deficit and debt reduction soon after Sarkozy's victory.[8] The new president subsequently explained to a Euro-group meeting of European partners why France would renege on the agreed timetable for restoring the public finances, delaying the elimination of the public deficit from 2010 to 2012 (Clift 2008: 205–7).

When the crisis hit, French debt had been coming down as a proportion of GDP for some years, reaching 64 per cent in 2007. The deficit was just over 3 per cent in 2008, and this gave pause for thought about how much 'fiscal space' the French authorities enjoyed in responding to the crisis.[9] Nevertheless, in the autumn of 2008, President Sarkozy played a high-profile role in garnering support for a bold, internationally coordinated fiscal stimulus, standing shoulder to shoulder with Gordon Brown on the European stage. Dominique Strauss-Kahn's Keynesian line since Davos in January 2008 had been that a fiscal stimulus was needed, part of the IMF's shift from the prior reliance on monetary policy to advocate a significant role for fiscal policy within economic stabilization. At Bercy, officials welcomed the part the Fund played in the 'rehabilitation of fiscal policy, in the case of big shocks, and when monetary policy is not efficient'.[10] In particular, the Fund line and commonality of view with the French on demand-oriented fiscal policy was helpful in dealing with the EC and Germany. Both were allergic to the Keynesian crisis narrative and interpretation, and its policy corollaries of fiscal stimulus. The Commission initially stuck steadfastly to SGP fiscal rules, leading to what one Sarkozy economic policy advisor called 'some debates' with the EC about fiscal stimulus.

The EC denied the crash constituted 'exceptional circumstances' permitting temporary relaxation of SGP debt and deficit targets. The Fund proved 'useful', as numerous Bercy officials put it, in convincing the Commission.[11] As Philippe Gudin, then Head of Macroeconomic Policy and European Affairs in the *direction générale du Trésor*, observed, 'the IMF played a very important role at that time in convincing the EC that these were exceptional circumstances, and fiscal stimulus to counteract the recession was warranted',

[7] 'Berlin critique la pause budgétaire française', *Le Monde*, 6 July 2007.

[8] 'Une politique économique qui hésite entre offre et demande', *Le Monde*, 5 June 2007.

[9] Interviews with French government advisors and Treasury officials.

[10] Interview with Anne Epaulard, former deputy assistant director at the Treasury Department at the French Ministry of Finance, Paris, September 2013.

[11] A term used by numerous Bercy officials, economists, and government economic policy advisors in interviews.

and also 'in convincing Germany to go for fiscal stimulus, and increased deficit in 2008–9'.[12] The European Central Bank, for its part, had raised interest rates in July 2008, focusing on price stability concerns. Both these key European authorities had, it seemed, failed to grasp the magnitude of the shocks, and non-linear threats of depression, deflation, and so on, facing the European economies. In this context, Sarkozy's economic policy advisor noted that the Fund's blessing was important in making initial fiscal stimulus possible.[13]

Two key contributions of the Fund noted by officials and advisors were firstly, resolving the delicate international coordination issue in avoiding the 'you first; no—you first' problem of one country having to be the first to say they needed a fiscal stimulus. As one senior Bercy economist put it, the Fund 'had a role—not because we were listening more, but because [the IMF] raised the question and helped the coordination on fiscal stimulus'. The IMF in this way 'was very helpful in making the discussion on stimulus, in late 2008, early 2009, possible and serious'.[14] Secondly, Fund advocacy of expansionary counter-cyclical fiscal activism provided the necessary legitimacy and intellectual seal of approval on the proposed response. Prior to the crisis, and to the Fund's intervention, 'it was not politically correct to talk about fiscal stimulus—it was no longer . . . in the toolbox of the regular policymaker, it was almost forbidden.' Yet if 'even these guys [at the IMF] say we need to do something' then it must constitute sound economic policy. 'In normal times you let monetary policy do the job, and then you have your automatic stabilizers, on the fiscal side, and that's more than enough—you don't have to add anything. So, [the shift to fiscal stimulus] was a big change, but the situation called for exceptional measures.'[15]

The Fund thus created some important conditions of possibility to advance the case for, and then enact, internationally coordinated fiscal stimulus. The French government duly delivered a relatively bold and successful fiscal stimulus, €38.3 billion in 2009 and €9.6 billion in 2010, representing roughly 2.5 per cent of GDP (OECD 2011: 48–9). The Fund's official initial assessment considered it 'temporary, well targeted, and [it] helped sustain domestic demand and avoid a sharper recession' (IMF 2010c). French automatic stabilizers, the increasing public expenditure, and the loss of output and tax revenues caused by the French economy falling substantially and enduringly below its potential growth rate, had a predictably adverse effect on the French public finances.

[12] Interview with Philippe Gudin, former Head of Macroeconomic Policy and European Affairs in the *direction générale du Trésor*, Paris, November 2013.
[13] Interview with Sarkozy's Economic Policy Advisor, Paris, November 2013.
[14] Interview with Anne Epaulard, former Deputy Assistant Director at the Treasury Department at the French Ministry of Finance, Paris, September 2013.
[15] Interview with Anne Epaulard, former Deputy Assistant Director at the Treasury Department at the French Ministry of Finance, Paris, September 2013.

Behind the scenes, there was some dissonance between the French authorities and the IMF on the conduct of French fiscal policy. There was conservative liberal resistance within the French Treasury as to whether fiscal stimulus was needed, linked to the habitual role of this ministry in curtailing spending. As Gudin noted, 'when we discussed [fiscal stimulus] in the Ministry of Finance in France, there were many who did not agree with the IMF. It was the time of Merkozy.'[16] Amongst those who did think some stimulus was required, numerous Bercy officials felt that Strauss-Kahn and the IMF were calling for *too large* a French stimulus in late 2008. French Treasury officials were also keenly mindful of the SGP's binding fiscal rules: 'we were not so sure, given the tie to European rules on the fiscal side. We were initially not very willing to do a fiscal stimulus at the end of 2008.'[17] Expansionary fiscal policy could have consequences for future room to manoeuvre in the form of the Excessive Deficit Procedure (EDP).[18] Furthermore, as Epaulard recalls, 'within the *Trésor* not everybody was convinced that a stimulus was what was needed', partly because 'if you have big automatic stabilizers, as we have in France, obviously, given the shock, we needed to do a little bit less'.[19] This coloured French views on the extent and scale of discretionary fiscal stimulus required.

In April 2009, leaders gathered for the London G20, where they expanded the IMF's resources and proclaimed the achievement of fiscal stimulus in averting another Great Depression. The IMF and some major advanced economies, notably the US and UK, were at this stage still pressing the case for more fiscal stimulus if necessary. Germany and the European authorities, on the other hand, were more focused on plans for exit from expansionary fiscal policy. In February, the European Commission had begun the EDP against France. The European Council called for the French deficit to be brought below the SGP target of 3 per cent of GDP by 2012. Despite this European pressure, the French line through the summer and autumn of 2009 was fixed on delaying the exit from fiscal stimulus (Sarkozy 2009). In that, they were closely aligned with the Fund Mission's thinking (IMF 2009e) and high-profile IMF interventions by the likes of Dominique Strauss-Kahn (see Chapter 5).

The Fund wanted a credible medium-term plan for fiscal sustainability given rising debt levels, but no immediate retrenchment. Indeed, the IMF was even prepared to countenance *additional* fiscal stimulus measures, albeit only 'in the event downside risks were to materialize'. The Mission counselled

16 Interview with Philippe Gudin, former Head of Macroeconomic Policy and European Affairs in the *direction générale du Trésor*, Paris, November 2013.

17 Interview with Anne Epaulard, former Deputy Assistant Director at the Treasury Department at the French Ministry of Finance, Paris, September 2013.

18 A point underlined by numerous Bercy officials, economists, and government economic policy advisors in interviews.

19 Interview with Anne Epaulard, former Deputy Assistant Director at the Treasury Department at the French Ministry of Finance, Paris, September 2013.

undertaking preparatory work on further future fiscal stimulus measures to be enacted should growth disappoint. Indicating the findings of Fund research on the optimal composition of fiscal adjustment, these plans should focus on 'measures with the largest impact on the economy, such as investment spending and targeted transfers' (IMF 2009e).

The EDP deficit reduction timetable set initially by the European Council—aiming for 3 per cent reduction in three years—was a very tight one. In December 2009, the Commission's estimate for French deficit was raised from around 5 per cent to 8.3 per cent, and the deadline was extended to 2013. The Fund Mission's thinking at the time was that France had 'weathered the current crisis better than most other large economies', but that 'the country remains in deep recession, and short-term policies to support recovery are essential', not least because 'Output has shrunk at an unprecedented rate and unemployment is rising steeply'. Whilst concerns about the health of major French financial institutions were looming, at this stage they were at moderate levels (IMF 2009e).

Turning Off the Taps

We have already established in this book how important crisis narratives can be in shaping policy responses. Up until 2010, Sarkozy consistently argued that this was a crisis of Anglo-Saxon capitalism, rooted in practices in the US and UK, and one that revealed the virtues of continental European capitalism. His platitudinous talk of 're-moralizing capitalism' was laced with critique of the financialization and securitization practices at the core of the Anglo-Saxon dominated financial services industry. French authorities were slow to acknowledge how steeped large French banks were in the same practices, with serious implications for the stability of the French economy.

Later, when it became clearer how deeply imbricated in the crisis France was, notably via its highly internationalized and high risk-taking big banks and their vast liabilities (IMF 2010f: 10–15, 2011i: 4, 6, 8, 23, 27), the crisis narrative changed. As the sub-prime crisis morphed into a banking and sovereign debt crisis centred on the Eurozone, Sarkozy's crisis narrative shifted from activism to restore demand and jobs in Europe to one more focused on fiscal prudence and soundness, standing shoulder to shoulder with Germany to do whatever it takes to save the euro and the Eurozone.

From 2010 onwards, the emphasis shifted in French fiscal policy circles—slowly at first, but with gathering intensity from the summer of 2011—towards first ending the stimulus and then enacting substantial fiscal consolidation. The immediate cause was the EDP, and deficit reduction promises made to the Commission. More broadly, the increasing political salience of fiscal sustainability was accentuated dramatically by the erupting Eurozone crisis from May 2010 onwards. The June 2010 G20 in Toronto, which followed shortly after the first Greek bailout programme was agreed, touted the notion of 'growth friendly fiscal consolidation' (see Chapter 5). Whilst the term didn't exactly catch on, deficit reduction became central within international economic policy discussion increasingly organized around a 'crisis of debt' interpretation.

Blanchard and Cottarelli, keen to feed their IMF line to the G20 fiscal debate, produced their '10 commandments' for fiscal adjustment, counselling against front-loading consolidation (Blanchard & Cottarelli 2010). A Sarkozy Economic Advisor prepared him a memo for Toronto indicating how French policy under his presidency was following all the lessons contained in Blanchard and Cottarelli's 10 commandments.[20] Around this time, the Fund's Article IV mission visited Paris, deeming the fiscal stimulus of 2009–10 'appropriate' (IMF 2010e: 30), and supporting the government's fiscal consolidation plans to cut the deficit to 3 per cent by 2013 (IMF 2010e: 15). The Fund Mission underscored the need to control local government spending, and endorsed government plans to reduce numbers of government employees. They echoed the '10 commandments' by reasserting recurrent recommendations for cost-containing pension reform and spending ceilings on healthcare (IMF 2010e: 16, 30).

Betraying a New Keynesian understanding of financial market psychology common at the Fund, the Mission noted that the goal of reaching the 3 per cent deficit target by 2013 was 'crucial to anchor expectations and avoid an unsustainable debt dynamics' (IMF 2010e: 30). This commitment presupposed a herculean effort of fiscal consolidation on the part of the French government, not least because the budget deficit stood at 7.7 per cent in 2010. French fiscal policy settings from 2010 onwards were not found wanting in terms of 'fiscal effort' to restore the public finances. Both key aspects of fiscal consolidation—increasing the overall tax take and curtailing public expenditure—were pursued boldly. There were commitments to medium-term fiscal sustainability, notably the 2010 pension reform increasing the pension age and lengthening contributions periods. This was a powerful signal; its aim was partly to reassure international financial market actors of the French government's preparedness to take tough action to reinforce fiscal rectitude and economic credibility.

This was important because of growing uncertainties about how successfully the French economy would weather the sovereign debt crisis, especially its knock-on effects on the liabilities of France's big banks. The 2010 Fund

[20] Interview with Sarkozy's Economic Policy Advisor, November 2013.

Mission were more concerned than the French authorities about the fragilities of the French banking sector. In particular, the Fund's analysis underlined that French banks had 'relatively large exposures to Greece, Ireland, Italy, Portugal, and Spain that account for seven percent of bank assets and 30 percent of GDP' (IMF 2010e: 6, 22).

Sarkozy's fiscal consolidation programme only got *more* ambitious as it was revised iteratively in the face of a deepening Eurozone sovereign debt and banking crisis. The Stability Programme for 2011–14 submitted to Brussels in April 2011 targeted a sizeable reduction of the deficit by €60 billion. Successive French executive directors at the IMF noted large agreement between the IMF and French authorities on how to approach fiscal consolidation, such that 'If growth is not there, don't add to the pressure on aggregate demand. This was discussed between the IMF and the French authorities, and basically there was a large agreement on the principles.'[21] Yet there were some ongoing differences of view. For some time the French state had been building up its multi-year budgeting framework to try and gain greater control of public expenditure (Bezes 2008; Le Lidec 2011; Cole 2008), something the Fund heartily approved of. Although this was seen as a move in the right direction, a perennial concern raised by every Fund Mission was that multi-year budgeting plans were based on over-optimistic growth forecasts (IMF 2009f; IMF 2010e: 16, 19–20; IMF 2011i: 8; IMF 2012n: 11–12, 16). This had the damaging effect of assuming away much of the pain of fiscal adjustment (Clift 2013).

These concerns grew as the Eurozone crisis drew on, and as growth continued to elude the Eurozone and France. The link between absent growth and debt sustainability concerns began to feed into the fiscal consolidation debate. Some, including within the Fund, began to ask whether securing growth should be afforded higher priority. The French fiscal adjustment was hampered by the depth and duration of the recession. Initially, in 2009, French Treasury officials were relatively confident growth would return to the French economy during the three to four years of the EDP process, and this would assist the task of fiscal adjustment. Indeed, they initially delayed some fiscal consolidation measures in anticipation of a recovery, rooted in Keynesian assumptions that executing fiscal adjustment once the recovery was already underway would prove less damaging to economic growth.[22] However, such hopes proved premature. Indeed, both the IMF and the French authorities significantly underestimated the depth and duration of the recession in France and the Eurozone which followed the GFC. When growth failed to materialize,

[21] Interview with French IMF Executive Director Hervé de Villeroche, June 2013; interview with former IMF Executive Director for France, Ambroise Fayolle, Paris, September 2013.

[22] Interviews with French government policy advisors, Paris, May, September, and November 2013.

it meant that harsher consolidation had to be planned when growth prospects were even worse.

In the summer of 2011, more significant differences of view emerged, which were reflected in different prioritizations attached to restoring the public finances on the one hand, and boosting aggregate demand to support economic recovery on the other. The IMF Mission took the view that the French Stability Programme agreed with the EC struck 'an appropriate balance between growth and sustainability concerns' (IMF 2011i: 12), yet French policymakers, officials, and advisors did not completely share this assessment. Successive French executive directors at the Fund noted how the French authorities' view of their fiscal space was much more constrained than Fund surveillance and commentary on the French economy recognized. While the IMF Mission identified significant French fiscal space, French policymakers were fixated on the threats Eurozone turmoil posed to their fiscal credibility and debt sustainability. French officials and advisors subsequently recognized that, as the Eurozone crisis deepened, it prompted them to consolidate 'too fast', beginning in November 2010 'in order to be seen by the markets as responsible players'.[23] This is an example of Fund attempts to use a particular construction of fiscal space—which emphasized not choking off the recovery—to try to influence and inflect French policy, but not succeeding. What is surprising is which side of the policy debate each side stood. The Fund were trying to impress more expansionary fiscal policy upon French authorities committed to harsher fiscal adjustment.

The spill-over effects of large French banks' enormous liabilities within troubled Eurozone periphery economies was especially disconcerting (IMF 2011i: 8) in the deepening European sovereign debt crisis. French borrowing costs were creeping upwards, and spreads between German and French bonds—a key indicator of investor confidence—were growing. As Fayolle recalls, 'in 2011 and early 2012, there was a risk that for the markets French debt would be seen as completely de-correlated (from German yields), and that we would become a credit risk.'[24] France could, French policymakers feared, soon resemble Italy or Spain in the eyes of bond market participants. In the summer of 2011 especially, French officials and policymakers were extremely anxious about this trajectory and the threats to French credibility it posed.[25] Hence, they were much less sanguine about available fiscal space, deciding on fiscal prudence grounds to use less of it for expansionary policy than the Fund Mission counselled. Further deterioration of French debt

[23] Interview with Sarkozy's Economic Policy Advisor, November 2013.

[24] Interview with Former IMF Executive Director for France, Ambroise Fayolle, Paris, September 2013.

[25] Interviews with many policy advisors and officials revealed these deep concerns.

dynamics was experienced by policymakers, officials, and advisors as a sword of Damocles over the heads of the French administration. The overwhelming priority for Sarkozy in this period was for France to be perceived as 'like Germany'—a source of stability in the Eurozone working towards the resolution of the crisis.[26]

At all costs, French officials needed France to be perceived as unlike the Southern European countries less trusted by financial markets and perceived as part of the problem. In pursuit of this objective, and in the face of widening spreads, fiscal consolidation was ramped up dramatically in August 2011—and then again in November. One proximate goal was to try and retain France's AAA sovereign bond status (IMF 2011i: 15–16, 38). This was seen at the time as a totem for French credibility and also essential for Sarkozy's hopes of securing re-election. Economic policy advisors noted how, after finding common cause with the IMF in the fiscal stimulus phase, by 2011 they felt the IMF went too far in the direction of advocating expansionary fiscal policies to tackle the downturn.

Sarkozy's conversion to the faith of fiscal rectitude and his commitment to restoring sound public finances came too late, according to Standard & Poor's. The bond ratings agency stripped France of its AAA rating in early 2012. This was not entirely surprising, given debt of around 90 per cent of GDP, low or no growth prospects for the French economy in the short to medium term, and extremely ambitious deficit targets which were unlikely to be met. Before all the major advanced economies started losing their AAA bond rating status in 2012 and 2013, retention of AAA status was seen as a very powerful virility symbol in French politics. Sarkozy reportedly said to aides in autumn 2011—prophetically as it turned out—that if France lost its triple 'A', he would lose the 2012 presidential election.

In truth, even after the downgrade, France remained a relatively safe haven within the Eurozone. In 2013, when the UK was downgraded, some commentators were seeing AA as the new AAA.[27] Given the declining number of remaining AAA sovereign bonds, French and UK bonds remained relatively safe and credible. According to former IMF Executive Director for France Fayolle, 'The combination of the support from the Germans to the French authorities, the changes in the French macro policy, and the confidence of investors in our issuing policy and the French government debt market has meant that we've been able to place the debt at very favourable funding

[26] Interview with Sarkozy policy advisor, November 2013; interview with Philippe Gudin, former Head of Macroeconomic Policy and European Affairs in the *direction générale du Trésor*, November 2013.

[27] 'Downgrade?... What downgrade?', *Financial Times*, 25 February 2013.

conditions.'[28] The adverse economic impact of the downgrade was thus less severe than some had predicted;[29] indeed, a year later French borrowing costs remained extremely low. Nevertheless, the symbolic political significance of the loss of AAA stratus was considerable. Being an early mover towards downgrade was certainly costly for Sarkozy in political and economic credibility terms.

In late 2011 and early 2012, key IMF figures such as Blanchard and Cottarelli made further important interventions in the international economic policy debate. Their aim was to influence the balance of prioritization between securing growth and cutting deficits (Blanchard 2012a, Cottarelli 2012a & b). IMF Chief Economist Blanchard's analysis in late 2011 (Blanchard 2011b) suggested that too rapid a fiscal consolidation might be perverse even in its own terms, as financial markets might see the adverse effects on growth of such *excessive* pace as reducing the credibility of such policies. This was a view also taken by some leading academic economists (Delong & Summers 2012). A lack of growth affects the denominator of debt/GDP ratios, meaning government debt levels get apparently higher, whilst tax revenues continue to fall or flatline. Moreover, bondholders get ever more concerned about the repayment prospects of governments in growth-less economies. As such, deficit fetishism might not be the route to restored credibility.

As the January 2012 *Fiscal Monitor Update* put it, further reductions in deficits 'could be undesirable not only from a growth perspective, but possibly from a market perspective as well' (IMF 2012a: 5). Advanced economies with more growth were 'benefiting from lower spreads', probably due to 'concerns about the feasibility of fiscal consolidation and solvency in an environment of very weak growth'. The upshot was that 'further tightening during a downturn could exacerbate rather than alleviate market tensions through its negative impact on growth' (IMF 2012a: 5–6). Blanchard called the attitude of financial investors 'schizophrenic', arguing that:

> They react positively to news of fiscal consolidation, but then react negatively later, when consolidation leads to lower growth... it does not take large multipliers for the joint effects of fiscal consolidation and the implied lower growth to lead in the end to an increase, not a decrease, in risk spreads on government bonds.

Governments, in feeling the need to respond to markets, 'may be induced to consolidate too fast, even from the narrow point of view of debt sustainability' (Blanchard 2011b).

[28] Interview with Former IMF Executive Director for France, Ambroise Fayolle, Paris, September 2013.

[29] The greatest significance of France's loss of AAA was perhaps felt within the Eurozone crisis management mechanism, the ESM, the firepower of which and ability to raise funds in the markets relied on, amongst other things, France's AAA status.

Citing IMF analytical work, Cottarelli also raised the concern about fiscal adjustment proceeding too fast and that it may prove counterproductive, given 'some evidence of a nonlinear relationship between growth and sovereign bond spreads'. Citing Standard & Poor's concern that fiscal austerity risks becoming self-defeating, Cottarelli noted: 'if growth falls enough as a result of a fiscal tightening, interest rates could actually rise as the deficit falls' (Cottarelli 2012a). The balance of emphasis in Fund thinking was that growth should not be jeopardized, because a lack of growth can do more harm in terms of fiscal credibility than any 'good' done by fiscal consolidation (Strauss-Kahn 2010: 4; Blanchard 2011b, 2012a; IMF 2012a & c; Cottarelli 2012a & b). French economic policy advisors noted how these lines of argument and insights from Cottarelli and Blanchard were picked up on in the French policy debate, and tempered the emphasis on austerity policies.[30] Nevertheless, the Fillon government's harsh fiscal consolidation, pursued because of the perception that fiscal space was lacking especially from 2011 onwards,choked off the post-GFC recovery of the French economy. The output gap increased, indicating how far the post-crisis French economy was falling short of its potential growth levels (IMF 2011i: 9–11).

Weak Growth and Fiscal Consolidation

The ongoing Eurozone crisis, and the financial market credibility concerns it generated, had shifted the tectonic plates of the politics of fiscal policy for France given its high debt and high deficit levels. This drastically narrowed the scope for substantive distance between left and right on public finances (see Clift 2013). The differences in the overall size of the French state and its displacement within French economic life were not dramatic between Sarkozy's and Hollande's 2012 presidential programmes (Heyer et al. 2012). Both Hollande and Sarkozy were agreed on the need to restore the public finances, and large swathes of the Fillon government's 2011–12 fiscal consolidation effort was not questioned. Hollande's campaign committed to erase the deficit and restore the public finances to balance by 2017, just one year later than Sarkozy promised.

That said, both candidates' planned fiscal adjustment programmes concealed the true scale of the pain of adjustment beneath over-optimistic 2–2.5 per cent growth assumptions over the next five years, compared to 1–1.5 per cent (at best) predicted by most economists, a fact consistently cited disapprovingly by IMF Missions, as noted above (see Clift 2013; IMF 2011e: 11;

[30] Interview with Philippe Gudin, former Head of Macroeconomic Policy and European Affairs in the *direction générale du Trésor*, Paris, November 2013.

IMF 2012n: 16). These apparently small differences in assumptions translate into enormous fiscal adjustment sums, assuming away the pain of the cuts in public spending and service provision which would inevitably accompany *actually* restoring balance to the public finances within five years. Indeed, French growth was very disappointing in this period, due to a combination of a very slow recovery, and the legacy of the earlier decision to delay the adjustment required by the EDP. This presented difficult conditions for even harsher fiscal adjustment.

Fund counsel here pulled in somewhat different directions in the short term as compared to the long term. The short-term advice of Blanchard, Cottarelli, and others was that macro policy should focus on supporting demand and growth, and slowing down fiscal adjustment. This seemed all the more pressing given France's very weak growth. The Fund Article IV Mission focused on longer-term suggestions for tackling the reduced potential growth rate which was one of the key adverse legacies of the crash prescribed more familiar Fund medicine (IMF 2012n: 4–7, 14–15, 19–26). The Mission's framing and couching its policy advice in terms of a narrative about the legacy of the crisis and how best to respond to it was used to package the same basic economic reform advice the IMF had been giving French governments for years. The French authorities were urged to make their labour, product, and services markets more competitive through liberalization and structural reform. They should, the Mission advised, make their pension and healthcare entitlements systems less generous and costly. Overall, the IMF advised reducing the size of the state, the number of civil servants, the scale of public expenditure, and the overall tax take in the economy (IMF 2011i: 10, box 4, IMF 2011j: 1–11; see also IMF 2013h). Even framed in the new terminology of the crisis legacy of lower potential growth, this agenda *still* failed to resonate deeply with the French authorities, as it had done many times before.

This lost growth potential arose partly from depressed demand and weak business confidence flowing from protracted recession and austerity policies. Hollande made a campaign theme of this lost growth potential. His solution was not the IMF's off-the-peg structural and market reforms, but rather a reorientation of European-wide economic policies recalling the 'Euro-Keynesianism' of Jacques Delors in the early 1990s, less focused on austerity and retrenchment (Hollande 2012; see Clift 2013; 2014b). Thus, the scope for national level expansionary policy to support demand was, in the Hollande administration's view, severely limited by fiscal credibility considerations.

Being able to follow Blanchard and Cottarelli's advice about more growth and demand-supportive macroeconomic policy required, Hollande thought, changes at the EU-level. This reflected the keen eye French officials and policymakers had on EU fiscal rules and the constraints they impose. Thus, Hollande sought to reorient macroeconomic policy of the Eurozone through reforms to its architecture, which could expand the fiscal space for European governments. He had claimed the Fiscal Compact would be renegotiated to reflect this change. Such reorientations, however, would require the assent of the EU authorities and the German and other governments. This issue came to a head early in Hollande's presidency when his growth plan was announced ahead of the Euro Area Summit in June 2012 (discussed below). Hollande found that renegotiation was not remotely possible—because the line on fiscal adjustment enshrined in the Compact, the substantive and procedural tightening of the SGP that it entailed, was a *casus belli* for the Germans.[31]

At the domestic level, Hollande's Keynesian thinking was tempered by market confidence concerns reflected in the assessments of limited French fiscal space. In their amendments to the 2012 budget and their drafting of the 2013 budget, the Socialist Ayrault government remained resolutely committed to the fiscal consolidation strategy. This had been the cornerstone of Hollande's programme even during the Socialist party primaries campaign in the summer of 2011. The balance of emphasis within the macroeconomic policy strategy set out for the Hollande *quinquennat* in July 2012 emphasized stabilizing and restoring the public finances, rather than with activist fiscal policy boosting demand and growth.

The Fund's first Mission visit with the new Socialist government questioned (along lines which recalled Blanchard's '10 commandments') the wisdom of the front-loaded fiscal consolidation. This sought to meet the 3 per cent deficit target by 2013 as promised to the European Commission to meet SGP and EDP requirements. These binding European obligations, much more than anything the Fund said, were in the forefront of French fiscal policymakers' minds.[32] French authorities defended policy as necessary for debt sustainability and financial market credibility reasons, whilst the Fund Mission urged a slower pace of consolidation, and raised concerns about the excessively procyclical policy stance (IMF 2012n: 15).

French authorities were well aware that fiscal multipliers meant that the adverse impact on growth would be considerable.[33] As Epaulard put it, 'We always knew. This is something that we always suspected... we are very happy that the Fund has been saying it. It's new because it's formalized... you have numbers behind it. What Olivier Blanchard did is very helpful for us. But we were not surprised by the result.'[34] Indeed this insight had guided an initial decision to delay the fiscal consolidation agreed in the context of EDP with the European Commission. Nevertheless, in the interests of French policy

[31] Interview with Sarkozy policy advisor, November 2013.
[32] A point made by numerous advisors, officials, and Bercy economists in interview.
[33] Interviews with numerous French policy advisors and officials.
[34] Interview with Anne Epaulard, former Deputy Assistant Director at the Treasury Department at the French Ministry of Finance, Paris, September 2013.

credibility, and of the wider euro area crisis resolution strategy, French policy-makers felt they had no choice (IMF 2012n: 15). As the final Article IV report put it, 'A more measured pace of fiscal consolidation would have been preferable on cyclical grounds, but market and euro area imperatives have reduced fiscal space' (IMF 2012n: 1). Again we see a markedly different construction of fiscal space by the Fund, with different policy corollaries, and its use by the IMF to try and alter policy settings and prioritizations.

In the 2013 Article IV consultations, discussions surrounded the pace and composition of fiscal adjustment, not the direction or necessity of fiscal adjustment, on which all were agreed. Once again, the Mission urged French authorities not to front-load fiscal consolidation, arguing that missing nominal targets was acceptable. Yet the French authorities did not think they had sufficient fiscal space to slow down the pace of fiscal consolidation. The Mission argued it did not make sense to heap further austerity on France's still fragile recovery. This was also rooted in the Fund's desire for less fiscal consolidation now, in the context of more later, built into the credible medium-term framework which it sees as the key to credibility (IMF 2013c).[35]

A second point of disagreement, which pointed in a rather different direction, was over the composition of adjustment. IMF concerns about the size of the French state and its tax take found expression in advocating a different mix between expenditures and revenues in how to pursue fiscal consolidation (IMF 2013c; IMF 2013h; IMF 2013g; see also IMF 2012n: 16). As the French Executive Director at the IMF put it in 2013,

> We are committed to do less on the income side and more on the expenditure side. The Fund more or less called on us to do all of the adjustment on the expenditure side. We do not think it is fully feasible, but we have a plan to share out 70% on the expenditure side and 30% on the income side.[36]

The Fund's Shaping of the European Fiscal Policy Debate 2012–13

In its direct advice to French authorities, both about front-loading and reducing the size of the state by focusing fiscal adjustment entirely on expenditure reduction, the IMF's view did not prevail. Nevertheless, the IMF did have a highly significant, if slightly more indirect, role to play in influencing the trajectory of French fiscal policy. As Epaulard recalls, 'the IMF was very helpful in changing the ideas of the European Commission, in easing the conditions

[35] This was confirmed in interviews with members of IMF French Article IV Mission, June 2013.
[36] Interview with French IMF Executive Director Hervé de Villeroche, June 2013.

that the European Commission was imposing on the country.'[37] This came through the Fund's successful efforts to persuade the EC to alter its thinking about agreed EDP deficit reduction timetables as the European-wide recession dragged on. In early 2013, Finance Minister Moscovici recognized that the Maastricht 3 per cent deficit target which had been a central plank of French policy since 2009 would not be met (Moscovici 2013). This was due to the ongoing weakness of French growth, and its adverse impact on government revenues. It also reflected over-optimistic growth assumptions built into France's multi-year planning of the public finances. Reneging on this totem of French fiscal credibility could have been interpreted as further evidence of French fiscal profligacy, with potentially dire consequences for French borrowing costs and fiscal sustainability. However, the ideational context had evolved significantly during 2012–13, thanks in no small part to the efforts of the IMF.

One manifestation of this was the prevailing wisdom about what kinds of fiscal objectives to target. Since the Maastricht Treaty, nominal targets—such as 3 per cent of GDP deficit at the core of the SGP—had been preferred by European authorities. The IMF had long argued for using *structural* (and therefore *cyclically adjusted*) targets to pilot fiscal policy (IMF 2012g: 1, 4–5). This was part of the Fund's long-standing critique of the damaging pro-cyclicality intrinsic to the nominal goals, which can induce spending cuts in a recession, or fail to induce restraint and the building up of fiscal buffers during upswings. In the Fund's advocacy of structural fiscal targeting, there was common ground with the French authorities, who advocated cyclically adjusted fiscal targets for the same reasons.[38]

The wind had begun to blow in this direction elsewhere in Europe—notably with the 2009 German 'Schuldenbremse' debt brake balanced budget amendment to Germany's Basic Law (constitutional law), which incorporated structural fiscal targeting. German attraction for structural targets was inspired more by 'sound finance'considerations, forcing governments to build up fiscal buffers in good times. For them the priority was not enabling more discretionary expansionary fiscal policy during recessions. On the greater prominence of structural targets within EU fiscal governance, the French Executive Director noted: 'we think that it's adequate to have structural targets and to keep on respecting those structural targets. But it's risky to have nominal targets. This view is wholly shared here at the Fund... I think the Fund has helped the European debate to change a little bit.'[39] In terms of the impact on fiscal policy

[37] Interview with Anne Epaulard, former Deputy Assistant Director at the Treasury Department at the French Ministry of Finance, Paris, September 2013.

[38] Interview with French IMF Executive Director Hervé de Villeroche, June 2013. This point was reaffirmed by numerous Bercy officials, economists, and French policy advisors in interview.

[39] Interview with French IMF Executive Director Hervé de Villeroche, June 2013.

conduct, former IMF Mission Chief for France noted the contrast between the Fund and the Commission on these fiscal issues: 'when you're telling [countries] in bad times perhaps you don't need to do quite as much [fiscal consolidation] as you originally planned because growth is actually weaker. I think where the Fund appears more activist is that it's certainly more tolerant than the EU fiscal rules.'[40]

The Fund found ways to set the economic policy agenda and shape thinking in European capitals and in EU institutions. Key figures such as Blanchard, Strauss-Kahn, and later Lagarde used interactions at the IMF's spring and autumn meetings, and at European summits where they were in attendance. This was particularly true of Blanchard and the evolution of approaches to fiscal consolidation through 2012 and into 2013. Gudin reported his first-hand experience:

> At the time the IMF's fiscal multipliers research was coming to light—even before the October 2012 *WEO*—in the 2012 spring meeting there was the first debate about the fiscal multipliers and there was a big disagreement between the European nation states and the IMF. This reached its height in Tokyo meetings in September—it was the big topic.[41]

In this period, protracted recessionary conditions, lost economic activity, and lost government revenues continued to impede efforts to restore the public finances. The upshot was that even fiscally hawkish countries like the Netherlands saw deteriorations in their public finances despite their steadfast pursuit of fiscal adjustment. This outcome seemed to support the view, espoused at the Fund and fed into the European debate, that fiscal consolidation can be self-defeating. This gave some policy elites who had hitherto advocated harsh austerity measures pause for thought. As French Executive Director at the IMF De Villeroche said, 'it is risky when growth is going down to pursue a nominal objective. The important thing is to reduce the structural deficit. The delay which has been given by the European Commission to France, to the Netherlands, and to other countries is very much based on this assessment.'[42]

Key IMF players sensed an opportunity presented by the difficulties experienced by fiscally sound 'good pupils' coinciding with the fruition of its own Keynesian-inspired fiscal research agenda. They leveraged the Fund's reputation for fiscal probity to intervene strategically in the European fiscal debate, notably through the work by Blanchard and Leigh on fiscal multipliers

[40] Interview with former IMF European Department Deputy Director Alessandro Leipold at the IMF, September 2013.

[41] Interview with Philippe Gudin, former Head of Macroeconomic Policy and European Affairs in the *direction générale du Trésor*, Paris, November 2013.

[42] Interview with French IMF Executive Director Hervé de Villeroche, June 2013.

(see Chapter 5). The Fund had assembled a combination of not just theoretical argument and qualitative evidence, but also quantitative evidence drawing on the IMF's wealth of cross-country experience. This was distilled in Blanchard and Leigh's 'natural experiment' research design regressing fiscal multiplier estimates against growth shortfalls. It found that the impact of fiscal policy on growth had been systematically underestimated by governments and institutions like the IMF and OECD. This work, and the policy issues it raised were much discussed in the IMF spring and autumn meetings in 2012 (IMF 2012j: 41–8; Blanchard & Leigh 2013a & b).

French economic policy advisors noted how the IMF built up momentum around its fiscal multipliers research. This, combined with the economic conjuncture which seemed to underline the prescience of the findings, enabled the IMF to play an instrumental role in convincing the European Commission to shift its thinking about the appropriate pace of fiscal consolidation.[43] French authorities equally made use of IMF thinking on fiscal multipliers and the growth/debt relationship. The Fund's position was helpful to French negotiations with the EC, since the IMF and the French were able to operate a kind of pincer movement. Both urged on the Commission a rethinking of the pace of fiscal consolidation, and a rebalancing of that priority alongside growth.

The Fund were shaping the ideational conditions in which the EC operated, and managed to get the Commission to revisit their assessment of fiscal multipliers, and its policy corollary—the timeframe for meeting the 3 per cent deficit target.[44] The French authorities, in their discussions with the Commission, promised more effort and movement on labour market and pension reform as quid pro quo for the longer deficit reduction timeline.[45] Both Cottarelli and Blanchard noted how they saw at first-hand how the Fund influenced the Commission's position on the size of fiscal multipliers, which in turn led them to revisit the appropriate pace of deficit reduction under EDP.[46] Gudin reported,

> I talked to a senior civil servant at the Commission and he evoked the IMF fiscal multipliers debate and said that as growth returns, fiscal multipliers are probably going to normalize—but over the recent period (2010–12), fiscal multipliers

[43] This point was reaffirmed by numerous Bercy officials, economists, and French policy advisors in interview.

[44] Interview with Sarkozy policy advisor; interview with Anne Epaulard, former Deputy Assistant Director at the Treasury Department at the French Ministry of Finance, Paris, September 2013.

[45] Interview with Sarkozy policy advisor; interview with Anne Epaulard, former Deputy Assistant Director at the Treasury Department at the French Ministry of Finance, Paris, September 2013.

[46] Interviews with Blanchard and Cottarelli, June 2013.

> probably have been much higher than what we had initially in mind. From that perspective it was justified to grant more time to France and other countries.[47]

The view of the Commission Directorate General for Economic and Financial Affairs was that, as growth returned to European economies, fiscal multipliers would probably normalize.

Another important marker in the 'growth vs austerity' debate in this period was the work of Reinhardt and Rogoff. In early 2010, former IMF Chief Economist Kenneth Rogoff, along with Carmen Reinhart, had published research claiming that, above a 90 per cent threshold, high debt had a strong adverse effect on medium-term growth (2010; see also Reinhart, Reinhart, & Rogoff 2012). The idea of such a debt threshold level had powerful salience for the politics of the European austerity debate. Its mooted existence seemed to tilt the balance of policy prioritization in favour of tackling debt over supporting growth above a debt level which many advanced economies were fast approaching or had exceeded. The 90 per cent threshold and the identification of an apparently mechanical relationship between higher debt and weaker growth prospects was widely evoked in support of a shift towards austerity policies. French officials and advisors noted how this 90 per cent threshold was used by the Commission, the German government, and others as one of the rationales behind encouraging more action on fiscal consolidation.[48]

However, at the same time as the timeframe for deficit reduction under the SGP being revisited, the intellectual underpinnings of the 90 per cent threshold were subjected to increasing scrutiny, as other researchers could not reproduce Reinhart and Rogoff's results. In 2013, their premises and research methods were critiqued and rejected, and the 90 per cent threshold findings discovered to be erroneous (Herndon et al. 2014), including by the Fund itself (Pescatori et al. 2014). This was part of a wider rethink about how high a priority should highly indebted advanced economy governments place on debt reduction (Ostry et al. 2015; Ostry et al. 2016). It was another instance of instrumental use of Fund research by French officials, who noted how 'helpful' it was to have the Fund and others discrediting the 90 per cent threshold. This meant that the Commission could no longer use that argument against the French position, or to justify more austerity. As sluggish economic performance drew on, especially in many Eurozone countries, the rejection of the 90 per cent threshold reignited parts of the politics of austerity debate. It opened up scope to revisit the balance of prioritization between tackling debt and supporting economic recovery.

[47] Interview with Philippe Gudin, former Head of Macroeconomic Policy and European Affairs in the *direction générale du Trésor*, Paris, November 2013.

[48] Interview with Anne Epaulard, former Deputy Assistant Director at the Treasury Department at the French Ministry of Finance, Paris, September 2013.

Franco-German Relations, the IMF, and Eurozone Crisis Narratives

These shifting positions on fiscal policy, growth, and debt fed into a febrile atmosphere of adversarial European austerity politics. Even though the Commission had relented in their deficit fetishism, the Germans in particular did not. Although convinced that structural fiscal targets were useful, the German authorities also saw a role for nominal targets as clear symbols of fiscal discipline, and they remained convinced that France and the Netherlands, as core countries, *had* to stick to and meet the nominal 3 per cent deficit target in 2013 in order to sustain the fiscal credibility of the Eurozone.[49] As one seasoned observed noted of EC and German authorities' approach to the SGP,

> in theory it's supposed to be structural targets, but in practice it actually never is. It's all about the 3 per cent nominal target... Whereas the Fund is more consistent in saying it does not matter if you have some nominal slippages. As long as you're just sticking to your underlying structural adjustment, that's perfectly fine.[50]

The French authorities, and by the end of 2012 also the EC, shared the IMF view that the damagingly pro-cyclical German attachment to nominal 3 per cent deficit target was misguided in the current conjuncture.

The German antipathy to expansionary fiscal policy is particularly deep-seated, rooted in the 'sound money' ethos of ordo-liberalism (see Bonefeld 2012; Dyson 1999; Dyson & Featherstone 1999: 261–2, 287–8, 293–4; Sally 1996).[51] This prioritized balanced budgets and fiscal prudence very highly, and was disinclined to see a positive short-term relationship between activist fiscal policy and growth. Rather, ordo-liberal thought focuses on long-term fiscal soundness, and the merits of balanced budgets. As one senior French Treasury official noted, this antipathy to Keynesian thinking is reflected in the German economic policy forecasting process:

> The Ministry of Economy together with the wise men do a scenario, a macroeconomic forecast, then they publish the forecast. Then they give it to the Ministry of Finance and they do the budget. There is no coordination, whatever the budget is, it's assumed it won't affect the economic forecast. They truly believe that whatever we do in terms of fiscal policy there is no impact. So they consider in their minds that fiscal multipliers are zero.[52]

[49] This point was reaffirmed by numerous Bercy officials, economists, and French policy advisors in interview.

[50] Interview with former IMF European Department Deputy Director Alessandro Leipold at the IMF, September 2013.

[51] The German state tradition focused on anti-inflationary macroeconomic policy and a constitutionally instituted competitive market order.

[52] Interview with Philippe Gudin, former Head of Macroeconomic Policy and European Affairs in the *direction générale du Trésor*, Paris, November 2013.

The IMF and French authorities' view that it is important not to *over-consolidate* was met with a refusal on the part of German authorities to recognize that, in the short-term, fiscal policy can have a significant impact on levels of economic activity.

Linked to this, the German interpretation of the Eurozone crisis more broadly saw it in terms of the competitiveness and sound finance failings of deficit countries within the Eurozone (see Jacoby 2015; Newman 2015; Varoufakis 2017). These countries had been insufficiently fiscally prudent, and had not undertaken the kinds of painful labour market and welfare reform which had boosted German competitiveness since the 1990s. There followed from this narrative a clear indication of who should bear the burdens of adjustment arising from the Eurozone crisis and efforts to resolve it. As Gudin put it, 'the focus had been exclusively on fiscal policies and public deficits. That was the German view that prevailed.'[53] This explains Germany's insistence on one-sided adjustment by deficit countries, seen in Berlin as a necessary quid pro quo for initiatives to address the crisis such as the European Stability Mechanism (ESM). This same difference of crisis interpretation underpinned the dissonance within the Troika about European programme design discussed in Chapter 5.

There was an alternative, more multi-causal interpretation about the roots of the Eurozone crisis, which had its advocates amongst the French authorities and some IMF staff. This saw German current account surpluses as every bit as much a problem, causing destabilizing imbalances, as the trade and budget deficits of Southern and periphery countries. This different narrative had the potential to alter how the burden of adjustment was shared in policies to address the crisis. Whist Lagarde was French Finance Minister, she was integral to the introduction of the 'macroeconomic imbalances procedure' (MIP) within Eurozone governance. This arcane and technocratic formula contained within it a frontal assault on Germany's Eurozone crisis narrative, and a challenge to German readings of its causes. The fiscal politics underpinning this different narrative had the potential to alter how the burden of adjustment was shared in policies to address the crisis.[54] The immediate policy corollary entailed the French Finance Minister urging Germany to stimulate domestic demand, and thereby boost European export markets, to tackle its sizeable current account surpluses (Barber 2010). The MIP sought to eradicate an asymmetry in the Eurozone's economic governance, proposing that *both* excessive deficits *and* excessive current account surpluses be considered a

[53] Interview with Philippe Gudin, former Head of Macroeconomic Policy and European Affairs in the *direction générale du Trésor*, Paris, November 2013.

[54] Interview with Philippe Gudin, former Head of Macroeconomic Policy and European Affairs in the *direction générale du Trésor*, Paris, November 2013; interview with Sarkozy policy advisor, November 2013.

problem which needed to be addressed. French officials noted how, in building up the case for tackling surplus countries as well, they drew on Fund work noting how crisis resolution required more effort to boost demand by surplus countries, with Germany repeatedly singled out.[55]

The MIP was introduced in 2011 as part of the 'Six Pack', the EU fiscal and macroeconomic surveillance mechanisms entailing stricter application of fiscal rules, strengthening both the preventative and corrective arms of the SGP. This entered into force in December 2011, its aim 'to identify, prevent and correct harmful imbalances by ensuring appropriate policy responses are adopted in Member States in a coordinated manner' (EC 2012: 10). This potentially required Member States to submit corrective action plans to the Commission indicating how these would be addressed. There was even the possibility of fines being levied if efforts to address the imbalances were deemed insufficient. The rebalancing to get surpluses as well as deficits to be considered as potentially 'harmful' was only partial. The threshold at which current account surpluses were deemed problematic was set at 6 per cent—rather higher than the 4 per cent for current account deficits.[56] Nevertheless, DG Ecfin's recognition that 'large and persistent current account surpluses can . . . be caused by market failures or policy settings that constrain domestic demand and investment opportunities' (EC 2012: 10) was important. German surpluses fell under its definition of 'harmful imbalances'. This challenged the prevailing German interpretation of the Eurozone crisis, and even critiqued German policy settings.

France's role in getting the tackling of surpluses on the political agenda of the Commission was a challenge to German power within the Eurozone. In this, they drew on Fund research and were supported by IMF interventions in the policy debate (IMF 2015f; IMF 2015d; IMF 2015e: 1–19; IMF 2015h). The German view was that supply-side reforms (following the German example) in the other economies would eventually restore competiveness and solve the Eurozone's imbalances problem. The French authorities and the Fund saw this as what Wren-Lewis calls 'demand denial' (Wren-Lewis 2011). In its way, the MIP also rejected the German view. Numerous interviewees noted how helpful to French authorities the IMF were in this period, working hard to convince Germany to look beyond the exclusive supply-side reform and fiscal consolidation approach to crisis resolution. Doing more to boost domestic demand, and private investment, including higher wages in Germany, could, the Fund

[55] Interviews with senior French government officials.

[56] Interview with Philippe Gudin, former Head of Macroeconomic Policy and European Affairs in the *direction générale du Trésor*, Paris, November 2013 <http://ec.europa.eu/economy_finance/economic_governance/macroeconomic_imbalance_procedure/scoreboard/index_en.html>.

Mission pointed out, be good for the German and Eurozone economies (IMF 2015d; IMF 2015f; Lagarde 2017).

The European banking and sovereign debt crisis, the IMF consistently noted, was not solely a supply-side problem, and could not be solved by getting the weaker Eurozone economies to observe the rules, undertake structural reforms, and wait for them to catch up. It was also a demand-side problem—and this required action by surplus countries to boost aggregate demand and economic activity. Calling upon 'excessive' surplus countries like Germany to do more to boost Eurozone aggregate demand was a recurrent theme of IMF commentary (IMF 2015f; IMF 2015d; IMF 2015e: 1–19; IMF 2015h). The Commission published MIP 'alerts mechanism' papers noting the very high German savings rate, very low private sector debt, and the adverse effect of these on private sector demand. These called for increased investment, and echoed Council of Ministers recommendations for Germany to do more to support domestic demand (EC 2013: 5–6). The Commission also published papers criticizing Germany's large surplus—indicating it required 'policy action', and noting the role played by German household investment and consumption practices in subduing demand in Germany and beyond (EC 2014: 11).

In the absence of direct leverage over non-borrowing advanced economies like Germany, there were limits to how much the IMF could affect policy settings. Nevertheless, within those limits, the IMF worked to impress an alternative crisis interpretation upon German and other European policymakers. They also played a role in building into the Eurozone's architecture the other policy concerns that flowed from this differing crisis interpretation.

The IMF, Breaking the 'Doom Loop', and the Politics of European Banking Union

The IMF, along with the French authorities, sought to advance an alternative crisis narrative at odds with the German version of both 'what's going on' and 'what is to be done'. The overarching goal for the French authorities and the Fund was to expand the fiscal space available for European governments to pursue macroeconomic strategies more supportive of demand and the recovery. The Fund had, ever since the Eurozone crisis first broke out in 2010, consistently urged the European institutions to do more to tackle contagion risks by putting in place effective and sufficiently powerful Eurozone backstops. As the sovereign debt crisis dragged on and deepened, Fund calls became more numerous and more urgent (IMF 2012f; IMF 2013k). This ranged from heavily hinting that the ECB should be doing more to buy up Greek and other sovereign debt in the secondary market (IMF 2011f: 9), to talking up and wishing into existence the 'permanent crisis management procedure' that the ESM would come to embody (IMF 2011c: 60; Lagarde 2012a & c).

Eurozone financial market dynamics reflected the fragilities of the European banking system. These compounded ongoing concerns about the liabilities of major banks with significant exposure to Eurozone periphery sovereign debt. This made what the IMF called 'the adverse feedback loop between weak sovereigns and financial institutions' (IMF 2011o: xvi) an especially pressing policy concern. One key possible solution took shape in the summer of 2012. In April 2012 Blanchard's foreword to the *WEO* urged that 'Measures should be taken to decrease the links between sovereigns and banks', notably including 'the creation of euro level deposit insurance and bank resolution' (Blanchard 2012b). Indeed, preparatory work and research had been undertaken by the IMF from early 2007 on the construction of financial sector firewalls (IEO: 2016: 24; Veron 2016; Chopra 2011b). This underpinned the proposals which crystallized into what came to be known as 'European Banking Union' at the Euro Area Summit in June 2012. This meeting signalled a potential step change, which promised to deliver on the agenda that Blanchard, amongst others, had set out. If successful, Banking Union had the potential to reduce the borrowing costs and the financial strain facing European governments, although at the cost of tighter banking supervision under the auspices of the ECB. Hollande, drawing on the IMF's groundwork, and supported by Italy and Spain, was at the centre of the Banking Union construction efforts.

If an EU- or Eurozone-level approach to resolving troubled financial institutions could be found, it could break the 'doom loop' linking weak sovereigns to failing banks. Struggling banks' liabilities need no longer end up on European governments' debt books. The summit's final statement advanced a Eurozone crisis resolution vision different from the German/ECB line. It echoed IMF sentiments, proclaiming 'it is imperative to break the vicious circle between banks and sovereigns'. This attempt to clearly distinguish the problem of bank debt from that of national debt had major implications for fiscal policy. Such a scenario could open up 'fiscal space' for growth-oriented macroeconomic policies. French economic policy advisors noted with approval the IMF's line on the need to break the sovereign/bank loop and their work on Banking Union.[57] This was partly because a successful Banking Union could, in short, have enabled Hollande to deliver on the Keynesian policy promises made during his campaign.

[57] Interview with Sarkozy economic advisor, Paris, November 2013; interview with Philippe Gudin, former Head of Macroeconomic Policy and European Affairs in the *direction générale du Trésor*, Paris, November 2013.

Proposals outlined included commitments for the ESM to engage in direct recapitalization of banks, and for the ECB to be involved in a single supervisory mechanism for European banks. The socialization of risks arising in European financial institutions could be managed in a way that no longer added to the debt burdens of Europe's sovereigns. Furthermore, there was scope for the new institutions to limit and mitigate financial market instability, notably by 'using the existing EFSF/ESM instruments in a flexible and efficient manner in order to stabilize markets' (Euro Area Summit Statement 2012). This agreement promised to deploy the €500 billion ESM bailout funds both directly to support troubled European banks (thus not adding to government debt) and also to purchase government bonds in order to lower borrowing costs. As the Banking Union took shape in the following years, it did not fully live up to French aspirations, not least due to German antipathy towards the radical implications for fiscal space.

More broadly, the IMF argued that more financial firepower for the ESM was crucial to addressing the Eurozone crisis. This should, in the Fund's view, include the ability to buy bonds in the primary market on a precautionary basis. So structured, the Fund argued, the ESM could be effective in 'preventing liquidity problems from casting doubts on a member state's capacity to fulfill its obligations' (see e.g. IMF 2011c: 60) . The IMF also repeatedly expressed admiration for proposals to introduce Eurobonds and forms of debt mutualization, with attendant strengthening of fiscal discipline (IMF 2011g; IMF 2012g: 9; IMF 2012h; Claessens et al. 2012; IMF 2012j). Bolstering the firepower of the Eurozone's fiscal backstop was seen by the Fund as key to mitigating short-term financial market instability and contagion risks. It could also address longer-term issues by reducing interest rate and liquidity shocks that could threaten debt sustainability. Blanchard's foreword to the April 2012 *WEO* urged 'the introduction of limited forms of Eurobonds, such as the creation of a common euro bill market' (Blanchard 2012b: xiv). This was in stark contrast to how the Eurobonds idea was viewed within the EC, ECB, and Germany. The overriding concern of the EC, ECB, and Germany was that effective backstops could reduce the pressure of struggling Southern European economies to pursue structural reforms and fiscal adjustment, which Germany deemed necessary to restore their competitiveness.

The French continued to bang the drum for Banking Union, Finance Minister Michel Sapin calling for full direct bank recapitalization at the April 2014 IMF spring meetings. This he harnessed to comments about getting surplus countries to do more to raise global demand and potential growth (Sapin 2014). For their part, Fund flagship publications rarely missed an opportunity to inveigh in favour of further movement in delivering on this agenda, noting that the June 2012 agenda 'will be critical to delink sovereigns' and banks' balance sheets... if implemented in full, [Banking Union] will help break these adverse links. In particular, once a single supervisory mechanism is established, the ESM would be able to recapitalize banks directly' (IMF 2012g: 8; see also IMF 2012n: 28).

The Fund's aspirations for 'full' Banking Union were articulated with increasing exasperation after the summer of 2012, as German and ECB resistance led to the proposals being watered down, and implementation delayed. Meanwhile, the crisis limped on. The October 2013 *Global Financial Stability Report* noted with regret the limited scope of ESM direct bank recapitalization. This placed 'the burden of raising capital firmly back on bank shareholders and creditors or on the sovereign'. In this way, the realization of Banking Union was falling short of the goal of breaking the bank/sovereign link. Indeed, the Fund feared that the approach to ESM direct recapitalization 'may not provide sufficient backstop should substantial capital shortfalls be found in economies with weak sovereign balance sheets' (IMF 2013l: 41).

Growth continued to elude the Eurozone, and problems of weak aggregate demand and broken financial transmission mechanisms endured. Progress on direct recapitalization, and on the single supervisory mechanism, was painfully slow (European Court of Auditors 2014). The Commission finally published proposals for European deposit insurance—another important element of Banking Union—in November 2015. At this stage the Banking Union was still being talked about by the Commission in the future tense (EC 2015). In the summer of 2016, the IMF was still calling for European deposit insurance (IMF 2016). A senior Fund economist noted with regret in 2014 'that sovereign bank link remains as tight as ever'.[58] The slow, halting progress was because the German government's particular interpretation of moral hazard concerns trumped financial market contagion fears (Newman 2015; Jacoby 2015).

Conclusion

The overriding impression from interviewing many French policy officials and advisors was that the IMF were respected by French authorities for their intellectual authority, and the quality of their research. The IMF's arguments carried weight. Fund work was, for example, held in higher esteem than the Commission's intellectual production. The shared worldview unearthed between IMF and Bercy chimes with Nelson's analysis of 'shared beliefs' (2014, 2017) as an important factor affecting Fund influence. It also echoes Woods' suggestion that the presence of sympathetic interlocutors can enhance IMF influence (2006). This influence, though, is contingent on policy

[58] Interview with Ajai Chopra, by then Senior Research Fellow at the Peterson Institute for International Economics, September 2014.

context and is episodic in ways which echo Pop-Eleches' findings about the interaction between domestic policy priorities and IMF prescriptions (2008). Thus, early in the crisis, close alignment saw French and Fund policy thinking pulling in the same direction. The intellectual legitimacy this conferred upon coordinated stimulus and macroeconomic activism to support growth was much welcomed in French policy circles.

The IMF had some success in 2008 in encouraging the embrace of fiscal stimulus, including in Germany. That said, the IMF—while it can shape the agenda—did not have direct power over non-borrowing countries. For example, the IMF Missions used fiscal space arguments to counsel *less* fiscal consolidation in 2011–12, yet the French government proceeded with front-loading against the Fund's better judgement, neglecting Blanchard and Cottarelli's '10 commandments' of fiscal adjustment (2010). Indeed, French officials extremely concerned to retain market credibility amidst rising sovereign debt anxieties complained that the IMF had, by the autumn of 2011 when French borrowing costs were rising, gone too far in its Keynesian embrace of more expansionary fiscal policy approaches. By 2012, a common position on how to expand fiscal space through reform of the Eurozone architecture saw a revival of IMF influence on French policy thinking.

The Fund's ability to use its seat at the table at numerous fora to encourage policymakers to rethink the premises of their policy thinking played a very important role in the Eurozone crisis, framing the debate for European policymakers. The Fund's traction was more amorphous than the EC's direct power over French policy through European treaties. As Fayolle puts it, 'what the IMF can do in terms of help is to make sure that the economic debate is set in good terms for the European policymakers to make the right decisions.'[59] The IMF's role of putting the right questions to policymakers to shape the dialogue amongst them was especially important because key centres of power, notably the German government, the European Commission, and the European Central Bank prioritized a 'crisis of debt' narrative. The policy corollaries of this were ever-tighter fiscal discipline and ramped-up austerity. The IMF is widely credited amongst French policy elites with creating the conditions wherein the EC shifted its fiscal policy thinking, accepting a longer time horizon for French deficit reduction, and acknowledging the Fund's case that fiscal multipliers were higher during recessions. This shift crucially bought more time for France and other Eurozone deficit countries to restore their public finances.

This testifies to the instrumental 'use' of IMF advice by French authorities, neglecting their advice when it does not accord with French policy priorities.

[59] Interview with Former IMF Executive Director for France, Ambroise Fayolle, Paris, September 2013.

At the same time, French policy elites draw upon the IMF, and make use of how Fund thinking carries weight vis-à-vis Germany. Yet that, too, had its limits. After 2012, hopes to infuse Eurozone economic governance with more fiscal activism in support of growth foundered. The Banking Union plan was built partly on Fund research, and answered recurrent calls from key Fund players and in Fund surveillance and flagship publications to break the 'doom loop' between troubled banks and weakened sovereigns. This indicates how the Fund can create the conditions of possibility for particular policies to emerge. However, the effective EU-level backstops which the Fund and French authorities hoped would emerge through realization of Banking Union failed to fully materialize. The intellectual legitimacy, research-based advocacy, and international coordination which the Fund contributed were not sufficient to see Banking Union prevail in its initial muscular Eurozone backstop form. This was due to lack of support from European partners, the European Commission, and the ECB.

8

Conclusion—IMF Intellectual Authority and the Politics of Economic Ideas after the Crash

Introduction

As this book has demonstrated, for all emphasis on technocratic and scientific practices, in carrying out their work, Fund economists are of necessity constantly making subjective judgements (Nelson 2017: ch. 2) about economic conjunctures and policies.[1] Notions of pursuing the 'right' economic policies are integral to Fund staff 's self-understanding of their role in dealing with and offering advice to national authorities (Boughton 2012; James 1996; Fischer 2001b). Encouraging and inducing policymakers to pursue 'sound' economic policy, to use a favoured Fund word (see e.g. Heller 2002), is what IMF staff economists see themselves as for. Fund staff see the institution as a, perhaps *the*, voice of economic policy reason in the world economy, and they use its knowledge bank, expertise, and mandate for surveillance and coordination to give life to the Fund's role as an arbiter of legitimate policy. The interpretive framework through which the IMF assesses and evaluates economic policy crucially shapes the view of 'sound' policy which the institution propagates.

Those who can make authoritative knowledge claims, such as the Fund, enjoy a privileged position within the inter-subjective process of constructing economic rectitude. The IMF has scope to shape and shift the boundaries of what constitutes 'legitimate' policy, and in doing so it can expand the policy space potentially available to many advanced economies. The Fund's intellectual framework for understanding economic policy—and in this instance for understanding the crisis and its implications in terms of appropriate policy

[1] Interviews at the IMF with Olivier Blanchard, David Lipton, Vivek Arora, Doug Laxton, Daniel Leigh, June and September 2013.

response—is the fulcrum of this surveillance relationship. The goal of shaping interpretive frameworks for thinking about the conduct of economic policy amongst national policy elites is at the heart of Fund surveillance and intellectual production (James 1996). Through multilateral and bilateral surveillance mandate (Pauly 1997, 2008) and other interactions with non-borrowing advanced economies, the Fund works to shape emergent inter-subjective understandings of appropriate economic policy and fiscal regimes.

Drawing selectively on particular sets of economic ideas, insights, and evidence, IMF bricoleurs work to develop and reproduce an interpretive framework of understanding economic policy (see e.g. Best 2010; Boughton 2004, 2012; Fourcade-Gourinchas & Babb 2002). The analysis presented in this book has penetrated the technocratic, apolitical façade of Fund prescriptive economic discourse to reveal normative underpinnings rooted in principles of political economy. Thus, for example, the 'New Classical'-inspired expansionary fiscal contraction thesis was rejected through recourse to Keynesian insights about fiscal policy.

Although surveillance of non-borrowing countries is what the IMF spends most of its time and effort doing, and the IMF has important relationships with non-borrowing countries, these have been neglected by IMF scholars more interested in conditional lending. This book has advanced *not only* a theory of internal ideational change at IMF, *but also* a systematic account of under what conditions the IMF is successful in gaining 'traction' with non-borrowing advanced economies for its economic policy thinking. Thus, the book has addressed two blind spots in the IMF literature, focusing on surveillance relations with *advanced* countries *not* borrowing from the Fund to provide novel insights into Fund authority—its scope, limits, and conditions for success.

As the analysis presented in this book demonstrates, the IMF made a series of carefully targeted interventions in the growth 'versus' austerity debate, deploying its intellectual authority and scientific reputation to advocate changes in policy settings. The interpretation offered here, gleaned from and corroborated by many interviews with Fund staff, and content analysis of large amounts of the Fund's intellectual production, is that Olivier Blanchard, Carlo Cottarelli, David Ostry, David Lipton, and others at IMF sought to influence the post-crash international economic debate, and shift underlying perceptions of appropriate economic policy. This was also how Strauss-Kahn and then Lagarde, the post-crash Managing Directors, saw the Fund's role and function.

This book has explored the politics of economic ideas in the wake of the crash—both within the international economic policy debate, and within the Fund. One central finding has been that it is wise not to presume too fixed, settled, or singular a set of views or understandings to be gleaned from economics. In the wake of the crisis, mainstream economics debates about fiscal policy were revived, and included a startlingly wide array of understandings of the economy and policy (see Alesina & Giavazzi 2013b). Many of these found themselves cited in Fund publications. One surprising facet of post-crunch economics is how relatively heterodox policy positions can find corroboration within 'New Consensus' macroeconomics (NCM) using orthodox methodologies (Auerbach & Gorodnichenko 2012, 2013a & b; Delong & Summers 2012; Ban 2015a; Eichenbaum et al. 2011; Nakamura & Steinsson 2014; see also Seabrooke et al. 2015). This is significant in the context of an internal scientific culture at the Fund which draws on a breadth of economic ideas (from traditional Keynesianism to the New Classical) within its repertoire accreted over decades of Fund thinking and practice. Fund staff in interview were not inclined to align with any particular paradigmatic position, but were prepared to draw on different economic insights in a more pragmatic fashion as they appeared relevant to the policies, issues and conjuncture at hand. For Doug Laxton, 'it is always a question of synthesis. You are taking the best ideas from different schools or camps.'[2] As Deputy Managing Director David Lipton put it, 'I don't think you'd find that many people here think of themselves as adherents to some school of thought.'[3] These characteristics of both the post-crash NCM, and the Fund's repertoire of economic ideas, open up scope for a variety of policy positions, or indeed underlying economic ideas, to be advocated, *provided* the case can be supported by a range of methods, and the evidence base can be garnered (see Chapters 2 and 3).

This enables Fund bricoleurs to deploy ideas and scholars in ways which support the policy prioritization they are seeking to champion in a given economic conjuncture. Thus, one desirable quality of a favoured economic idea is if the insight can be supported through reference to work by highly regarded academic economists. This provides ideas with the requisite level of intellectual authority required by the Fund's scientific norms and culture. The selection and framing of who to cite, and what policy implications to draw, are very important, used by key players within the Fund, for example in the Research department, to wield strategic ideational power. The IMF's unusual status as at once the equivalent of a large academic research institution, and a practical, operational lender and economic policy surveillance actor, gives its claims to ideational authority a distinctive, policy-oriented, and more empirically and practically grounded character.

[2] Interview with Doug Laxton, Division Chief of the Economic Modelling Division, IMF Research department, September 2013.

[3] Interview with IMF Deputy Managing Director David Lipton, September 2013.

The Construction of Economic Rectitude

Choosing economic policy settings is rarely if ever about ineluctable international economic imperatives. Restoring the contingency, and the politics, to discussions of economic policy choice, Constructivist Institutionalism (CI) sees ideas and interests as socially constructed, malleable, and emergent, rather than fixed and given. The same is true of crisis interpretations, and the economic orthodoxies which are reinforced by them. As ideationally attuned scholars have pointed out, how a crisis gets constructed and interpreted is vital for the politics of economic policy (Baker 2015; Gamble 2009, 2014; Hay 1996, 2013a & b). A crucial issue in the wider context within which the IMF operates and seeks to shape economic policy thinking is how the Global Financial Crisis (GFC) that began in 2007 came to be understood and what kinds of economic policy responses such an understanding supported.

Some authoritative voices in the world economy championed a 'crisis of debt' reading, with an attendant shift in prioritization towards speedy fiscal consolidation and restoring public finances. Gamble identifies a framing of 'orthodox narratives around debt, retrenchment and austerity [which] have for the most part defined the crisis and determined how it has been perceived' (Gamble 2014: 7). This 'demand denial' (Wren-Lewis 2011) was countered by the Fund's 'meta-Keynesian' understanding of the way that fiscal policy matters, and has impacts on the real economy.[4] The Fund was more persuaded by the 'crisis of growth' reading of the crisis itself, and focused on the crisis legacies of lost growth potential in advanced economies. These are examples of how the diagnosis of the crisis becomes framed in such a way as to recommend certain solutions to it, and rule out others.

What this research has underlined is how not only the crisis, but also how the crisis *legacy* was interpreted and characterized, was important. The interpretations of both crisis and legacy were used by the IMF to press the case for particular policy prioritizations. The Fund's increasingly differentiated approach to policy advice noted that advanced economies facing immediate financing constraints had little alternative but to focus on fiscal adjustment and debt and deficit reduction. The cruel irony for crisis-hit programme countries in the European periphery like Greece was that their absence of fiscal space meant the menu of more growth-supporting fiscal policies the Fund was advocating for others was not open to them—the countries that needed support for demand and growth the most. However, other advanced economies had more latitude to prioritize restoring demand and spurring economic recovery. The degree of fiscal space was the crucial intervening

[4] Interviews with Olivier Blanchard, Paolo Mauro, David Lipton, Alessandro Leipold, amongst others.

variable affecting how far the Fund deemed these policies open to governments. Fiscal space is a 'judgement call', a qualitative, subjective assessment, its' rule of thumb' quality revealing how far intuitions play a role in Fund decision-making (Nelson 2017).[5]

Advanced economies enjoying credibility and ready access to borrowing were encouraged to pursue unorthodox polices in support of boosting demand and fuelling the recovery. Linking to crisis legacies, the IMF highlighted 'non-linearities'—the threat of damaging policy spirals wherein protracted slumps lock in low or no growth. The IMF sought—with at best limited success—to challenge that austerity-oriented definition of the crisis, and appropriate policy responses for countries enjoying fiscal space.

In the heat of the crisis in 2008–9, with the system on the brink of collapse, and the threat of a Great Depression looming large, what constituted 'sound' economic policy was in flux. The Fund used its seat at the G20 table, its intellectual authority, and its strategic doctrinal flexibility to gain 'traction' for its calls for coordinated global fiscal stimulus to tackle aggregate demand deficiency. As the post-crash downturn dragged on and deepened, the IMF felt the need to maintain the short-term focus on growth and the recovery as many became more exercised by rising debt and deficit levels. The IMF's commitment to credible medium-term frameworks to restore the public finances enabled it to embrace an 'easy does it', 'less now, more later' approach to fiscal adjustment. More hawkish voices, by contrast, demanded harsh, front-loaded fiscal consolidation. Fund/government interactions are a repeated game, and through these recurrent consultations, Fund staff come to appreciate what and how policymakers are thinking. Fund actors alighted on a crisis legacy interpretation to maintain the emphasis on supporting growth, demand, and the recovery as the initial threat of economic catastrophe subsided. This also formed part of a strategy to make the case for fiscal activism which sidesteps standard oppositions from fiscal conservatives, both within the Fund and outside it.

One key crisis legacy for the Fund's macroeconomic policy recommendation which flowed from its meta-Keynesian outlook was that output gaps in the advanced economies would be large and persistent. The October 2009 *WEO* first set out how far and for how long economies were likely to be pushed below trend. In the eyes of senior Research department figures, this 'anchored thinking' that the bounce back to trend would not happen any time soon, and that once pushed away from trend, economies may grow slower persistently. Later, the Fund spelled out how non-linearities such as secular stagnation, associated with the post-crash political economic conjuncture, helped

[5] Interviews with Daniel Leigh, Vivek Arora, Doug Laxton, and Paolo Mauro.

account for these dynamics. Significantly, large and persistent output gaps provided a conducive environment for 'Keynesian' fiscal policies to boost demand to reduce the slack in the economy and hopefully help close the output gap. The presumed return to a steady state built into the linear assumptions of DSGE economic models was by no means assured. Indeed, staving off a protracted slump and deflation would require policy activism using a wider array of macroeconomic levers than had been appreciated pre-crash.

The Internal Politics of Economic Ideas within the IMF

This book advances a theory of internal ideational change at the IMF, arguing that ideational change requires the rethink of policy premises to get taken up within an internal politics of economic ideas by first- and second-tier leadership in key positions within the organization. Important for this ideational struggle is reconciling new thinking to the Fund's institutional and ideational context by passing through the four mechanisms recapped below.

Scholars revisiting Hall's seminal paradigms account have detected two main approaches for conceptualizing what is happening within ideational change. On the one hand there is a 'scientific' account, and on the other a more political, constructivist interpretation (Blyth 2013b; Wood 2015). The 'scientific' view focuses on a 'Bayesian' understanding of learning as rationalist evidence-based improvement. This views change as updating, assuming all the ideas in play are commensurable and operate within one paradigmatic plane. Blanchard, shortly before entering the Fund, characterized the evolution of macroeconomics not in terms of different schools—his view being that it had moved beyond earlier disputes, using evidence and theorizing to retain what was tenable and thereby arrive at NCM (Blanchard 2008a). He largely retained this view of the evolution of NCM economics as a science in the 2010 Fund Staff Position Note *Rethinking Macroeconomic Policy* (Blanchard et al. 2010: 10, 16). This kind of thinking implies that a single, 'objective' view of the right economic policy could be arrived at, and arguably posits a single possible construction of the economically rational. This view of economics was reaffirmed by many interviewees, and is how Fund staff choose to represent to themselves the evolution of Fund thinking (see e.g. Lagarde 2013). This conforms to a Bayesian, 'scientific' conception of rational updating, which aligns comfortably with IMF intellectual authority bound up in its scientific, technocratic, and apolitical reputation. Yet this does not capture the whole story of how prevailing ideas change within the IMF.

An alternative, more 'political', view sees that a number of different economic policy choices could be justified in any given conjuncture and setting given the indeterminacy of economic theory as a guide to policy (Kirshner

2003a & b). As noted in earlier chapters, fiscal policy evaluation is not a purely scientific exercise. Each approach entails making some prior assumptions which remain contestable within economics, such that differing views persist over fiscal policy's efficacy and desirability as an economic stabilization tool. IMF decision-making about economic policy is never as purely scientific or technocratic an exercise as the Fund's self-image presents it. Fund views on economic policy at the heart of its surveillance and programme work involve subjective judgements, intuitions, and judgement calls. Thus, fiscal policy assessment is never purely scientific, but always a matter of interpretation, rooted in prior assumptions about relationships between policy, growth, and output.

This suggests the applicability of the more political view of ideational change in the realms of assessing 'sound' fiscal policy. Such a reading is consistent with the CI approach of this book, foregrounding as it does contingency, discursive contestation, and constructivist insights about the importance of interpretation, framing, and 'arguments over meaning' (Widmaier et al. 2007: 756). It recognizes how a range of plausibly 'authoritative' claims, potentially from different paradigmatic planes, could be mobilized to justify different policy stances in any given context. In this more open-ended and indeterminate version of how economic ideas change, persuasive and interpretive struggles are understood to be shaped by power relations. Indeed, numerous staff economists, as well as academic visitors, describe the Fund as an intellectually lively environment with plenty of robust exchange in debates about economic policy thinking. In short, ideational change, on this reading, involves 'powering' as well as 'puzzling' (Blyth 2013b; Hall 1993: 289; Wood 2015: 6–8). Within the IMF, ideational evolution is not so exclusively 'scientific' as the Fund's self-image would have us believe.

In constructing a new prescriptive policy discourse, IMF bricoleurs use the building blocks of a range of economic perspectives to maintain a pragmatic relevance to current policy debates. The identification in this book of a range of acceptable doctrine from which key IMF bricoleurs select, then package and frame to garner support, also aligns more with the constructivist view of discursive struggles between competing sources of intellectual authority. All interviewees attested to the vibrant debates over economic policy thinking which characterized the Fund internal culture. One of the topics of these robust exchanges was appropriate post-crash fiscal policy. There was dissonance within the Fund between those espousing the post-crash more accommodating and expansionary fiscal policy line, and more conservative voices attached to earlier more 'sound finance'-centric fiscal policy thinking. Feedback loops provided by multiple internal fora for sharing ideas indicate which ideas, corroborations, and justifications are likely to garner support. In this way, they inform the internal politics of economic ideas.

The 'footprints' of these political struggles over Fund economic ideas are not always easy to discern. Interviewees often play down such dissonance, and IMF editorial practices and drafting style tend to obscure it. That said, the internal politics of economic ideas, and the more sceptical views on fiscal policy efficacy and activism are indicated by consistent caveats and qualifiers exerted into all Fund flagship publications. As regards the contours of these struggles, internally, the Keynesian-sympathetic subculture within the Fund enjoyed a revival and greater prominence due to the economic conjuncture and its powerful backers in positions of authority within the Fund—notably Strauss-Kahn and Blanchard. After a period of close alignment between the Research department and FAD between 2008 and 2010—as indicated in the 'duets' between Blanchard and Cottarelli—cracks began to appear. FAD became more focused on restoration of the public finances, whilst many in the Research department continued to underline the need for fiscal policy to do more in support of growth.

The Fund's ideational evolution, then, is more open-ended than the Bayesian rational updating view admits. Nevertheless, it remains institutionally circumscribed. One of the core contributions of this book is to set out how particular ideas get selected, specifying the mechanisms of internal ideational change, and the hoops that new ideas have to jump through. Firstly, the ideas need to be readily reconcilable to existing Fund standard operating procedures and sedimented Fund economic policy knowledge. Secondly, they have to be amenable to corroboration in a manner consistent with the Fund scientific norms of varied methodological techniques. Thirdly, the insights or ideas must be operationalized, that is, capable of being 'baked into guidance' and translated into new or revised operational frameworks, and technical guidance notes. Finally they require authoritative recognition—reinforced by citations from leading scholars and cutting-edge research in academic economics. These are important hoops to jump through for ideas to acquire 'social recognition' within the Fund (Park & Vetterlein 2010). The internal politics of economic ideas within the Fund is shaped by social, power-infused processes: packaging new ideas to channel them through the mechanisms of internal ideational change.

The mechanisms clarify *how* new thinking gains acceptance, but does not tell us all we need to know about why particular ideas get selected. This comes down to the strategic doctrinal flexibility afforded to senior IMF economists and management, in the way they give life to the Fund's role as an arbiter of 'sound' economic policy. Strategy involves discerning which ideational innovations will fly at Board level, and gain 'traction', as well as using the 'voice of the staff of the Fund' flagships to make pointed interventions in the policy debate. Blanchard notes the crucial combination of 'message' and 'opportunity'; 'if you have a clear message then you have some effect, and you clearly have more effect if it fits the agenda.'[6] It comes across in interviews that IMF staff see the goal of IMF surveillance as the promotion of 'good' policies, and to call out governments pursuing what the Fund consider to be 'bad' policies. The Fund seeks to encourage policymakers, as former Chief Economist Stanley Fischer once put it, to 'do the right thing' (2001b, 1998; see also Nelson 2017: 5). There was also an important sense in which the Fund's leading lights thought their Keynesian interpretation of the crisis and appropriate responses was right given the context and conjuncture (their interpretation and narrative of the crisis), and the more austerity-centric approaches of, for example, Germany and the ECB were misguided. Thus, part of the motivation was for the Fund to play its self-allocated role as a font of economic policy knowledge. In the major economic policy debates of the time, the IMF wants its policy advice to be 'on the right side of history'.[7]

New economic ideas get selected and amplified, or older ones revived, when their policy corollaries align with how leading Fund bricoleurs are seeking to shape the international policy debate. Is this a policy area where, in Fund bricoleurs' estimation, advanced economy governments need to revisit their policy thinking? To gain traction, the IMF also needed to present a clear and coherent line—which meant winning out in internal ideational struggles. Here the hierarchal nature of the organization plays its part, as with Blanchard's deliberate eradication of the term 'growth friendly fiscal consolidation', seized on by some leaders after 2010 Toronto G20 to imply that austerity might, via confidence effects, be good for growth, from Fund parlance and publications. Fund bricoleurs develop positions that can be corroborated using acceptable Fund scientific techniques, and use the Fund's knowledge bank to build up the evidence base and scientific case in support. Such an idea then has maximum chance of gaining salience within the Fund, and garnering the support of first- and second-tier management, from the Managing Director to Research department leadership. Both 'Will it Hurt's debunking of the expansionary fiscal contraction thesis in the October 2010 *WEO* and the October 2012 *WEO* exposure of the underestimation of fiscal multipliers were cases in point. Both played key roles in the politics of austerity.

The feedback loops also provide pointers as to how concepts can be strategically selected which offer interpretive latitude to Fund bricoleurs. The notion of fiscal space, which as discussed above is at the heart of Fund fiscal policy recommendations, is a useful concept for Fund fiscal revisionists to deploy in the internal politics of ideas, since it can diffuse standard 'deficit bias' objections suggesting an overwhelming focus on balanced budgets and

[6] Interview with IMF Chief Economist Olivier Blanchard, June 2013.
[7] Interview with Daniel Leigh, IMF Research department economist, June 2013.

fiscal sustainability. The long-standing instincts in FAD, under Vito Tanzi, (1981–2000) and then Teresa Ter-Minassian (2001–8) had been to prioritize deficit bias concerns and failings of governments to build up fiscal buffers, and to argue for fiscal discipline. In this context, fiscal space is an idea prioritized and foregrounded partly to justify the Fund's more differentiated policy advice. More importantly, it is used on a contingent basis to navigate around the inherent fiscal conservatism of many at the Fund, especially regarding countries with a reputation for being spendthrift. In perhaps the most pointed use of fiscal space to counsel a policy change, Deputy Director of the Research department Jonathan Ostry and colleagues brought together a range of IMF research and other work to highlight the adverse effects of austerity on inequality, and, through that, on growth (Ostry et al. 2016: 38–9).

The merits of neo-liberalism, they noted, had been oversold, and the effects of both fiscal consolidation and capital account liberalization had contributed to rising inequality and were jeopardizing a durable expansion (Lagarde 2012c & d). Highlighting another 'adverse feedback loop', and underscoring the non-linearities to which the post-crash Fund is increasingly attuned, the Fund's critique of neo-liberalism noted that higher inequality caused by 'the neoliberal policy agenda', both capital account liberalization and austerity, can hurt the very growth the policies are designed to support. Linking the advice back to the Fund's core mandate, Ostry et al. note 'strong evidence that inequality can significantly lower both the level and the durability of growth' (Ostry, Berg, & Tsangarides, 2014).

This critique of 'the neoliberal agenda' was an important intervention in the politics of austerity debates, much discussed in the *Financial Times* and selected broadsheets. Ostry et al. questioned the wisdom of prioritizing both fiscal consolidation and paying down public debt in all cases. Ostry et al. argue that for countries with 'ample fiscal space' (such as the UK and Germany), focusing on growth, rather than paying down public debt, would make more economic sense: 'the need for consolidation in *some* countries does not mean *all* countries—at least in this case, caution about "one size fits all" seems completely warranted' (Ostry et al. 2016: 38–9). Countries with a strong track record of sound fiscal responsibility—enjoying fiscal space—have 'latitude' not to cut productive spending or raise taxes when debt is high (Ostry et al. 2016; Ostry et al. 2010; Ghosh et al. 2013). Those countries enjoying this 'latitude' should use it because the benefits of paying down the debt, even for countries with very high debt levels, are 'remarkably small'. Indeed, the costs of paying down the debt 'could be large, much larger than the benefit' since cutting productive expenditure does excessive harm to growth. Thus, slowly reducing high debt through growth makes more economic sense than 'deliberately running budgetary surpluses to reduce the debt'; the IMF's considered view is that 'governments with ample fiscal space will do better by living with the debt' (Ostry et al. 2016: 40). This line was directly counter to the standard 'crisis of debt' line emanating from the German Government, and the UK Government between 2010 and 2015. The costs of austerity (lower output and higher unemployment) had been 'underplayed' and the benefits of countries with fiscal space focusing on growth to get high debt ratios to decline 'organically' had, Ostry et al. point out, been 'underappreciated'.

Through the repeated game of interactions with national authorities (through Article IV consultations and so forth), Fund staff came to understand the principal objections to their fiscal policy position. Fund bricoleurs made carefully calibrated interventions in the international economic policy debate to try and shift shared understandings of 'sound' economic policy towards a 'less now, more later' approach to fiscal consolidation for those countries enjoying the requisite fiscal space. They raised concerns about adverse feedback loops (such as that between higher inequality and lower growth), and highlighted other non-linear threats such as secular stagnation, deflation, and hysteresis to strengthen their case. Another aspect of Fund advocacy of activist fiscal policy which sidestepped some fiscally conservative objections was the call for public infrastructure investment, which would pay for itself through its positive growth effects, thus bringing debt down (IMF 2014e). Unlike the Fund of the new classical 'silent revolution' during the 1980s, which prioritized low inflation and austerity as necessary preconditions for growth (Boughton 2001; Babb & Buira 2005), post-crash, a more activist approach identifies supporting aggregate demand through counter-cyclical policy, infrastructure investment, and tackling inequality as key macroeconomic components of securing growth.

The IMF and Its Quest for Traction

This tells us much about how ideas come to prevail *within* the IMF as Fund economists work, as they see it, to promote good policy, and counsel against bad policy. Yet what is the likelihood that their efforts will prevail? Whether IMF policy ideas and advice will gain the 'traction' which all Fund staff seek for its work and thinking is an empirical question, to which the answer is always contingent upon historical circumstances and context. Under 'normal' conditions, non-borrowing advanced economies represent a less or least likely case for the success of Fund attempts to shape policy thinking. The nature of the surveillance relationship between the IMF and a non-borrowing country must respect 'the domestic social and political policies of members' (IMF 1993: 6), and Fund surveillance lacks any enforcement mechanisms (Pauly 1997). The norms of Fund/national authority interaction (see Chapters 4, 6, and 7), and the tension between the Fund's trusted advisor and independent auditor roles (IEO 2013) limit Fund traction. Fund staff need to maintain good working relations with national authorities to gain high-quality access to key policymakers, and to all relevant information.

The argument here is that the crisis and its aftermath presented relatively conducive conditions for the IMF to shape the climate of opinion. As many constructivist scholars have pointed out, what constitutes the economically sound is more 'up for grabs' in the middle of an economic crisis wherein uncertainty is heightened (Blyth 2002a; Widmaier et al. 2007). In our case, this offered institutions like the Fund greater scope to stabilize expectations, shape conventional understandings, and garner a revisiting of the premises of policy thinking on the part of advanced economy policymakers. Even with these comparatively favourable conditions, however, the Fund's ability to shape economic policy thinking in advanced economies had limits imposed by the nature of the surveillance relationship, the limited knowability of economic conditions and trajectories amidst the post-GFC uncertainty, and also the modest size of a Fund surveillance team for any given country.

Despite crises being widely seen as conducive environments for appropriate policy to be redefined, the post-crash environment proved a challenging one for the Fund to wield influence. Partly this was because self-aware Fund economists recognized the conditions of pervasive uncertainty, indeed Knightian uncertainty (Blanchard 2009, 2012c; Cottarelli 2013) under which they were operating. In all their policy advice, Fund staff face the limits of the knowability of economic policy effects, and of the cyclical position of the economy. As Nelson puts it, 'IMF judgements are shrouded in a fog of uncertainty (thicker in some contexts than in others, but always present)' (Nelson 2017: 165). This inherent uncertainty surrounding the Fund's forecasting that is a fulcrum of its surveillance limits how far the Fund can push its case for particular policy settings. IMF surveillance after the crash contained a wider range of alternative possible scenarios, and produced 'heat maps' identifying an extensive range of downside risks. More qualifiers had to be attached to Fund policy recommendations, and it was measured in its critique of existing policy settings.

Fund prescriptive policy discourse was accordingly channelled through the prism of numerous possible scenarios, with recommendations to adopt policy changes 'should growth disappoint', for example. These were indicators that there were limits on how far IMF economists could claim to know with great certainty what was happening in the economy, both in the present and in the near future. In such unusual conditions, Fund staff become all the more mindful of the limits of what predictive weight economic forecasting as a 'science' can bear. These qualifiers, and the backdrop of uncertainty, limited how firmly the Fund advocated its policy positions. These were matters of subjective expert judgement which have always been a central component of

IMF decision-making (Nelson 2017: 11–12), despite all the façade of a technocratic and systematic surveillance process.[8]

The asymmetry of information between a small Fund Mission team and large, well-resourced finance ministries and central banks can also affect surveillance interactions. Fund Missions deploy their political capital carefully, recognizing that there is no point banging their heads against a wall arguing for policies which stand no chance of being taken up by the authorities. Within those parameters, Mission members see it as their role to advocate good policies. The Fund at times sees the trade-offs between always difficult policy dilemmas in a different way to the national authorities. In such a context their aim is to plant a seed, to encourage a different way of thinking about a policy problem, and induce a revisiting of the premises of policy thinking.[9] The nature of Fund influence is not primarily about impressing upon national authorities policy ideas that had not occurred to them. Just as Fund economists were encouraged to 'think outside the box' as the crisis deepened, so country economists in the advanced economies were doing likewise. The Fund carrying out serious research on fiscal policy effects and efficacy under the specific conditions facing the advanced economies 'played onside' similar thinking, and policy initiatives, in a range of advanced economies. It was more about building stronger corroboration behind policies that national authorities were already contemplating.

One of the central theoretical claims of the book is that how Fund staff see themselves matters. They talk in terms of 'traction', not 'influence'. When asked what constitutes success in gaining traction, interviewees revealed that this can include getting their analysis and ideas taken up in op-ed pieces in the *Financial Times*. Others characterized gaining a wide readership for blog posts as traction. Another seasoned Fund figure, praising the influence of Reza Moghadam's blog on 'lowflation' which argued that the ECB should not be scared of QE, hinted that Fund internal review can be an impediment to traction: 'These blogs are less than 1,000 words, have a couple of nice pictures, and they get a lot more attention and traction. And they go through a lot less of a review process, which allows one to be bolder to inform and influence the public debate on controversial issues.'[10] That this constitutes success in their eyes gives some indication of the scale of the ambition of the IMF in shaping economic policy in non-borrowing advanced economies and the debates that surround it. Indeed, one striking feature of numerous Fund economists is the

[8] Interviews at the IMF with Vivek Arora, Daniel Leigh, Doug Laxton, September 2013.
[9] Interview with IMF First Deputy Managing Director David Lipton, September 2013.
[10] Interview with former IMF European Department Deputy Director Ajai Chopra, September 2014.

modesty of their ambition for effecting policy change. Blanchard talks of being able to 'move the compass a little bit'.[11]

With expectations of Fund influence calibrated accordingly regarding surveillance relations with non-borrowing countries, another major contribution of this book is to set out the conditions of possibility for the Fund to shape the climate of opinion and convince policymakers to adjust policy settings. Faced with the challenges of the limited knowability of the economy, and the nature of the surveillance relationship, self-aware Fund economists orient and frame their policy interventions where their intellectual authority is strongest in ways which maximize the chance of gaining 'traction'. Firstly, IMF bricoleurs carefully frame their intervention and justify it around the central Fund mandate for legitimacy reasons, notably with reference to one or more of international coordination, economic stability, and growth. This was why the Fund's post-crash reinterpretation of its mandate to redefine certain economic policy issues as 'macro-critical', notably inequality, was of such high political salience (IMF 2011l). The promise of international coordination can be especially effective since no other body is as well placed to deliver this within national or international economic policymaking.

Secondly, the chance of traction is enhanced by centring on policy questions where *the Fund itself* is in the vanguard of doing the policy-oriented research work. Where the Fund can itself provide corroboration of claims, and is doing the cutting-edge research, this can shift the asymmetry of information back in the Fund's favour. Senior Research department figures are very mindful of the potential adverse reputational effects of straying from where the economics evidence base is substantial.[12] To gain traction, Fund policy advice ideally requires a combination of theoretical argument, and also qualitative *and* quantitative evidence, drawing on the IMF's wealth of cross-country experience. The Fund's unique selling point and comparative advantage in world economic policy commentary is its knowledge bank and unrivalled cross-country economic policy experience. Its researchers trained their analytical guns and used the evidence base to improve the quality and depth of fiscal policy understandings, especially for advanced economies, after 2008.

One reason Blanchard and Leigh's upwards re-evaluation of multipliers in October 2012 gained such prominence was their 'natural experiment' research design, which proved persuasive and compelling. Even well-resourced central banks and Treasuries cannot devote extensive resources to this kind of background work on fiscal policy effects. At the Fund, by contrast, delivering numerous working papers, flagship chapters, and Staff Position Notes on this has been a central contribution of the Fund to understanding fiscal policy

[11] Interview with IMF Chief Economist Olivier Blanchard, June 2013.
[12] A concern recognized by many Fund staff in interview.

effects after the crash. Again, the central aim is to induce a re-evaluation of the premises of policy thinking, more so than specific policy recommendations by advanced economy policymakers. This research programme had built up knowledge about the state-dependent effects of multipliers (which were likely to be asymmetric across the economic cycle), and the likelihood of larger multipliers following a financial crisis. It also explored different multipliers associated with a variety of policies, informing understandings of the optimal composition of fiscal consolidation. All this strengthened the Fund's hand. The Fund also provided new analytical tools—such as its debt sustainaiblity analysis developed in 2011—which national authorities used to deepen their understanding of the debt and fiscal policy implications of large contingent liabilities (IMF 2011k).

Thirdly, the Fund mobilized and leveraged its 'arbiter of sound economic policy' role, using its unique ability to provide the intellectual 'seal of approval' on policy ideas. The Fund's independence and scientific, technocratic reputation was thus important within the post-crash fiscal policy rethink, not least because some of these ideas (like fiscal stimulus) lay outside the regular norms of policymaking during the 'Great Moderation'. The Fund can provide intellectual legitimacy and political cover for national authorities to embrace ideas not within the day-to-day economic management toolkit. In the case of coordinated stimulus, the Fund's intervention, and the seal of approval it conferred upon counter-cyclical fiscal policy, enabled national governments to avoid being the first to admit that their economy is in such dire straits that a fiscal stimulus was urgently needed.

Where expansionary fiscal policy in general is concerned, some countries (such as France) have a reputation for favouring more government spending. Calls for fiscal stimulus might provoke a 'they would say that, wouldn't they' response. Yet if they can align their call with the Fund's recommendation, French authorities can benefit from the IMF's reputation for fiscal probity. As one senior economist in the French Treasury put it, 'the Fund, usually, is not the one that advocates for fiscal stimulus. So, when you have the Fund saying you should do one, everybody listens more.'[13] Coming from the Fund, the case for fiscal policy activism carries more weight. The seal of approval and international coordination were contributions that only the Fund could make, national authorities could not. In these ways, the Fund was able to create the conditions of possibility for particular policies, and inflect policy settings, in addition to encouraging a wider re-evaluation of policy thinking.

[13] Interview with Anne Epaulard, former Deputy Assistant Director at the Treasury Department at the French Ministry of Finance, Paris, September 2013.

IMF Autonomy and Intellectual Authority—and Their Limits

IMF attempts to gain 'traction' also have to be understood in the context of the IMF's relations with powerful members, and the degree of autonomy enjoyed by staff and management. The Fund values its autonomy from its members, prizing its independence, and embracing its norm of even-handed treatment of all members. As noted in Chapter 4, those who decry the IMF as an arm of US foreign policy doing US government bidding underestimate all we have learned about Fund autonomy, and its ontological independence (Barnett & Finnemore 1999; 2004; Nelson 2017). Nevertheless, given its structure, and how power is distributed within it, the IMF cannot sustain a policy position diametrically opposed to *all* its major shareholders. The realms of 'thinkable' policy (Seabrooke 2010) to which its powerful members can be reconciled form the 'outer perimeter' (Woods 2006: 180) of viable Fund prescriptive discourse. Within those boundaries, IMF bricoleurs enjoy considerable latitude to alter the scope and limits of 'sound' policy, and can draw on a broad range of economic theories and concepts from within the Fund's repertoire in support of their position.

In this light, the commonality of view between the IMF and the US Treasury also played its part in terms of the coalitions behind a broadly Keynesian interpretation of the crisis and different appropriate responses. The Keynesian-sympathetic subculture—including in very high places within the Fund—gained succour from their alignment with key economic policy figures in the US administration. The arrival of the power couple of New Keynesian economics—Christy and David Romer—in Washington in late 2008 was significant given that they had co-authored important work on the US case highlighting large fiscal multipliers, and the efficacy of fiscal policy as a counter-cyclical tool (Romer & Romer 2007, 2010). Christy served on the Council of Economic Advisors, and David became a visiting researcher at the Fund, where he contributed to the landmark 'Will It Hurt?' WEO chapter (IMF 2010g: 93–113), amongst other things. This gives a flavour of a somewhat symbiotic relationship between the US Treasury and the Fund. The thinking of the two institutions on the crisis and appropriate responses was evolving in cognate directions, alive to the efficacy of counter-cyclical fiscal policy.

Yet not all advanced economies were thinking along these lines. One theme of this book has been the limits of the Fund's success in getting advanced economies to revisit their fiscal policy thinking in the direction counselled by the IMF. By redrawing our distinction between 'what is going on' and 'what is to be done' underpinning the Fund's post-crash intellectual production, this becomes clearer. In the early post-crash period, in 2008–9, the Fund's Keynesian reading on both fronts gained wide acceptance. For the

IMF, this was a crisis of deficient demand and confidence, and broken credit channels, calling for expansionary macroeconomic policy in the short term. A credible medium-term plan and framework to restore the public finances, targeting the structural fiscal balance, was sufficient to address any fiscal sustainability concerns.

Already in late 2009, Trichet and others, viewing the crisis as one of debt, were calling for a precipitate exit from fiscal stimulus. The IMF had played a key role in convincing Germany to go for fiscal stimulus in 2008. Yet, as one senior French official noted, for the Germans, 'then, very quickly afterwards, the priority became fiscal consolidation.'[14] By 2010, major economies such as Germany and the UK had shifted decisively towards fiscal consolidation. The Fund's 'easy does it' position was more nuanced (IMF 2012c: 12–17, 33–45). It agreed that targeting structural fiscal balance would require fiscal adjustment *at some point*. However, they argued firstly that it would be folly for all to consolidate at once, and secondly that, given ongoing recessionary conditions and weak demand, those with fiscal space should delay exit from stimulus, or pursue a 'less now, more later' approach to retrenchment (Blanchard & Leigh 2013b). The IMF's broadly Keynesian account of the crisis continued to foreground the themes of deficient demand, yet its crisis-defining and crisis legacy-defining ideas were not fully taken up.

Senior Fund figures are mindful that the IMF's intellectual authority is somewhat fragile, and could be undermined were it to consistently make strong policy recommendations that do not get taken up. To avoid the impression that it was being ignored, the language that IMF bricoleurs used to advance the case for a different approach to fiscal policy was measured, coded, and qualified. Nevertheless, it was clear that daylight emerged between Fund diagnosis and policy recommendations after 2010 and policies pursued by some advanced economies. The analysis is revealing of paths not taken due to limited traction of the Fund with key players—notably the UK coalition government's approach to the Great Recession, and the German government and ECB's approach to the Eurozone crisis.

As other Fund scholars have noted, the Fund's ideational power is enhanced when its policy thinking finds a favourable audience amongst national authorities, what Woods calls 'sympathetic interlocuters' (2006: ch. 3; see also Nelson 2017). Relatedly, Pop-Eleches identifies the alignment (or not) between 'IMF-style economic reforms' and the ideological persuasion of domestic governments, and powerful domestic economic interests as a crucial intervening variable affecting the extent of IMF influence (2008). Our findings broadly align with theirs—with the Fund's 'traction' at its zenith when pulling in the same direction as national policy elites, as during the autumn of 2008.

[14] Interview with Philippe Gudin, former Head of Macroeconomic Policy and European Affairs in the *direction générale du Trésor*, Paris, November 2013.

Lasting Change?

The final issue to address, having charted the evolution of IMF thinking on fiscal policy since the crash, is how enduring the shifts are likely to prove. After all, one take-home point of this book is to underscore how economic orthodoxy is historically contingent. The analysis reveals the malleability of conventional wisdoms about economic policy, and the processes of their social construction, drawing on a variety of economic assumptions.

Clearly, given the state of advanced economy public finances, and the debt and deficit positions of many of them, the politics of austerity is likely to pervade fiscal policy discussion for many years to come. A recent Institute for Fiscal Studies report noted that austerity and fiscal adjustment would continue to dominate UK macroeconomic policy until at least the mid-2020s (Emmerson et al. 2017; Treasury 2017), so the policy salience and political relevance of fiscal consolidation and adjustment ideas are not going away.

The rehabilitation of counter-cyclical fiscal policy established by the IMF in 2008–9 has been sustained for a decade. Indeed, there were successive waves of scholarship and policy recommendation, beginning with the *Fiscal Policy for the Crisis* in 2008, the 2010 debunking of the expansionary austerity thesis with 'Will it Hurt?', then the October 2012 *WEO*'s upwards re-evaluation of fiscal multipliers—and work revealing how fiscal multipliers vary across the cycle and are higher following financial crisis. Allied to this was the crucial underscoring of the view that fiscal consolidation can be self-defeating, and that—for many countries—fiscal retrenchment to pay down debt does not make sense as a policy prioritization. Thereafter came the counter-cyclical calls in *WEO* and *Fiscal Monitor* in 2014 for expanded public infrastructure investment which would pay for itself, contribute to growth, and help improve the debt positions of advanced economies. Maurice Obstfeld, Blanchard's successor as Chief Economist, then reasserted these central fiscal policy insights in September 2016 (Gaspar et al. 2016: 7, 10–14).

The September 2013 IMF Policy Paper *Reassessing the Role and Modalities of Fiscal Policy in Advanced Economies* provided an agreed summation of new fiscal policy thinking endorsed by the whole institution and the Executive Board. Yet an IMF Policy Paper does not have quite the same status as a new institutional positon, as was reached in the area of capital controls (see Chwieroth 2014; Moschella 2015; Gallagher 2015). This signalled that the shift on fiscal policy thinking was less thoroughgoing. Partly this is because the Fund, for all its attachment to even-handed treatment, views the fiscal policy debate differently for countries at different levels of development. The Policy Paper was, after all, specifically fiscal policy guidance for advanced economies. Since they were hardest hit by the crash, they faced a particular set of fiscal policy issues arising from it. Thus, the fiscal policy recommendations were context specific, not least because advanced economies are deemed to have fiscal policy institutions more capable of pursuing fiscal stabilization policy relatively efficiently and effectively.

The post-crash construction and deployment of fiscal space involves the IMF seeking to *expand* the policy space for a select group of advanced economies. In principle, this new fiscal policy agenda could also be extended to emerging economies. Historically, the IMF has been more risk averse, and more focused on fiscal sustainability considerations where they are concerned. Future work should explore whether the IMF's deployment of fiscal space arguments also expands policy space for some developing economies. This would be further evidence of how deep the new approach to fiscal policy goes within the IMF. Whether in emerging or advanced economies, however, IMF endorsement of activist counter-cyclical fiscal policy is not uniformly applicable but contingent upon fiscal space, and therefore a new institutional position or Fund-wide policy norm is unlikely to materialize.

The rehabilitation of fiscal policy as an active stabilization tool was in part justified as a special case under recessionary conditions, and in the context of the Zero Lower Bound rendering monetary policy ineffectual. The endorsement of Keynesian-inspired fiscal policy thinking was contingent upon both this context, and the fact of 'fiscal space' enjoyed by the country in question. Zero Lower Bound conditions have the potential to persist for some considerable time, and the category of advanced economies enjoying fiscal space is quite a large one. The September 2013 paper, endorsed by the Board, set the seal on a lasting recognition of the effectiveness of fiscal policy as a counter-cyclical tool. It underlined, amongst other things, how the 'cost of excessive frontloading or excessive postponement can be particularly large, even non-linear, during deep recessions' (IMF 2013j: 30). That said, the special case justification for enhanced counter-cyclical fiscal policy may set limits upon how far and how deep the rethinking of IMF economic policy premises goes. It could mean that, absent these Zero Lower Bound conditions, the short-term Keynesian recommendations would subside. The return of 'normal' conditions could mean a return to unreconstructed NCM models and approaches of old, targeting inflation using monetary policy, and guided by the non-accelerating inflation rate of unemployment (NAIRU) as in the pre-crash period.

Yet even if that proves to be the case, many of the aspects of the new fiscal policy thinking summarized in the paper extend their applicability beyond of the immediate post-GFC context. Crucially, the upwards re-evaluation of fiscal multipliers (IMF 2013j: 4, 17–21, 29–30) was 'baked into guidance' through the 'bucket' approach to fiscal multiplier assessment (Eyraud & Weber 2013). This evolved into guidance notes circulated to all desks (Batini et al. 2014b), sedimenting the new understandings of fiscal policy efficacy into

Fund standard operating procedures. It became part of how the Fund 'gets done' in the day-to-day work of desk economists. This procedural element is crucial to making enduring ideational change at the IMF.

Another enduring facet of Fund fiscal policy thinking was its attitude to the Eurozone crisis and the potential for its resolution. Shutting the door after the horse has bolted, the Fund highlights the need for Greek debt restructuring (IMF 2015c; Blanchard 2015c; Lagarde 2017). It also advocates debt mutualization, more active bond-buying by the ECB and ESM, and effective fiscal backstops to prevent financial market contagion risks (Moghadam 2014; Lagarde 2012c). This informed consistent and ongoing calls for Eurobonds and 'Full' Banking Union, as well as entreaties for the ECB and ESM to do more in terms of bond-buying on a precautionary basis, and for the ECB to be more active buying up government debt on the secondary market. The desire to sever the 'doom loop' between weakened sovereigns and troubled banks was an equally consistent refrain—underpinning calls for direct recapitalization of banks. More broadly, the Fund entreated European governments and institutions to complete the work to create a European banking resolution framework which would not leave national governments 'on the hook' for the costs of rescuing financial institutions. All these aspects of Fund fiscal policy conduct and crisis resolution became firmly embedded in IMF thinking and practice after 2008, and they survived a change of Managing Director *and* a change of Chief Economist.

Still more enduring are two other related aspects of new Fund thinking which each had important implications for fiscal policy. These were evolutions in IMF understandings of markets and stability, and its approach to inequality. The catalyst for both shifts was the GFC, and each is testament to a broader post-crash revisiting of IMF policy premises. The Fund has become more sceptical about the operation of financial markets and their relationship to economic stability. Official post-mortems on the Fund's failure to anticipate the 2008 crisis identified a hitherto prevailing faith in unfettered market forces as an important causal factor (see Moschella 2011). For example, the Fund's Independent Evaluation Office report on pre-crisis surveillance noted the dominant view amongst IMF staff 'that market discipline and self-regulation would be sufficient to stave off serious problems in financial institutions' and also unearthed issues of confirmation bias (IEO 2011: 17). There was also a common belief in the 'presumed ability of financial innovations to remove risks off banks' balance sheets' such that 'large financial institutions were in a strong position, and thereby, financial markets in advanced countries were fundamentally sound' (IEO 2011: 7); 'most staff saw financial markets as inherently stable' (IEO 2011: 10). Fund commentary and research had never wholly bought into the infamous efficient market hypothesis (Fama 1970), but Fund staff were too willing to trust market outcomes.[15] After 2008, the Fund became increasingly sceptical about financial markets and their properties, and IMF staff no longer presumed financial markets to be self-equilibrating. Fund understandings of the nature and potential scale of market instabilities and systemic risks posed by fragile financial systems have evolved markedly. So too has thinking about appropriate policy corollaries to counter this, including a revived role for capital controls (IMF 2012m; Chwieroth 2014; Gallagher 2015).

The post-crash IMF became more alive to adverse feedback loops, non-linearities, and systemic risks. José Viñals, its Financial Counsellor and Director of the Monetary and Capital Market department, amongst others, took the view that the financial system could no longer be relied upon to take care of itself (Viñals 2016). Nor did the Fund consider that leaving the market to its own devices was an adequate discharging of the IMF's duty to promote monetary and financial stability. The Fund's April 2009 *Global Stability Report* estimated overall losses to the global banking sector arising from the crash, putting total write-downs at $4.1 trillion (IMF 2009d: xi, 30). This arrestingly large figure was a spur to get national authorities to assess their own banks' losses, which was an important catalyst for the banking 'stress tests' that mobilized European and US authorities to recapitalize their banks.

Fund leadership recognized that they had previously been lacking the necessary elements in their policy toolkit to deal with systemic risk (Viñals 2010; 2011). This explains the focus and emphasis on financial stability, and on tools and policies to promote financial stability, as well as increased use of macroprudential and other regulation to limit, contain, and reduce systemic risks (IMF 2011m: ch. 3; IMF 2013d; Osinski et al. 2013). Its operationalization remained a work in progress, as Blanchard noted in June 2013: 'on macroprudential we are all on board—it looks like it has to be used, but we don't quite know how to use it.'[16] The Fund's re-enforced attention on the financial sector led to the development of a financial surveillance strategy in 2012 which presented the IMF as 'global macroprudential facilitator' and 'systemic risk advisor' (Lipton 2012; IMF 2013i). The IMF's spillover reports were designed to highlight systemic risks posed to the economy by financial sector developments. This was also the role of the beefed up *Global Stability Reports*, which every six months assess the key risks to financial stability and make policy recommendations on how to address them at the global level.

The Fund's default faith in the workings of financial markets has been shaken by the crash. IMF financial surveillance highlights the distortions, contingent liabilities, and a market failure to price risk, as well as tremendous fragilities and instabilities which financial market operations can entail. These

15 Interview with then FAD Director Carlo Cottarelli, June 2013.
16 Interview with IMF Chief Economist Olivier Blanchard, June 2013.

non-linear threats link to the recognition of multiple possible belief-driven equilibria, including 'bad debt' equilibria. Financial stability cannot be taken for granted, and certainly cannot be presumed to arise from the self-spontaneous working of the markets. Financial stability needs to be actively protected and nurtured, with an institutional and regulatory framework to guide markets in the right direction (Viñals 2011, 2016). The GFC and its aftermath underlined dysfunctionalities within what in Fund-speak are termed 'macro-financial interactions', the adverse feedback loops and spill-overs from the financial system to the real economy. Awareness grew that these can gather pace quickly and be devastating, as with sub-prime mortgages, or the bank/sovereign 'doom loop'.

The second broader shift is in relation to inequality. The Fund has for a very long time taken a stance of protecting poor and vulnerable social groups within its programmes, as well as within surveillance (see e.g. Tanzi, Chu, & Gupta 1999). Where there has been a clear evolution in Fund thinking is the level of prioritization this receives, highlighted by both Lagarde and before that Strauss-Kahn as Managing Directors. The post-crash Fund prioritized tackling inequality through macroeconomic and other policies in a way and to an extent which would have been unrecognizable a decade ago. The terminology used to discuss it has also evolved, framed by the Managing Director in terms of tackling 'excessive inequality' within capitalism and how 'more unequal countries tend to have lower and less durable economic growth' (Lagarde 2014a). From the 2011 triennial surveillance review onwards, there was explicit recognition of inequality as a so-called 'macro critical social indicator' (IMF 2011l). By establishing a link between inequality and growth, specifically, the duration of growth spells (Berg & Ostry 2011), income (re)distribution gets addressed *because of* the Fund's mandate. Thus, even if inequality is not per se part of the Fund's core mandate, the fact that high inequality can generate macroeconomic instability, and undermine growth, can render it close to a core mandate responsibility for the Fund.

Addressing inequality was also deemed crucial in the context of austerity and prolonged fiscal consolidation. As Deputy Director David Lipton pointed out in a speech to the 2013 Fiscal Forum, for protracted fiscal adjustment to be politically sustainable and socially viable, austerity must be understood to be 'fair' (Lipton 2013a). A reflexive Fund, keen to learn the lessons of past mistakes, recognized that these inequality considerations were not sufficiently to the fore in its tackling of the East Asian Financial Crisis in the late 1990s (IEO 2003: 40; Feldstein 1998; Chwieroth 2010: 6). Thus, the package of fiscal consolidation must be constructed in such a way that the burden of adjustment is equitably shared, and that it does not increase (and ideally reduces) inequality. Raising income taxes has, since the crash, become something the Fund cautiously advises governments to consider (see e.g. IMF 2010b: 44–6).

The IMF recommends policy which 'redresses the distributional impacts' including 'greater resort to progressive taxes and the protection of social benefits for vulnerable groups' as well as 'promoting education and training for low- and middle-income workers' (Furcedi & Loungani 2013: 27; Woo et al. 2013; Ball et al. 2011, 2013). A standard mantra of this IMF Managing Director and the last is that fiscal policy needs to focus 'not only on efficiency, but also on equity, particularly on fairness in sharing the burden of adjustment, and on protecting the weak and vulnerable' (Lagarde 2012b).

In relation to both of these enduring shifts in Fund thinking, fiscal policy plays a new and central role, notably as the primary tool for governments to affect income distribution (IMF 2014a). The more pervasive IMF view of financial markets as prone to instability makes stabilization policy a more pressing concern since the crash. This has implications not only for macro-prudential, but also for macroeconomic policy. Alongside unconventional monetary policy, fiscal policy plays a more pronounced role in stabilizing the economic cycle—both through automatic stabilizers and other policy measures. The counter-cyclical component of both macroprudential and macroeconomic policy has expanded since the crash, not least thanks to the IMF's efforts.

Coda

Economic orthodoxy is historically contingent. This analysis has revealed the malleability of conventional wisdoms about economic policy, and the processes of their social construction. The IMF's interpretive framework for evaluating economic policy is, we have seen, important within the construction of economic rectitude. The Fund uses its authoritative voice to fix meanings attached to appropriate post-crash fiscal policy. This reveals a crucial but underexplored connection between Fund economic ideas and room to manoeuvre for advanced economy governments. The IMF uses its knowledge bank, expertise, and mandate for surveillance and coordination to act as an arbiter of legitimate policy. It is engaged in pragmatic and reflexive processes of 'bricolage' (Campbell 2004) and 'layering' new ideas over old (Mahoney & Thelen 2010) to retain relevance to and 'traction' within pressing economic policy debates. There has been a notable rehabilitation of Keynesian insights, economic ideas which have long been accreted into IMF thinking and practice. This book has revealed the Fund's endorsement of activist, redistributive counter-cyclical fiscal policy which contrasts starkly with the IMF's reputation for austerity. As such, it substantially revises our understanding of the IMF's economic policy thinking and its relationship to government policy space.

Further work on this crucial but still underexplored connection between Fund economic ideas and room to manoeuvre for governments could analyse other policy areas, and other categories of countries. In analysing those Fund economic ideas, this book has demonstrated the value of disaggregating beyond the label 'neo-liberal' to reveal contours of evolutions in IMF policy thinking and practice. In a way which contests prevailing views of neo-liberal orthodoxy, this analysis reveals the wide range of economic insights—including unconventional and heterodox elements—reconcilable to mainstream economic thought. This affords key IMF actors hitherto-neglected scope to select and prioritize within this menu of respectable economic thinking. The Fund's reputation as a technocratic, scientific source of economic policy wisdom is important for its intellectual authority. Yet, as this book demonstrates, the Fund makes normatively driven interventions in ideologically charged economic policy debates.

Bibliography

Abiad, A., Furcedi, D., & Topalova, P. (2015). *The Macroeconomic Effects of Public Investment: Evidence from Advanced Economies*, IMF Working Paper WP/15/95. Washington DC: International Monetary Fund.

Adler, E., & Pouliot, V. (2011). 'International practices', *International Theory* 3(01): 1–36.

Ahamed, L. (2014). *Money and Tough Love: On Tour with the IMF*. Bristol: Visual Editions.

Alerkof, G. A., Blanchard, O., Romer, D., & Stiglitz, J. E. (2014). *What Have We Learned?: Macroeconomic Policy After the Crisis*. Cambridge, MA: MIT Press.

Alesina, A., & Giavazzi, F. (2013a). 'Introduction' in Alesina, A., & Giavazzi, F. (eds.). *Fiscal Policy After the Financial Crisis*. Chicago: University of Chicago Press.

Alesina, A., & Giavazzi, F. (eds.) (2013b). *Fiscal Policy After the Financial Crisis*. Chicago: University of Chicago Press.

Alesina, A. F. and Perotti, R. (2000). 'Budget deficits and budget institutions' in Lowry, R.C., Poterba, J. M., and von Hagen, J. (eds.), *Fiscal Institutions and Fiscal Performance*. Chicago: University of Chicago Press.

Alesina, A., & Perotti, R. (2010). 'Germany spending is not the cure' in Baldwin, R., Gros, D., & Laeven, L. (eds.), *Completing the Eurozone Rescue: What More Needs to Be Done?* Voxeu: Centre for Economic Policy Research, 79–83.

Alexander, S. (1952). 'Effects of a Devaluation on a Trade Balance', *IMF Staff Papers* 2: 263–78.

Annesley, C. & Gamble, A. (2003). 'Economic and Welfare Policy' in Smith, M. J. & Ludlam, S. (eds.), *Governing as New Labour*. Basingstoke: Palgrave.

Arestis, P. (ed.) (2007). *Is There a New Consensus in Macroeconomics?* Basingstoke: Palgrave.

Arestis, P. (2009a). 'The new consensus in macroeconomics: a critical appraisal'. Cambridge Centre for Economic and Public Policy CCEPP WP05-09. Department of Land Economy.

Arestis, P. (2009b). 'New Consensus macroeconomics and Keynesian critique' in Hein, E., Niechoj, T., & Stockhammer, E. *Macroeconomic Policies on Shaky Foundations—Whither Mainstream Economics?* (Vol. 12). IMK at the Hans Boeckler Foundation, Macroeconomic Policy Institute.

Arestis, P. (2011). 'Keynesian Economics and the New Consensus in macroeconomics' in Hein, E., & Stockhammer, E. (eds.), *A Modern Guide to Keynesian Macroeconomics and Economic Policies*. Cheltenham: Edward Elgar.

Arestis, P., & Sawyer, M. (1998). 'Keynesian economic policies for the new millennium', *The Economic Journal* 108(446): 181–95.

Arestis, P., & Sawyer, M. (2003). 'Reinventing Fiscal Policy', *Journal of Post Keynesian Economics* 26(1): 3–25.

Arestis, P., & Sawyer, M. (2006). 'The nature and role of monetary policy when money is endogenous', *Cambridge Journal of Economics* 30(6): 847–60.

Arestis, P., & Sawyer, M. (2008). 'A critical reconsideration of the foundations of monetary policy in the new consensus macroeconomics framework', *Cambridge Journal of Economics* 32(5): 761–79.

Arora, V. (2016). 'Five Lessons from a Review of Recent Crisis Programs', IMF Blog, iMFdirect, 11 July. available at: https://blogs.imf.org/2016/07/11/five-lessons-from-a-review-of-recent-crisis-programs/

Atkins, R. (2009). 'ECB Presses for Fiscal Exit Plan', *Financial Times*, 8 October.

Atkins, R. (2009). 'ECB Starts to Unwind Bank Liquidity Steps', *Financial Times*, 4 December.

Auerbach, A. J., & Gorodnichenko, Y. (2012). 'Measuring the output responses to fiscal policy', *American Economic Journal: Economic Policy* 4(2): 1–27.

Auerbach, A. J., & Gorodnichenko, Y. (2013a). 'Fiscal multipliers in recession and expansion' in Alesina, A., & Giavazzi, F. (eds.), *Fiscal Policy after the Financial Crisis*. Chicago: University of Chicago Press.

Auerbach, A. J., & Gorodnichenko, Y. (2013b). 'Output spillovers from fiscal policy', *The American Economic Review* 103(3): 141–6.

Babb, S. (2003). 'The IMF in sociological perspective: A tale of organizational slippage', *Studies in Comparative International Development* 38(2): 3–27.

Babb, S. (2007). 'Embeddedness, Inflation, and International Regimes: The IMF in the Early Postwar Period', *American Journal of Sociology* 113(1): 128–64.

Babb, S. (2013). 'The Washington Consensus as transnational policy paradigm: Its origins, trajectory and likely successor', *Review of International Political Economy* 20(2): 268–97.

Babb, S., & Buira, A. (2005). 'Mission creep, mission push and discretion: the case of IMF conditionality' in Buira, A. (ed.), *The IMF and the World Bank at Sixty*. London: Anthem Press.

Backhouse, R. E. (2002). *The Penguin History of Economics*. London: Penguin UK.

Backhouse, R. E. (2006). 'The Keynesian Revolution' in Backhouse, R. E., & Bateman, B. W. (eds.) *The Cambridge Companion to Keynes*. Cambridge: Cambridge University Press.

Baker, A. (2010). 'Austerity in the UK: Why it is not common sense but politically driven nonsense', Centre for Progressive Economics, www.centreforprogressiveeconomics.com.

Baker, A. (2013a). 'The new political economy of the macroprudential ideational shift', *New Political Economy* 18(1): 112–39.

Baker, A. (2013b). 'The gradual transformation? The incremental dynamics of macroprudential regulation', *Regulation & Governance* 7(4): 417–34.

Baker, A. (2015). 'Varieties of economic crisis, varieties of ideational change: How and why financial regulation and macroeconomic policy differ', *New Political Economy* 20(3): 342–66.

Baker, A., & Widmaier, W. (2014). 'The institutionalist roots of macroprudential ideas: Veblen and Galbraith on regulation, policy success and overconfidence', *New Political Economy* 19(4): 487–506.

Ball, L., Furcedi, D., Leigh, D., & Loungani, P. (2013). *The Distributional Effects of Fiscal Consolidation*, IMF Working Paper WP/13/151. Washington DC: International Monetary Fund.

Ball, L. M., Furceri, D., Leigh, M. D., & Loungani, M. P. (2011). 'Painful Medicine', *Finance & Development*, September, 48(3): 20–3.

Ban, C. (2015a). 'Austerity versus stimulus? Understanding fiscal, policy change at the International Monetary Fund since the great recession', *Governance* 28(2): 167–83.

Ban, C. (2015b). 'From Designers to Doctrinaires: Staff Research and Fiscal Policy Change at the IMF' in Morgan, G., Quack, S., & Hirsch, P. (eds.), *Elites on Trial*. Bingley: Emerald Group Publishing Limited.

Ban, C. (2016). *Ruling Ideas: How Global Neoliberalism Goes Local*. Oxford: Oxford University Press.

Ban, C., & Gallagher, K. (2015). 'Recalibrating policy orthodoxy: the IMF since the great recession'. *Governance* 28(2): 131–46.

Barber, T. (2010). 'Germany pressed to help cure imbalances', *Financial Times*, 1 April.

Barnett, M. N., & Finnemore, M. (1999). 'The politics, power, and pathologies of international organizations', *International Organization* 53(04): 699–732.

Barnett, M., & Finnemore, M. (2004). *Rules for the World: International Organizations in Global Politics*. Ithaca, NY: Cornell University Press.

Barnett, M., & Finnemore, M. (2005). 'The power of liberal international organizations' in Barnett, M., & Duvall, R. (eds.), *Power in Global Governance*. Cambridge: Cambridge University Press.

Barnett, M., & Duvall, R. (2005). 'Power in Global Governance' in Barnett, M., & Duvall, R. (eds.), *Power in Global Governance*. Cambridge: Cambridge University Press.

Barro, R. J. (1974). 'Are government bonds net wealth?', *Journal of Political Economy* 82(6): 1095–117.

Barro, R. J. (1989). 'The Ricardian Approach to Budget Deficits', *Journal of Economic Perspectives* 3(2): 37–54.

Batini, N., Callegari, G., & Melina, G. (2012). *Successful Austerity in the United States, Europe and Japan*, IMF Working Paper WP/12/190 Washington DC: International Monetary Fund.

Batini, N., Eyraud, L., Forni, L., & Weber, A. (2014b). *Fiscal multipliers: Size, determinants, and use in macroeconomic projections* (technical note, Fiscal Affairs Department). Washington DC: International Monetary Fund.

Batini, N., Eyraud, L., & Weber, A. (2014a). *A Simple Method to Compute Fiscal Multipliers*, IMF Working Paper WP/14/93. Washington DC: International Monetary Fund.

Baum, A., Weber, A., & Poplawski-Ribeiro, M. (2012). *Fiscal Multipliers and the State of the Economy*, IMF Working Paper WP/12/286. Washington DC: International Monetary Fund.

Baunsgaard, T., Mineshima, A., Poplawski-Ribeiro, M., & Weber, A. (2012). 'Fiscal Multipliers', unpublished paper.

Bayoumi, M. T., Dell'Ariccia, M. G., Habermeier, M. K. F., Griffoli, M. T. M., & Valencia, F. (2014). *Monetary Policy in the New Normal*, IMF Staff Discussion Note SDN/14/3. Washington DC: International Monetary Fund.

Bayoumi, T., Laxton, D., and Pesenti, P. (2004). 'GEM: A New International Macroeconomic Model', IMF Occasional Paper No. 239. Washington DC: International Monetary Fund.

Béland, D. (2009). 'Ideas, institutions, and policy change', *Journal of European Public Policy* 16(5): 701–18.

Béland, D. (2010). 'The idea of power and the role of ideas', *Political Studies Review* 8(2): 145–54.

Béland, D., & Cox, R. H. (2011). 'Introduction: Ideas and politics' in Béland, D., & Cox, R. H. (eds.) *Ideas and Politics in Social Science Research*. Oxford: Oxford University Press.

Bell, S. (2011). 'Do we really need a new "constructivist institutionalism" to explain institutional change?', *British Journal of Political Science* 41(04): 883–906.

Berg, A. & Ostry, J. D. (2011). *Inequality and Unsustainable Growth: Two Sides of the Same Coin?* IMF Staff Discussion Note SDN/11/08. Washington DC: International Monetary Fund.

Berg, A., Ostry, J. D., & Zettelmeyer, J. (2012). 'What makes growth sustained?', *Journal of Development Economics* 98(2): 149–66.

Best, J. (2003). 'From the top–down: The new financial architecture and the re-embedding of global finance', *New Political Economy* 8(3): 363–84.

Best, J. (2005). *The Limits of Transparency: Ambiguity and the History of International Finance*. Ithaca, NY: Cornell University Press.

Best, J. (2010). 'Bringing Power Back In: IMF's Constructivist Strategy in Critical Perspective' in Abdelal, R., Blyth, M., & Parsons, C. (eds.), *Constructing the international economy*. Ithaca, NY: Cornell University Press.

Best, J., & Widmaier, W. (2006). 'Micro-or macro-moralities? Economic discourses and policy possibilities', *Review of International Political Economy* 13(4): 609–31.

Bevir, M. (2002). *The Logic of the History of Ideas*. Cambridge: Cambridge University Press.

Bezes, P. (2008). 'The Reform of the State: the French Bureaucracy in the Age of New Public Management' in Cole, A., Le Galès, P., & Levy, J. (eds.), *Developments in French Politics 4*. Basingstoke: Palgrave.

Bezes, P., & Le Lidec, P. (2015). 'The French politics of retrenchment (2007–2012): Institutions and blame avoidance strategies', *International Review of Administrative Sciences* 81(3): 523–47.

Blanchard, O., & Cottarelli, C. (2008). 'IMF Spells Out Need for Global Fiscal Stimulus: interview with Olivier Blanchard and Carlo Cottarelli', *IMF Survey*, 29 December, available at: http://www.imf.org/external/pubs/ft/survey/so/2008/int122908a.htm

Blanchard, O. (2003). 'Comment on Inflation Targeting in Transition Economies: Experience and Prospects, by Jiri Jonas and Frederic Mishkin', presented at NBER Conference on Inflation Targeting, Bal Harbour, Florida, January. Cambridge, MA: National Bureau of Economic Research.

Blanchard, O. (2008a). 'The State of Macro', NBER Working paper 14259. Cambridge, MA: National Bureau of Economic Research.

Blanchard, O. (2008b). 'Cracks in the System: Repairing the damaged global economy', *Finance and Development* 45(4): 8–10.

Blanchard, O. (2009). '(Nearly). Nothing to fear but fear itself', *The Economist*, 29 January, available at: http://www.economist.com/node/13021961

Blanchard, O. (2010a). 'Interview with Olivier Blanchard: IMF Explores Contours of Future Macroeconomic Policy', *IMF Survey*, 12 February, available at: http://www.imf.org/en/News/Articles/2015/09/28/04/53/soint021210a

Blanchard, O. (2010b). 'Transcript of a Press Briefing on the International Monetary Fund's World Economic Outlook', 21 April, available at: http://www.imf.org/external/np/tr/2010/tr042110.htm

Blanchard, O. (2010c). 'A Problem Shared Is a Problem Halved: The G-20's "Mutual Assessment Process"', iMFdirect, 26 August, available at: http://www.economonitor.com/blog/2010/08/a-problem-shared-is-a-problem-halved-the-g-20s-mutual-assessment-process/

Blanchard, O. (2011a). Foreword to *World Economic Outlook*. September. Washington DC: International Monetary Fund.

Blanchard, O. (2011b). '2011 In Review: Four Hard Truths', IMFBlog, available at: https://blogs.imf.org/2011/12/21/2011-in-review-four-hard-truths/

Blanchard, O. (2012a). Driving the Global Economy with the Brakes On', IMFBlog, 24 January, available at: https://blogs.imf.org/2012/01/24/driving-the-global-economy-with-the-brakes-on/

Blanchard, O. (2012b). Foreword to *World Economic Outlook*. April. Washington DC: International Monetary Fund.

Blanchard, O. (2012c). Foreword to *World Economic Outlook*. October. Washington DC: International Monetary Fund.

Blanchard, O. (2013). 'Transcript of a Press Briefing', World Economic Outlook, 8 October, available at: http://www.imf.org/en/news/articles/2015/09/28/04/54/tr100813

Blanchard, O. (2014a). 'Where danger lurks', *Finance & Development* 51(3): 28–31.

Blanchard, O. (2014b). Foreword to *World Economic Outlook*. October. Washington DC: International Monetary Fund, xiii.

Blanchard, O. (2015a). 'Rethinking macroeconomic policy', Voxeu, 20 April, available at: http://voxeu.org/article/rethinking-macroeconomic-policy-introduction

Blanchard, O. (2015b). 'Ten Take Aways from the "Rethinking Macro Policy": Progress or Confusion?', iMFdirect blog, 1 May, available at: https://blogs.imf.org/2015/05/01/ten-take-aways-from-the-rethinking-macro-policy-progress-or-confusion/

Blanchard, O. (2015c). 'Greece: Past Critiques and the Path Forward', iMFdirect blog, 9 July, available at: https://blogs.imf.org/2015/07/09/greece-past-critiques-and-the-path-forward/

Blanchard, O., and Cottarelli, C. (2010). 'Ten Commandments for Fiscal Adjustment in Advanced Economies', IMFdirect, 24 June. available at: https://blogs.imf.org/2010/06/24/ten-commandments-for-fiscal-adjustment-in-advanced-economies/

Blanchard, O. J., Dell'Ariccia, M. G., & Mauro, M. P. (2010). *Rethinking Macro Policy*. IMF Staff Position Note SPN/10/03. Washington DC: International Monetary Fund.

Blanchard, O. J., Dell'Ariccia, M. G., & Mauro, M. P. (2013). *Rethinking Macro Policy II: Getting Granular*, Washington DC: International Monetary Fund.

Blanchard, O., & Galí, J. (2007). 'Real wage rigidities and the New Keynesian model', *Journal of Money, Credit and Banking* 39(1): 35–65.

Blanchard, O., and Leigh, D. (2013a). 'Growth Forecast Errors and Fiscal Multipliers', IMF Working Paper No. 13/1. Washington DC: International Monetary Fund.

Blanchard, O., and Leigh, D. (2013b). 'Fiscal consolidation: At what speed?', Voxeu, 3 May.

Blanchard, O., Romer, D., Spence, M., & Stiglitz, J. E. (eds.) (2012). *In the Wake of the Crisis: Leading Economists Reassess Economic Policy*. Cambridge, MA: MIT Press.

Blanchard, O. J., & Summers, L. H. (1986). 'Hysteresis in unemployment', *European Economic Review* 31(1–2): 288–95.

Blaug, M. (1990). *John Maynard Keynes: Life, Ideas, Legacy*. Basingstoke: Macmillan.

Blaug, M. (1996). *Economic Theory in Retrospect*. Cambridge: Cambridge University Press.

Blinder, A. S. (1988). 'The fall and rise of Keynesian economics', *Economic Record* 64(4): 278–94.

Blyth, M. (2002a). *Great Transformations*. Cambridge: Cambridge University Press.

Blyth, M. (2002b). 'Institutions and ideas' in Stoker, G., and David, M. (eds.), *Theory and Methods in Political Science*. Basingstoke: Macmillan.

Blyth, M. (2003a). 'Structures Do Not Come With An Instruction Sheet: Interests, Ideas, and Progress in Political Science', *Perspectives on Politics* 1(4): 695–706.

Blyth, M. (2003b). 'The political power of financial ideas'. in Kirshner, J. (ed.), *Monetary Orders: Ambiguous Economics, Ubiquitous Politics*. Ithaca, NY: Cornell University Press.

Blyth, M. (2007). 'Powering, puzzling, or persuading? The mechanisms of building institutional orders', *International Studies Quarterly* 51(4): 761–77.

Blyth, M. (2013a). *Austerity: The History of a Dangerous Idea*. Oxford: Oxford University Press.

Blyth, M. (2013b). 'Paradigms and paradox: The politics of economic ideas in two moments of crisis', *Governance* 26(2): 197–215.

Bonefeld, W. (2012). 'Freedom and the strong state: On German ordoliberalism', *New Political Economy* 17(5): 633–56.

Botman, D., Muir, D., Laxton, D., & Romanov, A. (2006). *A New Open-Economy Macro Model for Fiscal Policy Evaluation* IMF Working Paper WP/06/045. Washington DC: International Monetary Fund.

Botman, D. P., Karam, P. D., Laxton, D., & Rose, D. (2007). *DSGE Modeling at the Fund: Applications ands Further Developments*, IMF Working Paper WP/07/200. Washington DC: International Monetary Fund.

Boughton, J. M. (1997). *Modelling the World Economic Outlook at the IMF: A Historical Review*, IMF Working Paper WP/97/48. Washington DC: International Monetary Fund.

Boughton, J. M. (2001). *Silent Revolution. The International Monetary Fund 1979–1989*. Washington DC: International Monetary Fund.

Boughton, J. M. (2004). *The IMF and the force of history: ten events and ten ideas that have shaped the institution*. IMF Staff Papers. Washington DC: International Monetary Fund.

Boughton, J. M. (2012). *Tearing Down Walls: The International Monetary Fund, 1990–1999*. Washington DC: International Monetary Fund.

Boughton, J. M., & Lombardi, D. (eds.) (2009). *Finance, Development, and the IMF*. Oxford: Oxford University Press.

Braun, B. (2014). 'Central Bank Agency and Monetary Governability in the Euro Area: Governing Through Money, Trust And Expectations', PhD Thesis, University of Warwick.

Breen, M. (2013). *The Politics of IMF Lending*. Basingstoke: Palgrave.

Breen, M. (2014). 'IMF conditionality and the economic exposure of its shareholders', *European Journal of International Relations* 20(2): 416–36.

Broome, A. (2008). 'The importance of being earnest: the IMF as a reputational intermediary', *New Political Economy* 13(2): 125–51.

Broome, A. (2010a). 'The International Monetary Fund, crisis management and the credit crunch', *Australian Journal of International Affairs* 64(1): 37–54.

Broome, A. (2010b). *The Currency of Power: The IMF and Monetary Reform in Central Asia*. Basingstoke: Palgrave.

Broome, A. (2015). 'Back to basics: the great recession and the narrowing of IMF policy advice', *Governance* 28(2): 147–65.

Broome, A., & Seabrooke, L. (2007). 'Seeing like the IMF: Institutional change in small open economies', *Review of International Political Economy* 14(4): 576–601.

Broome, A., & Seabrooke, L. (2012). 'Seeing like an international organisation', *New Political Economy* 17(1): 1–16.

Broz, J. L., & Hawes, M. B. (2006). 'US domestic politics and International Monetary Fund in policy' in Hawkins, D. G., Lake, D. A., Nielson, D. L., & Tierney, M. J. (eds.), *Delegation and Agency in International Organizations*. Cambridge: Cambridge University Press.

Buchanan, J. (1975). *The Limits of Liberty: Between Anarchy and the Leviathan*. Chicago: Chicago University Press.

Buira, A. (ed.) (2005). *Reforming the Governance of the IMF and the World Bank*. London: Anthem Press.

Cameron, D. (2013). Economy speech, 7 March, available at: https://www.gov.uk/government/speeches/economy-speech-delivered-by-david-cameron

Campbell, J. (1998). 'Institutional Analysis and the Role of Ideas in Political Economy', *Theory and Society* 27(3): 377–409.

Campbell, J. (2001). 'Institutional Analysis and the Role of Ideas in Political Economy' in Campbell, J. L., & Pedersen, O. K. (eds.), *The Rise of Neoliberalism and Institutional Analysis*. Princeton, NJ: Princeton University Press.

Campbell, J. (2004). *Institutional Change and Globalization*. Princeton, NJ: Princeton University Press.

Campbell, J. (2010). 'Institutional Reproduction and Change' in Morgan et al. (eds.), *The Oxford Handbook of Comparative Institutional Analysis*. Oxford: Oxford University Press.

Campbell, J. L. (2002). 'Ideas, politics, and public policy', *Annual Review of Sociology* 28(1): 21–38.

Campbell, J. L., & Pedersen, O. K. (eds.) (2001a). *The Rise of Neoliberalism and Institutional Analysis*. Princeton, NJ: Princeton University Press.

Campbell, J. L., & Pedersen, O. K. (2001b). 'The rise of neoliberalism and institutional analysis' in Campbell, J. L., & Pedersen, O. K. (eds.), *The Rise of Neoliberalism and Institutional Analysis*. Princeton, NJ: Princeton University Press.

Carstensen, M. B. (2011a). 'Ideas are not as stable as political scientists want them to be: A theory of incremental ideational change', *Political Studies* 59(3): 596–615.

Carstensen, M. B. (2011b). 'Paradigm man vs. the bricoleur: bricolage as an alternative vision of agency in ideational change', *European Political Science Review*, 3(01): 147–67.

Carstensen, M. B. (2013). 'Projecting from a fiction: The Case of Denmark and the financial crisis', *New Political Economy* 18(4): 555–78.

Carstensen, M. B. (2015a). 'Institutional bricolage in times of crisis', *European Political Science Review* 9(1): 139–60.

Carstensen, M. B. (2015b). 'Bringing Ideational Power into the Paradigm Approach: Critical Perspectives on Policy Paradigms in Theory and Practice' in Hogan, J., & Howlett, M. (eds.), *Policy Paradigms in Theory and Practice: Discourses, Ideas and Anomalies in Public Policy Dynamics*. Basingstoke: Palgrave.

Checkel, J. T. (1998). 'The constructive turn in international relations theory', *World Politics* 50(2): 324–48.

Checkel, J. T. (2001). 'Why comply? Social learning and European identity change', *International Organization* 55(3): 553–88.

Chopra, A. (2011a). 'Union Jack: Be nimble, Be quick', iMFdirect, 1 August, available at: http://blog-imfdirect.imf.org/2011/08/01/union-jack-be-nimble-be-quick/

Chopra, A. (2011b). 'Strengthening the Financial Stability Framework of the EU', speech to the 2011 Dublin Economic Workshop, Kenmare, 15 October, available at: http://www.imf.org/en/news/articles/2015/09/28/04/53/sp101511

Chopra, A. (2012). 'Mind the Gap: Policies to Jump Start Growth in the U.K.', IMF Blog, 19 July, available at: https://blogs.imf.org/2012/07/19/mind-the-gap-policies-to-jump-start-growth-in-the-u-k/

Chopra, A. (2014). 'The IMF Was Right to Criticize UK Fiscal Policy', Peterson Institute for International Economics Realtime Economics Issues Watch blog, available at: https://piie.com/blogs/realtime-economic-issues-watch/imf-was-right-criticize-uk-fiscal-policy

Chote, R. (2013). 'Letter to the Prime Minister', March. London: Office for Budget Responsibility.

Chote, R., & Riley, J. (2014). 'Crisis and consolidation in the public finances', September, OBR Working Paper no. 7. London: Office for Budget Responsibility.

Chwieroth, J. (2007b). 'Neoliberal economists and capital account liberalization in emerging markets', *International Organization* 61(2): 443–63.

Chwieroth, J. M. (2007a). 'Testing and measuring the role of ideas: The case of neoliberalism in the International Monetary Fund', *International Studies Quarterly* 51(1): 5–30.

Chwieroth, J. M. (2010). *Capital Ideas: The IMF and the Rise of Financial Liberalization*. Princeton, NJ: Princeton University Press.

Chwieroth, J. M. (2013). '"The silent revolution": How the staff exercise informal governance over IMF lending', *Review of international Organizations* 8(2): 265–90.

Chwieroth, J. M. (2014). 'Controlling capital: the international monetary fund and transformative incremental change from within international organisations', *New Political Economy* 19(3): 445–69.

Claessens, S., Mody, A., & Vallée, S., (2012). *Paths to Eurobonds*, IMF Working Paper WP/12/172. Washington DC: International Monetary Fund.

Clegg, L. (2013). *Controlling the World Bank and IMF: Shareholders, Stakeholders, and the Politics of Concessional Lending*. Basingstoke: Palgrave.

Clift, B. (2006). 'The New Political Economy of *Dirigisme*: French Macroeconomic Policy, Unrepentant Sinning, and the Stability and Growth Pact', *British Journal of Politics and International Relations* 8(3): 388–409.

Clift, B. (2008). 'Economic Policy' in Cole, A., Le Galès, P., & Levy, J. (eds.) *Developments in French Politics 4*. Basingstoke: Palgrave.

Clift, B. (2012). 'Comparative capitalisms, ideational political economy and French post-dirigiste responses to the global financial crisis', *New Political Economy* 17(5): 565–90.

Clift, B. (2013). '*Le Changement?* French Socialism, the 2012 Presidential Election and the Politics of Economic Credibility Amidst the Eurozone Crisis', *Parliamentary Affairs* 66(1): 106–23.

Clift, B. (2014a). *Comparative Political Economy: States, Markets and Global Capitalism*. Basingstoke: Palgrave.

Clift, B. (2014b). *The Hollande Presidency, the Eurozone Crisis & the Politics of Fiscal Rectitude*. SPERI Paper No. 10.

Clift, B. (2015). 'The UK Macroeconomic Policy Debate and the British Growth Crisis: Debt and Deficit Discourse in the Great Recession' in Green, J., & Hay, C. (eds.), *The British Growth Crisis*. Basingstoke: Palgrave.

Clift, B., & Tomlinson, J. (2004). 'Capital Mobility and Fiscal Policy: The Construction of Economic Policy Rectitude in Britain and France', *New Political Economy* 9(4): 515–37.

Clift, B., & Tomlinson, J. (2007). 'Credible Keynesianism? New Labour macroeconomic policy and the political economy of coarse tuning', *British Journal of Political Science* 37(1): 47–69.

Clift, B., & Tomlinson, J. (2008a). 'Negotiating Credibility: Britain and the International Monetary Fund, 1956–1976', *Contemporary European History* 17(4): 545–66.

Clift, B., & Tomlinson, J. (2008b). 'Whatever happened to the balance of payments "problem"? The contingent (re)construction of British economic performance assessment', *British Journal of Politics and International Relations* 10(4): 607–29.

Clift, B., & Tomlinson, J. (2012). 'When rules started to rule: The IMF, neo-liberal economic ideas and economic policy change in Britain', *Review of International Political Economy* 19(3): 477–500.

Coddington, A. (1976). 'Keynesian economics: the search for first principles', *Journal of Economic Literature* 14(4): 1258–73.

Colander, D. (1992). 'New Keynesian Economics in Perspective', *Eastern Economic Journal* 18(4): 437–48.

Colander, D. (1996). 'Beyond New Keynesian Economics: Towards a Post Walrasian Macroeconomics', available at: http://cat.middlebury.edu/~colander/articles/Beyond%20New%20Keynesian5.pdf

Colander, D. (2005). 'The making of an economist redux', *The Journal of Economic Perspectives* 19(1): 175–98.

Colander, D. C. (2007). *The Making of an Economist, Redux*. Princeton, NJ: Princeton University Press.

Cole, A. (2008). *Governing and Governance in France*. Cambridge: Cambridge University Press.

Copelovitch, M. S. (2010). *The International Monetary Fund in the Global Economy: Banks, Bonds, and Bailouts*. Cambridge: Cambridge University Press.

Corsetti, G., Meier, A., & Müller, G. J. (2012). *What Determines Government Spending Multipliers?*, IMF Working Paper WP/12/150. Washington DC: International Monetary Fund.

Cottarelli, C. (2011). 'Challenges of Budgetary and Financial Crisis in Europe', Speech at the LSE, 18 November, available at: http://www.imf.org/external/np/speeches/2011/111811.htm

Cottarelli, C. (2012a). 'Fiscal adjustment: Too much of a good thing?', Voxeu, 8 February.

Cottarelli, C. (2012b). 'Fiscal Policy: Reconciling Fiscal Sustainability and Growth', PowerPoint presentation. Washington DC: International Monetary Fund, available at: http://www.imf.org/external/pubs/ft/fm/2012/update/01/pdf/cottarelli2.pdf

Cottarelli, C. (2013). 'From Here to Eternity: The Outlook for Fiscal Adjustment in Advanced Economies', Speech at Peterson Institute for International Economics, 20 May, available at: http://www.imf.org/external/np/speeches/2013/052013.htm

Cottarelli, C., Forni, L., Gottschalk, J., & Mauro, P. (2010). *Default in Today's Advanced Economies: Unnecessary, Undesirable, and Unlikely*. IMF Staff Position Note SPN/10/12. Washington DC: International Monetary Fund.

Cottarelli, C., Gerson, P., & Senhadji, A. (2014). *Post-Crisis Fiscal Policy*. Cambridge, MA: MIT Press.

Cottarelli, C., & Jaramillo, L. (2012). *Walking Hand In Hand: Fiscal Policy and Growth in Advanced Economies*, IMF Working Paper WP/12/137. Washington DC: International Monetary Fund.

Crouch, C. (2005). *Capitalist Diversity and Change*. Oxford: Oxford University Press.

Crouch, C. (2011). *The Strange Non-Death of Neo-Liberalism*. Cambridge: Polity.

Daniel, J., Davis, J., Fouad, M., & Van Rijckeghem, C. (2006). *Fiscal Adjustment for Stability and Growth*, IMF Pamphlet Series No. 55. Washington DC: International Monetary Fund.

David, W. L. (1985). *The IMF Policy Paradigm*. New York: Praeger.

Davidson, P. (2007). *Interpreting Keynes for the 21st Century: Volume 4: The Collected Writings of Paul Davidson*. Basingstoke: Palgrave.

De Vries, M. M. G. (1985). *The IMF, 1972–78: Cooperation on Trial*. Washington DC: International Monetary Fund.

De Vries, M. M. G. (1987). *Balance of Payments Adjustment, 1945 to 1986: The IMF Experience*. Washington DC: International Monetary Fund.

Decressin, J. (2012). 'Transcript of the World Economic Outlook Press Conference', 17 April, available at: https://www.imf.org/en/News/Articles/2015/09/28/04/54/tr041712

Decressin, M. J., & Laxton, M. D. (2009). *Gauging risks for deflation*. IMF Staff Position Note SPN/09/01. Washington DC: International Monetary Fund.

Dellepiane-Avellaneda, S. (2015). 'The political power of economic ideas: The case of "expansionary fiscal contractions"', *British Journal of Politics & International Relations* 17(3): 391–418.

DeLong, J. B., & Summers, L. H. (2012). 'Fiscal policy in a depressed economy', *Brookings Papers on Economic Activity* 2012(1): 233–97.

Dow, S. C. (2015). 'The role of belief in the case for austerity policies', *The Economic and Labour Relations Review* 26(1): 29–42.

Dreher, A., & Jensen, N. M. (2007). 'Independent actor or agent? An empirical analysis of the impact of US interests on international monetary fund conditions', *The Journal of Law and Economics* 50(1): 105–24.

Dyson, K. (1999). 'The Franco-German Relationship and economic and monetary union: using Europe to "Bind Leviathan"', *West European Politics* 22(1): 25–44.

Dyson, K., & Featherstone, K. (1999). *The Road to Maastricht: Negotiating Economic and Monetary Union*. Oxford: Oxford University Press.

Eatwell, J. (1995). 'The International Origins of Unemployment' in Michie, J., & Grieve Smith, J. (eds.), *Managing the Global Economy*. Oxford: Oxford University Press.

Eatwell, J., & Milgate, M. (2011). *The Fall and Rise of Keynesian Economics*. Oxford: Oxford University Press.

Ecofin (2009). 'Preparation of Eurogroup and Informal Economic and Finance Ministers Council, Göteborg (Sweden), 1 and 2 October 2009', MEMO/09/425 Brussels, 30 September, available at: http://europa.eu/rapid/press-release_MEMO-09-425_en.htm

Eichenbaum, M., Jaimovich, N., & Rebelo, S. (2011). 'Reference prices, costs, and nominal rigidities', *The American Economic Review* 101(1): 234–62.

El-Erian, M. A. (2010). 'Navigating the New Normal in Industrial Countries', Per Jacobsson Foundation Lecture, 10 October, available at: http://www.imf.org/external/np/speeches/2010/101010.htm

El-Erian, M. A. (2015). 'IMF Gets Smart about a Third Greek Bailout', *Bloomberg*, 31 July.

Elliot, L. (2013). 'George Osborne told by IMF chief: rethink your austerity plan', *The Guardian*, 18 April.

Emmerson, C., Johnson, P., Joyce, R., & Crawford, R. (2017). 'Neither Conservatives nor Labour are properly spelling out consequences of their policy proposals', IFS, 26 May, available at: https://www.ifs.org.uk/publications/9259

Engelen, E., Erturk, I., Froud, J., Johal, S., Leaver, L., Moran, M., Nilsson, A., & Williams, K. (2011). *After The Great Complacence: Financial Crisis and the Politics of Reform*. Oxford: Oxford University Press.

Euro Area Summit Statement (2012). 29 June, available at: http://www.consilium.europa.eu/uedocs/cms_Data/docs/pressdata/en/ec/131359.pdf

European Commission (2012). 'Current Account Surpluses in the EU', *European Economy* 9/2012. Brussels: European Commission.

European Commission (2013). 'Third Alert Mechanism Report on macroeconomic imbalances in EU Member States', 13 November. Brussels: European Commission, available at: http://europa.eu/rapid/press-release_MEMO-13-970_en.htm

European Commission (2014). 'Commission concludes in-depth reviews of 17 Member States to check for macroeconomic imbalances', 5 March. Brussels: European Commission, available at: http://europa.eu/rapid/press-release_MEMO-14-158_it.htm?locale=EN

European Commission (2015). 'European Commission—Fact Sheet Banking Union: restoring financial stability in the Eurozone', Updated version of first memo published on 15/04/2014—Brussels: European Commission, 24 November, available at: http://europa.eu/rapid/press-release_MEMO-15-6164_en.htm?locale=en

European Council (2010). 'Council Conclusions: Economic and Financial Affairs council Extraordinary Meeting Brussels 9/10 May 2010', available at: https://www.consilium.europa.eu/uedocs/cmsUpload/Conclusions_Extraordinary_meeting_May2010- EN.pdf

European Court of Auditors (2014). *European Banking Supervision taking shape—EBA and its changing Context.* Special Report no. 5. Luxembourg: European Court of Auditors, available at: http://www.eca.europa.eu/Lists/ECADocuments/SR14_05/SR14_05_EN.pdf

Evans, P., & Finnemore, M. (2001). 'Organizational Reform and the Expansion of the South's Voice at the Fund', G24 Discussion Paper Series, UNCTAD.

Eyraud, L., & Weber, A. (2013). *The Challenge of Debt Reduction during Fiscal Consolidation*, IMF Working Paper WP/13/67. Washington DC: International Monetary Fund.

Fama, E. F. (1970). 'Efficient capital markets: A review of theory and empirical work', *Journal of Finance* 25(2): 383–417.

Fama, E. F. (1991). 'Efficient capital markets: II', *Journal of Finance* 46(5): 1575–617.

Farrell, H., & Newman, A. L. (2010). 'Making global markets: Historical institutionalism in international political economy', *Review of International Political Economy* 17(4): 609–38.

Farrell, H., & Quiggin, J. (2012). 'Consensus, dissensus and economic ideas: The rise and fall of Keynesianism during the economic crisis', *Center for the Study of Development Strategies*: 1–52. available at: http://www.henryfarrell.net/Keynes.pdf

Faruqee, H., & Srinivasan, K. (2012). 'The G-20 mutual assessment process—a perspective from IMF staff', *Oxford Review of Economic Policy*, 28(3): 493–511.

Feldstein, M. (1998). 'Refocusing the IMF', *Foreign Affairs* 77(2): 20–33.

Finnemore, M., & Sikkink, K. (1998). 'International norm dynamics and political change', *International Organization* 52(4): 887–917.

Fioretos, K. O. (2011a). *Creative Reconstructions: Multilateralism and European Varieties of Capitalism after 1950*. Ithaca, NY: Cornell University Press.

Fioretos, O. (2011b). 'Historical institutionalism in international relations', *International Organization* 65(2): 367–99.

Fiscal Affairs Department (1995). *Guidelines for Fiscal Adjustment*, IMF Pamphlet Series no. 49. Washington DC: International Monetary Fund.

Fischer, S. (1998). 'The Asian Crisis: A View from the IMF—Address by Stanley Fischer', 22 January, available at: https://www.imf.org/en/News/Articles/2015/09/28/04/53/sp012298

Fischer, S. (2001a). The International Financial System: Crises and Reform', *The Robbins Lectures at the London School of Economics*, available at: https://piie.com/fischer/pdf/Fischer178.pdf

Fischer, S. (2001b). 'Farewell Dinner Speech First Deputy Managing Director', 29 August, available at: https://www.imf.org/en/News/Articles/2015/09/28/04/53/sp082901a

Fleming, J. M. (1962). 'Domestic financial policies under fixed and under floating exchange rates', *IMF Staff Papers* 9(3): 369–80.

Fourcade, M. (2009). *Economists and Societies: Discipline and Profession in the United States, Britain, and France, 1890s to 1990s*. Princeton, NJ: Princeton University Press.

Fourcade, M., Steiner, P., Streeck, W., & Woll, C. (2013). 'Moral categories in the financial crisis', *Socio-Economic Review* 11(3): 601–27.

Fourcade-Gourinchas, M., & Babb, S. L. (2002). 'The Rebirth of the Liberal Creed: Paths to Neoliberalism in Four Countries', *American Journal of Sociology* 108(3): 533–79.

Freedman, C., Kumhof, M., Laxton, D., & Lee, J. (2009). *The Case for Global Fiscal Stimulus*, IMF Staff Position Note SPN/09/03. Washington DC: International Monetary Fund.

Friedman, M. (1968). 'The role of monetary policy', *American Economic Review* 58(1): 1–19.

Fuchs, V. R., Krueger, A. B., & Poterba, J. M. (1997). *Why do economists disagree about policy?: The roles of beliefs about parameters and values* (No. 389). National Bureau of Economic Research.

Fuchs, V. R., Krueger, A. B., & Poterba, J. M. (1998). 'Economists' views about parameters, values, and policies: Survey results in labor and public economics', *Journal of Economic Literature* 36(3): 1387–425.

Furcedi, D., & Loungani, P. (2013). 'Who Let the Gini Out?', *Finance & Development* 50(4): 25–7.

G20 (2009). 'London Summit—Leaders' Statement', 2 April, available at: https://www.imf.org/external/np/sec/pr/2009/pdf/g20_040209.pdf

Gabor, D. (2010). 'The International Monetary Fund and its new economics', *Development and Change* 41(5): 805–30.

Galbraith, J. K. (1958). *The Affluent Society*. New York: New American Library.

Gallagher, K. P. (2015). 'Contesting the Governance of Capital Flows at the IMF', *Governance* 28(2): 185–98.

Gamble, A. (2009). *Spectre at the Feast*. Basingstoke: Palgrave.

Gamble, A. (2010). 'The Politics of the deficit: British politics and the financial crisis', paper prepared for APSA Conference, Boston Ma, September.

Gamble, A. (2012). 'The United Kingdom: The Triumph of Fiscal Realism?' in Grant, E., & Wilson, G. (eds.), *The Consequences of the Global Financial Crisis*. Oxford: Oxford University Press.

Gamble, A. (2014). *Crisis Without End?: The Unravelling of Western Prosperity*. Basingstoke: Palgrave.

Ganelli, G., & Tervala, J. (2016). *The Welfare Multiplier of Public Infrastructure Investment*, IMF Working Paper WP/16/40. Washington DC: International Monetary Fund.

Gaspar, V., Obstfeld, M., & and Sahay, R. (2016). *Macroeconomic Management When Policy Space is Constrained*, IMF Staff Discussion Note SDN/16/09. Washington DC: International Monetary Fund.

Gerson, P. (2014). 'Transcript of Conference Call on the 2014 United Kingdom Article IV Consultation', 28 July, Washington, DC, available at: http://www.imf.org/external/np/tr/2014/tr072814.htm

Ghosh, A., Kim, J., Ostry, J., Qureshi, M., and Mendoza, E. (2013). 'Fiscal Fatigue, Fiscal Space and Debt Sustainability in Advanced Economies', *Economic Journal* 123(566): 4–30.

Giavazzi, F., & Pagano, M. (1990). 'Can severe fiscal contractions be expansionary? Tales of two small European countries', *NBER Macroeconomics Annual* 5: 75–111.

Giavazzi, F. & Pagano, M. (1996). 'Non-Keynesian Effects of Fiscal Policy Changes: International Evidence and the Swedish Experience', *Swedish Economic Policy Review*, 3(1): 67–103.

Giles, C. (2009). 'Fiscal Stimulus: Weaned off the stimulus', *Financial Times*, 23 September.

Goldsbrough, D. (2007). 'Does the IMF constrain health spending in poor countries? Evidence and an agenda for action', *Center for Global Development*. Washington DC, available at: https://www.cgdev.org/doc/IMF/IMF_Report.pdf

Gonzalez-Paramo, J. M. (2009). 'Financial market failures and public policies: A central banker's perspective on the global financial crisis', *Revista de Economía Pública* 90(3): 127–56.

Goodfriend, M. (2007). 'How the world achieved consensus on monetary policy', *The Journal of Economic Perspectives* 21(4): 47–68.

Goodhart, C. A. (2009). 'The continuing muddles of monetary theory: a steadfast refusal to face facts', *Economica* 76(1): 821–30.

Gould, E. R. (2006). 'Delegating IMF conditionality: Understanding variations in control and conformity' in Hawkins, D. G., Lake, D. A., Nielson, D. L., & Tierney, M. J. (eds.), *Delegation and Agency in International Organizations*. Cambridge: Cambridge University Press.

Grabel, I. (2003). 'Ideology, power and the rise of independent monetary institutions in emerging economies' in Kirshner, J. (ed.), *Monetary Orders: Ambiguous Economics, Ubiquitous Politics*. Ithaca, NY: Cornell University Press.

Grabel, I. (2015). 'The rebranding of capital controls in an era of productive incoherence', *Review of International Political Economy* 22(1): 7–43.

Group of Independent Experts (1999). *External Evaluation of IMF Surveillance*, available at: https://www.imf.org/external/pubs/ft/extev/surv/eval.pdf

Hall, P. (1986). *Governing the Economy*. Cambridge: Polity.

Hall, P. (1989). 'Conclusion' in Hall, P. (ed.), *The Political Power of Economic Ideas*. Princeton, NJ: Princeton University Press.

Hall, P. (1993). 'Policy Paradigms, Social Learning and the State', *Comparative Politics* 25(3): 275–96.

Hall, P. A. (2012). 'The economics and politics of the euro crisis', *German Politics* 21(4): 355–371.

Hall, R. B. (2008). *Central Banking as Global Governance: Constructing Financial Credibility*. Cambridge: Cambridge University Press.

Hansen, A. H. (1934). 'Capital goods and the restoration of purchasing power', *Proceedings of the Academy of Political Science* 16(1): 11–19.

Hansen, A. H. (1949). *Monetary Theory and Fiscal Policy*. London: Mcgraw-Hill.

Hargreaves Heap, S. P. (1994). 'Institutions and (short-run) macroeconomic performance', *Journal of Economic Surveys* 8(1): 35–56.

Hawkins, D., Lake, D., Nielson, D., & Tierney, M. (2006a). 'Delegation under anarchy: states, international organizations and principal-agent theory' in Hawkins, D. G., Lake, D. A., Nielson, D. L., & Tierney, M. J. (eds.), *Delegation and Agency in International Organizations*. Cambridge: Cambridge University Press.

Hawkins, D. G., & Jacoby, W. (2006). 'How agents matter' in Hawkins, D. G., Lake, D. A., Nielson, D. L., & Tierney, M. J. (eds.), *Delegation and Agency in International Organizations*. Cambridge: Cambridge University Press.

Hawkins, D. G., Lake, D. A., Nielson, D. L., & Tierney, M. J. (eds.) (2006b). *Delegation and Agency in International Organizations*. Cambridge: Cambridge University Press.

Hay, C. (1996). 'Narrating Crisis: The Discursive Construction of the Winter of Discontent', *Sociology* 30(2): 253–77.

Hay, C. (2001). 'The "Crisis" of Keynesianism and the Rise of Neoliberalism in Britain: An Ideational Institutionalist Approach' in Campbell & Pedersen (eds.), *The Rise of Neoliberalism and Institutional Analysis*. Princeton, NJ: Princeton University Press.

Hay, C. (2004a). 'Credibility, competitiveness and the business cycle in "Third Way" political economy: a critical evaluation of economic policy in Britain since 1997', *New Political Economy* 9(1): 39–56.

Hay, C. (2004b). 'The normalizing role of rationalist assumptions in the institutional embedding of neoliberalism', *Economy and Society* 33(4): 500–27.

Hay, C. (2008). 'Constructivist institutionalism' in Rhodes, R. A., Binder, S. A., & Rockman, B. A. (eds.), *The Oxford Handbook of Political Institutions*. Oxford: Oxford University Press.

Hay, C. (2011a). 'Ideas and the Construction of Interests' in Béland, D., & Cox, R. H. (eds.), *Ideas and Politics in Social Science Research*. Oxford: Oxford University Press.

Hay, C. (2011b). 'Pathology Without Crisis? The Strange Demise of the Anglo-Liberal Growth Model', *Government and Opposition* 46(1): 1–31.

Hay, C. (2013a). 'Treating the symptom not the condition: Crisis definition, deficit reduction and the search for a new British growth model', *British Journal of Politics and International Relations* 15(1): 23–37.

Hay, C. (2013b). 'The British growth crisis: A crisis of and for growth', *SPERI Paper* (1): 1–27.

Hay, C. (2015). 'Good in a crisis: Constructivism's institutionalism and the political economy of dis-equilibrium', paper presented at the CES Conference, Paris, July.

Heilbroner, R. (1992). *The Worldly Philosophers*. New York: Touchstone Simon & Schuster.

Heilbroner, R. (1996). *Teachings from the Worldly Philosophy*. New York: W.W. Norton.

Helleiner, E. (2014). *The Status Quo Crisis: Global Financial Governance After The 2008 Meltdown*. Oxford: Oxford University Press.

Heller, M. P. S. (2005). *Understanding Fiscal Space*, IMF Policy Discussion Paper PDP/05/4. Washington DC: International Monetary Fund.

Heller, P. (2002). *Considering the IMF's Perspective on a 'Second Fiscal Policy'*, IMF Working Paper WP/02/08. Washington DC: International Monetary Fund.

Hemming, R., Kell, M., & Mahfouz, S. (2002). *The Effectiveness of Fiscal Policy in Stimulating Economic Activity: A Review of the Literature*, IMF Working Paper WP/02/208. Washington DC: International Monetary Fund.

Hemming, R., Mahfouz, S., & Schimmelpfennig, A. (2002a). *Fiscal Policy and Economic Activity During Recessions in Advanced Economies*, IMF Working Paper WP/02/87. Washington DC: International Monetary Fund.

Hemming, R., Mahfouz, S., & Schimmelpfennig, A. (2002b). 'Can Countries Always Spend their way out of recessions?', *IMF Survey* 31(14): 237–8.

Herndon, T., Ash, M., & Pollin, R. (2013). 'Does high public debt consistently stifle economic growth? A critique of Reinhart and Rogoff ', *Cambridge Journal of Economics* 38(2): 257–79.

Heyer, E., Plane, M., & Timbeau, X. (2012). 'Du social mais pas de sortie de crise' in 'Évaluation du projet économique du quinquennat 2012–2017', *OFCE les notes* 23, 26 juillet, 6–23.

Hicks, J. R. (1937). 'Mr. Keynes and the" classics"; a suggested interpretation', *Econometrica* 5(3): 147–59.

Hilbers, P. (2004). 'Interaction of monetary and fiscal policies: why central bankers worry about government budgets', *IMF seminar on current Developments in Monetary and Financial Law*. Washington DC: International Monetary Fund.

Holland, D., & Portes, J. (2012). 'Self-Defeating Austerity?', *National Institute Economic Review* 222: 1–8.

Hollande, F. (2012). *Le Changement C'est Maintenant: Mes 60 Engagements pour la France*. Paris: Parti Socialiste.

Hoover, K. (1984). 'Two Types of Monetarism', *Journal of Economic Literature* 22(1): 58–76.

Howarth, D. (2002). 'The France State in the Euro Zone' in Dyson, K. (ed.), *European States and the Euro-Zone*. Oxford: Oxford University Press.

IEO (2003). *IMF and Recent Capital Account Crises: Indonesia, Korea, Brazil*. Washington, DC: International Monetary Fund.

IEO (2011). *IMF Performance in the Run-Up to the Financial and Economic Crisis: IMF Surveillance in 2004–07*. Washington, DC: International Monetary Fund, available at: http://www.ieo-imf.org/ieo/files/issuespapers/Crisis_Final_Issues_Paper_Web.pdf

IEO (2013). *The Role of the IMF as Trusted Advisor*. Washington, DC: International Monetary Fund.

IEO (2014). *IMF Response to the Financial and Economic Crisis: An IEO Assessment*. Washington, DC: International Monetary Fund.

IEO (2015). *Possible Topics for Future Evaluation over the Medium Term*. Washington, DC: International Monetary Fund, available at: http://www.ieo-imf.org/ieo/files/workprogram/Possible_Topics_for_Evaluation_Over_the_Medium_Term%202015%201.pdf

IEO (2016). *The IMF and the Crises in Greece, Ireland and Portugal*. Washington, DC: International Monetary Fund.

IMF (1993). *Articles of Agreement*. Washington DC: International Monetary Fund.

IMF (1995a). *Unproductive Public Expenditures*, Fiscal Affairs Department IMF Pamphlet Series, No. 48 Washington DC: International Monetary Fund.

IMF (1995b). *Guidelines for Fiscal Adjustment*, Fiscal Affairs Department IMF Pamphlet Series, No. 49 Washington DC: International Monetary Fund.

IMF (2008a). *World Economic Outlook*, April. Washington DC: International Monetary Fund.

IMF (2008b). 'Euro Area Policies: 2008 Article IV Consultation—Staff Report', IMF Country Report No. 08/262. Washington DC: International Monetary Fund.

IMF (2008c). *World Economic Outlook*, October. Washington DC: International Monetary Fund.

IMF (2008d). 'Transcript of a Press Conference on the World Economic Outlook with Olivier Charles Collyns, and Jörg Decressin', 8 October, available at: https://www.imf.org/en/News/Articles/2015/09/28/04/54/tr081008

IMF (2008e). 'World Finance Chiefs Back Action Plan to Combat Crisis', *IMF Survey*, 11 October, available at: http://www.imf.org/en/News/Articles/2015/09/28/04/53/sopol101108a

IMF (2008f). 'World Leaders Launch Action Plan to Combat Financial Crisis', *IMF Survey*, 15 November, available at: https://www.imf.org/en/News/Articles/2015/09/28/04/53/sonew111508a

IMF (2009a). 'IMF Staff Note to the Group of Twenty Deputies', 5 February, available at: http://www.imf.org/external/np/g20/pdf/020509.pdf

IMF (2009b). IMF Urges G-20 States To Take More Decisive Action to Combat Crisis', *IMF Survey*, 5 February, available at: http://www.imf.org/external/pubs/ft/survey/so/2009/NEW020509A.htm

IMF (2009c). *World Economic Outlook*, April. Washington DC: International Monetary Fund.

IMF (2009d). *Global Financial Stability Report*, April. Washington DC: International Monetary Fund.

IMF (2009e). 'France—2009 Article IV Consultation Concluding Statement of the Mission', Paris, 16 June, available at: http://www.imf.org/external/np/ms/2009/061609.htm

IMF (2009f). 'France: 2009 Article IV Consultation—Staff Report; Staff Supplement; Public Information Notice on the Executive Board Discussion; and Statement by the Executive Director for France', IMF Country Report No. 09/232. Washington DC: International Monetary Fund.

IMF (2009g). *World Economic Outlook*, October. Washington DC: International Monetary Fund.

IMF (2009h). *The State of Public Finances Cross-Country Fiscal Monitor: November 2009*, IMF Staff Position Note SPN/09/25. Washington DC: International Monetary Fund.

IMF (2009i). *The G-20 Mutual Assessment Process and the Role of the Fund*, 2 December. Washington DC: International Monetary Fund.

IMF (2010a). *World Economic Outlook*, April. Washington DC: International Monetary Fund.

IMF (2010b). *Fiscal Monitor*, May. Washington DC: International Monetary Fund.

IMF (2010c). 'France—2010 Article IV Consultation Concluding Statement of the Mission Paris', 16 June, available at: http://www.imf.org/external/np/ms/2010/061510.htm

IMF (2010d). 'G-20 Mutual Assessment Process—Alternative Policy Scenarios G-20 Toronto Summit Toronto, Canada, June 26–27'. Washington DC: International Monetary Fund.

IMF (2010e). 'France: 2010 Article IV Consultation—Staff Report; Staff Supplement; Public Information Notice on the Executive Board Discussion; and Statement by the Executive Director for France', IMF Country Report No. 10/240. Washington DC: International Monetary Fund.

IMF (2010f). 'France: Selected Issues', IMF Country Report No. 10/243. Washington DC: International Monetary Fund.

IMF(2010g). *World Economic Outlook*, October. Washington DC: International Monetary Fund.

IMF (2010h). 'Transcript of a Conference Call on the 2010 Article IV Consultations with the United Kingdom', 9 November, available at: http://www.imf.org/external/np/tr/2010/tr110910.htm

IMF (2010i). 'IMF Executive Board Concludes 2010 Article IV Consultation with the United Kingdom', 9 November, Public Information Notice (PIN). No. 10/147, available at: http://www.imf.org/external/np/sec/pn/2010/pn10147.htm

IMF (2010j). 'United Kingdom: Selected Issues Paper', IMF Country Report No. 10/337. Washington DC: International Monetary Fund.

IMF (2010k). 'United Kingdom: 2010 Article IV Consultation—Staff Report; Staff Supplement; Public Information Notice on the Executive Board Discussion; and Statement by the Executive Director for the United Kingdom', IMF Country Report No. 10/338. Washington DC: International Monetary Fund.

IMF (2010l). *Fiscal Monitor*, November. Washington DC: International Monetary Fund.

IMF (2011a). *Fiscal Monitor*, update, January. Washington DC: International Monetary Fund.

IMF (2011b). 'Macroprudential Policy: An Organizing Framework', IMF Monetary and Capital Markets Department Policy Paper .Washington DC: International Monetary Fund.

IMF (2011c). *Fiscal Monitor*, April. Washington DC: International Monetary Fund.

IMF (2011d). 'United Kingdom—2011 Article IV Consultation Concluding Statement of the Mission', 6 June, available at: http://www.imf.org/external/np/ms/2011/060611.htm

IMF (2011e). 'France—2011 Article IV Consultation Concluding Statement of the Mission', 14 June, available at: http://www.imf.org/external/np/ms/2011/061411a.htm

IMF (2011f). *Fiscal Monitor*, update, June. Washington DC: International Monetary Fund.

IMF (2011g). 'Euro Area Policies: 2011 Article IV Consultation—Staff Report', 1 July, Report No. 11/184. Washington DC: International Monetary Fund.

IMF (2011h). 'United Kingdom: 2011 Article IV Consultation—Staff Report', IMF Country Report No. 11/220. Washington DC: International Monetary Fund.

IMF (2011i). 'France: 2011 Article IV Consultation—Staff Report', July, IMF Country Report No. 11/211. Washington DC: International Monetary Fund.

IMF (2011j). 'France: Selected Issues Paper', IMF Country Report No. 11/212. Washington DC: International Monetary Fund.

IMF (2011k). 'Modernizing the Framework for Fiscal Policy and Public Debt Sustainability Analysis', prepared by the Fiscal Affairs Department and the Strategy, Policy, and Review Department. Washington DC: International Monetary Fund.

IMF (2011l). *2011 Triennial Surveillance Review—Overview Paper* (approved by SPR). Washington DC: International Monetary Fund.

IMF (2011m). *Global Financial Stability Report*, September. Washington DC: International Monetary Fund.

IMF (2011n). *Fiscal Monitor*, September. Washington DC: International Monetary Fund.

IMF (2011o). *World Economic Outlook*, September. Washington DC: International Monetary Fund.

IMF (2012a). *Fiscal Monitor*, update, January. Washington DC: International Monetary Fund.

IMF (2012b). *World Economic Outlook*, update, January. Washington DC: International Monetary Fund.

IMF (2012c). *Fiscal Monitor*, April. Washington DC: International Monetary Fund.

IMF (2012d). 'United Kingdom—2012 Article IV Consultation Concluding Statement of the Mission', available at: http://www.imf.org/external/np/ms/2012/052212.htm

IMF (2012e). 'United Kingdom: 2012 Article IV Consultation—Staff Report', Country Report No. 12/90. Washington DC: International Monetary Fund.

IMF. (2012f). 'Euro Area Policies: 2012 Article IV Consultation—Staff Report', Report No. 12/181. Washington DC: International Monetary Fund.

IMF (2012g). *Fiscal Monitor*, update, July. Washington DC: International Monetary Fund.

IMF (2012h). *Global Financial Stability Report Market Update*. Washington DC: International Monetary Fund.

IMF (2012i). 'Transcript of a Conference Call on the 2012 Article IV Consultations with the United Kingdom', 19 July. Washington, DC, available at: http://www.imf.org/external/np/tr/2012/tr071912.htm

IMF (2012j). *World Economic Outlook*, October. Washington DC: International Monetary Fund.

IMF (2012k). *Fiscal Monitor*, October. Washington DC: International Monetary Fund.

IMF (2012l). 'IMF Note to G-20 Finance Ministers And Central Bank Governors November 4–5, Mexico City'. Washington DC: International Monetary Fund.

IMF (2012m). 'The Liberalization and Management of Capital Flows—An Institutional View'. Washington DC: International Monetary Fund.

IMF (2012n). 'France: 2012 Article IV Consultation—Staff Report; Staff Supplement; Public Information Notice on the Executive Board Discussion; and Statement by the Executive Director for France', IMF Country Report No. 12/342. Washington DC: International Monetary Fund.

IMF (2013a). *Fiscal Monitor*, April. Washington DC: International Monetary Fund.

IMF (2013b). 'Transcript of the UK Article IV Mission Concluding Press Conference with David Lipton', 22 May, available at: http://www.imf.org/external/np/tr/2013/tr052213.htm

IMF (2013c). 'France: 2013 Article IV Consultation—Concluding Statement of the Mission', Paris, 3 June, available at: http://www.imf.org/external/np/ms/2013/060413b.htm

IMF (2013d). 'Key Aspects of Macroprudential Policy'. Washington DC: International Monetary Fund.

IMF (2013e). 'Greece: Ex Post Evaluation of Exceptional Access under the 2010 Stand-by Arrangement', IMF Country Report No 13/156. Washington DC: International Monetary Fund.

IMF (2013f). 'United Kingdom: 2013 Article IV Consultation—Staff Report', Report No. 13/210. Washington DC: International Monetary Fund.

IMF (2013g). 'France: 2013 Article IV Consultation—Staff Report', IMF Country Report No. 13/251. Washington DC: International Monetary Fund.

IMF (2013h). 'Confidence, Competitiveness Key to Boost Recovery in France', *IMF Survey*, 5 August.

IMF (2013i). *The IMF's Financial Surveillance Strategy*. Washington DC: International Monetary Fund.

IMF (2013j). *IMF Policy Paper: Reassessing the Role and Modalities of Fiscal Policy in Advanced Economies*. Washington DC: International Monetary Fund.

IMF (2013k). 'More Fiscal Integration to Boost Euro Area Resilience', *IMF Survey*, 25 September, available at: http://www.imf.org/external/pubs/ft/survey/so/2013/CAR092513A.htm

IMF (2013l). *Global Financial Stability Report*, October. Washington DC: International Monetary Fund.

IMF (2014a). *Fiscal Policy and Income Inequality*, IMF Policy Paper. Washington DC: International Monetary Fund.

IMF (2014b). 'IMF note to Meetings of G20 Finance Ministers and Central bank Governors, February 22–23, Sydney, Australia'. Washington DC: International Monetary Fund.

IMF (2014c). *World Economic Outlook*, April. Washington DC: International Monetary Fund.

IMF (2014d). 'IMF note to Meetings of G20 Finance Ministers and Central Bank Governors, Cairns, Australia, September 20–21'. Washington DC: International Monetary Fund.

IMF (2014e). *World Economic Outlook*, October. Washington DC: International Monetary Fund.

IMF (2014f). 'IMF Staff note to Meetings of G20 Leaders' Summit, Brisbane Australia, November 15–16'. Washington DC: International Monetary Fund.

IMF (2015a). *Fiscal Monitor*, April. Washington DC: International Monetary Fund.

IMF (2015b). *World Economic Outlook*, April. Washington DC: International Monetary Fund.

IMF (2015c). 'Greece: An Update of IMF Staff's Preliminary Public Debt Sustainability Analysis', IMF Country Report No. 15/186. Washington DC: International Monetary Fund.

IMF (2015d). 'Germany: 2015 Article IV Consultation—Staff Report', IMF Country Report No. 15/187. Washington DC: International Monetary Fund.

IMF (2015e). 'Germany: Selected Issues', IMF Country Report No. 15/188. Washington DC: International Monetary Fund.

IMF (2015f). 'Germany Charts a Steady Course', *IMF Survey*, 15 July, available at: http://www.imf.org/external/pubs/ft/survey/so/2015/car071515a.htm

IMF (2015g). *World Economic Outlook*, October. Washington DC: International Monetary Fund.

IMF (2015h). '"Imbalances and Growth": Update of staff sustainability Assessments for G-20 Mutual Assessment Process', October. Washington DC: International Monetary Fund.

IMF (2016). 'Euro Area At The Crossroads No Time For Complacency', *IMF News*, 8 July, available at: http://www.imf.org/en/News/Articles/2016/07/08/19/56/NA070816-Euro-Area-At-The-Crossroads-No-Time-For-Complacency

IMF Research Department (2008). 'The Tasks Ahead' prepared by the Research Department, under the direction of Olivier Blanchard, IMF Working Paper WP/08/262, November. Washington DC: International Monetary Fund.

Jacoby, W. (2015). 'Europe's New German Problem' in Matthijs, M., & Blyth, M. (eds.), *The Future of the Euro*. Oxford: Oxford University Press.

Jahan, S., Mahmud, A. S., & Papageorgiou, C. (2014). 'What Is Keynesian Economics?', *Finance & Development*, September 3(51): 53–4.

James, H. (1996). *International Monetary Cooperation since Bretton Woods*. Washington DC: International Monetary Fund.

Jelveh, Z., Kogut, B., & Naidu, S. (2014). 'Detecting Latent Ideology in Expert Text: Evidence From Academic Papers in Economics' in *Proceedings of the 2014 Conference on Empirical Methods in Natural Language Processing*, 1804–9. Stroudsburg, PA: Association for Computational Linguistics.

Johnson, J. (2003). 'Past Dependence or Path Contingency? Institutional Design in Post-communist Financial Systems', in Ekiert, G., & Hanson, S. (eds.), *Capitalism and Democracy in Central and Eastern Europe*. Cambridge: Cambridge University Press.

Joyce, J. P. (2012). *The IMF and Global Financial Crises: Phoenix Rising?* Cambridge: Cambridge University Press.

Kahn, R. (1931). 'The Relation of Home Investment to Unemployment', *Economic Journal* 41(162): 173–98.

Kaya, A. (2012). 'Conflicted principals, uncertain agency: the International Monetary Fund and the Great Recession', *Global Policy* 3(1): 24–34.

Kentikelenis, A. E., Stubbs, T. H., & King, L. P. (2016). 'IMF conditionality and development policy space, 1985–2014', *Review of International Political Economy* 23(4): 543–82.

Keynes, J. (1937). 'The General Theory of Employment', *Quarterly Journal of Economics* 51(2): 209–23.

Keynes, J. M. (1936 [1964]). *The General Theory of Employment Interest and Money*. London: Macmillan.

Keynes, J. M. (1980). *The Collected Writings of J. M. Keynes: Vol. 2, Activities 1940–44: Shaping the Postwar World, The Clearing Union*, edited by Moggridge, D. Cambridge: Cambridge University Press.

Killick, T. (1995). 'Structural adjustment and poverty alleviation: an interpretative survey', *Development and Change* 26(2): 305–30.

Kirshner, J. (2003a). 'The inescapable politics of money' in Kirshner, J. (ed.), *Monetary Orders: Ambiguous Economics, Ubiquitous Politics*. Ithaca, NY: Cornell University Press.

Kirshner, J. (2003b). 'Explaining choices about money' in Kirshner, J. (ed.) *Monetary Orders: Ambiguous Economics, Ubiquitous Politics.*, Ithaca, NY: Cornell University Press.

Klaes, M. (2006). 'Keynes between modernism and post-modernism' in Backhouse, R., & Bateman, B. (eds.), *The Cambridge Companion to Keynes*. Cambridge: Cambridge University Press.

Klamer, A., & Colander, D. (1990). *The Making of an Economist.* Boulder, Co: Westview Press.

Knight, F. H. (1921). *Risk, Uncertainty and Profit.* New York: Hart, Schaffner and Marx.

Krugman, P. (2009). 'How did economists get it so wrong?', *New York Times*, 6 September.

Krugman, P. (2012). *End This Depression Now!* New York: WW Norton & Company.

Krugman, P. (2013). 'Osborne and the Stooges', *New York Times*, 19 December.

Kumar, M., Baig, M., Decressin, J., Feyzioglu, T., & Faulkner-MacDonagh, C. (2003). *Deflation: Determinants, Risks, and Policy Options,* IMF Occasional Paper No. 221. Washington DC: International Monetary Fund.

Kumhof, M., Muir, D., Mursula, S., & Laxton, D. (2010). *The Global Integrated Monetary and Fiscal Model (GIMF)—Theoretical Structure,* IMF Working Paper WP/10/34. Washington DC: International Monetary Fund.

Lagarde, C. (2011a). 'Statement by Christine Lagarde to the IMF Executive Board', 23 June, Press Release No. 11/253, available at: http://www.imf.org/en/News/Articles/2015/09/14/01/49/pr11253

Lagarde, C. (2011b). 'Don't Let Fiscal Brakes Stall Global Recovery', *Financial Times*, 15 August.

Lagarde, C. (2012a). 'Global Challenges in 2012', speech to the German Council for Foreign Relations, Berlin, 23 January, available at: http://www.imf.org/external/np/seminars/eng/2012/berlin/

Lagarde, C. (2012b). 'Cooperation and Connectedness', speech to the Associated Press, 3 April, available at: https://www.imf.org/en/News/Articles/2015/09/28/04/53/sp040312

Lagarde, C. (2012c). 'Completing the Task: Financial Sector Reform for Stability and Growth', speech hosted by the Süddeutsche Zeitung, 8 June, New York, available at: https://www.imf.org/en/News/Articles/2015/09/28/04/53/sp060812a

Lagarde, C. (2012d). 'Op-ed', *China Daily*, 28 December.

Lagarde, C. (2013). 'More Policy Work Ahead to Avoid Global Crisis Relapse', *IMF Survey* online, 17 January, available at: https://www.imf.md/press/News2013/news-130117.html

Lagarde, C. (2014a). 'Economic Inclusion and Financial Integrity—an Address to the Conference on Inclusive Capitalism', London, 27 May, available at: https://www.imf.org/external/np/speeches/2014/052714.htm

Lagarde, C. (2014b). 'Press Release: IMF Mission Completes the 2014 Article IV Consultation Discussions with the United Kingdom', 5 June, Press Release No. 14/263, available at: http://www.imf.org/en/news/articles/2015/09/14/01/49/pr14263

Lagarde, C. (2017). 'Transcript of an Interview with IMF Managing Director Christine Lagarde with the Leading European Newspapers Association', 12 April, available at: http://www.imf.org/en/news/articles/2017/04/17/tr041217-transcript-of-an-interview-with-imf-lagarde-with-lena

Laidler, D. (1981). 'Monetarism: an Interpretation and an assessment', *Economic Journal* 91(361): 1–28.

Lavelle, K. C. (2011). *Legislating International Organization: The US Congress, the IMF, and the World Bank*. Oxford: Oxford University Press.

Laxton, D. (2008). 'Getting to know the Global Economy Model and its philosophy', *IMF Economic Review* 55(2): 213–42.

Le Ledic, P. (2011). 'La décentralisation, la structure du financement et les jeux de transfert de l'impopularité en France' in Bezes, P., & Siné, A., *Gouverner (par). les finances publiques*. Paris: Presses de Sciences Po.

Leiteritz, R., & Moschella, M. (2010). 'The IMF and capital account liberalization: A case of failed norm institutionalization' in Park, S., & Vetterlein, A. (eds.), *Owning Development: Creating Policy Norms in the IMF and the World Bank*. Cambridge: Cambridge University Press.

Leiteritz, R. J. (2005). 'Explaining organizational outcomes: the International Monetary Fund and capital account liberalization', *Journal of International Relations and Development* 8(1): 1–26.

Lipsky, J. (2011). 'U.K. Must go for Top Quality Financial Supervision', *IMF survey*, 6 June, available at: http://www.imf.org/external/pubs/ft/survey/so/2011/CAR060611A.htm?id=33113

Lipton, D. (2012). 'Statement by IMF First Deputy Managing Director David Lipton on the IMF's Financial Surveillance Strategy', 21 September, Press Release No. 12/356, available at: http://www.imf.org/en/news/articles/2015/09/14/01/49/pr12356

Lipton, D. (2013a). 'David Lipton's opening remarks at fiscal Forum: The Evolving Role of Fiscal policy', International Monetary Fund, available at: http://www.imf.org/external/np/seminars/eng/2013/fiscal/

Lipton, D. (2013b). 'UK Should Restore Growth, Rebalance the Economy', *IMF Survey*, 22 May, available at: http://www.imf.org/external/pubs/ft/survey/so/2013/car052213a.htm

Lipton, D. (2014). 'IMF Holds High-Level Conference on Monetary Policy in the New Normal', 13 April, Press Release No. 14/170 , available at: http://www.imf.org/en/news/articles/2015/09/14/01/49/pr14170

Lombardi, D., & Woods, N. (2008). 'The politics of influence: An analysis of IMF surveillance', *Review of International Political Economy* 15(5): 711–39.

Lucas, R., & Sargent, T. (1978). 'After the Phillips Curve: The Persistence of High Inflation and High Unemployment' in *Federal Reserve Bank of Boston, Conference Series* (No. 19). Boston, MA: Federal Reserve Bank of Boston.

Lucas, R. E. (1977). 'Understanding business cycles', *Carnegie-Rochester Conference Series on Public Policy* 5: 7–29.

Lucas, R. E. (1980). 'Methods and problems in business cycle theory', *Journal of Money, Credit and Banking* 12(4): 696–715.

Lucas, R. E. (2003). 'Macroeconomic priorities', *The American Economic Review* 93(1): 1.

Lucas, R. E., and Sargent. T. (1981). 'After Keynesian Macroeconomics', *Rational Expectations and Econometric Practice* 1: 295–319.

Lütz, S., & Kranke, M. (2014). 'The European rescue of the Washington Consensus? EU and IMF lending to Central and Eastern European countries', *Review of International Political Economy* 21(2): 310–38.

Mahoney, J., & Thelen, K. (eds.) (2010a). *Explaining Institutional Change: Ambiguity, Agency, and Power*. Cambridge: Cambridge University Press.

Mahoney, J., & Thelen, K. (2010b). 'A theory of gradual institutional change' in Mahoney, J., & Thelen, K. (eds.), *Explaining Institutional Change: Ambiguity, Agency, and Power*. Cambridge: Cambridge University Press.

Mankiw, N. G. (2006). 'The macroeconomist as scientist and engineer', *The Journal of Economic Perspectives* 20(4): 29–46.

Mankiw, N. G., & Romer, D. (1991). *New Keynesian Economics: Coordination Failures and Real Rigidities* (Vol. 2). Cambridge, MA: MIT Press.

March, J. G., & Olsen, J. P. (1984). 'The new institutionalism: Organizational factors in political life', *American Ppolitical Science Review* 78(3): 734–49.

Martin, L. (2006). 'Distribution, information, and delegation to international organizations: The case of IMF conditionality' in Hawkins, D. G., Lake, D. A., Nielson, D. L., & Tierney, M. J. (eds.), *Delegation and Agency in International Organizations*. Cambridge: Cambridge University Press.

Masson, P. R., Symansky, S. A., & Meredith, G. (1990). 'MULTIMOD Mark II: A Revised and Extended Model', IMF Occasional Paper (No. 71). Washington DC: International Monetary Fund.

Matthijs, M., & McNamara, K. (2015). 'The euro crisis theory effect: northern saints, southern sinners, and the demise of the eurobond', *Journal of European Integration* 37(2): 229–45.

McNamara, K. R. (1998). *The Currency of Ideas: Monetary Politics in the European Union*. Ithaca, NY: Cornell University Press.

Meltzer, A. H. (2010). 'The IMF returns', *The Review of International Organizations* 6(3–4): 443–52.

Mendoza, E. G. (1991). 'Capital Controls and the Gains from Trade in a Business Cycle Model of a Small Open Economy', *IMF Staff Papers* 38(3): 480–505.

Merkel, A. (2009). Interview with Angela Merkel: 'Merkel warns on further stimulus', *Financial Times*, 27 March.

Mineshima, A., Poplawski-Ribeiro, M., & Weber, A. (2014). 'Size of Fiscal Multipliers' in Cottarelli, C., Gerson, P., and Senhadji, A. (eds.), *Post-Crisis Fiscal Policy*. Cambridge, MA: MIT Press.

Moghadam, R. (2014). 'Europe's Road to Integration', *Finance and Development* 51(1): 8–13.

Moghadam, R., Teia, R., & Berkmen, P. (2014). 'Euro Area — "Deflation" Versus "Lowflation"', iMFdirect, 4 March, available at: http://blog-imfdirect.imf.org/2014/03/04/euro-area-deflation-versus-lowflation/

Momani, B. (2004). 'American Politicization of the International Monetary Fund', *Review of International Political Economy* 11(5): 880–904.

Momani, B. (2005a). 'Recruiting and diversifying IMF technocrats', *Global Society* 19(2): 167–87.

Momani, B. (2005b). 'Limits on streamlining Fund conditionality: the International Monetary Fund's organizational culture', *Journal of International Relations and Development* 8(2): 142–63.

Momani, B. (2007). 'IMF staff: Missing link in Fund reform proposals', *The Review of International Organizations* 2(1): 39–57.

Momani, B. (2010). 'Internal or external norm champions: The IMF and multilateral debt relief' in Park, S., & Vetterlein, A. (eds.), *Owning Development: Creating Policy Norms in the IMF and the World Bank*. Cambridge: Cambridge University Press.

Moschella, M. (2009). 'When ideas fail to influence policy outcomes: Orderly liberalization and the International Monetary Fund', *Review of International Political Economy* 16(5): 854–82.

Moschella, M. (2010a). *Governing Risk: The IMF and Global Financial Crises*. Basingstoke: Palgrave.

Moschella, M. (2010b). 'International financial governance in hard times: tracing the transformations', *Contemporary Politics* 16(4): 421–36.

Moschella, M. (2011). 'Lagged learning and the response to equilibrium shock: the global financial crisis and IMF surveillance', *Journal of Public Policy* 31(2): 121–41.

Moschella, M. (2015). 'The institutional roots of incremental ideational change: The IMF and capital controls after the global financial crisis', *British Journal of Politics and International Relations* 17(3): 442–60.

Moschella, M. (2016). 'Negotiating Greece. Layering, insulation, and the design of adjustment programs in the Eurozone', *Review of International Political Economy* 23(5): 799–824.

Moscovici, P. (2013). 'Finance Minister Moscovici's communication to the French Cabinet, 27 February 2013', available at: http://discours.vie-publique.fr/notices/136000498.html?xtor=EPR-56

Müller, G., Meier, A., & Corsetti, G. (2012). *What Determines Government Spending Multipliers?* IMF Working Papers WP/12/150. Washington DC: International Monetary Fund.

Mundell, R. (1961). 'The Use of Monetary and Fiscal Policy for Internal and External Stability', 8 November, DM/61/27 (Departmental Memorandum). Washington DC: International Monetary Fund.

Mundell, R. (1962). 'The Appropriate Use of Monetary and Fiscal Policy for Internal and External Stability', *IMF Staff Papers* 9(1): 70–9.

Nakamura, E., & Steinsson, J. (2014). 'Fiscal stimulus in a monetary union: Evidence from US regions', *The American Economic Review* 104(3): 753–92.

Nelson, S. C. (2014). 'Playing favorites: how shared beliefs shape the IMF's lending decisions', *International Organization* 68(2): 297–328.

Nelson, S. C. (2017). *The Currency of Confidence: how Economic Beliefs Shaped the IMF's Relationship with its Borrowers*. Ithaca, NY: Cornell University Press.

Nelson, S. C., & Katzenstein, P. J. (2014). 'Uncertainty, risk, and the financial crisis of 2008', *International Organization* 68(2): 361–92.

Newman, A. (2015). 'The Reluctant Leader: Germany's Euro experience and the long shadow of Reunification' in Matthijs, M., & Blyth, M. (eds.), *The Future of the Euro*. Oxford: Oxford University Press.

NIESR (2014). National Institute of Economic and Social Research Estimates of Monthly GDP, 10 June, available at: http://www.niesr.ac.uk/sites/default/files/gdp0614press.pdf

Niskanen, W. (1971). *Bureaucracy and Representative Government*. Chicago: Aldane Atherton.

Oatley, T., & Yackee, J. (2004). 'American interests and IMF lending', *International Politics* 41(3): 415–29.

OECD (2011). *OECD Economic Surveys: France*. Paris: OECD.

Office for Budget Responsibility (2011). *Economic and Fiscal Outlook November 2011*, http://budgetresponsibility.org.uk/efo/economic-and-fiscal-outlook-november-2011/

Office for Budget Responsibility (2012). *Economic and Fiscal Outlook March 2012*, http://budgetresponsibility.org.uk/efo/economic-and-fiscal-outlook-march-2012/

Office for Budget Responsibility (2013). *Economic and Fiscal Outlook December 2013*, http://cdn.budgetresponsibility.independent.gov.uk/Economic-and-fiscal-outlook-December-2013.pdf

Office for National Statistics (2014). 'An International Perspective on the UK GDP', 24 April, http://webarchive.nationalarchives.gov.uk/20160105160709/http://www.ons.gov.uk/ons/dcp171766_360847.pdf

Oliver, M. J., & Pemberton, H. (2004). 'Learning and change in 20th-century British economic policy', *Governance* 17(3): 415–41.

Osborne, G. (2010). House of Commons 22 June 2010, Hansard, col. 166–7.

Osborne, G. (2011a). Speech by the Chancellor of the Exchequer, Rt Hon George Osborne MP, the Lloyd's of London Annual City Dinner, 6 September, available at: https://www.gov.uk/government/speeches/speech-by-the-chancellor-of-the-exchequer-rt-hon-george-osborne-mp-the-lloyds-of-london-annual-city-dinner

Osborne, G. (2011b). Opening remarks by the Chancellor of the Exchequer, Chatham House, Challenges for the global economy, 9 September 2011, availbale at: http://www.hm-treasury.gov.uk/speech_chx_090911.htm

Osborne, G. (2011d). Debate over the Autumn Statement, House of Commons, 29 November Col. 816.

Osborne, G. (2013). 'Chancellor speech on the economy', 9 September 2013, HM Treasury, available at: https://www.gov.uk/government/speeches/chancellor-speech-on-the-economy

Osborne, G. (2014). 'Chancellor's speech to the American Enterprise Institute', 11 April, available at: https://www.gov.uk/government/speeches/chancellors-speech-to-the-american-enterprise-institute

Osborne, G. (2011c). Autumn Forecast Statement by the Chancellor of the Exchequer, 29 November, 136/11, available at: http://www.hm-treasury.gov.uk/press_136_11.htm

Osiński, J., Seal, K., & Hoogduin, L. (2013). 'Macroprudential and Microprudential Policies: Toward Cohabitation', *IMF Staff Discussion Note*, SDN13/05. Washington DC: International Monetary Fund.

Ostry, J. Ghosh, A., & Espinoza, R. (2015). *When Should Debt Be Reduced?* IMF Staff Discussion Note SDN/15/10. Washington DC: International Monetary Fund.

Ostry, J. D., Ghosh, A. R., Kim, J. I., & Qureshi, M. S. (2010). *Fiscal Space*, IMF Staff Position Note SPN/10/11. Washington DC: International Monetary Fund.

Ostry, J. D., Loungani, P., & Furceri, D. (2016). 'Neoliberalism: oversold', *Finance & Development* 53(2): 38–41.

Ostry, M. J. D., Berg, M. A., & Tsangarides, M. C. G. (2014). *Redistribution, inequality, and growth*, IMF Staff Discussion Note SDN/14/02. Washington DC: International Monetary Fund.

Palaiologos, Y. (2015). 'Greece's Long and Painful Odyssey', *Wall Street Journal*, 23 April.

Park, S., & Vetterlein, A. (2010a). 'Owning Development: Creating Global Policy Norms in the World Bank and the IMF' in Park, S., & Vetterlein, A. (eds.), *Owning Development: Creating Policy Norms in the IMF and the World Bank*. Cambridge: Cambridge University Press.

Park, S., & Vetterlein, A. (eds.) (2010b). *Owning Development: Creating Policy Norms in the IMF and the World Bank*. Cambridge: Cambridge University Press.

Parker, J. A. (2011). 'On measuring the effects of fiscal policy in recessions', *Journal of Economic Literature* 49(3): 703–18.

Patinkin, D. (1959). 'Keynesian Economics Rehabilitated: A Rejoinder to Professor Hicks', *Economic Journal* LXIX: 582–7.

Patinkin, D. (1990). 'On different interpretations of the General Theory', *Journal of Monetary Economics* 26(2): 205–43.

Pauly, L. W. (1997). *Who Elected The Bankers? Surveillance And Control In The World Economy*. Ithaca, NY: Cornell University Press.

Pauly, L. W. (2008). 'The Institutional Legacy of Bretton Woods: IMF Surveillance 1973–2007' in Andrews, D. M. (ed.), *Orderly Change: International Monetary Relations Since Bretton Woods*. Ithaca, NY: Cornell University Press.

Pauly, L. W. (2009). 'The old and the new politics of international financial stability', *Journal of Common Market Studies* 47(5): 955–75.

Peet, R. (2009). *Unholy Trinity: the IMF, World Bank and WTO*. London: Zed Books.

Perotti, R. (2011). 'The "Austerity Myth": Gain Without Pain?', NBER Working Paper No. 17571. Cambridge, MA: National Bureau of Economic Research.

Pescatori, A., Sandri, D., & Simon, J. (2014). *Debt and growth: is there a magic threshold?* IMF Working Paper WP/14/34. Washington DC: International Monetary Fund.

Peters, B. G. (1999). *Institutional Theory in Political Science*. London: Continuum.

Phelps, E. S. (1967). 'Phillips curves, expectations of inflation and optimal unemployment over time', *Economica* 34(135): 254–81.

Phillips, A. W. (1958). 'The relation between unemployment and the rate of change of money wage rates in the United Kingdom, 1861–1957', *Economica* 25(100): 283–99.

Piketty, T. (2014). *Capital in the 21st Century*. Cambridge, MA: Harvard University Press.

Piketty, T. (2015). 'Putting distribution back at the center of economics: reflections on capital in the twenty-first century', *Journal of Economic Perspectives* 29(1): 67–88.

Polak, J. (1957). 'Monetary Analysis of Income Formation and Payments Problems', *IMF Staff Papers* 6(1): 1–50.

Polak, J. (1997). 'The IMF Monetary Model at 40', IMF Working Paper WP/97/49. Washington DC: International Monetary Fund.

Polak, J. (2001). *The Two Monetary Approaches to the Balance of Payments: Keynesian and Johnsonian*, IMF Working Paper WP/01/100. Washington DC: International Monetary Fund.

Pop-Eleches, G. (2008). *From Economic Crisis to Reform: IMF Programs in Latin America and Eastern Europe*. Princeton, NJ: Princeton University Press.

Portes, J. (2012). 'More on multipliers: why does it matter?', NIESR Blog, available at: https://www.niesr.ac.uk/blog/more-multipliers-why-does-it-matter

Portes, J. (2013). 'What Osborne won't admit: growth has increased because of slower cuts', *New Statesman*, 10 September.

Portes, J. (2014). 'Fiscal policy, "Plan A" and the recovery: explaining the economics', NIESR blog, 11 April, available at: https://www.niesr.ac.uk/blog/fiscal-policy-plan-and-recovery-explaining-economics

Portes, J., & Van Reenen, J. (2012). 'The UK should have waited to enforce austerity', *British Politics and Policy at LSE*, available at: http://blogs.lse.ac.uk/politicsandpolicy/waited-to-enforce-austerity-portes-van-reenen/

Prescott, E. C. (1986). 'Theory ahead of business-cycle measurement'. In *Carnegie-Rochester Conference Series on Public Policy* (Vol. 25, 11–44). North-Holland.

Quack, S., & Djelic, M. L. (2005). 'Reinforcement: The Story of Antitrust and Competition Law in Germany and Europe' in Streeck, W., & Thelen, K. A. (eds.), *Beyond Continuity: Institutional Change in Advanced Political Economies*. Oxford: Oxford University Press.

Quiggin, J. (2012). *Zombie Economics: How Dead Ideas Still Walk Among Us*. Princeton, NJ: Princeton University Press.

Radice, H. (2011). 'Cutting government deficits: Economic science or class war?', *Capital & Class* 35(1): 125–37.

Radice, H. (2014). 'Enforcing austerity in Europe: The structural deficit as a policy target', *Journal of Contemporary European Studies* 22(3): 318–28.

Rajan, R. (2004). 'Assume anarchy? Why an orthodox economic model may not be the best guide for policy', *Finance & Development* 41(3): 56–7.

Rajan, R. et al. (2004). 'GEM: A New International Macroeconomic Model', International Monetary Fund Research Department. Washington DC: International Monetary Fund.

Ramsden, D. (2012). 'The government's strategy for sustainable growth' in Giudice, G., Künzel, R., & Springbett, T. (eds.), *UK Economy: The Crisis in Perspective*. Abingdon: Routledge.

Reinhart, C. M., & Rogoff, K. S. (2010). 'Growth in a Time of Debt', *American Economic Review: Papers & Proceedings* 100 (May 2010): 573–8.

Reinhart, C. M., Reinhart, V. R., & Rogoff, K. S. (2012). 'Public debt overhangs: advanced-economy episodes since 1800', *The Journal of Economic Perspectives* 26(3): 69–86.

Reynaud, J., & Vauday, J. (2009). 'Geopolitics and international organizations: An empirical study on IMF facilities', *Journal of Development Economics* 89(1): 139–62.

Rivlin, A. M. (1987). 'Economics and the political process', *The American Economic Review* 77(1): 1–10.

Roaf, J. (2011). 'IMF Support Helping Restore Growth but Key Risks Ahead', *IMF Survey*, 15 April, available at: http://www.imf.org/external/pubs/ft/survey/so/2011/new041511a.htm

Robinson, J. (1974). 'What has become of the Keynesian Revolution?', *Challenge* 16(6): 6–11.

Robinson, J. (1978). 'Keynes and Ricardo', *Journal of Post Keynesian Economics* 1(1): 12–18.

Rogers, C. (2012). *The IMF and European Economies: Crisis and Conditionality*. Basingstoke: Palgrave.

Romer, C. D., & Romer, D. H. (2007). 'The Macroeconomic Effects of Tax Changes: Estimates Based on a New Measure of Fiscal Shocks', *NBER Working Paper Series*, 13264.

Romer, C. D., & Romer, D. H. (2010). 'The macroeconomic effects of tax changes: estimates based on a new measure of fiscal shocks', *The American Economic Review* 100(3): 763–801.

Romer, D. (1993). 'The new Keynesian synthesis', *The Journal of Economic Perspectives* 7(1): 5–22.

Romer, D. (2012). 'What have we learned about fiscal policy from the crisis?' in Blanchard, O. J., Romer, D., Spence, M., & Stiglitz, J. (eds.), *In the Wake of the Crisis*. Cambridge, MA: MIT Press.

Rosamond, B., & Hopkin, J. (2015). 'Deficit fetishism and the art of political bullshit: Part I', SPERI blog, 15 July, available at: http://speri.dept.shef.ac.uk/2015/07/15/deficit-fetishism-art-political-bullshit-part/

Ruggie, J. (1982). 'International Regimes, Transactions and Change: Embedded Liberalism in the Post-War Economic Order', *International Organization* 36(2): 379–415.

Ruggie, J. (1983). 'International Regimes. Transactions and Change: Embedded Liberalism in the Postwar Economic Order' in Krasner, S. (ed.), *International Regimes*. Ithaca, NY: Cornell University Press.

Ruggie, J. G. (1998). *Constructing the World Polity: Essays on International Institutionalisation*. London: Routledge.

Rutte, M., & Kees de Jager, J. (2011). 'Expulsion from the eurozone has to be the final penalty', *Financial Times*, 7 September.

Sachs, J. (2005). *The End Of Poverty: How We Can Make It Happen In Our Lifetime*. London: Penguin UK.

Sally, R. (1996). 'Ordoliberalism and the social market: Classical political economy from Germany', *New Political Economy* 1(2): 233–57.

Samuelson, P. A. (1997). 'Credo of a lucky textbook author', *The Journal of Economic Perspectives* 11(2): 153–60.

Samuelson, P. A., & Solow, R. M. (1960). 'Analytical aspects of anti-inflation policy', *American Economic Review* 50(2): 177–94.

Sapin, M. (2014). 'Statement at the International Monetary and Financial Committee', 12 April, available at: https://www.imf.org/External/spring/2014/imfc/statement/eng/fra.pdf

Sarkozy, N. (2009). 'Déclaration de M. Nicolas Sarkozy sur la politique menée face à la crise économique et financière, à Toulon le 1er décembre 2009', available at: http://discours.vie-publique.fr/notices/097003488.html

Schäuble, W. (2010a). 'Why Europe's monetary union faces its biggest crisis', *Financial Times*, 11 March.

Schäuble, W. (2010b). 'Maligned Germany is right to cut spending', *Financial Times*, 24 June.

Schäuble, W. (2011a). 'Why Austerity is the only cure for the Eurozone', *Financial Times*, 5 September.

Schäuble, W. (2011b). 'Dark Humour and Hard Talk at IMF Meetings', *Financial Times*, 25 September.

Schäuble, W. (2012). 'Building a Sturdier Euro', *Wall Street Journal*, 12 December.

Schäuble, W. (2013a). 'Banking union must be built on firm foundations', *Financial Times*, 12 May.

Schäuble, W. (2013b). 'Ignore the doomsayers: Europe is being fixed', *Financial Times*, 16 September.

Schumpeter, J. A. (1949). 'Science and ideology', *American Economic Review* 39(2): 346–59.

Schmidt, V. (2002). *The Futures of European Capitalism*. Oxford: Oxford University Press.

Schmidt, V. (2008). 'Discursive Institutionalism: The Explanatory Power of Ideas and Discourse', *Annual Review of Political Science* 11: 303–26.

Schmidt, V. A. (2010). 'Taking ideas and discourse seriously: explaining change through discursive institutionalism as the fourth "new institutionalism"', *European Political Science Review* 2(1): 1–25.

Schmidt, V. A. (2011). 'Reconciling ideas and institutions through discursive institutionalism' in Béland, D., & Cox, R. H. (eds.), *Ideas and Politics In Social Science Research*. Oxford: Oxford University Press.

Schmidt, V. A., & Thatcher, M. (eds.) (2013). *Resilient Liberalism in Europe's Political Economy*. Cambridge: Cambridge University Press.

Schwartz, M. J., & Rist, R. C. (2016). *The International Monetary Fund and the Learning Organization*. Washington DC: International Monetary Fund.

Scott, A. (2008). 'Making Fiscal Stimulus Effective During Downturns', *IMF Survey*, 2 October, available at: http://www.imf.org/en/news/articles/2015/09/28/04/53/sores100208b

Seabrooke, L. (2006). *The Social Sources of Financial Power: Domestic Legitimacy and International Financial Orders*. Ithaca, NY: Cornell University Press.

Seabrooke, L. (2010). 'Bitter Pills to Swallow: Legitimacy Gaps and Social Recognition of the IMF Tax Policy Norms in East Asia' in Park, S., & Vetterlein, A. (eds.), *Owning Development: Creating Policy Norms in the IMF and the World Bank*. Cambridge: Cambridge University Press.

Seabrooke, L. S., Ban, C., Helgadóttir, O., Nilsson, E. R., & Young, K. (2015). 'Embedding Group Think: Assessing the spread of neo-liberal ideas and influence', paper presented to the INET conference, Paris, April.

Searle, J. (1969). *Speech Acts: An Essay in the Philosophy Of Language*. Cambridge: Cambridge University Press.

Searle, J. (1995). *The Construction of Social Reality*. London: Penguin.

Sinclair, T. (2005). *The New Masters of Capitalism: American Bond Rating Agencies and the Politics of Creditworthiness*. Ithaca NY: Cornell University Press.

Sinclair, T. J. (1994). 'Passing judgement: credit rating processes as regulatory mechanisms of governance in the emerging world order', *Review of International Political Economy* 1(1): 133–59.

Skidelsky, R. (2009). *Keynes: The Return of the Master: Why, Sixty Years after his Death, John Maynard Keynes Is the Most Important Economic Thinker in the World*. London: Allen Lane.

Skidelsky, R. (2014). 'The Osborne audit: what have we learned?', *New Statesman*, 17 March, available at: http://www.newstatesman.com/politics/2014/03/osborne-audit-what-have-we-learned

Soederberg, S. (2004). *The Politics of the New International Financial Architecture: Reimposing Neoliberal Domination in the Global South*. London: Zed Books.

Solow, R. (2008). 'The state of macroeconomics', *Journal of Economic Perspectives* 22(1): 243–6.

Spilimbergo, A., Symansky, S., Blanchard, O., & Cottarelli, C. (2008). *Fiscal Policy for the Crisis*. IMF Staff Position Note SPN/08/01. Washington DC: International Monetary Fund.

Spilimbergo, A., Symansky, S., & Schindler, M. (2009). *Fiscal multipliers*, IMF Staff Position Note, SPN/09/11. Washington DC: International Monetary Fund.

Steinbruck, P. (2008). quoted in 'Berlin hits out at "crass" UK strategy', *Financial Times*, 23 October.

Steinmo, S., & Thelen, K. (1992). 'Historical institutionalism in comparative analysis' in Thelen, K. A., Longstreth, F., & Steinmo, S. (eds.), *Structuring Politics: Historical Institutionalism in Comparative Analysis*. Cambridge: Cambridge University Press.

Stiglitz, J. (1997). 'Reflections on the natural rate hypothesis', *The Journal of Economic Perspectives* 11(1), 3–10.

Stiglitz, J. E. (2002). *Globalization and its Discontents*. New York: WW Norton & Company.

Stiglitz, J. E. (2012). *The Price of Inequality: How Today's Divided Society Endangers Our Future*. New York: WW Norton & Company.

Stiglitz, J. E. (2015). 'The origins of inequality, and policies to contain it', *National Tax Journal* 68(2): 425.

Stockhammer, E. (2011). 'The macroeconomics of unemployment' in Hein, E., & Stockhammer, E. (eds.), *A Modern Guide to Keynesian Macroeconomics and Economic Policies*. Cheltenham: Edward Elgar.

Stone, R. W. (2002). *Lending Credibility: The International Monetary Fund and the Post-Communist Transition*. Princeton, NJ: Princeton University Press.

Stone, R. W. (2008). 'The scope of IMF conditionality', *International Organization* 62(4): 589–620.

Stone, R. W. (2011). *Controlling Institutions: International Organizations and the Global Economy*. Cambridge: Cambridge University Press.

Strauss-Kahn, D. (2008a). 'A systemic crisis demands systemic solutions', *Financial Times*, 25 September.

Strauss-Kahn, D. (2008b). 'Staving off a global depression', *The Guardian*, 3 November.

Strauss-Kahn, D. (2009). 'Take-Off or Holding Pattern? Prospects for the Global Economy', an Address to the Confederation of British Industry Annual Conference, 23 November.

Strauss-Kahn, D. (2010). Foreword to *Fiscal Monitor*, May. Washington DC: International Monetary Fund.

Streeck, W., & Thelen, K. A. (eds.) (2005a). *Beyond Continuity: Institutional Change in Advanced Political Economies*. Oxford: Oxford University Press.

Streeck, W., & Thelen, K. A. (2005b). 'Introduction: Institutional Change in Advanced Political economies' in Streeck, W., & Thelen, K. A. (eds.), *Beyond Continuity: Institutional Change in Advanced Political Economies*. Oxford: Oxford University Press.

Streeck, W., & Schäfer, A. (eds.) (2013). *Politics in the Age of Austerity*. Oxford: John Wiley & Sons.

Summers, L. (2013). 'On Secular Stagnation', *Reuters Analysis & Opinion*, blog available at: http://blogs.reuters.com/lawrencesummers/2013/12/16/on-secular-stagnation/

Summers, L. (2014). 'Reflections on the new Secular Stagnation hypothesis', Voxeu, 30 October, available at: http://www.voxeu.org/article/larry-summers-secular-stagnation

Tanzi, M. V., Chu, M. K. Y., & Gupta, M. S. (eds.) (1999). *Economic Policy and Equity*. Washington DC: International Monetary Fund.

Tanzi, V., & Zee, H. H. (1997). 'Fiscal policy and long-run growth', *IMF Staff Papers* 44(2): 179–209.

Tanzi, V., & Zee, H. H. (2000). *Tax Policy for Emerging Markets: Developing Countries*, IMF Working Paper WP/00/35. Washington DC: International Monetary Fund.

Taylor, J. B. (1993). 'Discretion versus policy rules in practice', *Carnegie-Rochester Conference Series on Public Policy* (39): 195–21.

Taylor, L. (1987). 'IMF conditionality: Incomplete theory, policy malpractice' in Myers, R. J. (ed.), *The Political Morality of the International Monetary Fund* (Vol. 3). New York: Transaction Publishers.

Taylor, P. (2015). 'IMF's "Never Again" Experience in Greece May Get Worse', *Reuters*, 10 June.

Ter-Minassian, T., & Schwartz, G. (1997). *The Role of Fiscal Policy in Sustainable Stabilization: Evidence from Latin America*, IMF Working Paper WP/97/94. Washington DC: International Monetary Fund.

Thacker, S. C. (1999). 'The High Politics of IMF Lending', *World Politics* 52(1): 38–75.

Thelen, K. A. (2010). 'Beyond Comparative Statics: Historical Institutional Approaches to Stability and Change in the Political Economy of Labor' in Morgan, G., Campbell, J., Crouch, C., Pedersen, O. K., & Whitley, R. (eds.), *The Oxford Handbook of Comparative Institutional Analysis*. Oxford: Oxford University Press.

Thirkell-White, B. (2005). *The IMF and the Politics of Financial Globalization*. Palgrave Macmillan.

Thompson, G. (1990). *The Political Economy of the New Right* London: Pinter.

Tovar, C. E. (2009). 'DSGE Models and Central Banks', *Economics: The Open-Access, Open-Assessment E-Journal* 3(2009–16): 1–31.

Treasury (2008). 'The case for a concerted international fiscal response', HM Treasury, November.

Treasury (2009). *Budget 2009 Building Britain's Future*, HC 407 London: HMSO.

Treasury (2010a). *Budget 2010 Securing the Recovery*, HC 451. London: HMSO.

Treasury (2010b). *Budget 2010*, HC 61. London: HMSO.

Treasury (2017). *Spring Budget 2017*, HM Treasury, HC 1025, available at: https://www.gov.uk/government/publications/spring-budget-2017-documents

Trichet, J.-C. (2010). 'Stimulate No More—It Is Now Time for All to Tighten', *Financial Times*, 7 June.

Trichet, J.-C. (2011). 'Building Europe, building institutions', Speech by Jean-Claude Trichet, President of the ECB on receiving the Karlspreis, Aachen, 2 June, available at: https://www.ecb.europa.eu/press/key/date/2011/html/sp110602.en.html

Tullock, G. (1965). *The Politics of Bureaucracy*. Boston: University Press of America.

Tullock, G. (1989). *The Economics of Special Privilege and Rent-Seeking*. Boston: Kluwer Academic.

Vail, M. I. (2014). 'Varieties of liberalism: Keynesian responses to the great recession in France and Germany', *Governance* 27(1): 63–85.

Van Reenen, J. (2015). 'Austerity in the UK: past, present, future', LSE Blog, 3 November.

Varoufakis, Y. (2017). *Adults in the Room: My Battle with Europe's Deep Establishment*. London: Bodley Head.

Veron, N. (2016). 'The IMF's Role in the Euro Area Crisis: Financial Sector Aspects', IEO Background Paper BP/16-02/10. Washington DC: International Monetary Fund.

Vetterlein, A. (2010). 'Lacking ownership: The IMF and its engagement with social development as a policy norm' in Park, S., & Vetterlein, A. (eds.), *Owning Development: Creating Policy Norms in the IMF and the World Bank*. Cambridge: Cambridge University Press.

Viñals, J. (2010). 'Towards a Safer Global Financial System', Speech at Center for Financial Studies, Goethe Universität, Frankfurt CFS Colloquium 2010 Series: 'Rebuilding Financial Markets', 9–11 November.

Viñals, J. (2011). 'Macroprudential Policy—Filling the Black Hole', iMFdirect, 8 April, available at: https://blog-imfdirect.imf.org/2011/04/08/macroprudential-policy-filling-the-black-hole/

Viñals, J. (2016). 'Reaching the "Great Normalization"—Overcoming Financial Stability Challenges in Advanced and Emerging Economies', Speech at the Reserve Bank of India, Mumbai, 10 March. available at: https://www.imf.org/en/News/Articles/2015/09/28/04/53/sp031016

Wade, R. (1996). 'Japan, the World Bank, and the Art of Paradigm Maintenance: "The East Asian Miracle" in Political Perspective', *New Left Review* 217(3).

Wade, R., & Veneroso, F. (1998). 'The Asian crisis: the high debt model versus the Wall Street-Treasury-IMF complex', *New Left Review* (228)3.

Wade, R. H. (2001). 'Capital and revenge: the IMF and Ethiopia', *Challenge* 44(5): 67–75.

Wade, R. H. (2002). 'US hegemony and the World Bank: the fight over people and ideas', *Review of International Political Economy* 9(2): 215–43.

Wade, R. H. (2003a). 'The invisible hand of the American empire', *Ethics & International Affairs* 17(2): 77–88.

Wade, R. H. (2003b). 'What strategies are viable for developing countries today? The World Trade Organization and the shrinking of "development space"', *Review of International Political Economy* 10(4): 621–44.

Warner, J. (2011). 'Lessons of Argentina Crisis Ignored in Handling Greece', *Daily Telegraph*, 4 July.

Watson, M. (2005). *Foundations of International Political Economy*. Basingstoke: Palgrave.

Watson, M. (2014). *Uneconomic Economics and the Crisis Of The Model World*. Basingstoke: Palgrave.

Watts, M. (2001). 'Development ethnographies', *Ethnography* 2(2): 283–300.

Weaver, C. (2008). *Hypocrisy Trap: The World Bank and the Poverty Of Reform*. Princeton, NJ: Princeton University Press.

Webb, R. (2000). 'The influence of international financial institutions on ISI' in Cardenas, E., Ocampo, J., & Thorp, R. (eds.), *An Economic History of Twentieth-Century Latin America: Volume I: The Export Age*. New York: Springer.

Widmaier, W. (2003a). 'The Keynesian Bases of a Constructivist Theory of the International Political Economy', *Millennium: Journal of International Studies* 32(1): 87–107.

Widmaier, W. (2003b). 'Constructing monetary crises: New Keynesian understandings and monetary cooperation in the 1990s', *Review of International Studies* 29(1): 61–77.

Widmaier, W. (2004). 'The social construction of the "impossible trinity": The intersubjective bases of monetary cooperation', *International Studies Quarterly* 48(2): 433–53.

Widmaier, W. (2016). *Economic Ideas in Political Time: The Rise and Fall of Economic Orders from the Progressive Era to the Global Financial Crisis*. Cambridge: Cambridge University Press.

Widmaier, W. W., Blyth, M., & Seabrooke, L. (2007). 'Exogenous shocks or endogenous constructions? The meanings of wars and crises', *International Studies Quarterly* 51(4): 747–59.

Williamson, J. (ed.) (1983). *IMF Conditionality*. Washington DC: Institute for International Economics.

Williamson, J. (1990). 'What Washington means by policy reform' in Weiss, L. (ed.), *Latin American Adjustment: How Much Has Happened*? Washington DC: Institute for International Economics.

Williamson, J. (2002). 'Did the Washington Consensus Fail?', Speeches, Testimony, Papers. Washington DC: Institute for International Economics.

Wolf, M. (2013). 'Osborne has now been proved wrong on austerity', *Financial Times*, 26 September.

Woll, C. (2008). *Firm Interests: How Governments Shape Business Lobbying on Global Trade*. Ithaca, NY: Cornell University Press.

Woll, C. (2010). 'Firm Interests in Uncertain Times: Business Lobbying in Multilateral Service Liberalisation' in Abdelal, R., Blyth, M., & Parsons, C. (eds.), *Constructing the International Economy*. Ithaca, NY: Cornell University Press.

Woo, J., Bova, M. E., Kinda, M. T., & Zhang, M. Y. S. (2013). *Distributional Consequences of Fiscal Consolidation and the Role of Fiscal Policy: What Do the Data Say*?, IMF Working Paper 13/195. Washington DC: Institute for International Economics.

Wood, M. (2015). 'Puzzling and powering in policy paradigm shifts: politicization, depoliticization and social learning', *Critical Policy Studies* 9(1): 2–21.

Woodford, M. (2003). *Interest and Prices: Foundations of a Theory of Monetary Policy*. Princeton, NJ: Princeton University Press.

Woodford, M. (2009). 'Convergence in macroeconomics: elements of the new synthesis', *American Economic Journal: Macroeconomics* 1(1): 267–79.

Woods, N. (2003). 'The United States and the international financial institutions: Power and influence within the World Bank and the IMF' in Foot, McFarlane and Mastanduno (eds.), *US Hegemony and International Organizations*. Oxford: Oxford University Press.

Woods, N. (2006). *The Globalizers: the IMF, the World Bank, and Their Borrowers*. Ithaca, NY: Cornell University Press.

Woods, N. (2010). 'Global governance after the financial crisis: a new multilateralism or the last gasp of the great powers?', *Global Policy* 1(1): 51–63.

Wren-Lewis, S. (2011). 'Lessons from failure: fiscal policy, indulgence and ideology', *National Institute Economic Review* 217(1): 1–16.

Wren-Lewis, S. (2013). 'The UKs macroeconomic battleground to come', 11 December, available at: http://mainlymacro.blogspot.co.uk/2013/12/the-uks-macroeconomic-battleground-to.html

Wren-Lewis, S. (2014a). 'Economic Standards', 4 January, available at: http://mainlymacro.blogspot.co.uk/search?updated-max=2014-01-22T14:41:00-08:00&max-results=7

Wren-Lewis, S. (2014b). 'Recovery rhetoric and reality', *Mainly Macro*, 29 April, available at: https://mainlymacro.blogspot.co.uk/2014/04/recovery-rhetoric-and-reality.html

Wren-Lewis, S. (2015). 'The Austerity Con', *London Review of Books* (February) 37(4), available at: http://www.lrb.co.uk/v37/n04/simon-wren-lewis/the-austerity-con vol-37

Wren-Lewis, S. (2016a). 'A general theory of austerity', Blavatnik School of Government Working Papers WP 2016/014, May 2016, available at: https://www.bsg.ox.ac.uk/sites/www.bsg.ox.ac.uk/files/documents/BSG-WP-2016-014.pdf

Wren-Lewis, S. (2016b). 'What Brexit and austerity tell us about economics, policy and the media', SPERI paper no. 36, December 2016.

Index

absorption approach (balance of payments) 74
academic economics 9, 11–14, 24, 37–8, 40, 56–87, 120, 210, 215
academic journals 37, 40, 59
accountability 15, 88, 94
adaptive expectations 69
adverse feedback loops 121, 140–1, 162, 203, 217, 218, 228, 229
agency 32, 33, 54, 91–2
aggregate demand, *see* demand
Akerlof, George 70
Alesina, Alberto 85, 129, 130
a priori assumptions 11–12, 64–5, 69, 70, 78, 87
Arestis, Philip 73
Arora, Vivek 17, 45, 46, 53–4, 63, 92–3
Articles of Agreement 88, 93–4, 95
Asset Purchase Facility (Bank of England) 169
asymmetric fiscal multipliers 171–2
Auerbach, Alan J. 85
austerity:
  Austria 123, 135
  Denmark 130
  and economic orthodoxy 16, 211
  and the European Central Bank 3, 26, 122–4, 132, 135, 142, 148, 178
  and the European Commission 26, 123, 148
  expansionary 129–32, 148, 157–8, 161–2, 173, 177, 186, 216, 225
  Finland 123, 135
  and fiscal space 16–18, 106–10, 112, 114, 127, 164–6, 211–12, 217–18
  France 185–9, 191–4
  Germany 3, 26, 106, 111–12, 115, 122–4, 126–7, 129, 132, 135, 142, 148, 178–9, 199–202
  Greece 126–8, 133, 148
  and growth 5, 35, 124, 128–35, 139, 142–3, 148, 157–64, 186, 209, 211, 216, 217, 218
  IMF position on 3, 5, 16–18, 22–3, 25, 35, 106–11, 112–36, 139, 142–5, 147–8, 157–66, 171–3, 179, 185–94, 196–8, 209, 211–12, 230
  and inequality 22–3, 114–15, 143–4, 217, 229–30
  Ireland 130
  longevity of 225
  Netherlands 115, 123, 132, 135, 178
  and the Troika 126–8, 148, 200
  United Kingdom 3, 25–6, 106, 111–12, 123, 129, 135, 150–1, 157–66, 170–7, 225
  see also fiscal consolidation
Austria 123, 135
authoritative recognition 7, 23, 29, 37, 40–1, 50, 55–6, 59, 86, 96, 105, 215
authority, *see* institutional authority; intellectual authority
automatic stabilizers 73, 76–8, 98, 116, 134, 158, 165–6, 171, 183–4, 230
autonomy:
  of the IMF 6, 24, 28, 54, 89, 90, 91–3, 223–4
  of IMF staff 28, 32, 33, 89, 92–3, 98, 223
autumn meetings 97, 196, 197

backstops 20, 25, 115, 136, 138–41, 148, 202, 204, 207, 227; *see also* firewalls
bad debt equilibria 138, 141, 148, 228
bad debt spirals 53
bail-outs, *see* banks: bail-outs; sovereign bail-outs
Baker, Andrew 15, 30
balance of payments 74
Ball, Larry 70, 143, 145
Ban, Cornel 48
Banking Union proposal 140–1, 179, 203–5, 207, 227
Bank of England 158, 159, 160, 169–70, 174
banks:
  bail-outs 125
  direct recapitalization 138, 140, 179, 204–5, 227, 228
  and DSGE modelling 61, 72, 83–4
  ECB supervision 203–4
  fragility of sector 136–8, 140, 179, 187, 203–5, 228
  France 185, 186–7, 188
  measures to break sovereign/bank link 140–1, 179, 203–5, 207, 227
  proposed Banking Union 140–1, 179, 203–5, 207, 227

banks: (*cont.*)
  runs on 19
  stress tests 228
  write-downs 228
Barnett, Michael 122
Barro, Robert J. 79
Barroso, José Manuel 122
Bayesian rational updating 213, 215
beauty contest analogy 107
belief-driven equilibria 20, 52, 228
Bercy, *see* French Treasury
Bernanke, Ben 98–9
Best, Jacqueline 11, 59, 63, 76
big government 13, 85
Blanchard, Olivier:
  appointment of 9, 48
  on austerity 26, 151
  on crisis legacies 144
  on economic modelling 61, 84
  on expansionary austerity 129, 132, 216
  on fiscal consolidation 129, 130, 131, 132–5, 157, 158, 172–3, 179, 186, 190, 196, 206
  fiscal multipliers research 6, 39, 133–4, 135, 171, 196–7, 221–2
  and fiscal policy 78, 81–2, 116–18, 146, 192–3
  on fiscal stimulus 119
  on growth 139, 144, 192–3
  hysteresis theories 99
  on ideational change 8, 38, 45, 81, 213
  and IMF crisis responses 102–3, 117–18, 119, 120, 122, 209
  on IMF influence 6, 196, 215–16, 221
  on inflation control 73
  on infrastructure investment 146
  and intellectual authority 179, 180
  and internal debate 46
  and Keynesianism 9, 10, 16, 70, 75, 81, 117, 120, 122, 215
  on market efficiency 19
  on non-linearities 20, 48
  on output gaps 120
  on sovereign/bank links 203
  on stabilization 78
  'Ten Commandments' 130, 131, 157, 158, 186, 206
  on UK fiscal policy 26, 151, 168, 172–3
  work with Cottarelli 81, 130, 131, 157, 158, 186, 206, 215
Blaug, Mark 69
Blyth, Mark 11, 101–2, 113, 124, 129
bond markets 20, 53, 138, 139, 141, 148, 157, 164, 169–70, 204, 227
bond ratings 169, 189–90
borrowing costs 17, 77, 108, 129, 150, 164, 169–70, 190, 195, 203, 204, 206
Boughton, James 74, 95
Bretton Woods Agreement 18, 88, 94
bricolage 7, 23, 29, 32–3, 40–1, 50–4, 230
Brisbane G20 summit (2014) 146, 149
Brown, Gordon 99, 122, 182
bucket approach (fiscal multipliers) 39, 226
Budget Ministry (France) 180
buffers, *see* fiscal buffers
Bundesbank 122

Cameron, David 25–6, 132, 150, 164, 165, 173, 177
Campbell, John 7, 31, 32–3, 75
capital account liberalization 217
capital controls 18, 21, 57, 117, 225, 228
capital flows 18, 38, 49
Carstensen, Martin B. 50
Case for Global Fiscal Stimulus (Staff Position Note) 119–20
case study methods 40, 61
central banks 2, 13–14, 20, 85, 96, 102, 114, 141, 148; *see also* Bank of England; Bundesbank; European Central Bank
China 118, 129
Chopra, Ajai 128, 136, 140–1, 143–4, 153, 156–7, 158–9, 161, 175
Chote, Robert 169
Chwieroth, Jeffrey M. 40, 47, 48, 57, 59, 62, 64, 96
Clegg, Liam 36, 90, 97
Clegg, Nick 26
Coddington, Alan 67, 172
cognitive filters 7, 28, 33, 34, 36–7, 41, 42, 53, 54, 55
Colander, David 65, 67
comparative political economy (CPE) 4, 7, 48
competitiveness 124, 129, 135, 139, 148, 181, 192, 200, 201, 204
confidence 2, 10, 12, 38, 67, 102, 117, 124–5, 128–32, 136, 138–9, 151, 158, 160, 162, 169, 192, 224; *see also* fiscal credibility
Conseil d'Analyse Economique 180
consensus-building 15, 89, 104
conservatism, *see* fiscal conservatism
consolidation, *see* fiscal consolidation
constitutive rules 34–5
constructivism 4, 7, 23, 27, 31–41, 92, 213, 214, 219
Constructivist Institutionalism (CI) 7, 23, 27, 29, 31–41, 54, 62, 91, 93, 98, 101, 211, 214
contagion 19, 20, 103, 114–15, 136–41, 148, 202, 204, 227
contingency planning 126, 135, 154, 157, 159, 161
contingent liabilities 19, 137, 140, 146, 153, 228
conventions 13, 20, 34, 52–3, 56, 72, 102, 107
Copelovitch, Mark S. 91

corroboration 7, 23, 29, 37, 39–41, 50, 55–6, 59, 62, 86, 105, 215, 221
Corsetti, Giancarlo 83
Cottarelli, Carlo:
  on fiscal consolidation 130, 131, 142–3, 157, 158, 186, 191, 192, 206
  and fiscal policy 81, 82, 98, 119, 121
  on ideational change 9–10, 58
  and IMF crisis responses 117, 119, 121, 125, 126
  on IMF influence 94, 95, 97, 153, 197, 209
  and Keynesianism 82
  on Ricardian equivalence 13, 84
  'Ten Commandments' 130, 131, 157, 158, 186, 206
  work with Blanchard 81, 130, 131, 157, 158, 186, 206, 215
Council of Economic Advisors 99, 223
counter-cyclical policies:
  and deficits 66
  and demand management 5, 13, 17, 35, 123, 218
  and economic stabilization 66, 68, 99, 135, 148
  and employment levels 74, 76
  fiscal policy as tool for 38, 66, 78, 80, 81–2, 99, 116, 119, 135, 148, 223, 225–6, 230
  and fiscal stimulus 2, 183
  and infrastructure investment 145–6, 149
  and Keynesianism 10, 13, 35, 38, 66, 68, 80, 99, 125
  revival of 86, 103, 144–9, 225–6
credibility, *see* fiscal credibility
credit channels 2, 81, 116, 119, 160, 224
creditworthiness (of states) 17, 107, 108, 137, 138, 188
crisis legacies 8, 16, 102, 106, 144, 148–9, 162, 176, 192, 211–12
crisis of debt narratives 8, 25–6, 123–4, 126, 146, 151, 164, 176, 178, 186, 206, 211, 218
crisis of growth narratives 123, 125, 126, 151, 176, 178, 211
cross-border leakages 14, 76, 116, 121

Darling, Alistair 99
Davos world economic forum 115, 182
debt, *see* public debt
debt benchmarks 139
debt limits 108
debt mutualization 204, 227
debt restructuring 11, 25, 127–8, 148, 227
debt sustainability 18, 35, 122, 127–8, 137, 139, 153, 158, 187, 193, 204, 222
debt sustainability analysis (DSA) framework 137, 153, 222
Decressin, Jorg 118, 121
deficits:
  deficit bias 13, 14, 18, 77, 80, 98, 107, 116, 125, 126, 216–17
  deficit fetishism 133, 190, 199–201
  discourses of 16, 150, 164, 168–9, 176
  France 181–2, 184–5, 186, 187, 189, 191, 193, 195, 206
  IMF position on 3, 16, 19–20, 76, 77, 80, 106, 179, 199–201
  and Keynesianism 66
  prioritization of 2, 3, 16, 106, 112–14, 129, 133, 135, 139, 164, 174, 184–6, 199–201, 211
  United Kingdom 155, 157, 160, 164, 168–9, 174, 176
deflation 2, 20, 53, 116, 121, 138, 142, 147, 176, 183, 218
de Jager, Jan Kees 133, 139
DeLong, Brad 9, 145, 161
Delors, Jacques 192
demand:
  and counter-cyclical policies 5, 13, 17, 35, 123, 218
  deficiencies in 9, 10, 12, 16, 20, 82, 102, 117, 125, 144, 151, 161, 162, 176, 212, 224
  'demand denial' 171, 173, 177, 201, 211
  and employment levels 66, 67, 71, 74, 76, 84, 144
  and fiscal policy 12–13, 17, 65, 66, 75, 102, 104, 120, 159
  France 188, 192
  Germany 114, 129, 134, 146, 200–2
  and hydraulic Keynesianism 67
  and interest rates 65, 67
  and Keynesianism 12–13, 65, 66, 75, 80, 120, 159, 177, 178–9
  management of 2, 3, 5, 12–13, 17, 22–3, 35, 65–7, 74–5, 80, 102, 104, 106–7, 114, 120, 122, 126, 132, 134–5, 144, 146, 159, 177–9, 188, 192, 202, 212, 218
  and monetary policy 12–13, 159
  and New Classical Macroeconomics 68–9
  and New Keynesianism 71
  surplus countries encouraged to boost 3, 112, 114, 129, 134, 146, 200–2
  United Kingdom 151, 161, 162, 176
Denmark 130
deposit insurance scheme 140, 203, 205
de Villeroche, Hervé 196
diabolical loops 20–1, 142
Dijsselbloem, Jeroen 133
direct recapitalization 138, 140, 179, 204–5, 227, 228
discursive institutionalism (DI) 35–6
'doom loop' 140, 179, 203, 207, 227, 229
Draghi, Mario 136, 138, 141
dynamic stochastic general equilibrium (DSGE) modelling 52–3, 61, 72, 79, 80, 82–4, 162, 213

East Asian crisis 44, 114, 229
'easy does it' approach (fiscal consolidation) 133, 212, 224
Ecofin meetings 123
economic crises:
  assessing impact of future crises 137
  construction of 7–8, 15–18, 101–2, 211–13
  legacy of 8, 16, 102, 106, 144, 148–9, 162, 176, 192, 211–12
  narratives of 7–8, 26, 90, 101–2, 105–6, 123–4, 135–6, 164, 176, 185, 192, 211–13
  as norm, not exception 19, 21, 137
  provide opportunity for IMF influence 6, 101–6, 219
economic cycle 38, 83
economic forecasting 111, 125, 132–4, 154, 160, 199, 219–20
economic modelling 52–4, 60, 61, 68–70, 79, 83–4, 87, 172, 213
economic orthodoxy:
  and academic economics 11–14, 24, 56–87
  and austerity 16, 211
  construction of 4–8, 15–18, 211–13, 225, 230–1
  and the IMF 3, 4–8, 15–18, 56, 58, 98, 154, 210
economic stability:
  automatic stabilizers 73, 76–8, 98, 116, 134, 158, 165–6, 171, 183–4, 230
  and counter-cyclical policies 66, 68, 99, 135, 148
  and financial markets 3, 18–21, 57–8, 65, 103, 227–9
  and financial sector fragility 137, 228
  and fiscal policy 3, 10, 13–14, 16, 37–8, 66, 73–4, 76–82, 85–6, 99, 109, 115–26, 134–5, 148, 182, 226, 230
  France 183–4
  and inequality 21–2, 229
  and interest rates 9, 13, 85
  and Keynesianism 65–6, 76, 80, 99
  and monetary policy 9, 13–14, 16, 66, 73, 77–8, 80, 85, 119, 148, 182, 226
  non-linear threats to 20–1, 48, 52–3, 103, 121, 142, 162, 176, 183, 212–13, 218, 228–9
  role of central banks 13–14, 20, 85
  role of the IMF 20–1, 228
  stabilizing norms 20, 102
  and systemic risks 137, 228
  United Kingdom 165–6, 171
efficient market hypothesis 3, 12, 19, 84, 87, 227–8
employment levels 11–12, 17, 19, 22–3, 38, 65–70, 73–6, 82–4, 144, 161–3, 177, 218
entitlement reform 136, 186, 192, 197
Epaulard, Anne 184, 193, 194–5
equilibria, *see* bad debt equilibria; belief-driven equilibria; multiple equilibria
Eurobonds 140, 141, 204, 227
European Central Bank (ECB):
  austerity 3, 26, 122–4, 132, 135, 142, 148, 178
  and Banking Union proposals 140–1, 179, 203–5, 207, 227
  bond purchasing by 138, 141, 148, 202, 227
  crisis of debt narratives 26, 123, 178
  and debt restructuring 127–8
  and the Eurozone crisis 126–8, 135, 138, 139, 140–2, 148, 202, 203–5, 207, 224, 227
  and expansionary austerity 129
  and fiscal stimulus 122, 123–4, 182–3
  and Greece 126–8, 148, 202
  and interest rates 115–16, 183
  as lender of last resort 138
  prioritizing of fiscal consolidation 132
  and quantitative easing 138, 220
  reliance on private sector 124
  responses to the global financial crisis 26, 115–16, 122, 123–4
  and structural reform 135, 139
  supervisory role 203, 204
  see also Troika
European Commission (EC) 26, 123, 126–8, 135, 148, 179, 180, 182–5, 193–7, 199–202, 204–7; *see also* Troika
European Financial Stability Facility (EFSF) 138, 204
European Stability Mechanism (ESM) 115, 138, 140, 200, 203, 204, 205, 227
European Summits 106, 138, 140, 193, 196, 203
European Union (EU) 139, 140, 192–3; *see also* European Commission (EC)
Eurozone crisis 7–8, 20, 25, 115, 126–8, 134–44, 148, 173, 185–9, 200–6, 224, 227
Excessive Deficit Procedure (EDP) 184–5, 187, 192, 193, 195, 197–8
Executive Board 28, 42, 47, 91, 93, 98, 99, 158, 225
exit strategies (fiscal stimulus) 110, 123–4, 147, 155, 224
expansionary austerity (EA) 3, 129–32, 148, 157–8, 161–2, 173, 177, 186, 216, 225
externalities 68, 70

Fama, Eugene 10
Fayolle, Ambroise 179, 188, 189–90, 206
feedback loops:
  adverse 121, 140–1, 162, 203, 217, 218, 228, 229
  and ideational change 5, 23, 28, 42, 46–7, 48–9, 54, 214, 216
  sovereign–bank feedback loops 21, 140–1, 179, 203–5, 207, 227
  and surveillance interactions 95, 99, 118, 133, 152–3

Fillon, François 191
financial bubbles 84, 174
financial markets:
  bond markets 20, 53, 138, 139, 141, 148, 157, 164, 169–70, 204, 227
  and contagion 19, 20, 114, 136, 137, 138–41, 148, 202, 204, 227
  and economic stability 3, 18–21, 57–8, 65, 103, 227–9
  efficiency of 3, 9, 12, 19, 84, 87, 227–8
  failures of 12, 16, 37–8, 57, 67, 68, 70, 71–2, 228
  and full employment 11, 12, 19, 38, 65, 66, 67–8, 70, 83
  and growth 19, 57
  and herd behaviour 19, 20, 72
  and iniquitous outcomes 21–3
  and irrational exuberance 19, 72
  and Keynesianism 5, 10, 12, 37–8, 57–8, 64–5, 67–8, 87, 99, 117
  market scepticism 5, 10, 12, 18–22, 37–8, 57–8, 64–5, 67–8, 87, 99, 137, 142–3, 227–9
  responses to fiscal consolidation 142–3, 190
  and socially optimal outcomes 9, 11, 12, 69, 71
  sovereign debt markets 20, 137–8, 155, 202
  Walrasian model of 19, 65, 68–70
financial programming 53, 62, 74
financial sector fragility 136–8, 140, 179, 187, 203–5, 228
Financial Times 124, 217, 220
Finland 123, 135
Finnemore, Martha 122
firewalls 20, 114, 138–41, 148, 203; *see also* backstops
Fiscal Affairs Department (FAD) 9, 37, 39, 45, 58, 60, 76–7, 81, 104, 117, 119, 125, 129–30, 137, 171, 215, 217
fiscal buffers 77, 107, 109, 116, 126, 137, 195, 217
Fiscal Compact 178, 193
fiscal conservatism 2–4, 25–6, 47, 54, 102, 116–17, 119, 123, 125, 212, 214, 217
fiscal consolidation:
  Blanchard and Cottarelli's 'Ten Commandments' 130, 131, 157, 158, 186, 206
  dangers of too much or too little 142–5
  'easy does it' approach 133, 212, 224
  and fiscal space 16–18, 114, 127, 133–4, 143, 148, 164–6, 188, 193–4, 206, 211–12, 217–18, 224
  France 185–9, 191–4, 206
  front-loading of 130, 139, 142, 151, 157–8, 175, 193, 194, 206, 212
  Germany 3, 26, 111, 114, 132, 224
  Greece 127–8, 133, 148
  and growth 3, 25–6, 114, 128–35, 139, 142–3, 148, 150, 156–64, 171–5, 186–8, 190–4, 196–7, 211, 216, 217
  IMF position on 3, 16–18, 22–3, 25, 104–5, 110–12, 114–15, 126–35, 142–5, 148, 156–66, 171–3, 179, 185–94, 196–8, 206, 211–12, 217–18, 224
  and inequality 22–3, 114–15, 143–4, 217, 229–30
  and international coordination 3, 104–5, 112, 114, 126
  'less now, more later' approach 3, 25, 104–5, 115, 134, 143, 171, 212, 218, 224
  market responses to 142–3, 190
  Netherlands 132
  'not too far, not too fast' approach 3
  post-crisis focus upon 16–18, 110–11, 112, 126–35, 211–12
  as self-defeating 114, 143, 146–7, 148, 191, 196, 225
  United Kingdom 3, 25–6, 111, 151, 155–66, 168–9, 171–7, 224
  see also austerity
fiscal credibility 77, 106–7, 130, 135–6, 150–1, 156–7, 164–5, 169–70, 176, 188–93, 195
Fiscal Monitor 10, 63, 93, 97–8, 102, 104, 125, 137, 168, 171, 190, 225
fiscal multipliers:
  asymmetric 171–2
  Blanchard and Leigh's research 6, 39, 133–4, 135, 171, 196–7, 221–2, 226–7
  bucket approach 39, 226
  European Commission reassessment of 197–8, 206
  and fiscal stimulus 39, 104
  France 193–4, 197–8, 206
  Germany 122, 171, 199
  higher during recessions 25, 85–6, 104–5, 131, 143, 150, 168, 171, 206, 225
  increased by international coordination 106, 120
  and Keynesianism 16, 38, 39, 66, 76–7, 120
  Romer's work on 81, 99, 223
  United Kingdom 151, 158, 162, 171–2, 176–7
  upwards re-evaluation of 38, 39, 128, 133, 148, 221–2, 225, 226–7
fiscal policy:
  assessing impacts of 12, 214
  as counter-cyclical tool 38, 66, 78, 80, 81–2, 99, 116, 119, 135, 148, 223, 225–6, 230
  and demand management 12–13, 17, 65–6, 75, 102, 104, 120, 159
  and growth 25–6, 35, 77, 80, 86, 102–3, 115, 120, 126
  IMF positions on 3, 10, 13–14, 24, 37–8, 60–1, 74–87, 98–100, 104–26, 132–5, 150–77, 178–207, 208–31

fiscal policy: (*cont.*)
implementation lags 14, 78, 115
interaction with monetary policy 120
and Keynesianism 12–13, 24, 37–8, 65–6, 74–7, 80–7, 116–17, 177, 209, 226
proposed EU control of 139
range of acceptable positions on 10, 12–15, 24, 85–7, 214
and redistribution 82, 114–15, 229–30
as stabilization tool 3, 10, 13–14, 16, 37–8, 66, 73–4, 76–82, 85–6, 99, 109, 115–26, 134–5, 148, 182, 226, 230
Fiscal Policy for the Crisis (Staff Position Note) 119, 225
fiscal risks 19–20, 137, 153
fiscal space:
and austerity 16–18, 106–10, 112, 114, 127, 164–6, 211–12, 217–18
and the Banking Union 203, 204
demonstrates IMF influence 109–10
and fiscal consolidation 16–18, 114, 127, 133–4, 143, 148, 164–6, 188, 193–4, 206, 211–12, 217–18, 224
France 26, 178, 179, 182, 188–9, 191, 193–4
and growth-oriented policies 26, 106, 114, 127, 140, 148, 178, 211–12, 217–18
and public debt 146–7, 217–18
and range of policy options available 17–18, 58, 90, 107–9, 127, 133, 148, 211–12
social construction of 17, 106–7, 112, 113
and subjective judgement 17–18, 108–9, 212
United Kingdom 151, 158, 164–6, 169–70
fiscal stimulus:
and central banks 2, 85
efficacy of 116
and the European Central Bank 122, 123–4, 182–3
and the European Commission 182
exit strategies 110, 123–4, 147, 155, 224
and fiscal multipliers 39, 104
France 99, 105, 182–5, 186, 206, 222
Germany 114, 118, 122, 123, 182–3, 206, 224
international coordination 14, 16, 17, 98, 102, 104, 110, 112, 115, 117–21, 155, 182–3, 206, 212, 222
and Keynesianism 16, 102, 104, 112, 116, 118
leaking of 14, 116, 121
and Ricardian equivalence 13, 70
target figure for 118–19
United Kingdom 99, 122, 154–5, 184
United States 81, 98–9
fiscal sustainability 16–17, 77, 107–8, 114, 116, 122, 125, 137–8, 145, 169, 179, 181–2, 185–6, 195, 217, 224, 226
fiscal targeting 195–6, 199
Fischer, Stanley 59, 70, 215
Fitch Ratings 109
flagship publications:
and academic economics 24
discussion of Banking Union 204–5, 207
discussion of boosting growth 144
discussion of fiscal consolidation 111
discussion of fiscal policy efficacy 10, 215
discussion of infrastructure investment 145
discussion of non-linearities 142
as expressing staff voice 63, 92–3, 121, 215
and ideational change 43
and IMF influence 1, 15, 43, 96, 97–8, 104, 154
and internal review processes 43
and publication of IMF research 104
and theoretical pluralism 52, 60
see also *Fiscal Monitor*; *World Economic Outlook* (*WEO*)
Fleming, Marcus 74, 75
France:
austerity 185–9, 191–4
Banking Union proposal 140–1, 179, 203–5, 207, 227
banks 185, 186–7, 188
borrowing costs 190, 195, 206
deficits 181–2, 184–5, 186, 187, 189, 191, 193, 195, 206
demand management 188, 192
and economic stabilization 183–4
fiscal consolidation 185–9, 191–4, 206
fiscal credibility 188–90, 192, 193, 195
fiscal space 26, 179, 182, 188–9, 191, 193–4
fiscal stimulus 99, 105, 182–5, 186, 206, 222
growth 187–8, 189, 191–4, 195
influence on the IMF 91
Keynesian thinking 192–3
loses AAA bond rating 189–90
output gap 191
pension reform 186, 192, 197
public debt 182, 188–9
public spending 180, 186, 187, 192, 194, 222
relationship with Germany 179, 181–3, 185, 193, 199–202, 207
relationship with the IMF 25, 26, 105, 178–207
responses to crisis 25, 26, 99, 105, 123, 181–94
sovereign debt securities held by 138
taxation 181–2, 186, 192, 194
unemployment 185
French Treasury (Bercy) 105, 180, 182, 183–4, 205, 222
Friedman, Milton 69
front-loaded fiscal consolidation 130, 139, 142, 151, 157–8, 175, 193–4, 206, 212
full employment 11, 12, 19, 38, 65, 66–8, 70, 74, 75, 83, 144, 177
Fund staff:
academic backgrounds 47–8, 78

agenda-setting capacity 24, 28, 43, 89, 93
autonomy 28, 32, 33, 89, 92–3, 98, 223
and cognitive filters 7, 28, 33, 34, 36–7, 41, 42, 53, 54, 55
compared with economics academics 59–61
diversity 47–8
and ideational change 7, 8, 10, 36, 37, 39, 41–54
and IMF influence 100, 101, 108–10, 220–1
and internal debate 45–7, 214
and internal review processes 42–6
and power relations 41–8
publishing in academic journals 37, 40, 59
recruitment practices 47–8, 81, 96
self-understanding 7, 10, 23, 27, 36, 51, 61, 63–4, 90, 97, 208, 220–1
voice expressed through flagship publications 63, 92–3, 121, 215

Galbraith, J.K. 56
Gali, Jordi 73
Gamble, Andrew 16, 113, 211
GEM model 79
General Theory (Keynes) 37–8, 65, 66, 67–8, 70, 72, 82, 117
generational change 57
German Economic Council 122
Germany:
austerity 3, 26, 106, 111–12, 115, 122, 124, 126–7, 129, 132, 135, 142, 148, 178–9, 199–202
crisis of debt narratives 26, 123, 178, 206, 218
current account surpluses 200–2
deficit fetishism 133, 199–201
and demand management 114, 129, 134, 146, 200–2
and expansionary austerity 129
fiscal consolidation 3, 26, 111, 132, 224
fiscal multipliers 122, 171, 199
fiscal stimulus 114, 118, 122, 123, 182–3, 206, 224
fiscal targeting 195, 199
influence on the IMF 91
labour market reform 124, 200
opposition to Banking Union proposals 140, 204–5
ordo-liberalism 199–200
relationship with France 179, 181–3, 185, 193, 199–202, 207
responses to crisis 3, 5, 26, 106, 111–12, 122–4, 126–7, 129, 132, 135, 142, 148, 178–9, 182–3, 199–202, 206, 224
welfare reform 124, 200
Gerson, Philip 173
Global Financial Stability Report 179, 205, 228
Gorodnichenko, Yuriy 85
Great Moderation 80, 81, 82, 114, 118, 222
Greece 6, 17, 126–8, 133, 135, 140, 148, 186, 187, 202, 211, 227
Group of Five (G5) 91
Group of Seven (G7) 91, 117, 155
Group of Twenty (G20) 2–3, 6, 10, 15, 91, 102, 104, 110–11, 118, 121, 123, 128–31, 146, 149, 155, 157, 184, 186, 212, 216
groupthink 47
growth:
and austerity 5, 35, 124, 128–35, 139, 142–3, 148, 157–64, 186, 209, 211, 216, 217, 218
crisis of growth narratives 123, 125, 126, 151, 176, 178, 211
and financial markets 19, 57
and fiscal consolidation 3, 25–6, 114, 128–35, 139, 142–3, 148, 150, 156–64, 171–5, 186–8, 190–4, 196–7, 211, 216, 217
and fiscal policy 25–6, 35, 77, 80, 86, 102–3, 115, 120, 126
France 187–8, 189, 191–4, 195
and inequality 21–2, 35, 115, 143–4, 217, 229
and infrastructure investment 145–6, 149, 174, 177, 218, 225
and low inflation 5, 35, 144, 218
and monetary policy 102–3
and public debt 139, 147, 156, 198
supporting of 3, 16, 106, 114, 124–6, 134, 139–40, 142–6, 149, 159, 162, 168, 192, 212
and taxation 147
United Kingdom 25–6, 150, 151, 155–68, 170–7
growth-friendly fiscal consolidation, *see* expansionary austerity
Gudin, Philippe 182–3, 184, 196, 197–8, 200

Hall, Peter A. 30, 213
Hall, Rodney Bruce 106–7
Hansen, Alvin 38, 67
Hay, Colin 36
healthcare reform 130, 136, 192
Heller, Peter 60–1, 75, 76, 79, 107
Help to Buy scheme 174, 175
Hemming, Richard 79
herd behaviour 19, 20, 38, 72
Hicks, John R. 38, 66–7
hierarchical structures 5, 9–10, 23, 27, 43–5, 48–50, 63, 82, 86, 91, 116–17, 216
historical institutionalism (HI) 31–2, 33
historical methods 40, 61–2
Hollande, François 140, 179, 191, 192–3, 203
housing prices 174
hydraulic Keynesianism 13, 67
hysteresis 20–1, 53, 61, 71, 84, 99, 142, 162–3, 171, 176, 177, 218

ideational change 7, 15, 23, 27–55, 62, 80–7, 116, 119, 209, 213–18, 225–30

ideational power 6, 15, 90, 93–8, 210, 224
imperfect competition 70
imperfect information 70, 71, 72
implementation lags 14, 78, 115
incremental change 7, 15, 28, 29, 31, 33, 52
Independent Evaluation Office (IEO) 8, 44, 46, 47, 128, 227
inequality:
  and austerity 22–3, 114–15, 143–4, 217, 229–30
  and fiscal consolidation 22–3, 114–15, 143–4, 217, 229–30
  and growth 21–2, 35, 115, 143–4, 217, 229
  IMF emphasis on tackling 4, 5, 21–3, 35, 114–15, 143–4, 218, 221, 227, 229–30
  and progressive taxation 77, 144, 229–30
  and stability 21–2, 229
inflation:
  controlled through monetary policy 73, 79, 226
  and growth 5, 35, 144, 218
  inflation targeting 59, 226
  and interest rates 73, 116
  and New Consensus Macroeconomics 72–3
  prioritization of low inflation 2, 5, 35, 79, 122
  and unemployment 67, 69
  United Kingdom 159
  see also deflation
influence:
  of the IMF 2, 6, 8, 10, 15–16, 24–5, 41, 44, 63, 90, 93–8, 100–6, 109–12, 151–4, 179–81, 194–8, 202, 205–9, 212, 215–16, 218–22, 224, 230
  of member states on the IMF 91–3
information asymmetries 70
infrastructure investment 5, 35, 145–6, 149, 151, 159, 168, 170, 174, 176–7, 218, 225
iniquitous outcomes 21–3
Institute for Fiscal Studies 225
institutional authority 93–5, 118, 151–2
institutional memory 4, 62, 94
intellectual authority 3, 6, 8, 15, 24–5, 40, 44–5, 54–5, 57, 59, 88, 90, 93, 95–8, 101, 112, 126, 151–4, 170, 179–81, 205–6, 209–10, 212, 214, 222, 224, 231
intellectual framework 15, 30, 89, 90, 96–8, 107, 208–9
inter-elite persuasion 101–2
interest rates 9, 13, 18, 39, 65, 67, 73, 85, 87, 116, 131, 138, 145, 183, 191, 204
internal culture 36–7, 45–7, 50, 54, 56, 63–4, 210, 214
internal debate 45–7, 214
internal politics 4, 5, 23, 27–8, 41–8, 55, 56, 119, 213–18
internal review processes 23, 27, 29, 40, 42–6, 48, 63, 116, 118–19, 220
international coordination 3, 14, 16, 88–9, 94, 102–6, 110–12, 114, 117–18, 120–1, 126, 183, 221
International Monetary and Financial Committee (IMFC) 117
international political economy (IPE) 4, 7, 48
international public goods 103–4
Ireland 127, 128, 130, 140, 187
irrational exuberance 19, 72
IS-LM model 67, 74
Italy 137–8, 187, 188, 203
iterative processes 4, 7, 41, 42, 54, 119–20

Jacoby, Wade 126
James, Harold 94, 95, 97
Japan 91
Jaramillo, Laura 142
Jobs and Growth working group 143
Joint Vienna Institute 97
Joyce, Joseph P. 91

Kahn, Richard 66
Keynes, John Maynard 11, 12, 15, 18–19, 37–8, 56, 65–8, 70, 72, 82, 107, 117
Keynesian fine-tuning 13, 67
Keynesianism:
  beauty contest analogy 107
  and conventions 20, 34, 56, 72, 107
  and counter-cyclical policies 10, 13, 35, 38, 66, 68, 80, 99, 125
  and demand management 12–13, 65, 66, 75, 80, 102, 120, 159, 177, 178–9
  displaced by monetarism 30
  dominant position from 1940s to 1970s 12
  and economic stability 65–6, 76, 80, 99
  and fiscal multipliers 16, 38, 39, 66, 76–7, 120
  and fiscal policy 12–13, 24, 37–8, 65–6, 74–7, 80–7, 116–17, 121–2, 177–9, 209, 226
  and fiscal stimulus 16, 102, 104, 112, 116, 118
  and French policies 192–3
  hydraulic 13, 67
  IMF relationship with 2, 5, 8, 10, 12, 16, 24, 37–8, 52, 57–8, 60, 64–5, 74–7, 80–7, 99–100, 102–3, 112, 116–17, 121–2, 147, 177–9, 182, 186, 209, 211–13, 215, 216, 223–4, 226, 230
  and IMF subcultures 5, 10, 48, 58, 82, 87, 99, 102, 112, 215, 223
  integration into academic mainstream 37–8, 71
  key features of 65–6
  and market scepticism 5, 10, 12, 37–8, 57–8, 64–5, 67–8, 87, 99
  meta- 120, 211, 212
  and the neo-classical synthesis 66–8

New 20, 47, 52, 58, 60, 64–5, 70–2, 77–9, 81, 83, 86–7, 99, 121, 147, 154, 177, 186, 223
and New Consensus Macroeconomics 83–4, 85–6, 87
overview 65–6
post- 64–5, 83
and responses to crisis 2, 5, 16, 29–30, 81–5, 99–103, 112, 116–17, 121–2, 147, 182, 211–16, 223–4
Kirschner, Jonathan 10, 86
Knight, Frank 19, 35, 48, 102, 219
Krugman, Paul 10, 47
Kuhn, Thomas 30

labour market reform 124, 197, 200
Lagarde, Christine 7, 8, 22, 47, 99, 113–14, 138, 141, 168, 174, 196, 200, 209, 229
Laxton, Doug 51, 60, 61, 121, 210
layering, of ideas 7, 33, 41, 52, 230
Leading Economists Re-assess Economic Policy (Blanchard et al.) 45
legitimacy:
of economic ideas 43, 46, 54, 105, 183, 206
of the IMF 39, 44, 47, 103–6, 112, 208, 221
Leigh, Daniel 39, 82, 130–1, 133–4, 143, 145, 171, 172, 196–7, 221–2
Leipold, Alessandro 76, 180
'less now, more later' approach (fiscal consolidation) 3, 25, 104–5, 115, 134, 143, 171, 212, 218, 224
Lipsky, John 160
Lipton, David 10, 51, 60, 81, 131–2, 135–6, 168, 170, 173–4, 209, 210, 229
liquidity traps 16, 119
loan conditionality 2, 89
London G20 summit (2009) 121–2, 123, 184
Loungani, Prakash 143
lowflation 21, 220
Lucas, Robert E. 9, 10, 13, 68, 70, 72, 73, 86

Maastricht Treaty 195
macroeconomic imbalances procedure (MIP) 200–2
macro-prudential economic governance 21, 57, 228
Mahoney, James 31, 33
market efficiency 3, 9, 12, 19
market failure 12, 16, 37–8, 57, 67, 68, 70, 71–2, 228
market scepticism 5, 10, 12, 18–22, 37–8, 57–8, 64–5, 67–8, 87, 99, 137, 142–3, 227–9
markets, *see* financial markets
materialism 33–4
Mauro, Paolo 5, 49, 61–2, 75, 80, 85, 120, 131
meanings, fixing of 6, 15, 97, 107, 122, 154, 230
medium-term fiscal frameworks 20, 104, 114, 122, 194, 212, 224
Meier, André 83
Merkel, Angela 122, 123, 126, 129, 133, 139
meta-Keynesianism 120, 211, 212
methodological pluralism 40, 61–2
modelling, *see* economic modelling
Moghadam, Reza 220
Momani, Bessma 30, 47
monetarism 30, 69
monetary policy:
and demand management 12–13, 159
and growth 102–3
and inflation control 73, 79, 226
interaction with fiscal policy 120
as stabilization tool 9, 13–14, 16, 66, 73, 77–8, 80, 85, 119, 148, 182, 226
moral hazard 11, 26, 127, 128, 140, 141, 148, 178, 205
Moschella, Manuela 101
Moscovici, Pierre 195
Müller, Gernot 83
MULTIMOD model 79
multiple equilibria 20, 52, 53, 71–2, 87, 112, 136, 154, 177
Mundell, Robert 74, 75, 86
Mundell/Fleming approach (economic adjustment) 74
mutual assessment process (MAP) 104, 110–11

narrative methods 40, 61
National Institute for Economic and Social Research 170
Nelson, Stephen C. 64, 205, 219
Neo-Classical Synthesis (NCS) 12, 38, 58, 66–8, 75–6, 79, 83, 86
neo-liberalism 4, 57, 64, 78, 79, 217, 231
Netherlands 115, 123, 132, 133, 135, 139, 178, 196, 199
New Classical Macroeconomics 5, 13, 37, 47, 52, 58, 60, 68–71, 73, 77–9, 83, 86, 159, 177, 209, 218
New Consensus Macroeconomics (NCM) 9, 14, 58, 72–4, 79, 80–7, 210, 213, 226
New Keynesian Macroeconomics (NKM) 20, 47, 52, 58, 60, 64–5, 70–2, 77–9, 81, 83, 86–7, 99, 121–2, 147, 154, 177, 186, 223
Newman, Abraham 126–7
'new normal' 35, 44, 80, 107, 112, 137
Nickell, Steven 163
non-linearities 20–1, 48, 52–3, 103, 121, 142, 162, 176, 183, 212–13, 217, 218, 228–9
norm advocates 29
'not too far, not too fast' approach (fiscal consolidation) 3

Obstfeld, Maurice 70, 225
Office for Budget Responsibility (OBR) 151, 158, 161, 163–4, 166–7, 169, 171–3, 176–7
open-mindedness 45–6, 47, 49–50, 64
operationalization 7, 23, 29, 37, 38–9, 40–1, 55, 62, 86, 215, 226–7
ordo-liberalism 199–200
Organisation for Economic Cooperation and Development (OECD) 95, 120, 181, 197
Osborne, George 25–6, 132, 156–60, 164, 165, 168, 170, 172–5, 177
Ostry, Jonathan 3, 17, 21–2, 57, 81–2, 107, 113–15, 143, 146–7, 217, 218
output gaps 73, 75, 120, 126, 134, 144, 151, 156, 159, 161–7, 174, 176, 191, 212–13
Outright Monetary Transactions 138

paradigm change 7, 23, 29, 30–1, 50–2, 55
Park, Susan 29
path contingency 50
path dependency 31, 32, 50, 54–5
Patinkin, Don 68
Pauly, Louis 28, 88, 94
peer review, *see* internal review processes
pension reform 130, 136, 186, 192, 197
perfect information 68, 70, 71
Perotti, Roberto 129
Peters, B. G. 32
Phillips, William 67
Phillips curve 67, 69, 73
Piketty, Thomas 22
Pisani-Ferry, Jean 180
Pittsburgh G20 summit (2009) 104
pluralism, *see* methodological pluralism; theoretical pluralism
Polak model 62, 74
policy ineffectiveness proposition 13, 69, 78–9, 85, 177
political economy principles 2–3, 11–15, 24, 64–5, 209
Pop-Eleches, Grigore 100, 206, 224
Portes, Jonathan 170, 172
Portugal 17, 127, 140, 187
Post-Crisis Fiscal Policy (Cottarelli et al.) 45, 82
post-Keynesianism 64–5, 83
power relations:
  between the IMF and states 91–3, 100, 125–6, 151–4, 223
  within the IMF 4, 5, 24, 27, 28, 41–8, 50, 214
pragmatism 4, 7, 10, 14, 52, 54, 55, 60–1, 63–4, 210, 214, 230
price mechanism 19, 68
price rigidities 70–1
principal/agent (PA) analysis 89, 91–2, 98
private sector 11, 124, 126, 128, 129, 151, 157, 161–2, 177
productive power 15, 40, 59, 96–7, 107
progressive taxation 77, 82, 86, 144, 229–30
public choice theory 14
public debt:
  assessments of prudent levels of 19–20, 137, 146–7
  benchmarking of 139
  crisis of debt narratives 8, 25–6, 123–4, 126, 146, 151, 164, 176, 178, 186, 206, 211, 218
  debt limits 108
  and fiscal space 146–7, 217–18
  France 182, 188–9, 194
  Greece 127–8, 148, 227
  and growth 139, 147, 156, 198
  IMF position on 3, 16, 19–20, 77, 106, 137, 139, 146–7
  measures to break sovereign/bank link 140–1, 179, 203–5, 207, 227
  mutualization of 204, 227
  prioritization of 3, 16, 106, 112–14, 122, 135, 139, 155, 164, 174, 186, 198, 211, 217–18
  restructuring of 11, 25, 127–8, 148, 227
  speed of debt reduction 146–7
  sustainability of 18, 35, 122, 127–8, 137, 139, 153, 158, 187, 193, 204, 222
  United Kingdom 155–6, 160, 164, 169, 174, 176
public goods 103–4
public spending 3, 12–14, 66, 77, 85, 123–4, 128–30, 133, 145–6, 151, 155–6, 160, 177, 180, 186–7, 192, 217, 222

quantitative easing (QE) 121, 138, 158, 159, 160, 163, 169, 220

Ramsden, Dave 155, 160, 164
rational expectations 13, 20, 33, 68–70, 71–2, 79, 83
Real Business Cycle (RBC) modelling 52, 60, 69, 73, 79
real economy 58, 76, 103, 122, 125, 133, 137, 174, 211, 229
Reassessing the Role and Modalities of Fiscal Policy in Advanced Economies 225–6
reconciliation 7, 23, 29, 37–8, 40–1, 55, 62, 86, 116, 215
recruitment practices 47–8, 81, 96
redistribution 22, 77, 82, 114–15, 143–4, 229–30
reflexivity 44–5, 50, 54, 101, 230
regulative rules 34–5
Reinhart, Carman 198
Research Department 37, 39, 49, 58, 81, 87, 96, 104, 119, 125, 129–30, 210, 212, 215, 221–2
resonance (of economic ideas) 24, 90, 99, 101, 106, 119, 121, 205

Rethinking Macro Policy (Staff Position Note) 44, 78, 213
Ricardian equivalence 13, 70, 73, 78–9, 84, 85–6, 151, 177
Ricardo, David 11, 13, 79
Ricardo/Barro effect 79
risk, *see* fiscal risks; systemic risks
Robinson, Joan 68
Rogoff, Kenneth 198
Romer, Christy 86, 99, 223
Romer, David 70, 81, 86, 99, 130, 223
Rutte, Mark 133, 139

Samuelson, Paul 67, 69, 75
Sapin, Michel 204
Sargent, Thomas J. 10, 13, 68
Sarkozy, Nicolas 99, 122, 181–2, 183, 185–7, 189–90, 191
Sawyer, Malcolm 73
Say, Jean-Baptiste 11, 12
Say's law 12, 21, 65, 67, 68, 129
scenarios 111, 154, 159, 161, 219
Schäuble, Wolfgang 122, 128, 129, 132, 133, 139
Schmidt, Vivien A. 32, 35–6
Schumpeter, Joseph A. 12
Seabrooke, Leonard 6, 98
Searle, John 34–5
secular stagnation 20–1, 53, 111, 144–5, 160–2, 176, 212–13, 218
Securities Market Programme 138, 141
self-censorship 42
Shiller, Robert J. 10
silo thinking 46, 47
'Six Pack' 139, 201
Smith, Adam 11
social facts 34, 35
socially optimal outcomes 9, 11, 12, 69, 71
sociological institutionalism (SI) 32
Solow, Robert 67, 69, 83
sovereign bail-outs 11, 127, 186
sovereign–bank feedback loops 21, 140–1, 179, 203–5, 207, 227
sovereign debt markets 20, 137–8, 155, 202
Spain 137–8, 187, 188, 203
special case framing 37–8, 67, 68, 119, 226
Spilimbergo, Antonio 82
spillovers 103, 125, 137, 138, 174, 229
spring meetings 10, 97, 168, 196, 197, 204
stability, *see* economic stability
Stability and Growth Pact (SGP) 178, 181–2, 184, 193, 195, 198, 201
Staff Discussion Notes 60, 79, 146
Staff Position Notes 60, 106, 119–20, 213, 221
stagnation 2, 20–1, 53, 111, 144–5, 147, 160–2, 176, 212–13, 218
Standard and Poors 189, 191
state intervention 11, 12, 14, 65, 69, 124, 177
Steinbruck, Peer 122
Stiglitz, Joseph 10, 22, 84
stimulus, *see* fiscal stimulus
Stone, Randall 91
Strategy, Policy and Review (SPR) department 43–4, 45, 63, 137
Strauss-Kahn, Dominique 7, 9–10, 16, 22, 48–9, 81–2, 102, 105, 113–19, 123–5, 143, 182, 184, 196, 209, 215, 229
Streeck, Wolfgang 31, 33
stress tests 228
structural fiscal balance 75, 109, 224
structural reforms 127, 134–6, 139, 140, 181, 192, 204
subcultures 4, 5, 9–10, 27–8, 48, 51, 58, 62, 82, 87, 99, 102, 112, 215, 223
subjective judgements 17, 39, 53–4, 108–9, 112, 208, 212, 214, 219–20
sub-prime mortgages 103, 185, 229
sudden stops 19, 53
Summers, Larry 9, 81, 99, 145, 147, 161
surveillance:
  absence of enforcement mechanisms 15, 24, 90, 95, 153, 218
  as channel for IMF influence 2, 6, 10, 89, 93–8, 100–4, 111–12, 152–4, 208–9, 218–21
  of France 26, 178–207
  and inequality 114–15, 229
  and internal review processes 43, 45, 46
  mandate for 15, 93–5, 100, 103–4, 111, 152, 208–9, 229
  resources dedicated to 2, 6, 89, 94, 209
  of the United Kingdom 25–6, 150–77
sustainability, *see* debt sustainability; fiscal sustainability
systemic risks 9, 25, 136, 137–8, 228

Tanzi, Vito 77, 217
taxation 77, 80, 82, 85–6, 122, 144, 147, 156, 159, 162, 181–2, 186, 192, 194, 229–30
Taylor rule 73
'Ten commandments' (Blanchard and Cottarelli) 130, 131, 157, 158, 186, 206
Ter-minassian, Teresa 77, 217
Thelen, Kathleen 31, 33
theoretical pluralism 60–1, 64
'thinkable' policy 6, 24, 28, 54, 89, 98–100, 223
third-order change 30
Tobin, James 67
Toronto G20 summit (2010) 2–3, 128–9, 130, 131, 157, 186, 216
traction, *see* influence; legitimacy
training programmes 97
translation 32, 40–1

Treasury (UK) 154–5, 163, 165, 171, 177
Trichet, Jean-Claude 115, 122, 123–4, 128, 129, 132, 133, 139, 224
Troika 25, 126–8, 148, 200
Troubled Asset Relief Program 98

uncertainty 19–2, 35, 38, 48, 52, 71, 72, 82, 102, 117, 137, 154, 219–20
unemployment 17, 61, 66–7, 69–71, 74, 82, 84, 117, 131, 161–3, 185, 218
United Kingdom (UK):
  austerity 3, 25–6, 106, 111–12, 123, 129, 135, 150–1, 157–66, 170–7, 225
  borrowing costs 150, 164, 169–70
  debt and deficit discourses 150–1, 164, 168–9, 176
  deficits 155, 157, 160, 164, 168–9, 174, 176
  demand deficiency 151, 161, 162, 176
  economic policies of 1970s and 80s 30
  economic stabilization 165–6, 171
  and expansionary austerity 129, 157–8, 161–2, 173, 177
  fiscal consolidation 3, 25–6, 111, 151, 155–66, 168–9, 171–7, 224
  fiscal credibility 150, 151, 156–7, 164–5, 169–70, 176
  fiscal multipliers 151, 158, 162, 171–2, 176–7
  fiscal space 151, 158, 164, 165–6, 169–70
  fiscal stimulus 99, 122, 154–5, 184
  growth 25–6, 150, 151, 155–68, 170–7
  hysteresis 162–3, 176, 177
  impact of crisis upon 98
  inflation 159
  influence on the IMF 91
  infrastructure investment 151, 159, 168, 170, 174, 176, 177
  loses AAA bond rating 169, 189
  output gap 151, 156, 159, 161, 162–3, 164–5, 166–7, 174, 176
  public debt 155–6, 160, 164, 169, 174, 176
  public spending 151, 155, 156, 160
  relationship with the IMF 25–6, 112, 150–77
  responses to crisis 3, 25–6, 99, 106, 111–12, 123, 129, 135, 150–1, 154–77, 224
  stagnation 160–2
  taxation 122, 156, 159, 162
  unemployment 161, 162, 163
United States 91, 93, 98–9, 103, 112, 118, 122, 123, 184, 223

Van Reenan, John 170, 172
VAR models 83
Vetterlein, Antje 29
vicious cycles 20–1, 121, 142, 203
Viñals, José 46, 58, 228
Virginia School 14

Wade, Robert 18
wage rigidities 68, 70–1
Walras, Leon 19
Walrasian market model 19, 65, 68–70
Washington Consensus 7, 18, 54, 79
Watson, Matthew 53
Weaver, Catherine 38
welfare 124, 130, 136, 200
What Have We Learned? (Alerkof et al.) 44
White, Thirkell 18
Widmaier, Wesley 11, 16
'Will it Hurt?' (Leigh) 130–1, 132, 134, 173, 216, 223, 225
Woerth, Eric 182
Woods, Ngaire 99, 205, 224
World Bank 95
World Economic Outlook (*WEO*):
  on crisis legacies 144, 176, 212
  on expansionary austerity 130–1, 132, 134, 173, 216, 223, 225
  and expression of staff voice 63, 92–3
  on fiscal consolidation 130–1, 132, 134, 173, 216, 223, 225
  on fiscal multipliers 39, 131, 133–4, 135, 171–2, 196, 216, 225
  Fiscal policy as a counter-cyclical tool 116–17
  on fiscal policy efficacy 37, 116–17, 119, 148, 225
  on fiscal stimulus 115, 116, 123
  and IMF influence 10, 94, 97, 102, 104
  on infrastructure investment 145, 146
  on sovereign–bank links 203, 204
  'Will it Hurt?' 130–1, 132, 134, 173, 216, 223, 225
Wren-Lewis, Simon 170, 171, 172, 173, 201

Zero Lower Bound 9, 39, 85, 87, 119, 131, 226